THE HISTORY OF DEVONSHIRE

by

Richard Polwhele

Volume 3

Introduction by

A. L. Rowse

KOHLER AND COOMBES

DORKING

1977

First edition published 1793 – 1806

This edition published Dorking 1977 by Kohler & Coombes

Introduction © A. L. Rowse 1977

The publishers are indebted to Devon Library Services for all their help in making this project possible and for providing the original copy of Polwhele from which this reprint has been made. They also provided the original manuscript of the Davidson Index which is in the Westcountry Studies Library at Exeter.

ISBN 0 903967 04 9

Printed and bound in Great Britain by The Scolar Press Ltd., 59–61 East Parade, Ilkley, Yorkshire.

THE

HISTORY

OF

DEVONSHIRE.

———————

IN THREE VOLUMES.

By the Reverend RICHARD POLWHELE,
Of POLWHELE in CORNWALL, and late of CHRIST-CHURCH, OXFORD.

VOL. III.

PRINTED BY TREWMAN AND SON,
FOR MESSRS. CADELL AND DAVIES, LONDON.

———

M,DCCC,VI.

ARCHDEACONRY

OF

BARNSTAPLE.

———◆———

DEANRIES

OF

CHULMLEIGH,

SOUTHMOLTON,

SHERWELL,

BARNSTAPLE,

TORRINGTON,

HERTLAND.

ARCHDEACONRY of BARNSTAPLE.

GENERAL CHOROGRAPHICAL DESCRIPTION.

IN marking the general face of the country within the Archdeaconry of Exeter, I ſtopt ſhort at Bamton. Purſuing my route, I have now to obſerve, that the land between Bamton and the river Mole, is coarſe and mooriſh; of which nature are the pariſhes of Witheridge, Rakenford, Crekam, Meſhaw, Romanſleigh, Knowſton, Biſhop's Nymton, Eaſt and Weſt Anſty, Molland, and Twitchin.

The road from Bamton to South-Molton (at leaſt the laſt ten miles) lies on a high ridge, which has on each ſide a commanding proſpect. The pariſhes of Anſty ſtand high. From the eaſtern parts, the rivulets run into the Mole; from the weſtern, into the Exe. Here, the land is coarſe, ſhelfy, and inclinable to furze; the upper coat a clay.

The river Mole runs in a deep and narrow valley, and through a coarſe, furzy, and incloſed country. The ſides of the hills near the river are covered with wood.

In the pariſh of Molland there is a great deal of oak wood, and ſome good land.

The pariſhes of Molland, Twitchin, and North-Molton border on Exmoor, which ſtretches weſtward to the rivulet called Bray, and is bounded by the pariſhes of Eaſt-Buckland, Charles, High-Bray, Chollacombe, and Parracombe.

In Chollacombe riſes the river called North-Yeo, which runs by Sherwell, Stoke-Rivers, and Goodleigh, in its way to Pilton, where it diſcharges itſelf into the Taw: And another rivulet joins it below Sherwell, which riſes in the pariſh of Kentiſbury, and runs by Eaſt-Down, Arlington, and Lockſore.

The country between theſe pariſhes and the Briſtol Channel, is for the moſt part high, and conſiſts in a great meaſure of downs, which are terminated, on the weſt, by the pariſhes of Bittaden, Weſtdown, and Marwood; on the north, by Ilfracombe, Berrynarber, and Comb-Martin; to the eaſt, by Eaſt-Down and Sherwell; and to the ſouth, by Goodleigh.

The country between this and the river Taw is uneven and incloſed. That part of it which lies near Barnſtaple is very rich land, abounding in graſs; but that near the North Sea, in the pariſhes of Mortho and Georgeham, coarſe.

The

The coaſt, from the headland of Santon, which forms the eaſtern part of Barnſtaple Bay, to the extremity of the county at Counteſbury eaſtward, is very high, rocky, and ſteep. That within land is full of hills and narrow vales; and in the pariſhes of Ilfracombe, Berry-Narber, and Comb-Martin ſufficiently fertile. The pariſhes of Trenſow, Linton, and Counteſbury are rocky and indifferent land.

The country between the rivers Taw and Torridge is hilly and incloſed; but level near the junction of the rivers. Further up, it is more uneven, though the hills are not high. The ſoil is clay on a ſhelfy bottom: and there is a good quantity of underwood on it. Towards Torrington the hills are higher, and the country more open.

The weſt ſide of the Torridge, from Bideford to Hertland, is coarſer than the eaſtern ſide, excepting only the three pariſhes of Bideford, Northam, and Abbotſham, which are good corn land.

The ſea coaſt from Appledore, almoſt to Portledge, declines greatly towards the ſea: But from Portledge quite to the weſtern extremity of the county, the cliffs are very high and ſteep.

The pariſh of Alwington is coarſe land; and ſo is the greateſt part of Clovelly and Vowelſworthy—the ſoil a ſtrong clay—the incloſures and the hedgerows weak and ſcrubby.

The pariſh of Hertland ſtands very high: But in general the land is much better, and the country more populous.

The country to the ſouthward of Parkenham and Vowelſworthy is tolerably level—very coarſe—full of moors, ſprings, and bogs, open with few and low fences, and thinly inhabited.

In this part riſes the river Torridge; and, as it runs along, it leaves a ſtring of pariſhes on each ſide, where the land is better in itſelf, and more cultivated.

The river Torridge, from Bradford to Torrington, runs in a deep valley, amidſt hills, the ſides of which are covered with large oak woods. The dark brown tinge of its waters, owing to the moory country in which it takes its riſe, and through which it paſſes, added to the gloom of theſe umbrageous hills, gives a melancholy appearance to the river. This woody country continues, for the moſt part, from Torrington to Bideford.

The river Torridge, from its riſe to Appledore, where it falls into the ſea, forms a ſemicircle, in the centre of which is a ſmall ſpot of level moory country, lying between the pariſhes of Merland, Merton, and Padſtow, about three miles in breadth. It reſembles the Somerſetſhire moors. The large bed of pipe clay found under it, has not been unnoticed in the natural hiſtory.

Of the ſix deanries within this archdeaconry—Chulmleigh, South-Molton, Sherwell, Barnſtaple, Torrington, and Hertland, the firſt in order is Chulmleigh.

ARCHDEACONRY

DEANRY OF CHULMLEIGH.

IN this deanry are contained the parifhes of Chulmleigh, Burrington, Chaw-leigh, Eggesford, Wemworthy, Lapford, Brufhford, Bondleigh, Coleridge, Nymet-Rowland, Zeal, Northtawton, Broad-nymet, Nymet-tracey, Clannaborough.*

Of thefe parifhes, a few only have a claim to further notice.

CHULMLEIGH is a large parifh, extending four miles from the S. S. E. point to the N. N. W. and about feven miles from W. S. W. to E. N. E. It is divided from Chawleigh by the little river Dart. The manor of Chumleigh is poffeffed by Sir Jacob Wolff, bart. of Mellyfent, Somerfet. Waddington, in Chulmleigh and King's-Nymton, belongs to John Bawden, gent. The church is handfome and fpacious; 84 feet long and 48 feet wide;—the tower 86 feet high.†

VOL. III.   C   The

---

* " *Benefices remaining in charge:*

First Fruits. £. s. d.				Yearly Tenths. £. s. d.		
10	17	8½	Boneleigh or Bondleigh R. [St. James] Rep. B. Proc. vi*s*. viii*d*. Syn. & Cath. ii*s*. v*d*. A. D. Proc. vi*s*. viii*d*. r. V. 90*l*. Patr. Hon. Percy Wyndham	1	1	9
13	11	3	Burrington V. [Holy Trinity] Rep. B. Proc. vi*s*. viii*d*. Syn. & Cath. ii*s*. v*d*. A. D. Proc. vi*s*, viii*d*. r. V, 120*l*. Patr. and V. Mr. Nicolas Hole.	1	7	1½
2	4	2	Broadnymet R. Rep. none in charge. r. V. 35*l*. - - - - - - - Patr. John Lethbridge, efq.	0	4	5
4	8	4	Brokeland P. in Chulmleigh. Rep. none in charge - - - - - - - Patr. and P. Mr. Richard Hole.	0	8	10
25	14	2	Chawleigh R. [St. James] Rep. B. Proc. vi*s*. viii*d*. Syn. & Cath. ii*s*. v*d*. A. D. Proc. vi*s*. viii*d*. r. V. 240*l*. Patr. Henry Arthur Fellowes, efq.	2	11	5
20	18	1½	{ Chulmleigh R. [St. Mary Magdalene] formerly a collegiate church. Rep. B. Proc. vi*s*. viii*d*. Syn. & Cath. ii*s*. v*d*. A. D. Proc. vi*s*. viii*d*. r. V. 260*l*. - - - - - - - } Patr. and R. Mr. Richard Hole.	2	1	9¾
5	17	3½	Clannaborough R. [St. Petrock] Rep. B. Proc. iii*s*. iv*d*. Syn. & Cath. ii*s*. v*d*. A. D. Proc. iii*s*. iv*d*. r. V. 130*l*. Patr. The KING.	0	11	8¾
4	6	8	Denes P. in Chulmleigh.——Patr. and P. Mr. Richard Hole - - - - - - -	0	8	8
5	13	4	Higherline P. in Chulmleigh.——Patr. and P. the fame - - - - - - -	0	11	4
5	0	0	Lowerline P. in ditto.——Patr. and P. the fame - - - - - - -	0	10	0
5	0	0	Penell P. in ditto.——Patr. and P. the fame - - - - - - -	0	10	0
15	1	10½	Lapford R. [St. Thomas Becket] Rep. B. Proc. vi*s*. viii*d*. Syn. & Cath. ii*s*. v*d*. A. D. Proc. vi*s*. viii*d*. r. V. 240*l*. Patr. and R. Mr. John Radford.	1	10	2½
32	4	7	North-Tawton R. [St. Peter] Rep. B. Proc. vi*s*. viii*d*. Syn. & Cath. ii*s*. v*d*. A. D. Proc. vi*s*. viii*d*. r. V. 280*l*. Patr. and R. Mr. Richard Hole.	3	4	5½
19	8	9	{ Nymet-tracie alias Bow R. [St. Bartholomew] Rep. B. Proc. vi*s*. viii*d*. Syn. & Cath. ii*s*. v*d*. A. D. Proc. vi*s*. viii*d*. r. V. 160*l*. - - - - - - - - - - } Patr. Mrs. Marfhal.	1	18	10½
17	8	9	{ Sele alias Zele Monachorum R. [St. Peter] Rep. B. Proc. vi*s*. viii*d*. Syn. & Cath. ii*s*. v*d*. A. D. Proc. vi*s*. viii*d*. r. V. 160*l*. - - - - - - - - - } Patr. John Parker, efq.	1	14	10½
11	13	4	Wemworthy R. [St. Michael] Rep. B. Proc. vi*s*. viii*d*. Syn. & Cath. ii*s*. v*d*. A. D. Proc. vi*s*. viii*d*. r. V. 100*l*. Patr. and R. Mr. John Toffel Johnfon.	1	3	4

Difcharged.

King's Books.				Certified Value.		
0	0	0	Brufhford Cur. [Ded. unc.] Rep. iv*s*. iv*d*. Syn. ii*s*. v*d*. A. D. Proc. iii*s*. iv*d*. r. V. 30*l*. - - - Patr. Mr. Luxton.	8	0	0
7	8	9	Colerudge V. [St. Mary] Rep. B. Proc. vi*s*. viii*d*. Syn. & Cath. ii*s*. v*d*. A. D. Proc. vi*s*. viii*d*. r. V. 90*l*. Patr. Bifhop of Exeter.	45	17	1
7	18	9	Eggesford R. [Ded. unc.] Rep. B. Proc. iii*s*. iv*d*. Syn. & Cath. ii*s*. v*d*. A. D. Proc. iii*s*. iv*d*. r. V. 100*l*. Patr. Henry Arthur Fellowes, efq.	38	7	4
6	1	3	{ Nymet-Rowland R. [St. Bartholomew] Rep. B. Proc. iii*s*. iv*d*. Syn. & Cath. A. D. ii*s*. v*d*. Proc. iii*s*. iv*d*. r. V. 35*l*. - - - - - - - - - } Patr. and R. Mr. Arundel Radford.	30	0	0

Thes. Eccles. Prov.

† See Chapple's *Rifdon*, p. 249, and *Prince*, p. 307.

The parifh of EGGESFORD is fmall, not exceeding two miles in length or breadth, its fituation in general high and hilly. It ftands on the principal road leading from Northtawton, Okehamton, &c. to Chawleigh, Chulmleigh, &c. The parifh is inclofed by common hedges, well wooded with all kinds of foreft trees, the moft flourifhing of which are the beech and oak, embellifhing the vales with a variety of beautiful fcenes. The whole parifh is in the manor of Eggesford, a confiderable part of which is kept in hand by the lord of it, the reft diftributed into fmall farms; the houfes built chiefly with mud walls, a few with ftone, and thatch'd, furnifhed with the ufual appendages of gardens and orchards, and in a moderate ftate of cultivation.* There is one gentleman's feat in the parifh and manor of Eggesford, built about the year 1718, of brick, much increafed and improved by the prefent poffeffor, who has alfo laid out the grounds about it with much elegance and tafte, under the direction of the late Mr. Richmond: woods well interfperfed, confiderable plantations, and the river Taw contributing much to enrich and beautify the fcene. This manfion, with a large appendant property, belongs to Henry Arthur Fellowes, efq. whofe grandfather purchafed it of St. Leger, Lord Vifcount Doneraile. In the year 1596 it appears to have been in the poffeffion of John Copleftone, efq. whofe only fon and heir was buried in the parifh church in that year. On the death of the faid John Copleftone it defcended to his only daughter Ann, married to Edward Lord Vifcount Chichefter, of the kingdom of Ireland, whofe fon and heir, Arthur, was promoted to the earldom of Donegall.† The church is fituated at the northern extremity of the parifh, near the principal manfion: the walls are of ftone, the body of the church covered with fhingle, the chancel with flate. The church confifts only of the body, without any aifle, is about 22 feet high, 18 broad, and about 50 feet long. The tower fquare, built chiefly with moor-ftone, about 40 feet high, has three bells.‡

On the weft fide of the Taw ftands *Bonleigh*, or BUNDLEIGH, which the Englifh Saxons called *Bonelega*, or *good pafture ground*. Here Ulmer, a Saxon, poffeft lands in the time of Edward the Confeffor. After the Conqueft, Wm. Poilgi had inheritance, by the Conqueror's gift; and Sir Robert de Campell, the 10th of Richard 1ft. William de Campell granted his land of *More*, in this parifh, to Robert Prior, for the fum of fixteen fhillings, giving a gold ring to Mary his wife. The manor belongs (fays Chapple) to a fon of the late Lord Egremont, the patron of the living. It has been long in that family.

COLRIDGE

* The total number of inhabitants about 160; the farmers all rack-renters; paupers who receive conftant relief 9 or 10, others occafionally; the lower order of the parifhioners employed either in hufbandry or the woollen manufacture; they are in general healthy, and furnifh many inftances of longevity.

† For their family hiftory, fee the infcription on two monuments erected to their memory in a fmall building adjoining the north-fide of the chancel: which, with other particulars, are accurately ftated in Prince's Worthies. This property is faid to have paffed from the Donegall family into that of St. Leger, Lord Vifcount Doneraile, of Ireland, on the death of Lady Ann Chichefter, by claim of inheritance; and in the year 1718 was purchafed by William Fellowes, efq. a mafter in chancery, and grandfather of the prefent poffeffor.

‡ Befides the monuments of the Chichefter family, there is a fmall ftone in the wall to the memory of John Copleftone, efq. as mentioned in Prince; and alfo an handfome one for William Fellowes, efq. the grandfather of the prefent Mr. Fellowes, recording his integrity in the difcharge of his office of mafter in chancery, his marriage, family, and the dates of his age and death. In the church-yard, which is fmall, is a tomb, under which are buried the late Coulfon Fellowes, efq. one of the reprefentatives of the county of Huntingdon in feveral parliaments, fon of the former, and father of the prefent Mr. Fellowes; and near him Mrs. Mary Fellowes, his eldeft daughter, by Urania, fifter of the late Earl Powis: The infcriptions mention the excellence of their characters, and the dates of their deaths and ages.

COLRIDGE or Colrudge is derived, (according to Rifdon) *de frigido jugo.**

NORTH-TAWTON taketh name of the river Taw, and its fcite from South-Tawton, from which the whole hundred hath denomination.†

CLANABOROW was held by Sir Alan Dacus, in the days of Henry 3d, of which family three defcents fucceeded. At the fame time William Punchardon held lands in this tything, Walfton and Thorn. The barton and Walfton belong to Boringdon and Lethbridge.

* Here Sanlf, a Saxon, was feized of lands in the time of the conqueft. Ralph de Sackville, lord of this manor in the reign of Richard the 1ft, gave Wefcott a part of it, to William England in frank marriage with Alice his daughter, and fold the reft to Sir Henry Champernowne. Sir *Ralph Sackville* confirmed his father's grant of the manor, to Sir Wm. Champernowne, Sir Henry's fon. The laft of this family had iffue two daughters his heireffes; Elizabeth, firft married to Polglas, fecond to John Sergeaux, and Katherine, wife of Sir Walter Woodland, who died without iffue. By a daughter of Polglas, thefe lands came to Sir John Herle, her hufband; whofe fon, Sir John, died without iffue. And the Lord Wm. Bonville procured this land, and left it to his pofterity. But by the Duke of Suffolk's attainder, the manor came to the crown: And Queen Mary beftowed the fame upon her fervant, James Baffet, whofe fon fold it to Dunf-combe. *Rifdon.*—The manor now belongs to Montague Parker, efq. *Chapple.*

† The principal mannor of which place did in elder ages belong unto Sir Joell Valletort, a younger fon of Sir Roger de Valletort, and Joan the daughter of Richard Earl of Cornwall, whofe moated fort adjoining to the church-yard, as yet appeareth, now called Court-Green. The barton of Bathe was in ancient time the inheritance of Sir Walter Bathe, knight. Margaret, the daughter of Auguftine his fon, was the wife of Sir Andrew Medfteed, knight; of latter days, the lands and dwelling of Marke Slader, a branch tranfplanted hither from a family at Barhamdown in Kent. In which barton there is a pit of large circumference, and fo deep in the center, as the heigth of a man well mounted on horfe-back; whereout fometimes a fpring breaketh, by fome called a *Borne*, which filleth the pit, and fo continueth full for many days together, taken to be a fore runner of forrow to enfue, (as hath been obferved) by the death of fome noble perfonage; not unlike that borne in Hertfordfhire, prefaging fome fad event, when it breaketh out of the earth, thereof called *Woomere*, which in the time of King Edward 4th, did run from February until June; whereof fome do affirm natural reafons thereof, as the caufe; it may be there may be fome fupernatural myftery in it. This parifh containeth divers tythings. Robert Burnell had his dwelling in Croke-Hamlet, in King Henry the 3d's time, where he inherited. In the fame tything, Roger Week was feized of lands, as by this appeareth. *Noverint me Roger Weeke Conceffiffe Johanni Wey unum Ferlingum terre in Stone, in Decima de Croke Burnell, una cum* Pafturam *in la Moore de Croke, ad omnia Avaria fua Teftibus Hugh Samford, Thomas Barry, Richard Cocktree. Dat. apud Stone,* 14 *Hen. VI. Rifdon.*

ARCHDEACONRY

ARCHDEACONRY OF BARNSTAPLE.

DEANRY OF SOUTHMOLTON.

THIS Deanry includes the following pariſhes: Southmolton, Warkleigh, Saterleigh, George-Nymet, Biſhop's-Nymet, Marianſleigh, Romanſleigh, King's-Nymet, Meſhaw, Cheldon, Weſt-Worlington, Eaſt-Worlington, Thelbridge, Wolfardiſworthy, Puddington, Cruwys-Morchard, Waſhford-pyne, Witheridge, Rackenford, Studeley, Okeford, Creacombe, Roſeaſh, Knowſtone, Molland, Eaſt-Anſty, Weſt-Anſty, Twitchen, North-Molton.*

Among

* " *Beneſices remaining in charge:*

Firſt Fruits. £.	*s.*	*d.*		*Yearly Tenths.* £.	*s.*	*d.*
21	11	8	Cruwys-Morchard R. [Holy Croſs] Rep. B. Proc. vis. viii*d.* Syn. iis. v*d.* A. D. Proc. vis. viii*d.* r. V. 280*l.* Patr. and R. Cruwys.	2	3	2
18	19	7	Eſraffee, or Roſeaſh R. [St. Peter] Rep. B. Proc. vis. viii*d.* Syn. iis. v*d.* A. D. Proc. vis. viii*d.* r. V. 140*l.* Patr. and R. Southcombe.	1	17	11½
11	0	0	Eaſt-Anſty R. [St. Michael] Rep. B. Proc. iiis. iv*d.* Syn. iis. v*d.* A. D. Proc. iiis. iv*d.* r. V. 100l. Patr. Tidboald.	1	2	0
7	15	10	Eaſt-Worlington R. [St. Mary] Rep. B. Proc. iis. ii*d.* ob. Syn. iis. x*d.* A. D. iis. ii*d.* ob. r. V. 120*l.* Patr. Fellowes.	0	15	7
26	10	10	Knoweſton [St. Peter] with Molland V. [St. Mary] Rep. B. Proc. xiiis. iv*d.* Syn. ivs. x*d.* A. D. Proc. xiiis. iv*d.* r. V. 120*l.* Patr. John Chicheſter, eſq. Cath.	2	13	1
20	7	3½	Nymet Biſhop's V. [Ded. unc.] Rep. none in charge. Pec. of the Bp. r. V. 180*l.* Patr. Biſhop of Exeter.	2	0	8¾
9	19	2	Nymet St. George's R. Rep. B. Proc. iis. ii*d.* ob. Syn. iis. v*d.* A. D. Proc. iis. ii*d.* ob. r. V. 110*l.* Patr. Sir Thomas Acland, bart.	0	19	11
28	6	8	King's Nymet R. [St. James] Rep. B. Proc. vis. viii*d.* Syn. iis. v*d.* A. D. Proc. vis. viii*d.* r. V. 200*l.* Patr. John Southcombe, clerk.	2	16	8
24	0	0	Okeford R. [St. Peter] Rep. B. Proc. ivs. v*d.* Syn. iis. v*d.* A. D. Proc. ivs. iv*d.* r. V. 150*l.* Patr. and R. Mr. Richard Haydon.	2	8	0
6	8	1½	Podington, alias Puddington R. [St. Thomas Becket] Rep. B. Proc. is. viii*d.* Syn. is. v*d.* A. D. Proc. is. viii*d.* r. V. 100*l.*	0	12	9¾
19	17	3½	Rakingford R. [All Saints] Rep. B. Proc. iis. v*d.* Syn. iis. v*d.* A. D. Proc. iis. ii*d.* ob. r. V. 80*l.* Patr. Thomas Melhuiſh, clerk.	1	19	8¾
10	14	9½	Romanſleigh R. [St. Rumon] Rep. B. Proc. iis. ii*d.* ob. Syn. iis. v*d.* A. D. Proc. iis. ii*d.* ob. r. V. 100*l.* Patr. Sir Thomas Dyke Acland, bart.	1	1	5¾
20	0	2½	Stodeleigh, alias Studley, R. [St. Margaret] Rep. B. Proc. vis. viii*d.* Syn. iis. v*d.* A. D. Proc. vis. viii*d.* r. V. 180*l.* Patr. Matthew Brickdale, eſq.	2	0	0¼
10	6	5½	Tilbridge alias Thelbridge R. [St. David] Rep. B. Proc. iis. ii*d.* ob. Syn. is. v*d.* A. D. Proc. iis. ii*d.* ob. r. V. 80*l.* Patr. Mr. Pierce.	1	0	7¾
14	4	7	Warkleigh R. [St. John] Rep. B. Proc. iis. ii*d.* ob. Syn. iis. v*d.* A. D. Proc. iis. ii*d.* ob. r. V. 100*l.* Patr. and R. Beavis.	1	8	5½
8	15	10	Weſt-Worlington R. [St. Mary] Rep. B. Proc. iis. ii*d.* ob. Syn. iis. v*d.* A. D. Proc. iis. ii*d.* ob. r. V. 90*l.* Patr. George Buck, eſq.	0	17	7
9	19	4½	Wolfardiſworthy R. [Holy Trinity] Rep. B. Proc. iiis. iv*d.* Syn. iis. x*d.* A. D. Proc. iiis. iv*d.* r. V. 140*l.* Patr. and R. Walrond.	0	19	11¼
23	10	5	Wytheridge V. [St. John Baptiſt] Rep. B. Proc. vis. viii*d.* Syn. iis. x*d.* A. D. Proc. vis. viii*d.* r. V. 120*l.* Patr. and R. Melhuiſh.	2	7	0½

Diſcharged.

King's Books. £.	*s.*	*d.*		*Certified Value.* £.	*s.*	*d.*
4	18	6½	Cheldon R. [St. Mary] Rep. B. Proc. iis. ii*d.* ob. Syn. iis. v*d.* A. D. Proc. iis. ii*d.* ob. r. V. 90*l.* Patr. Henry Arthur Fellowes, eſq.	28	6	11
4	18	9	Creacomb R. [St. Michael] Rep. B. Proc. iis. v*d.* A. D. Proc. is. v*d.* r. V. 50*l.* Patr. William Harris, eſq.	25	4	0
7	4	2	Meſhaw R. [St. John Baptiſt] Rep. B. Proc. iis. ii*d.* ob. Syn. iis. v*d.* A. D. Proc. iis. ii*d.* ob. r. V. 70*l.* Patr. and R. Tanner,	44	2	10½
16	16	3	North-Molton V. [All Saints] Rep. B. Proc. vis. viii*d.* Syn. iis. v*d.* A. D. Proc. vis. viii*d.* r. V. 70*l.* Patr. John Parker, eſq.	20	16	8
4	0	2	Satterleigh R. [St. Peter] Rep. B. Proc. iis. ii*d.* ob. A. D. Proc. is. v*d.* r. V. 60*l.* Patr. and R. Beavis.	31	9	6
6	0	2½	Waſhford-Pyne R. [St. Peter] Rep. B. Proc. is. vi*d.* Syn. is. v*d.* A. D. Proc. is. viii*d.* r. V. 70*l.* Patr. Lamb.	49	7	6
10	6	8	Weſt-Anſty V. [St. Petrock] Rep. B. Proc. iiis. iv*d.* Syn. iis. v*d.* A. D. Proc. iiis. iv*d.* r. V. 75*l.* Patrs. Dean and Chapter of Exeter.	37	17	5

Not

Among the parifhes enumerated, SOUTHMOLTON holds the principal place. The town takes its name from the river Moul, or Mole, which rifeth about five miles diftant to the north-ward, on the foreft of Exmoor, and runs thro' the parifh from north to fouth, and at a few miles diftance falls into the river Taw. Its length, from eaft to weft, exceeds half a mile, and from north to fouth it is nearly the fame. It confifts of two large wide ftreets, befides two others of a fmaller extent.*

About the year 1780, the inhabitants of the town and parifh did not exceed 2500. In the late return under the population act, they were 2753. The fituation is efteemed healthy. The ruins and poor remains of fome gentlemen's feats are ftill fubfifting;† but as they have been alienated, and fold to different people, who do not refide upon them, they are dwindled into farm-houfes, and of courfe not worthy of notice. Indeed two genteel houfes have of late been built and inhabited by Mr. Handford and Mr. Sharland.‡ The church is fituated at

Vol. III.   D   the

Not in charge.

	Certified Value.
	£. s. d.
Anfty St. Mary's, alias Marianfleigh Ch. Rep. B. Proc. ii*s*. ii*d*. ob. Syn. ii*s*. v*d*. A. D. Proc. ii*s*. ii*d*. ob. r. V. 40*l*.	24 0 0
Patrs. Mayor and Chamber of Exeter.	
South-molton Cur. [St. Mary Magdalen]. This was a rectory, valued at 67*l*. 3*s*. 4*d*. Rep. B. Proc. vi*s*. viii*d*. Syn. ii*s*. v*d*. A. D. Proc. vi*s*. viii*d*. r. V. 80*l*.	20 0 0
Patrs. Dean and Canons of Windfor.	
Twitchen, [St. Peter] Ch. to North-molton.	

* At the eaftern end is a ftone bridge of arches, which parts the parifh from Bifhop's Nymett. About two miles diftance from the town, on the fouth, is another ftone bridge of arches, which parts it from Marianfleigh; another in the fame manner between this parifh and Chittlehamton; a fourth not far diftant between this town and Filleigh. Thefe bridges are repaired partly by particular eftates, and partly by the adjoining parifhes. Some good and valuable woods lie within its limits, confifting of the ufual produce of this part of the country. Roads not to be highly extolled—the beft are turnpike; but even thefe in fome meafure indifferent. Within this parifh are feveral good farm-houfes, and valuable eftates belonging to them: Only two villages, both on the weftern fide; their names Hill and Shallow ford.

† " This town was written *Snotmoulton*, when holy King Edward held it in demefne, as the roll of Winchefter relateth. William Lord Martin held this land in King Edward 1ft's age, by ferjeancy, to find a man with a bow and three arrows to attend the Earl of Gloucefter when he goeth to Gower to hunt; which lands defcended to James Lord Audleigh, and by an entail by him made to the heirs males of his body, the remainder to the king. After the death of Nicholas Lord Audleigh, that died the 15th of King Richard 2d, this mannor came to the king. Since when the burgeffes have bought the borough, which hath a mayor for its chief magiftrate, a recorder, town-clerk, with ferjeants, and a Saturday's market, with fundry fairs well frequented and furnifhed with neceffaries, from which town the hundred hath name. The lord of the royalty, is Hatch, an ancient family fo named of their houfe in this parifh; which land, with de la Leigh, Jeffery Hatch his daughter, by her marriage, brought to William Worlington in the reign of King Henry 3d, whofe grandchild William had divers daughters, whereof Joan was wedded to William Atwater, and had this land for her portion. Thomas, the fon of William and Joan, was called Hatch of his habitation; of which family many generations fucceeded, and it hath lords at this prefent fo furnamed. Arthur Hatch married the daughter of Sir John Chichefter, his grand-father the daughter of Fortefcue.

Aure or *Aller*, had John de Aure or Allar for lord the 24th of King Edward 1ft, whom William Aller his fon fucceeded, whofe daughter Clayes was married to Gilbert Hatch, and brought this land unto that family in King Edward 2d's time, which hath been enjoyed by that name ever fince to this prefent fome ten defcents.

Clotworthy lieth likewife in this parifh of South-moulton, which had Robert Furlong for its lord in the time of King John, whofe grandchild Robert, in the end of King Henry 3d's time, affumed the name of his dwelling, which ever fince hath continued the furname of that family, even fourteen generations.

Black-Pole, happily of fome ftanding water of a black colour, is a tything in Moulton, where Pollard, Gambon, and Huifh, held lands; fome are of opinion, that a mannor divided between coheirs, each of them hath a mannor.

Thomas Barkley was lord of lands in the hamlet of *Eaft Bray*, about the beginning of King Henry 3d's reign. Mathew Crawthorn was feized thereof in King Edward 2d's age, which inheritance afterwards came to the Cornews."—*Rifdon.*

" In this parifh is *Bremridge*, originally the lands of Raleigh; from whom they came to the Lord Martin; thence to Fortefcue; and at length to Giffard of Brightley, who fold them to Judge Dodderidge. Here the judge built a genteel houfe about the year 1622; but having no iffue of his own, at the time of his death, he left it to his brother Pentecoft Dodderidge, of Barnftaple, merchant, from whom it defcended to his fon John Dodderidge, who was bred to the law, and became very eminent in his profeffion. He was thrice married—firft to Jane, the daughter of Hele, of South-Hele; fecondly, to Martha, daughter of Sir Thomas Dacus, of Hereford, knight; thirdly, to Judith, daughter of Goardon, of Afhington hall, Suffolk. He had a fon named John, who died young, and was buried in the church of Barnftaple, in 1663; but at his death left no furviving iffue. He confiderably improved his houfe at Bremeridge, which, together with his other eftate, fell among his three fifters; who were thus difpofed of in marriage—Mary, to John Martin, of Exeter, merchant; Dorothy, firft to John Clarke, of Exeter, merchant, and fecondly to John Lovering, of Barnftaple, merchant; and Elizabeth Dodderidge, to Richard Croffing, of Exeter, merchant; whofe youngeft daughter, Sarah Croffing, married to John Blundell, of Tiverfon, efq. brought Bremeridge into that family."—*Prince's Worthies.*

‡ At Southmolton are two endowed fchools; one for latin, arithmetick, and writing, and the other a charity fchool, with houfes and a falary to the refpective mafters and miftrefs—one meeting-houfe—one chapel within the parifh, (not licenced nor confecrated, within remembrance, by any bifhop), duty in it once a month, with an eftate annexed to fupport it, and to anfwer the purpofes of its founder.

the northern extremity of the town, a handfome and venerable fabrick, dedicated to the Virgin Mary, with an organ, and fome decent monuments.*

Thro' WARKLEIGH,† SATERLEIGH,‡ GEORGE-NYMET, (George-Nymton, or
Nymet St. George),§ and BISHOP'S NYMET,‖ we haften to KING'S NYMET, or
KING'S NYMTON. This laft, in length about five miles, and in breadth about the
fame, is an enclofed parifh, and well wooded. The farms are, in general, not
very large, and are moftly well wooded.¶ Henry the 1ft gave his lands at King's-
Nymet to Joel de Mayne; which King John, on the feparation of Normandy
from England, feized into his hands again.*† Henry the 3d beftowed them on
Roger le Zouch; from whom Geofrey Lucy received them. In the time of Edw.
3d, Sir Geofrey Cornwall, knight, was lord of King's-Nymton; during the minority of whofe heir, Ingram Coucy, Earl of Bedford, held the fame. Sir
Bryan Cornwall and Sir John de Cornwall, knights, poffeft this place in the
reigns of Henry the 4th and 5th. King's-Nymton hath fince been the feat of
the Pollards, a numerous race, and allied to noble families. Sir Hugh Pollard
married a daughter of Sir John Chichefter, knight. Sir Lewis Pollard, his fon,
(in Rifdon's time),‡§ enjoyed here a fair demefne, with a park and manor; and

was

* " 1547, Oct. 7th. To the dean and canons of the King's free-chapel of St. George, within the caftle of Windfor, for exchange of the
manor and rectory of Iver, and of the manor of Damary Court, and divers other lands and tenements, to King Henry given and made
over, and divers others furrendered by the dean and chapter, were granted the rectories and churches of *Bradwynch, Northam, Iplepen,
Affington,* and *South-Moltcn,* in the county of Devon," &c. *Strype's* Ecclefiaftical Memorials, vol. ii. p. 75.

† The Raleighs of WARKLEIGH flourifhed there from the days of Henry 2d. to thofe of Edw. 2d, when John Raleigh fold to William
Lord Martin, the manors of Warkley and Saterley, with all his rents in Sidbury, Wootton, North Bray, South Bray, Blackpole, Barnftaple, Southmolton, Bremeridge, Blackwell, Haddircombe, Hill, Calcote, and Honigton, (qu. Honiton). From the Lord Martin this
eftate defcended to the noble family of Bourchier Earl of Bath; and thence to the heirs general. *Prince.*

‡ " The Bray carrieth his courfe by *Saterley,* which mannor did anciently belong to the Raleighs, and did defcend in that name, from
King John's time, unto the 16th year of King Edward the 2d. John Raleigh, the fon of Peter, fold it unto William Lord Martin. In
this parifh, Richard de Down granted a farthing of land to Walter le Hopper, in the time of King Edward the 3d. *Tefte Gervaife Raleigh
Mil. Roger de la Hill, Ralph de Saterleigh.*" *Rifdon.*

§ Broom-houfe, in *George-Nympton,* formerly poffeffed by John Hale, gent. now belongs to Thomas Gay, gent. a defcendant from
Matthew Gay, M. A. who was deprived about the year 1645 of the living of Bratton-Fleming, under fequeftration. The tower to the
church of George-Nymet was built with *brick,* in the year 1671. It is 39 feet high.

‖ " *Nimet Epifcopi,* the ancient land of the bifhops of this diocefs. In which parifh ftands *Grilfton,* that had anciently lords furnamed De
Grilfton, a family that continued from King John's time, unto the reign of King Richard 2d, when the only inheritrix of Robert Grilfton
was married to John Vauitort of Clift St. Laurence; and by Elizabeth, daughter and heir of his grandchild, this inheritance came to Sir
Hugh Pollard, knight, who was the fon of that reverend judge, Sir Lewes Pollard, which dwelt here in the days of King Henry the 7th,
now owned by his great grand-child, Sir Lewes Pollard, baronet.—*Rawefton* was the ancient inheritance of Ralph de Dodifcombe, and
Walter Nymet who alfo held Kippingcot, the 28th of King Henry the 3d, after whom, Thomas de Horton was feized thereof. *Beamport*
within this parifh, had William de Brome, and Gilbert fo furnamed, for its lords in the time of King John, with lands in Uppecot. Since
it became the Raleighs inheritance; in which place Sir Henry Raleigh feated himfelf in King Edward 1ft's age, which Raleighs were diftinguifhed by this houfe from other families of that name; of whom Joan the heir general, was married to Sir Thomas St. Albin, knight.—
In this parifh, is *Whitechapel. Acres thre. Amys John Blake, Joan le feme Will. Baffet, Chivaler, Salutz in Dieu pur ceo que jeo ai grant a Thome
Champernoon Otis Bodragon, Thome Collin & Thome Cottisford, Parfon de St. Illogan & a James Gerveis les Rents & Service; & la revercon. de
vous John Blake, & Joan votre feme de Ter. que tenet de Moy in le Mannor de* White-chapel, *in le Com. de Devonfhire. Dat. a Tebedy la Merkdy,
in la feft du Nat. du St. Jean Baptift. Lan. du Regn Rich.* 2. *Sifme* 6." *Rifdon.*

" In Nymet church Judge Pollarde lyeth honourably interred, having a monument erected to his memory; a window of which church,
whereunto he was a benefactor, fheweth his name, marriage, office, and iffue, with his effigies, and his ladies, figured fairly in glafs, he
having *ten fons* on the one fide, and fhe fo many daughters on the other, a fair off-fpring; with this infcription :—*Orate pro bono ftatu
Lodovici Pollard Militis, unius Jufticiar. Domini Regis de Banco, & Elize Uxor. ejus, qui iftam feneftram fieri fecerunt.*" *Rifdon.*

¶ The defcription of King's-Nymton will fuit many other parifhes in this deanry.

*† Whether Dr. Jafper Mayne, archdeacon of Chichefter and chaplain in ordinary to Charles the 2d, a native of Hatherleigh, was de-
fcended or not from this Joel de Mayne, is uncertain.

‡§ Here Sir Lewis Pollard, the judge, in the reign of Henry the 7th, purchafed a confiderable eftate, and built a good houfe on it, and
inclofed a large park adjoining to the manfion. He married Agnes, daughter of Thomas Hext, of Kingfton, in the parifh of Staverton;
by whom he had eleven fons, and as many daughters. Four of his fons, according to Dr. Fuller, were knighted, Sir Hugh, Sir John, Sir
Richard, and Sir George. The others flourifhed in their feveral ftations, particularly John, archdeacon of Barum, and canon of the church
of Exeter. The daughters were married into families of confequence; as, the firft, to Sir Hugh Stukeley, of Affton; the fecond, to Sir
Hugh Courtenay, of Powderham; the third, to Sir Hugh Pawlet, of Sampford Peverel; the fourth, to Sir John Crocker, of Lineham.—
The pofterity of Sir Lewis Pollard, the judge, continued in this parifh for about five defcents. His grandfon Lewis was an eminent lawyer
in the time of Edward the 6th. There were three knights in a direct line, and two baronets; the laft of whom was Sir Hugh Pollard,
baronet, a gentleman of a noble mind, fpirited, hofpitable, and benevolent. Sir Hugh Pollard married the Countefs Dowager of Berkfhire, fifter to Henry, Earl of Oxford, and left only one daughter. He fold King's-Nymton to Sir Arthur Northcote, baronet, who was
fucceeded by Sir Francis Northcote. His baronetfhip defcended to his younger brother Sir Amias; but very little, if any, of the ancient
eftate. *Prince.*—The Pollard arms: *Argent a chevron B. between three mullets gules.*

was confpicuous for his fumptuous hofpitality. He married a daughter of Sir Henry Berkeley, knight; his fon, the daughter of Vere, Earl of Oxford, the Countefs of Berkfhire. From the Pollards the eftate paffed by purchafe to the Northcotes; who fold it to James Buller, efq. This gentleman built the prefent manfion, New-place, or King's-Nymton Park.* The prefent poffeffor is John Buller, efq. March 5th, 1798, died, in her 75th year, the Hon. Lady Jane Buller, relict of James Buller, efq. (who died in 1765) daughter of Allen, E. Bathurft, and mother of Sir F. Buller.

In W. WORLINGTON, *Afton* was formerly the refidence of the *Stuckleys*, a family of fome diftinction, but now extinct. The laft female branch and heirefs of this manor, was the mother of George Buck, efq. of Daddon, near Bideford. A fmall part only of the ancient houfe is ftanding, with the gateway; which, however, denotes the whole to have been a large building, in the caftle form.‡

In WOLFARDISWORTHY the manor was, for upwards of 150 years, in the poffeffion of the Walronds of Bradfield. It was offered to fale in 1788; the eftates were purchafed by the different occupiers; and the manerial rights, royalty, cottages, and waftes, with the perpetual advowfon of the rectory, by John Hole, the prefent incumbent.

CRUWYS-MORCHARD appears by Domefday, to have been the land of Wm. Chievre, taken from Ailward Tochifone foon after the conqueft. Rifdon in his MSS. Survey of Devonfhire, fays it was the inheritance of Warinus, in the Saxons' time, which Ailward Tochifone wrongfully wrefted from him at the conqueft. How long it was fpelt Morchet, and when it was firft named Cruwys-Morchard, is uncertain. It appears, on an inquifition taken 24th Edward 1ft, 1296, by Kirkby's Feodary, that Robert Cruwys, knight, then held the manor of Cruwys-Morchard by one knight's fee of the Earl of Cornwall, as of the honour of Braynz, (i. e. Bradninch). Cruwys-Morchard is fituated about five miles W. S. W. from Tiverton, amongft hills and moors, and the wildeft part of it has been cultivated as rye ground. There is no account of this parifh worthy of being recorded, (except that the family of the Cruwys's have been feated there for many centuries paft), till the year 1689, when on the 13th day of February, the church, which was built 20th Henry the 8th, 1529, was confumed by lightning.§

WITHERIDGE

---

* The park formerly contained a confiderable number of deer; but of late years it has been difparked, and is now in a courfe of tillage. The eftate abounds with woods; in fome of which is good timber. The fituation is retired and rural. The houfe confifts of four fronts, with five windows in one, and a portico before it. The houfe ftands on a very fteep hill.

‡ *Weft-Worlington* was anciently William Worlington's lands, whom Sir Matthew his fon fucceeded; whofe fon left iffue two daughters his heirs, the one married to William Atwater in Molton, the other to Robert de Crawthorne, to whofe part this land fell; which, after two defcents in that name, went to Walter Marwood, by marriage of Thomazin his wife, who fold the fame unto Thomas Affeton the 24th year of King Edward 3d. for the performance whereof, the faid Marwood was bound unto the faid Affeton, that his wife fhould confirm the bargain when fhe fhould come unto her full age. In which king's reign, Thomas Affeton was fheriff of Devon, and dwelt at *Affeton*, fometime a parifh of itfelf, now united to Weft-Worlington, and remaineth a tything in North-Tawton hundred. Katherine, the only heir of the laft of this line, was linked in wedlock to Sir Hugh Stuckley, fon of Richard Stuckley in Huntingdonfhire, and of Elizabeth, lady of Chuton. Her fecond hufband was William Bourchier, Lord Fitz-Warren; fince which time, this family have made their principal dwelling at Affeton. John Stuckley, the now inheritor, married to his firft wife, the daughter of Halfe, fecondly, the daughter of Coade; his father Sir Lewis Stuckley, the daughter of Monk; his grandfire the daughter of Sir John St. Leger, knight." *Rifdon.*

§ On the 23d of the fame month a rate was made for re-building the church, tower, and cafting the bells. An eftimate having been made of the expence of re-building, cafting the bells, and erecting the pews, and it amounting to the fum of £.1800 and upwards, it was refolved to petition Sir Jonathan Trelawney, bart. the then bifhop of the fee of Exeter, for leave to collect a charitable contribution throughout his diocefe; which petition was figned by all the principal inhabitants of the parifh of Cruwys-Morchard. His lordfhip

moft

WITHERIDGE is an extenfive parifh, the head of a hundred. It is fituate on a ridge of land which runs from Chawleigh to Templeton and Stoodleigh, in a line with the ridge of land whence it derives its name. Its principal river is the Dart. The good land is inclofed with hedges, the moor land open.* The Melhuifh family have poffeffed the fpiritual manor, and the Chichefter family, Lord Donegal, the temporal. His lordfhip fold the temporal manor to the Fellowes family, who now poffefs it.‡

STOODLEIGH,† which ftands high, from eaft to weft feven miles; OAKFORD,§ remarkable for its oak forefts; ROSE-ASH,‖ the refidence of Effe and Southcombe; KNOWSTONE ¶ and MOLLAND,*§ well wooded with oak, afh, and beech; and

NORTH-

moft gracioufly received the petition, and in confequence thereof figned a recommendatory letter to the clergy throughout the diocefe, defiring them " to promote the good end thereof, by their own example, and ftirring up the hearts of their people to a liberal contribution " to fo good a work, on fo fad and ftrange an occafion." In confequence of this petition and letter, the parifhioners, by an eafy rate, were enabled to build the upper part of their tower, new roof the church, and erect pews in the manner it now ftands. The church was completed in the year 1702.

* It has two hamlets, called Heales and Dryford, where there is a bridge over the Dart, confifting of three arches. The houfes are thatched farms about a hundred a year, and from thence down to twenty pounds a year. The inhabitants were about * fix hundred in 1790. They are long lived, frugal and healthy, moftly farmers and day labourers: two carry on the manufactory of wool, three fhopkeepers, three maltfters, one furgeon. Near one hundred farms, about fifty paupers, many rackholders, many leafeholders and freeholders.

‡ " Here Reginald was feized of lands, at the conqueft time, by the name of *Wederidge.* Sir Robert Fitz-Payne held this mannor, and the honour of the hundred, the 30th year of King Henry the 3d. William Poleine held half a knight's fee there, the 8th of Edward the 2d. Roger Marchant was lord of lands in this tything, and held the hundred the 19th of King Edward the 3d. The Lord William Botereaux dyed feized of this manor and hundred, in King Richard the 2d's reign, with the royalty thereof, whofe fon the Lord William, fucceeded him. This burrough hath a fair on the feaft-day of St. John the Baptift." *Rifdon.*

† " On the weft-fide of the Ex ftands *Stodley,* a place well ftored with woods, which were the lands of Roger de Campeaux in King Henry 2d's time. In the time of King Henry 3d, Robert de Campeaux did grant half a knight's fee, and the advowfon of the church, unto Sir Roger Fitz-Payne. knight, which from that family, by Anftile and Kelly, came unto the Carews, who enjoy a large demefne in this parifh, with a fair inheritance. Edith, the daughter of Thomas Kelly, married Humphry Cawoodleigh, which man, to gain his wife's inheritance, brought his concubine inftead of his contemned wife, and levied a fine in the name of the faid Edith; but fhe dying without iffue, the heirs-general of Kelly recovered Stodley, and much other lands. In this parifh is an high hill, called *Warbrighfley.* On the top thereof ftandeth a beacon; the fetting up of which was ordained in the time of King Edward 2d, when he doubted of the landing of his Queen Ifabel and Sir John of Henold. Here, by the declining of the country, the current of a river there arifing, may be turned to the North or South Sea. Ralph de Alabafter held lands here, and in Blackworthy, the 27th of Henry the 3d, which by Agnes, the heir of that name, came to Adam Sachvile, which Adam, in King Edward the 3d's reign, gave to John Grilfton and William Carden the rents and fervices of divers his free tenants and villains." *Rifdon.*

§ The name of the parifh in old deeds and writings is Okeford, but at prefent commonly fpelt Oakford. It feems to derive its name from the great quantity of oak in it, and the two rivers that bound it on the eaft and fouth. It is about five miles and a half in length, and two miles and a half in breadth. Its fituation is high: It abounds in fprings. It has a bridge of feven arches over the river Exe, built of ftone, with wooden rails on each fide. The bridge is kept in repair, one half by the parifh of Bamton, the other half by fix or feven eftates belonging to the manor. The parifh is for the moft part inclofed, and well-wooded on the eaft and fouth fides. It has about 500 acres of coppice and timber wood at prefent, and probably contained much more formerly. The moft flourifhing trees are the oak. The roads, as yet, are but in an indifferent condition, but from the attention lately paid them, may be faid to be in an improving ftate. The vallies, thro' which the Exe winds, with the furrounding hills, of different fhapes, and varioufly cloathed, fome with coppice, and others with large timber trees, prefent feveral picturefque views.—The houfes are for the moft part built of ftone, and thatched, are tolerably neat and compact, with generally fmall gardens and orchards belonging to them. The farms are moderately large, and in an improving ftate of cultivation.—The inhabitants amounting in number to about 450, are in general healthy and long-lived.—The manor of Oakford was granted by James the Ift, in the tenth year of his reign, to Richard Hill, alias Spurway, a younger brother of the family of that name. Henry Spurway, the fon of William, the laft of his male defcendants, died in 1680, leaving four daughters, between whom the manor was divided. —— Sanford, efq. of Warford, Somerfet, is in poffeffion of one part of the manor, and the Rev. Mr. Parkin, great grandfon of the above Henry Spurway, of the other; and who is alfo patron of the rectory. The advowfon is an appendage of the manor. Spurway was the ancient feat of the elder branch of the family of the Spurways. It was burnt down a few years fince, but has been fince rebuilt for the ufe of the tenant on the eftate. The barton or manor houfe, adjoining to the church-yard, belongs to the Rev. Mr. Parkin —Hightly St. Mary, as it is generally named, is looked on as an extra-parochial place. Its fituation is high. It is a manor, and the fee of it belongs to Rolle. There was formerly a chapel in it, the ruins of which are ftill to be feen. Two or three perfons were buried there about 60 years fince. The inhabitants are not more than three or four families. They attend divine fervice at Oakford, where they marry, baptife, and bury, but pay no tithes.

‖ " The lake which comes from Knowfton, leads me to *Rofe-Afh,* corruptly fo called for *Effe-Raph,* of the lords thereof. Sir Ralph de Effe, that dwelt there in the days of King Henry 3d, defcended from Wagerus de Effe, that had this inheritance in the beginning of King Henry the 2d's time. A tribe that hath been eminent in this fhire, which the places to which their name remaineth plainly prove, and flourifheth even from the firft time of the Normans government, unto the reign of King Edward the 3d. William Ingaret, the inheritrix of Sir Aland Effe, was married unto Giffard." *Rifdon.*

¶ " The Taw receiveth much increafe from Moule, whofe current is augmented by a brook that cometh from *Knowfton,* anciently *Cuntefton,* of which mannor Ailmer de Brett was lord in King Henry the 2d's reign, who granted the fame to Richard Beaple, whofe pofterity made this place their dwelling; of which family were divers knights. Sir Ralph Beaple, the laft of that houfe, had iffue one daughter his heir, married to Sir Neal Loring, one of the premier knights of the order of the garter, that had iffue Elizabeth, wife of the Lord Harrington, and Margaret married to Thomas Payner. This mannor fell to the Lord Harrington's part, whofe inheritrix, by match, brought the fame to the Lord Bonvile, and by the duke confequently to the crown; which was purchafed by Robert Pollard, a younger fon of Sir Lewis Pollard,

* On the late return, 875.

NORTH-MOLTON,* large and populous, are the only remaining parifhes that need detain us.

Pollard, knight, where he inhabited, and his pofterity enjoyed it after him. In the conqueror's time, Ulfe held *Wadham*, after him Bret, from whom it came to Beaple; and in the time of King Henry the 4th, Sir John Wadham poffeffed both Eaft and Weft-Wadham, from whom this land defcended to the heirs general of Nicholas Wadham. Wadham was a freeholder of it, in the time of Edward the 1ft." *Rifdon.*

*† " *Molland,* the king's demefne at the conqueft. Since, Ralph Sarazenus was feized of lands in this tything; and in the time of Edw. the 1ft, Ralph Champeaux was lord of lands, and fixed his dwelling here, hence called Champefton. He was fucceeded by many of that name. Since, this land hath been fome defcents in the name of Columbe; of which family, three fucceffively have been called Hugh. The prefent poffeffor married the daughter of Courtney, his father the daughter of Fortefcue, his grandfire the daughter of Frye. *Botreaux-Park,* was the ancient lands and dwelling of Botreaux in Devonfhire, a name that hath continued in thefe our weftern parts, from the conqueft, unto the reign of King Henry the 6th. At which time, John Botreaux, a younger fon of William Lord Botreaux, captain of Charenton in Normandy, in the time of King Henry the 5th, enjoyed this land, who fighting valiantly at St. Albans, was flain by the Duke of York, the 23d day of May, 33 Henry 6th. William Botreaux, the firft I find of this name, was in great favour with King Henry the 1ft, and married Alice, daughter and coheir of Robert Corbett, fifter of Amafia, on whom that king begot Reginald, Earl of Cornwall. Afterwards Sir Philip Courtney, fecond fon of Sir Philip and Elizabeth, the Lord Hungerford's daughter, had this land diftinguifhed from other families of that name, by his houfe. From whom iffued a large offspring, who defcending from the earls of Devon, were ingrafted into that family again; which name continueth lord of this land, and flourifheth here to this day." *Rifdon.*

" Sir Philip, the fecond fon of the fecond Sir Philip Courtenay, of Powderham-caftle, had Molland for his portion. He married a daughter of Robert Hingefton, of Wonewell, and had iffue by her two fons and two daughters. His firft fon was John, who fucceeded his father in the eftate, and married Joan, daughter of Robert Brett, of Pilton, in the parifh of Pilton, and died in the year 1510. This John Courtenay had a fon named Philip, who was fixteen years old, when his father died; and it was he that continued the family. Sir Philip Courtenay of Molland's fecond fon was called William: he was feated at Loughter, in the parifh of Plymton St. Mary. Sir Philip Courtenay of Molland's firft daughter Elizabeth, was married to Sir Edward Courtenay, made Earl of Devonfhire by Henry the 7th; the fecond daughter, Margaret, was married to Sir John Champernowne of Modbury. The family of Sir Philip Courtenay, of Molland, who was fheriff of Devon, the 10th of Edward the 4th, flourifhed for many generations, to the year 1732; when John Courtenay, of Molland, the laft male of the family, died without iffue: and his brother George, a little before, died iffuelefs. They left only two fifters." *Cleveland.*

* *North-Molton* is very extenfive, the fituation high, adjoining the foreft of Exmoor, on the fouth fide. It is well wooded, the moft flourifhing trees oak. There are feveral manors in the parifh, which belong to Lord Boringdon and Sir Charles Bampfylde. The houfes are principally thatched. The inhabitants of the town confift chiefly of combers and weavers, on which account the parifh poor-rates are very large. The number of inhabitants are 1541, are very healthy, and live in general to a great age. The church is dedicated to All-Saints: it is very well feated, large, and built of excellent ftone, raifed in the parifh. There are two good monuments erected in the church, an ancient one to the memory of Sir Amias Bampfyld's family, and a modern one to John Burgefs, efq. of Upcott, in the fame parifh. The tower is a lofty well-built ftructure, fame ftone as the church, and contains fix new bells. The church is very large; on the weft-fide adjoining is a well built houfe, belonging to Lord Boringdon; on the eaft-fide is a fmall one, (Sir Charles Bampfylde's); and on the fouth is the vicarage houfe, which is a very ancient, low building. It is an impropriated living, (Lord Boringdon the rector. Four miles diftant from North-Molton church, eaftward, is the fmall parifh-church of TWITCHEN, dedicated to St. Peter;—it is called a chapelry, annexed to North-Molton, and is ferved by the fame vicar, who is paid a fmall annual ftipend, (i. e. £.32 6s. 8d.) for the care of both.

ARCHDEACONRY OF BARNSTAPLE.

DEANRY of SHIRWELL.

I HAVE here to enumerate the parifhes of Shirwell, Afhford, Heanton-Punch-ardon, Braunton, Marwood, Eaftdown, Bittadon, Georgeham, Weftdown, Morthoe, Ilfracombe, Berrynarber, Kentifbury, Combmartin, Trentifhoe, Mar-tinhoe, Lynton, Countefbury, Brendon, Parracombe, Challacombe, Arlington, Loxore, Bratton-fleming, Stoke-rivers, Highbray, Charles, Eaft-Buckland, Weft-Buckland, Goodleigh.*

SHIRWELL

* " Benefices remaining in charge:

First Fruits. £. s. d.			Yearly Tenths. £. s. d.
13 18 1½	Arlington R. [St. James] Rep. B. Proc. vis. viiid. Syn. iis. vd. A. D. Proc. vis. viiid. r. V. 110l. -	- 1 7 9¾	
	Patr. John Chichefter, efq. Ca.		
34 15 10	Berry-narber R. [St. Peter] Rep. B. Proc. vis. viiid. Syn. iis. vd. A. D. Proc. vis. viiid. r. V. 300l. -	- 3 9 7	
	Patrs. Reprefentatives of the four daughters of —————————, efq.—Mrs. Pearfe, the fecond daughter, devifed her turn to the bifhop of Exeter, for ever.		
29 15 5	Bratton Fleming R. [St. Peter] Rep. B. Proc. vis. viiid. Syn. iis. vd. A. D. Proc. vis. viiid. r. V. 240l. - 2 19 6½		
	Patrs. Mafter and Fellows of Gonvil and Caius College, Cambridge.		
16 3 6¼	Braunton V. [St. Brannock] a Pec. of the Dean of Exeter. Rep. none in charge. r. V. 160l. - - - 1 12 4¼		
	Patr. Dean of Exeter.		
9 10 0	Charell alias Charles R. [St. John Baptift] Rep. B. Proc. vis. viiid. Syn. iis. vd. A. D. Proc. iiis. ivd. r. V. 120l. 0 19 0		
	Patr. H. Vivian, clerk.		
11 9 2	Chollacombe R. [Holy Trinity] Rep. B. Proc. vis. viiid. Syn. iis. vd. A. D. Proc. iiis. ivd. r. V. 80l. - 1 2 11		
	Patr. Earl Fortefcue.		
38 8 9	Comb-Martin R. [St. Peter] Rep. B. Proc. vis. viiid. Syn. iis. vd. A. D. Proc. vis. viiid. r. V. 200l. - - 3 18 10½		
	Patr. Mr. John Unwin.		
9 1 8	{ Eaft-Buckland R. [St. Michael] united to the R. of Filleigh, in D. of Barnftaple. Rep. B. Proc. iiis. ivd. } 0 18 2 { Syn. iis. vd. A. D. Proc. iiis. ivd. r. V. 90l. - - - - - - - }		
	Patr. Earl Fortefcue.		
18 3 9	Eaft-Downe R. [St. John Baptift] Rep. B. Proc. vis. viiid. Syn. iis. vd. A. D. Proc. vis. viiid. r. V. 160l. - 1 16 4½		
	Patr. John Pine, clerk.		
40 17 11	Georgeham R. [St. George] Rep. B. Proc. vis. viiid. Syn. iis. vd. A. D. Proc. vis. viiid. r. V. 270l. - 4 1 9½		
	Patr. Sir John Chichefter, bart.		
14 19 4½	Goodleigh R. [St. Peter] Rep. B. Proc. is. ivd. A. D. Proc. is. vd. r. V. 120l. - - - 1 19 11¼		
	Patr. Mrs. Churchward.		
22 7 11	{ Heamton, alias Heaunton Punchardon R. [St. Auftin] Rep. B. Proc. vis. viiid. Syn. iis. vd. A. D. Proc. } 2 4 9½ { vis. viiid. r. V. 180l. - - - - - - - - - - }		
	Patr. Baffet.		
14 6 8	Highbray R. [All Saints] Rep. B. Proc. vis. viiid. Syn. iis. vd. A. D. Proc. vis. viiid. r. V. 140l. - - 1 8 8		
	Patr. Oxenham.		
12 10 7½	Kettefbury alias Kentifbury R. [Ded. unc.] Rep. B. Proc. vis. viiid. Syn. iis. vd. A. D. Proc. vis. viiid. r. V. 140l. 1 5 0¾		
	Patr. Mr. Sweet.		
9 14 4½	Loxore R. [St. Michael] Rep. B. Proc. ivs. vid. Syn. iis. vd. A. D. Proc. iiis. ivd. r. V. 100l. - - 0 19 5¼		
	Patr. John Chichefter, efq.		
24 8 6¼	{ Marwood R. [St. Michael] Pri. Plymton Penf. vs. Rep. B. Proc. vis. viiid. Syn. iis. vd. A. D. Proc. vis. } 2 8 10¼ { viiid. r. V. 300l. - - - - - - - - - }		
	Patrs. St. John's College, Cambridge.		
13 10 10	Parracombe R. [Ded. unc.] Rep. B. Proc. vis. viiid. Syn. iis. vd. A. D. Proc. vis. viiid. r. V. 130l. - - 1 7 1		
	Patr. —— St. Aubyn, efq.		
30 3 11½	Shirwell R. [St. Peter] Rep. B. Proc. vis. viiid. Syn. iis. vd. A. D. Proc. vis. viiid. r. V. 260l. - - 3 0 4¾		
	Patr. Sir John Chichefter.		
14 14 7	Stoke Rivers R. [St. Bartholomew] Rep. B. Proc. vis. viiid. Syn. iis. vd. A. D. Proc. vis. viiid. r. V. 130l. - 1 0 5		
13 13 4	Weft-Buckland R. [St. Peter] Rep. B. Proc. iiis. ivd. Syn. iis. vd. A. D. Proc. iiis. ivd. r. V. 130l. - - 1 7 4		
	Patr. Francis Baffet, efq.		

Difcharged.

King's Books.			Certified Value.
0 0 0	Afhford V. [St. Peter] Rep. B. Proc. iis. iid. ob. A. D. Proc. viid. r. V. 60l. • - -	- 38 0 0	
	Patr. The KING.		
5 2 8½	Bittadon R. [St. Peter] Rep. B. Proc. iis. iid. ob. Syn. iis. vd. A. D. Proc. iis. iid. ob. r. V. 35l. -	- 32 0 0	
	Patr. —— Barbor, efq.		
9 4 2	Brendon R. [St. Brendon] Rep. B. Proc. vis. viiid. Syn. iis. vd. A. D. Proc. vis. viiid. r. V. 70l. -	- 50 0 0	
	Patr. Sir John Chichefter.		
50 4 4½	Ilfordcombe V. [Holy Trinity] Rep. B. Proc. vis. viiid. which is paid by Impr. r. V. 70l. - -	- 50 0 0	
	Patr. Prebendary thereof in the church of Sarum.		

Martinhoe

SHIRWELL lies about three miles to the N. E. of Barnſtaple.* The principal place in this pariſh, is *Youlſton*, the ſeat of Sir John Chicheſter, bart.†

The Iſle of LUNDY (about four leagues from Hertland-point) is included in the deanry of Shirwell. It is five miles long, and about two broad.‡

HEANTON PUNCHARDON (ſo called from its ancient lords, the Punchardons,) lies on the north-ſide of the river Taw. § The Punchardons‖ flouriſhed at Heanton for ſeveral generations; afterwards the Beaumonts; then the Baſſets.¶ Heanton, or Heanton-court, is a pleaſant ſeat.*‡

BRAUNTON

King's Books.				Certified Value.		
£.	s.	d.		£.	s.	d.
8	10	10	Martinhoe R. [St. Martin] Rep. B. Proc. ivs. vid. Syn. iis. vd. A. D. Proc. ivs. vid. r. V. 50l. - -	- 47	0	0
			Patr. John Chicheſter, eſq. Cath.			
9	19	4½	Morthoe V. [St. Mary] Rep. B. Proc. vis. viiid. Syn. iis. vd. A. D. Proc. vis. viiid. r. V. 48l. -	- 40	0	0
			Patrs. Dean and Chapter of Exeter.			
8	8	4	Trentiſhoe R. [St. Peter] Rep. B. Proc. iis. iid. ob. Syn. viid. A. D. Proc. iis. iid. ob. r. V. 50l. -	- 35	0	0
			Patr. John Rogers, eſq.			
9	0	7½	Weſt-Downe V. [Holy Trinity] Rep. B. Proc. vis. viiid. Syn. iis. vd. A. D. Proc. vis. viiid. r. V. 80l.	- 45	0	0
			Patr. Biſhop of Exeter.			

Not in charge.

Lynton and Counteſbury, Rep. B. Proc. xs. Syn. ivs. xd. A. D. Proc. xs. Together r. V. 60l. - - 10 0 0
Patr. Archdeacon of Barnſtaple.

* " *Sherwell, fons limpidus,* ſo named of the clear ſprings which bubble up here; a place which Alfred ordained to be honoured with the name of a hundred. Where, at the conqueſt, lands were allotted unto William Poilgi or Pola, a follower of the conqueror's." *Riſdon.*

† *Youlſton* was anciently the property and dwelling-place of Roſceline de Beaumont, Viſcount Main, who married Conſtance, a natural daughter of Henry the 1ſt; by which marriage he became poſſeſt of the chief manor of South-Tawton. By her, he had Richard, Lord Main, who gave this manor of South-Tawton with his daughter Conſtance, to the Lord Toni, Baron of Flamſtead, in Hertfordſhire. This gentleman was in great favor with Henry the 2d; inſomuch, that the king was graciouſly pleaſed to provide a royal huſband for his other daughter, Ermegand, and beſtowed her in marriage upon William, King of Scotland, ſurnamed the Lion: and Henry was himſelf preſent at the ceremony, which was ſolemnized at his expence. The noble family of Beaumont, or Bellemont, (as Dugdale calls it) flouriſhed at Youlſton from the days of Henry the 1ſt, to thoſe of Henry the 7th, nearly 400 years. They were lords of the manor and hundred of Sherwell, and poſſeſt a vaſt eſtate, by marrying into the families of Punchardon, Crawthorn, Stockey, Poteſford, Willington, Champer-nowne, Palton, and others. The family of Beaumont, about the time of Henry the 7th, iſſued into female heirs; in whom this ancient name, in the direct line, expired. After the death of Hugh Beaumont, the laſt heir male of this houſe, there aroſe three powerful com-petitors for the eſtate—Baſſet, who had married Joan, daughter of Sir Thomas Beaumont, the father—Chicheſter, who had taken to wife Margaret, the daughter and heirefs of Hugh Beaumont, a younger ſon by a ſecond wife—and John Bodrugan. How Bodrugan came by his title, may be worth relating. William, the eldeſt ſon of Sir Thomas Beaumont, married a young lady of an honourable houſe in this county, but in a ſhort time deſerted her, and died in London about two years after they had parted. In the mean time ſhe formed a connexion, in conſequence of which ſhe proved with child, and a ſon was born, who was bred up in ſecreſy. On the deceaſe of her huſband, Philip, his brother, ſucceeded to his eſtate, as next heir; and he died quietly poſſeſt of it; having firſt, for want of iſſue in himſelf, ſettled it on Thomas his next brother, by a ſecond wife. Thomas Beaumont alſo dying without iſſue, the eſtate came to Hugh, his younger brother; whoſe daughter and heirefs, Margaret, married into the family of the Chicheſters. Hugh, the laſt heir male being dead, John, the ſon of Joan, wife of William the elder brother, entered upon the lands of Beaumont, and claimed his right to the eſtate, as heir to William his father—and it was proved that he was born in wedlock. Many ſuits, however, commenced on this oc-caſion, and the ſubject was brought before parliament, in the time of Henry the 7th, who reſolved: *Nolumus leges Angliæ mutari*—or, that they would not make a baſtard of one born in wedlock. But this, it ſeems, was ſo plain a caſe, that the pretended heir was named by proclamation, John, the ſon of Joan Bodrugan, (Bodrugan her ſecond huſband), and ſo deemed a baſtard. Yet a compromiſe, at length, took place between all parties: and there was allotted to John, the ſon of Jane Bodrugan, an hundred pounds per ann. rent of affize; a part of which was Gittiſham, near Honiton, where he reſided: and he reſumed the name of Beaumont, which continued in his family for three generations. Heanton, and ſome other eſtates, fell to the ſhare of Baſſet, whoſe habitation there is called Court. Sherwell, Youlſton, and other lands, valued at 200 marks per ann. old rent, fell to the portion of Chicheſter; and Sir Arthur Chicheſter, bart. re-ſided there in Prince's time. " He hath made a very noble dwelling of Youlſton, ſays Prince, where he lives in great repute, worthy of that honourable ſtem from whence he is deſcended."—Of Chicheſter, three diſtinct families remain, in the north of Devonſhire: Sir John Chicheſter, of Youlſton, baronet;—Chicheſter, of Arlington, a Catholic;—Chicheſter, of Hall, " an old Engliſh gentleman." Sir J. Chicheſter, bart. is a bachelor: his heir is his firſt couſin, John Chicheſter, eſq. ſon of his father's younger brother, the Rev. William Chicheſter, M. A. rector of Sherwell.

‡ In William of Worceſter's time, it was uninhabited. Riſdon ſays: " In former time this iſland had governors; for Sir Ralph Wel-lington, the ſon of Sir Ralph Wellington, and the lady Joan Champernon had the cuſtody of *Londey* committed unto him. And after he was diſcharged thereof, it was committed to the keeping of Humphry de Bohun. This iſland in the reign of King Edward the 3d, was the lands of the Lutterels, now of the Grenviles, wherein, as in Ireland, no venomous worm or beaſt liveth; and therefore queſtionable to whether kingdom it appertaineth." *Riſdon.* It now belongs to Mr. Clevland.—See *Chapple's* Parochialia under Braunton, p. 1.

§ See *Chapple's Paroch.* p. 192.

‖ " *Heanton,* the dwelling of William de Punchardon, in the days of King Richard the 1ſt, who held four knights fees in this county, whoſe ſon Roger ſucceeded him. He granted to Robert Deandon one farthing of land in Wracheton, whereunto were witneſſes, Hugh de Chagford, and Philip de Doune. Of this family were divers knights; amongſt whom, Sir Richard Punchardon, performed worthy ſervice in the French wars, under King Edward the 3d. Sir John Punchardon, the laſt of this line, that lived in this place, left iſſue three daughters, Ermengard, the wife of Sir Philip Beaumont, Mable married unto Sir Henry Raleigh, and Margery unto Sir Richard Beaple. This mannor and manſion came to be part of Beaumont's portion, which after divers deſcents in that lineage, by Joan the daughter of Sir Thomas Beaumont, and Philip his wife, daughter of Sir John Dinham, deſcended unto the Baſſets." *Riſdon.*

¶ Oſmond Baſſet came into England with William the Conqueror: and from this gentleman deſcended the Baſſets of Drayton, in Staf-fordſhire; of Sapcote, in Leiceſterſhire; Hedendon, in Oxfordſhire; Wycomb, in Buckinghamſhire; of Heanton-court, in this county; and of Tehidy, in Cornwall. Of this noble family, Thomas Lord Baſſet, brother and heir to Gilbert Lord Baſſet, of Hedendon, poſſeſt
the

BRAUNTON, (or *St. Brannock's-Town*) is a large parifh, by computation nearly nine miles from N. E. to S. W. and fix miles from E. S. E. to W. N. W.* This parifh is confpicuous in the legends of the faints;† as are its proprietors, in the annals of families.‡ The church is very large and fpacious, unfupported by any pillar.§

In

the manors of Colyton and Whitford, in the fouth-eaft part of Devon, which were given him by Richard the 1ft. This gentleman left three daughters, his heireffes; Philippa, the wife of Henry Earl of Warwick, afterwards of Richard Seward; Joan, of Reginald Valetort; and Alice, of John Biffet. Sir Alan Baffet, (another branch of this family), was the fon of William, by Cicely his wife, daughter of Alan de Englefield, who was the fon of John Baffet; who was the fon of Ofmond Baffet, the owner of Ipifden and Stoke-Baffet, in the time of Henry the 1ft. The above Sir Alan married Lucia, the fifter of Sir William Peverell, of Sanford, through whom he poffeft White-chappel and La Hayne, in the parifh of Bifhop's Nymton. This part of the Baffet family long refided at Whitechapel; till in the time of Henry the 8th, John, the fon of Sir William Baffet, married Joan, daughter of Sir Thomas Beaumont, and fifter and heir of Philip Beaumont, of Shirwell, who brought two noble feats into the family, Umberleigh and Heanton-court. At firft the Baffets made Umberleigh their place of refidence; but afterwards removed to Heanton-court. Here lived Sir Robert Baffet, who being, by his grandmother, defcended from the Plantagenets, and of the blood-royal, afpired to the crown of England in the beginning of James the 1ft's reign; but not being able to make good his pretenfions, he was obliged to fly into France to fave his head. To compound for which, Sir Robert greatly exhaufted his eftate; felling off, with White-chappel, the ancient houfe, no lefs than 30 manors of land. Colonel Arthur Baffet, the fon of Sir Robert, married one of the daughters and coheirs of Leigh, of Barrow, in the parifh of Northam. This gentleman fuffered, among others, in the civil wars; and he facrificed a part of his eftates to his loyalty. " As to his ftature (fays Prince) he was fomewhat fhort, but of an high creft, and noble mind. As to his religion, he did not boaft great matters; but loved them. Deferving this true character, that as the red rofe, though outwardly not fo fragrant, is yet inwardly more cordial than the damafk; fo the moft excellent perfons virtues are more inwardly folid between God and their own fouls, than outwardly vaunting in the fight of man—he being as plain in his foul, as he was in his garb, which he refolved fhould be proud of him, rather than he of it." He died in the 75th year of his age, and was buried in his parifh church of Heanton Punchardon.—" Colonel Arthur Baffet, born here in 1597, was the eldeft fon of Sir Robert Baffet, by Elizabeth, fecond daughter and coheir of Sir William Perream, knight; who was the eldeft fon of Sir Arthur Baffet, by Elinora, daughter of Sir John Chichefter, of Raleigh; who was the eldeft fon of John Baffet, of Umberleigh and Heanton-court, by Frances his wife, daughter and coheir of Arthur Plantagenet, Vifcount of Lifle, natural fon to King Edward the 4th." *Weftcote.*—Colonel Arthur Baffet prefented to the church of Heanton, in 1669; John Baffet, in 1720, and died in 1757; and Colonel Francis Baffet, (fon of John) prefented in 1772, and lately deceafed.

*‡ " A fweet and pleafant feat. The houfe is a handfome pile, well furnifhed with every variety of entertainment which the earth, fea, and air can afford." *Prince.*—Heanton-court is fituated at the bottom of a park, very near the river; a new front of eleven windows, and two ftories, with battlements, and a tower at each end.

* A pretty large river runs thro' the parifh : It fwells to a confiderable height, from rains. It has four bridges, built of ftone; *Knolle*, of two arches; *Corf*, of two arches; the *Dean's*, of four arches; and *Cane-bridge*, of four arches. They are repaired by the parifh.

† " *Branton*, of fome called *Branockfton*, fo named of St. Brannock, the king's fon of Calabria, that lived in this vale; and, as appeareth in the book of his commemoration of the place, arrived here in the days of Malgo Conanus, King of the Britons; and 300 years after Chrift, began to preach his holy name in this defolate place, then overfpread with brakes and woods. Out of which defart, now named the Boroughs, (to tell you fome of the marvels of this man) he took harts, which meekly obeyed the yoke, and made of them a plow to draw timber thence to build a church. Which may gain credit, if it be true hiftorians write, that in foreign countries they caufe red deer to draw, and milk their hinds. Of which Giraldus maketh no wonder, but avoucheth, that he hath feen the fame often ufed in Wales, where he did eat cheefe made of hind's milk. I forbear to fpeak of his cow, his ftaff, his oak, his well, and his fervant Abel; all which are lively reprefented in a glafs-window of that church; than which you fhall fee few fairer of one roof." *Rifdon.*

‡ " In King Edward the Confeffor's age, *Braunton* was the king's demefne; and not long after the conqueft, by the procurement of William Warweft, a great counfellor of ftate, and chaplain to the conqueror and his two fons, as alfo Bifhop of Exon, the chief mannor was obtained for the church of St. Peter's in Exon. King Richard the 1ft, gave to Odo de Cario, the fon of William Fitz-Gerald, a mannor in this parifh, with the honour of the hundred of Braunton. From which Odo, iffued that noble family of the Carews, which have been fo famous in Ireland, Wales, and England, where, for the moft part, they have inhabited, fince the time of King Edward the 1ft, after the marriage of Sir William Mohun's daughter.—The tything of *Lobb*, had lords furnamed thereof, fo ancient as King Edward the 1ft; which, after fundry fucceffions in that tribe, the daughter and heir of the laft brought the fame to the Berrys.—*Beare* was the ancient dwelling of Richard de Charteray, who held 14 knights-fees in the reign of King Henry the 2d, whom fucceeded Symon de Charteray; Sir John Charteray was lord thereof in King Edward the 1ft's time, and his fon Sir John lived there in King Edward the 2d. Afterwards this land came to the Lord Martin; and from him, by the Lords Audleigh, Fitz-warren, and Hankford, unto the Earl of Bath.—*Lufcot* gave name to its ancient owners; amongft whom, William de Lufcot lived here in the time of King Edward the 3d, who was learned in the laws, and bore rule in the county. He much increafed his anceftor's eftate, as well by his own induftry, as by the marriage of the fifter and heir of Michael Lerchdecon : Which William Lufcot left his eftate to Alice his only daughter and heir, married unto Sir John Arundel of Lanhern, in whofe name and iffue this land lately was.—*Santon* is in the parifh of Braunton, not unaptly fo termed by the fand that hath over-blown many hundred acres of land. And near this hamlet, the country-people had fo undermined a hill of fand, by digging it to carry it into their grounds, that a great quantity thereof fell down, difcovering the top of a tree, which, by farther fearch, was found to be 30 foot in length. So that it plain'y appeareth, this circuit of marfh-land (now of the fands over-blowing, called the Burrows) was in elder ages ftored with woods and tall timber-trees,—for *Ex ungue Leonem*—. This dwelling is daintily feated towards the fouth, the hills guarding it from the north, having a fair demefne thereunto belonging, and had fometime inhabitants fo furnamed, being the feat of Thomas de Santon, whofe fon's daughter Melior was married to Robert de Stockey, which two Sir Robert Stockey fucceeded. Joan, the daughter and heir of the laft of this tribe that lived here, by her marriage, carried thefe poffeffions to Crawthorn : And Joan, their only daughter, brought the fame, by her match, to Sir John Beamont, knight. She was fecondly married to Sir William Efturmy; but this land defcended in the line of Beamont, to the family of the Chicheſters, and was by John Chichefter, knight, given to Sir Arthur Chichefter his younger fon, a man of excellent worth, Lord Deputy of Ireland, Baron of Belfaft, and Vifcount Carrickfergus, who fold this ancient feat unto John Lutterel, defcended of a younger brother of Dunfter-Caftle, and is now become the manfion-houfe of Sir Edward Southcot, knight, defcended of an ancient family in this fhire, who married the relict of the faid Lutterel, the daughter of Sir Edward Gorges of Wraxhal, knight. It is now time to make an end of Braunton, a parifh fo fertil for foil, that it is reported for credit, fome fields there are never uncultured, bearing barley with great increafe, of which grain there is abundant ftore." *Rifdon.*—In Braunton are, the town of Braunton, Saunton, North Lobb, South Lobb, Upcott, Nethercot, Knolle, Higher and Lower Winfhams, Halfinger, Beercharter, Pippacott. Its manors are, Braunton-Abbots, Braunton-Dean, Braunton-Gorges, Buckland, Saunton-court, Beercharter. Buckland and Incledon were inhabited by the Incledon family, from the reign of Richard the 3d, till 1759, when Phil. Webber, efq. married

Mary,

In the parifh of MARWOOD, *Weftcote* * was a place of diftinction. There is a tradition, that the church † was built by the Marwoods.

The parifh of EAST-DOWN takes its name from the family of Down.‡

VOL. III.   F   WEST-

Mary, one of the coheirefles of J. Incledon, efq. The houfe is modern, having feven windows on a floor, the offices all behind. It is fituated in a hollow on the top of a hill, and furrounded by hills on every fide, except to the fouth-eaft; where it opens into a pleafant vale, thro' which runs a ferpentine river. It has a beautiful lawn in front. The country around it, hilly and romantic, affords delightful profpects of the fea. Some of the hills are fkirted with plantations of fir and other wood, not half a mile from the church.—*Lifcott*, inhabited by a family of that name, afterwards Collamore, then came to Incledon, then Webber.—*Afh*, by Bellew, Bere, Chichefter, Bury Lamley, Baffet by purchafe.—*Saunton-court*, by Chichefter, Luttrell, Clevland by purchafe.

§ The church is fituated in a vale near the river, with fhady walks of elms, limes, and fycamore. It is a large and lofty pile, in the fhape of a crofs, its length in the clear 79 feet. The chancel is 28 feet long. The breadth of the church and chancel is 34 feet. A fpire, on the fouth, anfwers to a fmall aifle on the north, to form the crofs. By the chancel is another aifle belonging to three different eftates, Lifcott, Afh, and Chapple-Hill Tenement. Here are two handfome monuments of the Incledon family; one of Hales, defcended from Sir Thomas Hales, of Kent; one, of Shepherd alias Hooper, from whom Sir Nicholas Hooper, knight, was defcended. A chapel, dedicated to St. Brannock, ftands on a hill above the town, commands an extenfive profpect, and is a fea-mark: The walls are perfect. Another chapel in the Sand-burroughs leading from Saunton to Appledore, the walls to the eaft ftanding, dedicated to St. Anne. Another in the fanctuary ground, in ruins, as are all the buildings adjoining to it, except the old kitchen, the chimney of which ftill remains. One at Afh, its walls ftanding. One at Buckland, in ruins. A crofs, in the church yard, called the Palm-crofs, kept up at a great expence, till 1557. The walls which fupported it, are ftill preferved.

* It was the ancient feat of the Weftcotes. The manor houfe feems to have been no inconfiderable one. The fide next the water has a very thick wall, with huge buttreffes. The arms of the Chichefters remain in plaifter in the hall; but the ftructure feems to be as old as the Weftcotes. The moft diftinguifhed of this family were the abbot of Hertland, John Weftcote, born at Weftcotehoufe, about 1270, and who was one of the canons refidentiary of St. Peter's church, and warden of St. John's hofpital, Exeter; and Thos. Weftcote, efq. born alfo at Weftcote, in this parifh. This laft gentleman was a foldier, and greatly beloved by Henry the 4th and 5th. He married Elizabeth, daughter and heirefs of Sir Thomas Littletou, of Frankley, in Worcefterfhire, knight; but could not obtain her father's confent to the marriage, without a promife that their male iffue, enjoying the mother's inheritance, fhould be called by her name. Accordingly, Mr. Weftcote, having a fon by this lady, he was called Thomas Littleton, afterwards the famous Sir Thomas Littleton, one of the judges of the common pleas, in the time of Edward the 4th. Thomas Weftcote, the famous antiquary, was of the fame name and family.

† Richard Harding, the rector in 1782, was obferved, as an incumbent, to be not only the father of this diocefe, but probably of the kingdom. He was inftituted to Marwood 3d of June, 1714. He died May 8th, 1782, aged about 96, after an incumbency of near 68 years. His fucceffor was Samuel Ryder Wefton.

‡ " *Eaft-Down* is fuppofed to take its name from the family of Down, formerly proprietors of the manor of Eaft-Down, by an heirefs of whom it came into the family of Pine, and has regularly defcended through thirteen generations, to the prefent poffeffor, the writer of this. The parifh extends eaft and weft about 5 miles, north and fouth only between 2 and 3, and takes in two large hills, which unite at the weftern extremity. It confifts moftly of good land in the valleys and fides, and good pafture on the tops of the hills. The general run is from 15*s.* to 20*s.* per acre for pafture and tillage land, and 30*s.* or upwards for meadow. Moftly inclofed, either by high banks, well planted, or what are called ftone ditches, the country abounds with beautiful woods, hanging on the fides of hills, and variegated rich picturefque views, both of fea and land. There is only one ftone bridge, of one arch, over the Yeo, maintained at the joint expence of Eaft-Down and Arlington. There are three fmall villages, Church hill, Brockham, and Shortacombe. in former days a church or chapel ftood in the former, of which fome traces may yet be diftinguifhed; however, the church ftands at prefent almoft at the eaftern extremity of the parifh, a few yards from the manor houfe; and tradition fays: The north aifle was a chapel to the houfe, but (that at Churchill proving ruinous) was given to the parifh, who built the north aifle and tower. It is a very neat church, well feated with wainfcot oak; has a very well carved oak fcreen, which divides the chancel and my pew from the body of the church. The latter is ftill repaired by the family, both within and without. On the fouth-fide of the pew is a fmall marble monument of an anceftor of this family, with two bufts carved in bafs-relief of him and his wife. There is a table of black marble in the window, in memory of Elizabeth, daughter of John Pointz, of Greenham, in Somerfetfhire, who married one of the anceftors of this family. There are no other monuments, tho' many tombftones of the family, and others, particularly one to the memory of John Spooner, who died aged 90, 60 years of which he was rector of this parifh. The prefent rector, Edward Pine, (my uncle) is in his 80th year, and has been rector about 55 years. The parfonage houfe is a very inconvenient old ruinous building, covering a deal of ground, without one tolerable room in it, and is full three quarters of a mile from the church. The glebe is a very good one, worth about £.60 a year, and appears to have been taken out of Eaft-Down manor. It is fuppofed that on this account the barton was excufed from tythe, from which it claims exemption, and never paid any, tho' it was once contefted by law by Mr. Spooner, when rector. The church is dedicated to St. John the Baptift, and on that day a revel is held at Churchill, where the old church ftood. They alfo hold another revel on St. Peter's-day, at a place called Twifthead. I never could learn the origin of this revel, but fuppofe the other church was dedicated to St. Peter. About 80 years ago Sir Stafford Northcote's family had a large feat in this parifh, on an eftate which ftill bears his name, and where the ruins are ftill vifible. It was then burnt by accident. The family fold the eftate in parts and parcels, and removed to Pines, near Exeter, which was once the family feat of the Pines, but was feized by the crown, together with a very large property elfe, lying in the parifhes, bearing the name of Pine. It was forfeited for killing one of the king's favorites, a privy councellor, in a duel, fought without the king's leave. Pine married the heirefs of Down, by which he got this eftate, with feveral other manors. The family originally came from Denmark, (fee the Herald's Books) and fettled at Ham, in the parifh of Morwenftowe, in Cornwall; but afterwards, that houfe being burnt, removed to Upton Pine, where they remained till it was loft by forfeiture. Eaft-Down, with other manors, being then under fettlement, efcaped. This forfeiture, I believe, muft have happened in Henry the 8th's reign, as I have a fmall filver coin or medal with this infcription:—" Pyne de Upton Pyne in Devon, efq." The word efq. being turned upfide down, forms the date 1513.—By this Upton Pyne was then in the family. They loft eftates valued in £.3000 a year at that time, out of which £.2 15 4 a year continued to be paid the family, till I fold it a few years fince. Lord Chief Juftice Pyne, who wrote the Reports which bear his name, was of this family, and by his will intailed his eftate on it, fhould his only daughter die unmarried, whom he left a minor under the guardianfhip of the then Lord Chancellor. He married her to his fon, when fhe was in fo deep a confumption, that fhe lived only one month after; but long enough to defeat the intail. On the north-fide of the parifh is an eftate, which, tho' now inclofed, ftill bears the name of Mattocks-Down, from a fight there under the general of that name, during the civil wars. On Berry-down are feveral tumuli, and a beacon. This down, as well as all in this country, fhew evident marks of having been once in tillage, tho' we have no account when. From the church to Barnftaple is 7 miles, about the fame to the port of Ilfracombe, and 3 from Combmartin, once a market town, but now fallen to decay." From Mr. *Pine*, now *Pine Coffin*, efq.

WEST-DOWN, from its ancient Lords *de Columbariis*, is called alfo *Down-Columbers*.*

Morte Bay is fo called from Morte, anciently MORTHOE.†

ILFRACOMBE is an extenfive parifh, containing feveral manors.‡ Sir Bourchier Wrey, bart. is the prefent lord of the manor of Ilfracombe. Its church is a large old fabrick.

There

---

* " *Weft-Down*, in ancient time the lands of William Columbers, from whom iffued Sir Philip Columbers, knight, that married Elea-nor, one of the daughters of William Lord Martyn, Baron of Barnftaple, Camois, and Dartington. In this tything, Ralph Moring held lands in King Henry the 3d's time, which Ralph Beaple inherited the 24th of King Edward the 1ft.—The barton of *Bradwell* is in this parifh, whereof William de Pyne was lord, and of Crakway, in the beginning of King Henry the 3d's reign, which by Margaret, the heir of the family of Yeo, that had formerly affianced Joan the inheritrix of that tribe, about the reign of King Henry the 4th, is lineally de-fcended unto Sir Samuel Rolle, knight.—*Stofford*, a very ancient place in this tything, was (as fome dream) the dwelling of Thomas de la Wayt, who, as they fay, lieth buried in the north-ifle of Weft-Down church; but more probable it is, that it was the dwelling of the anceftors of Sir John Stowford, one of the judges of the common pleas, and that its inhabitants took name thereof; he was a judge in the time of King Edward the 3d. *Rifdon*.—" Judge Stowford, full of days and good deeds, put off with his robes his rags of mortality, at his houfe at Stowford, which laft were carefully depofited in the north-aifle of the parifh-church of Weft-Down. To his memory is there erected a fair and large monument, reprefenting his effigies in fcarlet robes, with his lady lying by him, Joan, coheir of Tracey, of Wolla-combe Tracey." *Prince*.

† " *Julian la Cruke*, in her widowhood, granted lands here unto Hugh Vaultort and Luce his wife, before dates of deeds; whereunto were witneffes, Sir Thomas Raleigh, Sir Robert Beaple, Sir John Charteray, knights.—In this parifh ftandeth a noted ftone, named of the place Mortftone, which hath occafioned, forfooth, a notable conceit, that all fuch whofe wives have the fovereignty, fhould go to fhoulder with that ftone; but hitherto a fufficient number cannot be marfhalled to remove it.—And here are the hamlets of *Over* and *Neather Wollacombe*, whereof an open bay hath taken the name of *Wollacombe-Sands*; and whereof an ancient family, that fometime dwelt here, deriveth their name, and inheriteth here to this day. In this remote place, Sir William Tracy, fon of Oliver Lord Tracy, lived a private life, after he, with others, had flain Thomas Becket, arch-bifhop of Canterbury, in King Henry the 2d's time; of whom this report goeth, that, after this fact, wind and weather were ever againft him, a proverb applied to the unfortunate. The punifhment of a prieft-killer, (as in fome authors is to be feen) was not then death of body by execution, but of the foul by excommunication, until about the 23d year of that king's reign, when it was yielded, that fuch perfons fhould alfo fuffer lofs of life. Certain it is, he withdrew himfelf hither; here he fpent the remainder of his life, and lieth buried in an ifle of this church, by him built, under an erected monument, with his pourtraiture engraven on a grey marble ftone, having thefe armories cut on the fide thereof: firft, 3 *lyons paffant gardant*, fecond, 3 *bends*, and the third, *a faltier*. On whofe mangled monument I found this fragment of a French infcription, in this ancient character:

SYRe ..... mE Dec TRACE,
mae eeys ..... meeRCy."   *Rifdon*.

In the Magna Britannia, the infcription is faid to mean:
Sir William de Tracy,
May I find mercy.

" When the late Dean Milles, (fays Badcock), faw the tomb and the infcription, he at once pronounced that the tradition was groundlefs: that it was not Sir William de Tracy, (fo diftinguifhed in the Hiftory of Hen. 2d.) who was buried at Mort, but fome clergyman of that name: for the clergy at that period had the appellation of *Syre*. Hiftory, indeed, contradicts, or at leaft doth not fanction the tradition; and in many refpects it is improbable. But tho' the learned dean furmifed that the tomb and infcription originally belonged to the parfon of the parifh, yet he could not prove it by any pofitive memorial. I think I have difcovered a record which put it out of all doubt, and eftablifhes the dean's hypothefis. Turning over Prynn's *Papal Ufurpations*, or *Hiftory of King John*, I found by mere chance the following record:—K. Edw. 1ft, An. 25. Rogerus de Mortho et Ricardus de Sparkwyll de Comitat. Devon: recogn: et oblig: 11 Regi pro *Wilhelmo de Tracy* perfona Ecclefiæ de Mortho Exon: Dioces."—This is a conjecture of Badcock, in a letter to Sir George Yonge. I cannot fay that it is, to me, fatisfactory. The murderer of Thomas a Becket is faid by Will. of Worcefter to have retired in *occidentalem partem*: And *occidentalem* is taken for Yorkfhire by fome hiftorians—which I fhould much rather call *feptentrionalem*. Surely the word points out the weft of England. Befides, the tradition of the country, that Tracey retired hither, ought to have fome weight with us; to fay nothing of Rifdon's pofitive affurance, that he fpent at Mortho the remainder of his life.—" This fepulture, continues Rifdon, was violated in our memory by fome that hoped for gain; but difappointed of their prey, they carried thence the lead wherein the dead was wrapt; who being men of fome fubftance, it was obferved, that their wealth wafted, and they did not profper afterwards. This Sir William Tracy left one only daughter, married to Sir Gervaife Courtenay, by whom fhe had iffue William, which took the name of Tracy; from whom, by his fon Oliver, defcended Henry Lord Tracy, Baron of Barnftaple. John Tracy, the laft of the name that dwelt in this place, left his inheri-tance unto his two fifters Ifabel and Joan; Ifabel was thrice married, firft, unto Sir Herbert Morice; fecondly, unto Sir Edmond Boteler, and from him divorced; thirdly, unto Sir Simon Rogus. This mannor of Wollacombe-Tracy, in the reign of King Edward the 3d, came to be the inheritance of Sir John Stowford, knight, whofe feoffees, the 18th year of the fame king, conveyed this, among other lands, unto William Fitz-warren of Brightly, their fon. In the time of King Henry the 3d, William Lord Hardefhull, with confent of Matilde his wife, granted unto Matthew de Bofton all his lands in Mortho. And Robert Beaple granted to Sir William Tracy, patron of the church of Mortho, all his land of Cheglinch, as certain marks bound it between the land of Dene, and the land of Weft-down towards the eaft, in the prefence of Sir Thomas de Raleigh, then fheriff of Devon, John de Charteray, Henry de Merwood, John de Lufcot, Pegan de Malcot, Tempore Edward the 1ft, 33." *Rifdon*.

‡ " *Alfrincombe*, *Ilfridcombe*, vulgarly *Ilfarcombe*, of which ancient name evidences make mention, was in the tenure of one Robert, in Edward the Confeffor's time, and guilded after one hide and one farthing of land. At this place there is a harbour for fhips by means of a pile built; and, for failors better direction, a light is there maintained, inftead of a watch-tower, no doubt, *ad Speculum Walliæ* over againft.—This parifh is large, and containeth divers tythings and mannors; the chief whereof was in the reign of King Richard the 1ft, the inheritance of the Lady Roife, wife of Sir Henry Champernon, knight, whom divers of that knightly family fucceeded. The laft Sir William left iffue two daughters, Elizabeth wedded to William Polglas within three days of her father's death; and Katherine, wife of Sir Walter Woodland, which died *fans* iffue. Elizabeth, after the death of Polglas, was re-married to John Sergeaux within two days after her firft hufband's death, by whom fhe had iffue Richard Polglas, an ideot, who died of the plague in an abby in Yorkfhire, where-unto he was privily conveyed; and Margaret his fifter was married unto Sir John Herle, who had this mannor, and all Champernon's inhe-ritance.—*Lincombe* or *Lindefcombe*, in the time of William the Conqueror, was held by the forefaid Robert; unto which mannor was added land, called *Laerda*, that was rated after one hide. The family of Witchalfe, that flourifhed fometimes at Chidleigh, were lately lords of this mannor. And in this hamlet of Lincombe, the abby of Donkfwell had lands belonging unto it.—The tything of *Burgh* lieth in this parifh,

There are fo many large *barrows* in BERRY-NARBER, (fays Bifhop Lyttelton) that, I fufpect, they gave name to the parifh.*

COMBMARTIN† is a fmall town, on the Briftol Channel, about five miles to the eaft of Ilfracombe.

The mountainous parifh of LYNTON, its impetuous river, and its "valley of ftones," have been already the fubject of picturefque defcription.‡

In the parifh of ARLINGTON, near Barnftaple, the feat of John Palmer Chichefter, efq. was rebuilt, a few years fince, by Meadows.‖

LOXORE lies to the fouth of Arlington.§

STOKE-RIVERS ftands between two ftreams; whence, as fome fuppofe, it took the addition of *Rivers*: But it received that adjunct from its ancient lords, the Rivers, Earls of Devon.¶

CHARLES lies high; a well wooded parifh. From an eftate called Shutfcomb, we have a beautifully picturefque view of Brayford, the village of Highbray, and the parfonage and glebe.*†

In

parifh, and is a parcel of the mannor of Braunton-Abbot, which had for its Lord Thomas-de Britton. Neither would the hamlet of Molecot be omitted, that many ages paft was held by Paganus de Molecot.—William Fitz-Morice held *Haginton* by one knightly fee, the 27th of King Henry the 3d; and William Camvill, fon of the Lord Jeffery Camvill, that enjoyed the barony of Barnftaple during his wife's life, and after by the courtefy of England, had lands in this tything in the time of King Edward the 2d. And in this parifh, Cutliffe hath inheritances and inhabitance. The prefent inheritor married the daughter of Chichefter.—The town of Ilfarcombe confifteth of one ftreet, lying fcatteringly at moft a mile in length from the church to the harbour; where, in the church-yard, was a chapel confecrated to the honour of the lady of Thorn, as they give out, now almoft demolifhed." *Rifdon.*

* " *Berry-narber*, the lands of John de Lidford, William Bickleigh, and Henry Annet, who held one knight's fee there in King John's time. After whom, Richard de Biry was lord of this manor in the time of Edward the 1ft, whofe pofterity, (fays *Rifdon*) have dwelt here twelve defcents, and have advanced their eftate by the marriage of the heirs of Damerell, Giffard, and Bowden." *Watermouth*, in this parifh, belongs to Davie, of Orleigh.

† " *Martins-combe*, vulgarly *Combe-Martin*, bears the adjunct of its ancient landlords the Martins, whofe inheritance it was many ages paft; which lieth low, as the name implieth, and near the fea, having a cove for boats to land: A place noted for yielding the beft hemp in all this country, and that in great abundance: But in former times famous for mines of lead, (and that which is better merchandife) filver hath been there found fince our remembrance, tho' Cicero denieth there is any in Great Britain. Thefe filver mines were firft found in the 22d year of King Edward the 1ft; at which time were taken up in the wapentakes of the Peak in Derbyfhire, 337 men, and brought hither to work in thefe mines. Afterwards, in the age of King Edward the 3d, they yielded the king great profit towards the maintenance of his French wars, as appeareth upon record. This mannor from the Lords Martins, defcended to the Lords Audleighs; and for want of iffue-male, by the death of Nicholas Lord Audleigh, came to the crown, which King Henry the 8th gave unto Sir Richard Pollard, a younger fon of Sir Lewis Pollard, the judge; whofe fon, Sir John Pollard, fold the fame to the particular tenants, and the demefne thereof to William Hancocke, his fervant, who left it unto Edward Hancocke, his fon, recorder of the city of Exeter, a gentleman of good hopes, who died in his flourifhing age, leaving iffue, by the daughter of Sir Amias Bampfield, knight, a fon called William. To this place, the faid Edward Hancocke, efq. purchafed a Tuefday's market, and a fair on Whitfun-Monday.—In this parifh is *Orchard*, the dwelling in ancient times of a family fo named. The laft of this line left his heritage to his only daughter and heirefs, Jane, who was married to John Prowfe, of Chagford." *Rifdon.*

‡ " *Lyn*, a pretty lake, ftreameth out of the Exmoor-hills, and in his paffage to the fea communicateth his name to *Linton*, where, when William the Conqueror had expulfed the Englifh, he beftowed thefe lands on William Chievre, one of his captains, together with Crynton, Wolvecomb, Bocheland, and much more hereabouts. Jeffery de Lyn was feized of land in this parifh, the 24th of King Edward the 1ft.—Henry de Hallefworth held *Eaft-Lyn* and *Weft-Lyn*, in the reign of King Edward the 2d; and *Wolbanger*, in this tything, was the ancient lands of Ralph Pyne, in the age of King Edward the 1ft. *Stokes* in this mannor of Lyn, was, by Reginald fo furnamed, given to Alan his fon, in the time of King Henry the 3d, which Richard Thorgar afterwards held with Furfhil. And in the 19th of King Edward the 3d, Richard Lovering was lord of thefe lands.—Where the lake Lyn fheddeth itfelf into the fea, the place thereof taketh to name *Lynmouth*; of late years notable for the marvellous plenty of herrings there taken. A kind of fifh, which in our forefathers days kept, as it were, their ftation about * Norway; but in our time, not without divine Providence, take their courfe round about this ifle of Great Britain by fhoals in great numbers. And from September until Chriftide, offer themfelves to the fifhers' nets, to the no little benefit of this land; which we may not mention without the acknowledgment of God's great goodnefs towards us." *Rifdon.*

‖ " *Arlington*, or *Alrington*, the ancient poffeffion of the Raleighs. In this family it remained many defcents; when the heir general was married to Chichefter, one of whofe houfe gave the manfion-houfe and manor to a younger fon, whom he had by a fecond wife; by which lineage it is now inherited." *Rifdon.*—It ftill continues in this family.

§ " *Loxhore*, *Lochefhore*, anciently, when Godwin held half a hide there. This land fince belonged to the Beamonts, and was given by Sir Richard Beamont, knight, to William his younger fon, who had iffue Richard, the father of Sir John; to whom all Beamont's inheritance, (the iffue male of the elder houfe failing) defcended. From the Beamonts it paffed to the Chichefters." *Rifdon.*

¶ " This manor was by Baldwin, Earl of Devon, given to Atavis his daughter, married to Gilbert Solers, who dwelt at Umberleigh, in the time of Henry the 2d. By Champernowne and Willington it defcended to Beaumont. In the time of Edward the 1ft, the Lady Joan Champernowne granted an eftate in Stoke to Sir Peter Fifhacre, and the Lady Beatrife his wife." *Rifdon.*

*† " *Charles*, in old deeds *Charels*, the inheritance of the Punchardons. The laft of this line, Sir John Punchardon, knight, left iffue three daughters, his heirs, Mabill, married unto Henry Raleigh, a younger fon of Sir William Raleigh, of Raleigh, unto whofe part this land was allotted. From whom the Raleighs of Warwickfhire are defcended, that were lately lords of this mannor; in which place Sir John Raleigh, knight, dwelt in the days of King Edward the 3d, at which time there lived no lefs than fix knights of that name in this fhire. I fay not of one family, for they bare different armories." *Rifdon.*

● This note is a miftake.

In WEST-BUCKLAND, the beech and fycamore are not lefs flourifhing than the oak and afh.

GOODLEIGH has been, for ages, famous for its gardens of black and red cherries: The black are the largeft and moft lufcious.*

---

* " *Goodleigh*, in the Saxons time and tongue, was named *Goodlega* ; by which name, the Conqueror gave the fame to Robert de Albemarle, that was formerly Ulward's inheritance ; a parifh fertile both in grain and grafs, yielding in great abundance a fruit called mazards here, elfewhere black cherries ; at the time of whofe ripenefs, people flock hither, as to the prime place of fuch fruit. Roger Giffard and the Prior of Cannington held lands in this tything, about the time of King Henry the 3d ; fince the heirs of the Lord Brewer, then John de Stanton, by whofe co-heirs it defcended to Dennis and Crewkern, now the Carys inheritance." *Rifdon*.

ARCHDEACONRY

ARCHDEACONRY OF BARNSTAPLE.

DEANRY of BARNSTAPLE.

IN this deanry the parifhes of Barnftaple, Pilton, Afhford, Lankey, Bifhop's-Tawton, Swimbridge, Filleigh, Chittlehamton, Atherington, Bickington, Hunfhaw, Yarnefcombe, Newton-Tracey, Horwood, Weftleigh, Tawftock, Inftow, and Fremington, for the moft part, require a particular furvey.*

BARNSTAPLE lies on the river Taw, pleafantly fituated among hills, in the form of a femicircle, to which the river is a diameter. It has a ftone bridge, of 16 arches. The ftreets are clean and well paved, and the houfes of ftone.†

VOL. III.   G   PILTON

* " Benefices remaining in charge:

First Fruits.				Yearly Tenths.		
£.	s.	d.		£.	s.	d.
26	2	1	{ Adrington alias Athrington R. [St. Mary] Rep. B. Proc. vis. viiid. Syn. & Cath. iis. vd. A. D. Proc. vis. viiid. } r. V. 140l. - - - - - - - - - - - Patr. Baffet.	2	12	2½
29	7	6	{ Buckington alias High-Buckington R. [St. Mary] Rep. B. Proc. vis. viiid. Syn. & Cath. iis. vd. A. D. Proc. } vis. viiid. r. V. 200l. - - - - - - - - - - Patr. Stawell.	2	18	9
34	18	11½	Chettlehamton V. [St. Urith] Rep. B. Proc. vis. viiid. Syn. & Cath. iis. xd. A. D. Proc. vis. viiid. r. V. 160l. - Patr. Rolle.	3	9	10¾
12	5	2½	{ Filleigh R. [St. Paul] Rep. B. Proc. iiis. ivd. Syn. & Cath. iis. vd. A. D. Proc. iiis. ivd. united to Eaft } Buckland, in the deanery of Shirwell. r. V. 190l. - - - - - - Patr. Fortefcue.	1	4	6¼
20	0	5	{ Fremington V. [St. Peter] Rep. B. Proc. vis. viiid. Syn. & Cath. iis. vd. A. D. Proc. vis. viiid. Abb. Hertland } Penf. xls. [qu? obs.] r. V. 140l. - - - - - - - - Patr. Charles Hill, clerk.	2	0	0½
11	7	1	Hunfhaw R. [St. Mary Magdalene] Rep. B. Proc. vis. viiid. Syn. & Cath. iis. vd. A. D. Proc. vis. viiid. r. V. 120l. Patr. Orford.	1	2	8½
69	11	10½	Tawftock R. [St. Peter] Rep. B. Proc. vis. viiid. Syn. & Cath. iis. vd. A. D. Proc. vis. viiid. r. V. 300l. - Patr. Sir Bourchier Wrey, bart.	6	19	2¾
21	0	0	Tawton-Bifhop's V. [St. John Baptift] formerly the Bifhop's fee. Pec. of the Bifhop. Rep. none in charge Propr. and Patr. Dean of Exeter.	2	2	0

Difcharged.

King's Books.				Certified Value.		
8	13	9	Afhford V. [St. Peter] Rep. B. Proc. iis. iid. ob. A. D. Proc. viid. r. V. 45l. - - - Patr. The KING.	38	0	0
15	8	9	Barnftaple V. [St. Peter and St. Paul] Rep. B. Proc. vis. viiid. Syn. & Cath. iis. vd. A. D. Proc. vis. viiid. r. V. 80l. Patrs. Lord and Lady Bute.	47	0	0
7	8	4	Horwood R. [St. Michael] Rep. B. Proc. viid. A. D. Proc. viid. r. V. 60l. - - - - Patr. Mr. John Dene.	40	0	0
12	17	3½	Inftow R. [St. John Baptift] Rep. B. Proc. iiis. ivd. Syn. & Cath. iis. vd. A. D. Proc. iiis. ivd. r. V. 90l. - Patr. Humphrey Sibthorpe, M. D.	45	0	0
5	8	1½	Newton Tracy R. [St. Thomas Becket] Rep. B. Proc. viid. A. D. Proc. viid. r. V. 40l. - - Patr. The KING.	27	0	0
0	0	0	Pilton Impr. [St. Margaret] Rep. none in charge. r. V. 35l. - - - - Impr. and Patr. Baffet.	7	10	0
8	2	1	Weftleigh V. [St. Peter] Rep. B. Proc. vis. viiid. Syn. & Cath. iis. vd. A. D. Proc. vis. viiid. r. V. 70l. Patr. Dean and Chapter of Exeter.	47	17	2
0	0	0	Landkey Cur. [Holy Trinity] Pec. of the Bifhop. Rep. none in charge Impr. and Patr. Dean of Exeter.	20	0	0
0	0	0	Swymbridge Cur. [St. James] Pec. of the Bifhop. Rep. none in charge Impr. and Patr. Dean of Exeter.	20	0	0
7	12	1	Yarnefcombe V. [St. Andrew] Rep. B. Proc. vis. viiid. Syn. & Cath. iis. xd. A. D. Proc. vis. viiid. r. V. 40l. Patr. The KING.	34	0	0

† " Barftaple, a borough right ancient, bordereth here upon the eaft-bank of Taw, a town of mart, fo much Staple fignifieth in the Saxon fpeech; Bar is Britifh, and betokeneth the mouth of a river. To conclude with this compound, it is the chief town of merchandife next the river's mouth, or outlet into the fea; the original whereof, I conjecture, was the caftle, (for even provinces have taken names of caftles) which, as tradition tells us, was built by King Athelftane, being but at firft, of fmall circuit; for it was once walled, the foundation of whofe walls, could they be traced out, doubtlefs the town would appear nothing fo large; which if now walled, fo fair built, and populous withal, would prove little inferior to fome cities; for it hath liberties and privileges, as in a city, and is pleafantly and fweetly fituate amidft hills, in form of a femi circle upon the river, as it were a diameter, whofe ftreets, in whatfoever weather, are clean, and fairly paved; wherein I obferved three principal ornaments of building, the bridge on the fouth, croffing the river, fair and ftrongly built by one Stamford of London, after fome, or, as others will, by a ferry there kept; only three pillars were built by the bounty of
maids,

PILTON is a pretty village, in the parifh of that name.* Pilton-houfe, the feat of Incledon, lies on the fcite of Barnftaple-Priory. A part of an old wall,

that

maids, *aut fama eft Mendax.* Towards the north, the reliques of a caftle are to be feen, which, by common report, King Athelftane, but by fome, Indaell, of Totnefs, built. Indeed William the Conqueror beftowed this, with Totnefs, on Indaell, for the defence whereof, fundry men held lands hereabouts, and yielded a cuftom called Caftle-guard. The third principal building, is a religious houfe toward the eaft, erected by Joell, (*potius* Indaell, as before) fon of Alured, Earl of Britany, which was confecrated to St. Mary Magdalene, for monks of the order of Cluniacke, after the manner of the houfe of St. Martins de Campis in Paris. In which convent, he purpofed to have entered their profeffion during his life; unto which he gave large poffeffions, in accomplifhment of a vow, as appeareth by the copy of the donation. This was fometimes a cell to St. Martins in the Fields, near Paris; which, at the furrender, was worth by the year £.223 6s. and 7d. whereof Robert Thorne was the laft prior; who, for his devife, bare a row-buck leaning to a hawthorne, in an efcotcheon, with the word *Bert* interpofed, and this under-written,

Caprum cum fpina protegat divina poteftas.

In the garden of which priory, was lately, the proportion of a knight, lying crofs-legged with his fword and fhield, feeming to be one of thofe that had vowed a voyage into the holy land for that facred warfare, removed out of the church doubtlefs at the diffolution.

In the Conqueror's time, the borough of Barftaple had 40 burgeffes, and nine without; and Baldwin the baron had feven burgeffes here. It did no fervice on any expedition, but when Exeter did, and was gildable in all fervices by land or fea, as Totnes or Lidford. It was incorporate by King Henry the 1ft, who endowed the place with many privileges, and King John with more. A mayor and two bailiffs for a long time it had; but Queen Mary ordained two aldermen, and a council of twenty-four. This borough maintaineth two burgeffes in parliament; hath a Friday's market, for frequency of people, and choice of all commodities, the chiefeft in this tract. The inhabitants profefs merchandize, and through traffick have much inriched themfelves. A haven they have, and that but fhallow, fo that it hardly beareth fmall veffels; yet in the year 1607, it fuffered a kind of inundation amongft divers other in the Severn fide, at a fpring tide, driven by a very ftrong perry, from the ocean fo high fwelling, that it fubverted houfes, drowned beafts, and deftroyed people; of whom fome, to fave their lives, were conftrained from their upper rooms to take boat, and be gone. This river, at fome changes and full of the moon, fo overflowed the marfhes, that the town feems to be a demy-ifland. The greateft glory the place had, was a barony; which honour the lord once had, from whom it came to the Tracys, and from them defcended to the Lords Martyns and Audleighs; which, for want of iffue in Nicholas Lord Audleigh, came to Richard the 2d, who gave it to his half-brother John Holland, Duke of Exeter, who, failing of iffue, it again reverted to the crown, and was by Queen Mary beftowed on Thomas Marrow, of Warwickfhire. In this town were anciently divers chapels, when I fuppofe the church was not built." *Rifdon.*—The fon of Thomas Marrow fold the manor of Barnftaple to the Chichefters.—Sir John Dodderidge, one of the judges of the court of king's bench, in the time of James the 1ft, was born (not at Southmolton as Weftcote intimates, but) at Barnftaple, the fon of Richard Dodderidge, an eminent merchant of that town, by Joan Badcock, of Southmolton. He had fucceffively three wives. His firft was a daughter of Germin; his fecond wife was a daughter of Culme, of Canonfleigh; his third wife was Dorothy, the daughter of Sir Ames Bampfylde, of North-molton, knight, and the relict of Edward Hancock, efq. of Combmartin, whofe refidence was fometime at Mount Radford, near Exeter. In right of his laft wife, Hancock's widow, Mount Radford became the habitation of Judge Dodderidge. He had one fon by his laft wife, who died before his father, in the flower of his age.— " There is but one paroch chirch, in the town, fays *Leland*. There have beene 4 chapelles yn the town; of the which one was at the eft end of the bridge, dedicate to Thomas Beket, now profanid. The other 3 yet ftand, one of Alhallowes at the north-gate, another of St. Nicolas, at the weft-gate, as I remembre. One Holman, vicar of the paroche chirch in Barftaple, made a fair chapelle and founded a *Cantuarie* in it, in the paroche chirch yard in Barftaple."—" The church at Barftaple, which is dedicated to St. Peter and St. Paul, fays *B. Willis*, had, before the reformation, feveral chauntries founded in it; as our lady's chauntry, founded by one Thomas Holman, in a chapel of our lady; and St. Anne's, founded by one Henry Admyn, in a chapel of our lady in the church-yard; befides which were St. Nicholas's chauntry, and a free chapel built upon the end of the bridge—all which I find mention of in the chauntry rolls, in the furvey taken 37th of Henry the 8th."

To the memory of Mifs Burton, who died there Nov. the 2d, 1771.

Underneath

The library of this church

Refteth

Until the Archangel's trump

Shall fummon her to appear

On an immortal ftage,

The body of

ELIZABETH BURTON, comedian;

Formerly of Drury-lane,

But late of the Exeter Theatre;

Who exchanged time for eternity

On All-Souls day, 1771,

Aged 20 years.

Life's but a walking fhadow,

A poor player,

Who ftruts its hour or two upon the ftage,

And then is heard no more.

This fmall tribute,

To the memory of

An amiable young woman,

An innocent cheerful companion,

And moft excellent actrefs,

Was placed here by J. Foote,

Manager of the Theatre.

* " *Pilton,* which Sir John Chichefter, grand-father of Sir Robert Chichefter, knight, purchafed; who married the daughter of Sir William Courtney, knight; his fon Sir John, the daughter of Sir Robert Dennis, knight; his grand-child Sir Robert, firft Frances, fifter and heir of John Lord Harrington; his fecond wife was Mary, the daughter of Robert Hill, efq. which family have been lords of Raleigh, (a fair feat adjoining) ever fince John Chichefter married Thomafin, the heir of that name, that wrote themfelves anciently *de Ralega, & de Raleia.* In the time of King Edward the 3d, one Robert Chichefter, a learned man, wrote a chronicle, beginning it from the firft coming of the Saxons into this land, anno 449, and continued it unto the year 1348.—*Pilland* is in this parifh, whofe Lord was William Favell, in the time of King Henry the 2d. After fome defcents in that tribe, this tything had inheritors, furnamed thereof, in King Edward the 1ft's age; of which family, many fucceffions did enjoy the fame, unto the time of King Henry the 6th. Then the heir of Pilland was married unto Brett, who made his dwelling there in King Edward the 6th's time. This land Sir Alexander Brett fold unto

John

that belonged to the priory, ſtill remains at the north end of the manſion. This houſe is pleaſantly ſituated in a paddock, commanding a view of Barnſtaple, at a ſmall diſtance. Raleigh, a very pleaſant ſeat, lies about half a mile to the eaſt of the town of Barnſtaple.*

On the South-Yeo lieth LANKEY.✝

In BISHOP's-TAWTON, " the church (ſays Riſdon) ſtands ſomewhat inconve-nient for the inhabitants: But ſo it pleaſed the firſt founders. It is a place of large limits, lying in length from S. to N. upon the Taw."‡

At SWIMBRIDGE § is one of the neateſt country churches in Devonſhire. The ſcreen is of excellent carved wood-work, painted and gilt, and in fine preſerva-tion.

John Walton, biſhop of Exon. And ſo near neighbour is Pilton to Barnſtaple, that to the beholders it ſeems to be one town, conjoyned by a long bridge over the North-Yeo, with few arches; built by Sir John Stowford, knight, one of the judges of this land, in the age of King Edward the 3d, upon remorſe of one there drown'd, (as they have by tradition)." *Riſdon.*—" Athelſtan gave Pilton lordſhip to Malmeſ-bury. The abbot of Malmeſbury had the parſonage of Pilton, and kept a cell there." *Leland.*

* " *Raleigh*, anciently written *de Ralega* and *de Raleia*, the ancient ſeat of the Raleighs. The firſt was Walter de Raleia, then William, then Sir William de Ralega, who lived in the days of King John; then another Sir William; then Sir Thomas, and ſeveral others—in all eight generations. And then Thomaſin, the daughter and heireſs of John Raleigh, brought this eſtate to her huſband, John Chicheſter, in which family it continued, till Sir John Chicheſter, bart. ſold it to Arthur Champneys, merchant, a younger ſon of a family ſo called, in the pariſh of Yarnſcombe." *Prince.*—*Upcote* belongs to Robert Harding, eſq.

✝ " *Lankey*, in old deeds *Landkey*, in King Henry the 2d's reign was the lands and dwelling of Reginald Beaple; from which family, by Margaret, daughter of Sir Neal Loring, married unto Thomas Peiner, iſſued Paul Peiner, lord ſteward of the houſe to King Henry the 3d, who left a ſon called Paul, whoſe wardſhip the lady bought; but the Lord Grey paid the money, being 500 marks, and married him to his daughter, at his mannor of Keyton; and ſhortly after, at London, he married the mother. The 35th of Henry the 3d this inheritance deſcended unto Mary their daughter, firſt married unto St. Maur, ſecondly, unto John Broughton. Robert, the laſt, after ſeven deſcents in that line, left his two ſiſters his heirs. Katherine was wife of William Lord Howard, of Effingham, which had this mannor in portion, who had iſſue Agnes, married to William Paulet, Marquis of Wincheſter, which lady gave this mannor unto Sir Thomas Dennis, knight, that married her daughter.—In this pariſh is *Acland*, pleaſantly ſituated againſt the ſouth, on the ſide of a hill, which hath given name to its ancient dwellers, that have continued in that place from the time of King Henry the 2d, unto this preſent. Of which lineage, five of the firſt were called Baldwin, whoſe written name anciently was Accelena. This family have increaſed their heritage, by marrying the daughters and heirs of divers houſes. The now lord of this place married the daughter of Sir Francis Vincent, baronet, his father Sir Arthur, the ſiſter and heir of John Mallet, his grandſire the daughter of Monk, of Potheridge." *Riſdon.*—*Acland-Houſe.* The Acland family derive their name from their ſeat, *Aukeland* or *Acland*, ſignifying an *oaken grove*, near which it is ſituated againſt the ſouth, on the ſide of a hill. As a confirmation of this conjecture, I find in ancient times, ſo far back as Richard the 2d's days, that this family bore on their ſeal, *three oak leaves on a bend, between two lions rampant.* " This family hath flouriſhed in this place from the time of Henry the 2d, to this day," ſays *Prince.*—The chriſtian name of the Aclands was, for the moſt part, Baldwin. They have been connected with many houſes of diſtinction, ſuch as Cruwys, Monk, Prideaux, Mallet, Radcliff. John Acland, of Acland, ſerved in the French wars, 9th Richard the 2d, 1385, as appears by a deed dated the ſame year, in which is expreſſed a condition for the raiſing of money towards his redemption, if he happened to be taken priſoner, without ſelling his lands. At this time he was in poſſeſſion of eſtates in Akelene, Reweton, Gratton, Barnſtaple, Hawkeridge, Little Bray, Southmolton, and other places.—*Olim Capella de Tawton.* Cloſe to the north wall lie two recumbent figures, of a man and his wife, the former croſs-legged, and therefore a knight of the holy voyage: Part of his ſhield remains; but no arms, or any other token by which we can diſcover who he was. The tradition is, that he was once Lord of Lankey.

‡ " *Hall* was the ancient habitation of a tribe ſo ſurnamed; of whom Simon Hall, a man very learned in the laws, grew ſo gracious with the biſhop, that he procured his father's dwelling for his inheritance, being before parcel of the mannor, and left it unto Thomazin, his daughter and heir, married to Richard Chicheſter, a younger ſon of Raleigh-houſe; which family hath enjoyed the ſame divers de-ſcents, which is now the ſeat of Sir John Chicheſter, knight, who hath annexed much fruitful land thereunto. He married firſt the daughter of Sir William Stroude, knight; ſecondly, the daughter of Sir Lewis Pollard, baronet; his father the daughter of Sir Arthur Baſſet, knight; his grandſire the co-heir of Marwood.—*Pill* had anciently lords ſo named; which place, by the daughter of Michael de la Pill, in the age of King Edward the 2d, came to Robert Fulk of Halmſton, from whoſe co-heir, married to Thomas Perot, after ſome ſucceſſions in that tribe, Travers, deſcended of an ancient family in Hampſhire, was inveſted therewith. And *Welleſley* was the inheri-tance of Cauſey, which by Alice, the inheritrix of that houſe, hereditarily deſcended to the Giffards. *Halmſton* in this tything, was the land of Fulk in King Edward the 3d's time, by whoſe co-heir Alice, Baldwin Acland was inveſted therewith, which deſcended to Joan her heir, married to Thomas Mules, ſecond ſon of Thomas Mules of Erneſborough, in King Henry the 5th's time, and ſo lineally, after ſix deſcents, to John Mules, the late lord thereof, that married the daughter of Chafe, his father the heir of Yeomans of Northampton-ſhire. His only daughter and heir Anne, was married to Bennet. In this pariſh is an high hill, called *Coddon*, which affordeth a fair proſpect both to ſea and land; whereof ſome verſifieth thus:

Here *Coddon*, king of hills, doth chryſtal *Taw* o'erlook;
How he attended comes, with many a pretty brook;
And how the fertile fields about the *Taw* do lie,
It ſeeth from its top, e'en with an amorous eye." *Riſdon.*

More than 40 towers and ſteeples, (it is ſaid), may be ſeen from this hill.

§ " The brook that here tumbleth into Taw, deſcendeth from *Swimbridge*, ſo termed happily of the waters full flowing to the bridge there; for ſeated it is ſomewhat low by the lake-ſide, the hills overlooking it in every quarter; in which pariſh is *Erneſborough*, which, as the name imports, is a principal place or court-houſe in the lord's mannor, and ſo this ſeems by the ruins yet remaining. Baldwin de Ernſborough was lord thereof, in the beginning of King Henry the 3d's reign, whom three of that ſurname ſucceeded. After that, it was the fair ſeat of the Flavels, whoſe inheritrix brought this heritage, with a goodly patrimony, to Sir Roger Mules, ſecond ſon to the Lord Mules, Baron of North-Cadbery in Somerſetſhire: A family that flouriſhed there divers deſcents, until that honour, by Mariell and Iſabel, the heirs-general of that houſe, paſſed unto the noble families of Courtney and Botreaux. Of this tribe, was John Lord Mules, one of the 94 barons that in a parliament holden at Lincoln, in the reign of King Edward the 1ſt, A.D. 1301, ſubſcribed a letter, denying the Pope's
pretended

tion. The roof of the north-fide of the chancel contains fome coats of arms and emboffments, which were revived with frefh colours a few years fince. The pulpit is an excellent piece of ftone-work—the outfide divided by compartments, in each of which, within niches, are ancient figures—on the whole, in a good gothic tafte, apparently coeval with the church; which I guefs to to have been erected in the time of Edward the 3d. *

Caftle-hill, in the parifh of FILLEIGH, hath attracted the obfervation of various travellers or tourifts. The houfe is a fine ftructure: Its Grecian hall has a ftriking effect. The grounds, from their inequalities, and from the wood and water in profufion there, afford fufficient fcope for the difplay of a picturefque imagination. Much was done by the predeceffors of the prefent lord, particularly Lord Clinton, but not all judicioufly. The imitation of an old caftle on the hill (whence the name was changed from Filleigh-houfe to Caftle-hill) the hermitage, and park-bridge, were well conceived and executed. But the terrace before the houfe, and the ftrait lines of trees on the hills, were not capable of adding beauty to the landfcape. We are pleafed with the hermitage at the end of the park, where the wood begins to grow thick, and the river Bray winds its foaming courfe: And park-bridge is roughly hewn out of the rocks, correfponding with the genius of the place.†

CHITTLEHAMTON is a very large parifh, on the river Taw. The principal place is *Brightley.*‡

At

pretended title to the kingdom of Scotland." *Rifdon.*—Hole, of Roborough, is the prefent owner of Swimbridge —" *Dinington*, with *Woodland*, was in former times given by the bifhop to the anceftors of Martin Fifhacre, knight; of whom Philip de Dinington held the fame in King Henry the 3d's reign, which continued in that name, unto the end of King Henry the 3d's time. Since it hath been the lands and habitation of the name of Hanford, and lately devolved on a branch of the Chichefters, by the fifter and heir of the laft of that line.—The hamlet of *Stowford* did fometime belong to the dutchy of Lancafter. In this place was Hieritha, patronefs of Chittlehampton, born; who, as the legend of her life makes mention, fuffered the next year after Thomas Becket, in the reign of King Henry the 2d, in which the name of her parents are fet down." *Rifdon.*—Near Ernefborough, is a place called *Tower*, which, tradition fays, was formerly the habitation of the Mules's.—" *Accott* anciently belonged to the bifhops of this diocefe; which one of them gave to Drogo de Teigne. It afterwards came to coheirs; two parts whereof the lord of Landkey, and the third, Simon Hall held, which defcended to Chichefter, by the match of his heir. The two former parts were by the Lady Marchionefs of Winton given to Drake of Wifcombe, who fold the fame to Chichefter." *Rifdon.*—*Marfh* is the property of Rolle: And at the S. E. of Kefcot-hill, is Kefcot, an eftate belonging to the Rev. W. Hole.

* The churches of *Swimbridge* and *Landkey* are faid to have been formerly chapels of eafe to Bifhop's-Tawton. Thefe three parifhes, at prefent, always join in the expence of repairing any public buildings. The north-aifle of this church was built by Sir John Mules, of Ernefborough; as the infcription in a window, and the roof, once fairly painted, and gilded, with the arms and matches of that family make evident—unto the maintenance whereof he gave to that church his lands, called Furfe, in the parifh of Chittlehamton. There were other lands in Furfe, given by Sir John Norberry towards the maintenance of St. Bridget's chapel, to find lights, and fing mafs for the fouls of Sir John Norberry and Joan his wife, and other benefactors to the church of Swimbridge, for ever. There were lands, alfo, given, for the fupport of the nave of this church, and of the poor and impotent of this parifh, Rabfcot in North-Molton, Eaft-Brailey in Eaft-Buckland, and feveral cottages in the church-town of Swimbridge.

‡ " Whence the family of Filleigh took their origin. Simon de Filleigh held half a knight's fee here, in the time of Henry the 2d. And the Filleighs continued lords thereof, unto the reign of Henry the 4th; when Elizabeth, the daughter of John, the laft of that line, was married to William Trawen, of Wear, whofe only inheritrix Joan, took to hufband Richard Denfell, whom his fon Richard fucceeded; and his daughter and heir, was married to Martin Fortefcue, eldeft fon of Sir John Fortefcue, chief juftice; which name inheriteth thefe lands unto this day; where they enjoy large demefne, with a park thereunto belonging; where the franknefs of the houfe-keeper confirms the welcome of friends." *Rifdon.*—The fame praife is juftly due to the prefent poffeffor of *Filleigh-houfe*, now *Caftle-hill*, viz. Matthew Fortefcue, Earl Fortefcue, Vifcount Ebrington, and Baron Fortefcue. His lordfhip was born March 12, 1753; married May 4, 1782, Hefther Grenville, fifter to the Marquis of Buckingham, by whom he had a fon (the heir apparent) Feb. 13, 1783. He has fince had feveral children. For further particulars of this family, fee the peerages.

‡ " *Brightley*, about 8 miles fouth of Barnftaple, was anciently the dwelling of William Filius Warini, in the reign of King Richard the 1ft, who was the fon of Fulk Fitz-Warren, that had this land from his father in the time of King Henry the 2d; which family afterwards affumed the name of Brightley from their dwelling. Of which tribe, there were fix called William, amongft whom one flourifhed in knight's degree. Another William de Brightley was well learned in the laws, and a governor of the county; and in the 39th year of King Edward the 3d, was chofen one of the knights of fhire. From which name, by the Carews, this land came to the name of Cobleigh; whofe only daughter and heir Margaret, was married to Sir Roger Giffard, a flourifhing branch of Halfberry-houfe, who made the place a dainty feat, with a park thereunto belonging; which is now inherited by John Giffard, that married the daughter of Sir John Windham, his father the daughter of Leigh, his grandfire the daughter of the Earl of Dorfetfhire." *Rifdon.*—Brightley was a pleafant feat before it was pulled down and rebuilt as a common farm-houfe: Nothing of the old building remains but one room and the chapel. The arms of the Fitzwarrens, however, were preferved. They were over the porch, cut in ftone, and put up again in the porch or front of the new building.

At Chittlehamton-Church is a remarkably handfome tower. It is built in the fame tafte as that of St. Mary Magdalene at Tawton, and of Bifhop's-Lydiard near Taunton—poffibly by the fame architect. *

The parifh of Aldrington or Atherington (as Rifdon fays) in ancient deeds, was formerly written Afherington. Its length and breadth are nearly the fame, about two miles and half. The church, fituated in the center of the parifh, confifts of two aifles, 56 feet in length—the chancel and Umberleigh aifle are each 30 more, making together 86—the breadth 34—the tower from the top of the battlements is 76 feet. There is befide a fmall fouthern aifle, formerly belonging to and repaired by the barton of Buriat. The fcreen which interfects the north aifle, parting it from that called Umberleigh aifle, was very handfome —fome part of it is ftill remaining, which is richly carved, and highly ornamented. In the chancel are two recumbent figures of Sir Arthur Baffet and Elinora his wife.†

Vol. III.   H   Befides

building. The chapel was, a few years ago, kept in repair, tho' not ufed for divine fervice. A gold cup of the Cobleigh's (called Cobleigh's cup) is preferved to this day, and always produced at the court baron of this manor, wherein the tenants drink to Cobleigh's memory. The park had been difparked before the houfe was pulled down; but the then remaining trees ferved to fupply timber for the new farm-houfe. From the Giffards, Brightley came to the Rolles, who at prefent poffefs it.—A branch of the ancient ftock of Acland-houfe, was planted at *Hawkridge*, in this parifh; and " liking the foil well, flourifhed here to the prefent age." " Of which Hawkridge, fays Prince, I have heard it reported, that when any one defcended from this family, firft enters the houfe, he immediately falls into a fwoon." John Acland defcended from the family of Hawkridge, married Elizabeth, the daughter of Mr. Duck, of Heavitree, and refided at Exeter as a merchant.

* " This parifh, fays Rifdon, is graced with a fair church, and a ftately tower; and, in times paft, hath been notable for that Hierytha, canonized a faint, was here interred. To her memory the church was dedicated; and fhe efteemed to be of fuch fanctity, that you may read of many miracles afcribed to her holinefs in his book that penn'd her life."—In the north-aifle of this church Colonel Giffard erected a monument of alabafter, to the memory of his grandfather; where his effigies in armour is reprefented to the life: The whole is adorned with efcutcheons of the family; and on a handfome table we have a Latin infcription: See *Prince*, p. 344, 345.

† On a flab adjoining the monument is the following infcription: Part of the ftone is fcaled off, it is therefore fomewhat imperfect.

Here lie the bodies of the right

———— the 2d April, 1586—the latter
———— buried the 10th of July, 1585
———— behind them 5 fons & 2
————ters—Requies-cant in pace—

of Sr John Chichefter of Rawleigh

He that is 3 in 1 & 1 in 3
ft made us 2 then 1—this one were we
One love, one life we liv'd—1 Year 1 Death
Rock'd us afleep by borrowing but 1 breath
Grave the bed that holds us both—the Stone
hides us covert—the bed is one
1 Heaven contains our Souls—1 trump 1 day
raife our bodies from this bed of clay
Death which ufeth over to diffever
once united us for ever—

worthipful & worthy knight Sr Arthur Baffet

and Elinora his wife, daughter

Over the chancel door is a fmall monument, with this infcription:

In Obitum Magiftri Ludovici Vicary
Hujufce Ecclefiæ nuper Rectoris—Qui ex hac vitâ
Emigravit 3 die Febrii. Ætatis 64.
Et Janæ uxoris fuæ cariffimæ—Quæ obiit 13 die
Decembris—Annos nata. 55—1662.

Conjugium quale hoc! vivos et morte cadentes
    Endomus una duos, Lectulus unus habet.
Occidit uxor amans, et amabilis inde fecutus
    Vir facer, Angelicís femper adeffe Choris
Rectorem hic roftri rapuit fibi Rector Olympi
Poft raptam uxorem ut fit utrique Maritus eorum.

O Love how ftrong doft thou tie knots
That Death can't folve them with his plots.
Death with thy fting t'haft loft thine art
For man and wife thou canft not part.
True Love made us one heart to live and die
Our bodies reft below—our fouls on high.

Befides the large manor of Umberleigh, which extends itfelf into the adjoining parifh of Bickington, (the patronage of which church, as well as of Atherington, being an appendage to it), there are two other fmall manors in this parifh; that of Wootton, formerly the lands of the Giffards, but now belonging to a Mrs. Melhuifh, of Saterleigh, and that of Atherington annexed to the rectory. This, as well as another manor belonging to the rectory of Bickington, was founded, according to Rifdon, by King Athelftan, who gave to God, and to each of thefe churches, one hide of land.* Tradition tells us, that Umberleigh was the palace of Athelftan; and that this king built a chapel there, to the honor of the Bleffed Trinity, for the ufe of his own family and the neighbourhood. After Athelftan, this chapel lay long neglected; when Lady Champernowne allowed lands for the maintenance of a chaplain.†

HUNTSHAW

Nec non in memoriam Magiftri Johannis Vicary prædicti Patris indulgentiffimi et præcedentis hujus Ecclefiæ Rectoris et uxoris fuæ Joannæ—Qui fepulti fuerunt—Ille die Decemb⁵. 31, 1644—et illa Aprilis die 20, 1622—Quorum Corpora cum Prioribus hoc fimul dormiunt Cancello—Animis ad Deum evolatis.

On flabs within the rails of the communion table, are the following infcriptions:

Mors janua vitæ
Here lieth the body of
George Fairchild, Rector of Atherington
19 years—who departed this Life the 9th Day of
April 1728—Ætatis fuæ 55.

M: S:
Rev^di: Gulielmi Mervin
Collegii Exonienfis olim Socii
S. T. B.
Tam Clare Portionis in Tiverton
Quam hujus Ecclefiæ
Rectoris
Obiit Decr. 17—An: Dom: 1759
Ætatis 77.

Here is depofited what remains of Baple Yeo, A. B.
Rector of this Church, who fuddenly departed
this Life June 18, 1764—Aged 44.

There are in the body of the church grave-ftones in memory of the Pollards of Langley Barton adjoining this parifh; as alfo of the Chichefters and Ifaacs, formerly of Buriat Barton, given to one of their anceftors by Sir Ralph Willington, in the reign of King Henry the 3d. This eftate now belongs to Gonvil and Caius College, Cambridge, by the donation of a Mrs. Pinkcombe, who bequeath'd a very confiderable eftate to this and other charitable ufes.

Near the defk is the following:
Mors Janua Vitæ
Under refteth enterr'd, in hopes of a joyful refurrection, the
body of Grace the Wife of William Stevens of Great Torrington,
Gent: by whom he had iffue 3 Sons and 2 Daughters—She
departed this Life the 6th day of Novr. in the Year of our Lord
1652 in the year of her Age 70.
Per Chriftum refurgam
What though inclos'd in filent cell
Grace for a fpace with worms may dwell
This truth we find in facred ftory
Earth cannot long keep Grace from Glory.
Chriftus via ad Cœlum.

* He gives a copy of the donation for its antiquity, but mentions not where he faw it :—" Iche Atheftan King Grome of this home geve and graunt to the Prefts of thus Chirch one yoke of land frelich to holde Wode in my holt houfe to buyld, byt graffe for all his Beafts, fuel for hys hearth, pannage for his Sow and puggis World without end."

† " This chaplain, Peter Quivil Bifhop of Exeter confirmed." In another part of his furvey, Rifdon has introduced the copy of in all probability this very deed :—" There was an agreement, he fays, made between Ralph Willington and Joan his wife of the one party, and Hugh de Loges of the other party, for Buckenholt, in the prefence of the Lord Henry Tracy and Sr Hugh Chagford, knight, in the time of King Henry the 3d—and Sr John Willington gave Weefkland, in this tything, unto Robert Tolla—cum 40 Somagia annuatim capiend in Buckenholt (fo be the words of the grant) in the time of King Edward 1ft"—then follows—" Johannes de Campo Arnulphi Salutem-noveritis me in viduitate meâ, divinæ Charitatis intuite pro Salute Animæ mee et Anteceflorum meorum nec non pro Salute animarum Domini Will de Campo Arnulphi Patris mei et Eve Matris mee the Parents of Lady Joan Champernon et puerorum noftrorum Concef. totam terram de Niara ad Suftentationem Capelle ad Præfentationem noftram et Hæredum ad Celebrand Divina in Capellâ noft. de Umberley—Hiis Teftibus John de Punchardon, Nicolao de Filleigh, Roberto Beaple, Matth. de Wolington, Milit. Sans Date—Robert de Querry ad petitionem Regis Johannis Conftitut. Olimpi ad neptem fuam Jil. Wilmoi Franchevalier Uxor. Radulphi Willington Hæred. Medietat—Jette Eaklington Hiis Teftibus Petro Stoke, Senefcall Domini Regis Fulk Kau. Jo. Actim Robert Repleigh."—" In this chapel, after the eftate became the habitation of the Baffetts, many of them were there interred, where they had fair fepulchres, on whofe tombs
fome

TAWSTOCK HOUSE.

To Sir Bourchier Wrey Bart. this Plate is Inscribed

By his Obliged

Servant, R. Polwhele.

Drawn and Engraved by J. Bonnor.

Published by A. Published May 1 1794.

HUNTSHAW was, anciently, famous for its woods.*

YARNSCOMBE, fix miles fouth of Barnftaple, lies detached from the four other parifhes in the hundred of Hertland.

HORWOOD is a fmall parifh, near four miles to the eaft of Bideford.†

The parifh of WESTLEIGH would here be paffed in filence, but for the elegant feat of the Clevlands, which is very pleafantly fituated,‡ and commands an extenfive view of the Briftol Channel.

At TAWSTOCK, it has been obferved, are the beft manor, the nobleft manfion,§ and the moft curious church in the county. Tawftock, in the time of Henry the 2d, was the joint poffeffion of William de Brewes and Oliver de Traci: and the manfion was afterwards inhabited by Henry de Tracy. The Lords Martyn and Audelegh poffeffed it in hereditary fucceffion; till in failure

of

fome of their proportions were curioufly cut. But Tempus edax rerum—now only 2 of them remain, upon one of which is the effigies of a knight and his lady, adorned with their armories, and other noble families, their allies, richly guilded, whereon the Courtneys, Grandifons, Willingtons, Whalfborowes did not long time fince appear;—on the other was a proportion completely arm'd, lying crofs legg'd, after the manner of fuch as in elder ages went to war in the Holy Land; but neither of them have any infcription left to teftify who they were. Near unto was a chantry, a facred edifice, created for divine fervice, daily to be faid for the founder's foul."—In the " Mitred Abbies" I find among the chauntries in Devon, Umberleigh, and that at its diffolution five pounds were allowed to John Weye, incumbent. This chapel is 59 feet 6 inches long, and 20 feet 6 inches wide.—About a century ago a new roof and covering were beftowed upon it, but fince that time it has been much neglected—almoft every flate is gone, but the arch timber work ftill remains, and ferves as a fupport to the ivy which has fpread itfelf almoft over the whole roof, and in feveral places in the chapel hangs down in long waving traces, and produces a ftriking and picturefque appearance. The houfe was formerly an extenfive building, and the hall a very large and fpatious one, with fine carv'd work; but on modernifing the houfe, about 80 years fince, it was deftroy'd. Scarce any thing remains of the old houfe but the porch, where are Queen Elizabeth's arms, with thofe of the Baffetts, Granvilles, and fome other families.—" This manor, (fays Rifdon) according to the mutation of times, hath had lords out of fundry families. The firft that comes within the compafs of my knowlege, was Afculphde Soleigney, who dwelt at Umberley in the time of Henry the 2d, whom his fon Gilbert fucceeded, that married Avis, fifter to Richard Rivers, Earl of Devon, and dwelt here alfo. This Gilbert had iffue Mabill, his daughter and heir, married to Jordan Champernon, from whom iffued the Lord Jordan their fon, whom fucceeded the Lord William Champernon; whofe only daughter the Lady Joan was married to a knight of Gloucefterfhire, called Sᵣ Ralph Willington, by whom fhe had many fons, which lady ftill retained her own name, and in all her charters and grants is ftill ftiled the Lady Joan Champernon, and all her fons left the arms of Willington, and gave their mother's arms."—" From the Willingtons, Umberleigh came to the family of Wroth, from Wroth to Palton, from Palton to Beaumont, and from Beaumont to Baffet, in which family it ftill remains." See Sir Wm. Pole.—The regifter for baptifms begins in 1538, for marriages in 1548, for burials in 1570.—The parifh is rated 927 pounds, and pays land-tax at 4s.—£,130 0 2.

* " Huntfhaw, or the Hunter-fhaddow; for Shaw with our forefathers fignifieth a fhadow; fo as this place may be termed the Hunters-fhadow, and that not unaptly; being not altogether deftitute of trees, tho' not furnifhed with fuch goodly woods former ages afforded. In the time of King Henry the 3d, Henry Fitz-Reginald was lord of this mannor, fince the Champernons; then the Wellingtons. In the reign of King Richard the 2d, Joan Wellington was lady of this mannor; of later times the inheritance of the Beaumonts, by which name it came to the Chichefters." Rifdon.

† Horwood was the ancient inheritance of Cornu. Here Alan Cornu lived in the reign of Edw. the 1ft. William Cornu, the laft of this family, dying without iffue, and leaving his inheritance to his two fifters, Elizabeth, married to Walter Pollard, and Margaret to William Wolford, this land defcended to the Pollards.—Here Walter Pollard lived 27th Hen. 3d; after that another Walter, 24th of Edw. 1ft; then Joel; then John; then Walter the third; then John the fecond; who by Eleanora, daughter of John Copleftone, of Copleftone, efq. had iffue Walter and Robert; from the laft of whom iffued Sir Lewis Pollard, one of the judges of the common pleas in the reign of Henry the 7th. The pofterity of Walter Pollard flourifhed at Horwood fix or feven generations, after his time, when in the iffue male it became extinct.—Weft-Horwood, or Church-Horwood, fituated in the wefternmoft part of the parifh, adjoins to the hamlet of Eaftleigh. It was the inheritance of Richard Lamprey, in the time of Henry the 2d: and in the reign of Edward the 2d came by marriage to the Paflews, who long continued there. Robert Paflew, one of Henry the 3d's favourites, entered into a confpiracy to murder William Marfhall, Earl of Pembroke. On the difcovery of the plot, he took fhelter, with the reft of the confpirators in the new temple. " This Robert Paflew was fo fhaken by the court tempeft, that he became parfon of Deerham, in Norfolk." Rifdon.—Weft-Horwood was, lately, the feat of John Dene, efq.—" It is written in a window of Pollard's aifle, in this church: Orate pro bono ftatu Johannis Pollarde et Wilmote Uxor. ejus, qui iftam Guildam fieri fecerunt. In this window Pollarde impaleth a griffon ramp. fub. in a field arg. This griffon (report fays) was borne by a Duke of France, with whofe daughter one of the Pollards grew fo enamoured, that tho' fhe belonged to a nunnery, he determined to marry her—and obtained a difpenfation from the king for the fame purpofe." Rifdon.

‡ " Weftleigh, in the Saxons time and tongue, Weftlega, fell to the fhare of Robert de Albamara, upon whom the Conqueror beftowed much land in this county. From which family the Lord Hugh Courtney purchafed this mannor, of whom Mauger le Grant held the fame, whofe fon William le Grant was lord thereof. And his grand-fon William left iffue Elizabeth married to John Monke of Potheridge.—The hamlet of Eaft-Leigh, was the lands of Galfride de Leigh in the time of King John, whofe daughter and heir was married to John Barry of Winfcott, with whom he had that mannor, whofe fon gave one farthing of land in Wych to John, furnamed of the place of his dwelling. And in this place William Wilmer had inheritance, and his pofterity a fair feat. The laft of the Wilmer's dying iffuelefs about the reign of Henry the 7th, left his eftate to divers perfons." Rifdon.—The lands of Wilmer, which were the manor of Weftleigh and hamlet of Eaftleigh, came by conveyance to the Berrys, a family of good antiquity. Berry married a Giffard—his fon one of the coheireffes of Leigh. The Berrys ftill poffefs thefe lands.—" The manor of Tapley, (anciently Apley) was in former times the lands of Baudrope. Since, it was held by Walter, furnamed Tapley. His heir general was married to Grant—from whom it defcended to Cobley; whofe inheritrix, Margaret, was married to Giffard of Brightley." Rifdon.—Giffard fold this place to William Clevland, efq. defcended from an ancient family in Scotland. His fon was fecretary to the admiralty: His grandfon, John Clevland, efq. M. P. for Barnftaple, is the prefent owner of Tapley.

§ Owing to a fire which happened in 1787, and confumed the principal part of the houfe, it has fince been rebuilt; and the grounds much improved. The whole was executed from Sir B. Wrey's own defigns—which do honor to his tafte and judgment.

of male iffue it became by fpecial entail the property of Margaret, daughter and heirefs of the laft Lord Audelegh; from whom by her marriage with Fulk Lord Fitzwarren, the property defcended to the family of the Bourchiers Lord Fitz-warren and Earls of Bath; from whom Sir Chicheſter Wrey,* by his marriage with Anne, coheir of Edward Earl of Bath, inherited this place: and his iffue male ftill enjoy it.†—The church and monuments at Tawftock are remarkable.§

INSTOW

* By the blood of heirs female, we derive the Wreys from Charlemagne:

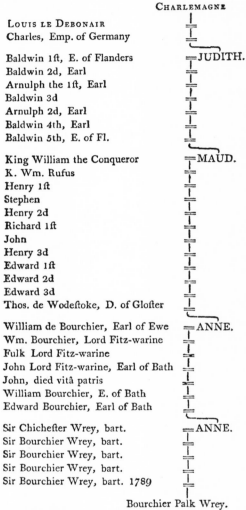

CHARLEMAGNE

Louis le Debonair
Charles, Emp. of Germany

Baldwin 1ft, E. of Flanders   =JUDITH.
Baldwin 2d, Earl
Arnulph the 1ft, Earl
Baldwin 3d
Arnulph 2d, Earl
Baldwin 4th, Earl
Baldwin 5th, E. of Fl.

King William the Conqueror   =MAUD.
K. Wm. Rufus
Henry 1ft
Stephen
Henry 2d
Richard 1ft
John
Henry 3d
Edward 1ft
Edward 2d
Edward 3d
Thos. de Wodeftoke, D. of Glofter

William de Bourchier, Earl of Ewe   =ANNE.
Wm. Bourchier, Lord Fitz-warine
Fulk Lord Fitz-warine
John Lord Fitz-warine, Earl of Bath
John, died vitâ patris
William Bourchier, E. of Bath
Edward Bourchier, Earl of Bath

Sir Chichefter Wrey, bart.   =ANNE.
Sir Bourchier Wrey, bart.
Sir Bourchier Wrey, bart.
Sir Bourchier Wrey, bart.
Sir Bourchier Wrey, bart. 1789

Bourchier Palk Wrey.

See " *The Englifh Baronetage*," Vol. II. pp. 84, 85, 86, 87. [Edit. 1741.]

† Sir Bourchier Wrey, bart. fucceeded his father in 1784. In 1786 he married Mifs Palk, only daughter of Sir Robert Palk, bart: She died in 1792, leaving two fons and a daughter. In 1793 he married Mifs Ofborne, of Glocefterfhire, by whom he has no iffue. The late Sir B. Wrey, in 1755, married Mifs Threfher, of Wiltfhire. now living, by whom he had fix children, the prefent Sir Bourchier, and the Rev. Bourchier William; a daughter, married to the Rev. Mr. Winfield, of Bedfordfhire; another, married to Robert Harding, of Upcot, efq; another, married to Richard Long, of Wiltfhire, efq.; and another, married to —— Foke, of Kent, efq.

§ At the eaft-end of the fouth aifle, is a monument adorned with 3 Corinthian pillars, under which is the effigies of a lady, and this infcription:

Here lieth buried Francis Lady Fitz warren the daughter of Sʳ Thoˢ. Kitfon, kᵗ. & wief to John Lᵈ Fitz warren the fon, and heir apparent of John Earl of Bath, by whom fhe had iffue Thomas, John, Margaret, & William now Earl of Bath. She patiently departed ͨ mortality of this lyf in the trew faith on Efter day 1586. Eliz: Reginæ: XXVIII.

Another monument in the fame church:

Hic fitus eft Dom. Henricus Bourychier Comes Bathonienfis qui longa propagine, & numerofo ftemmate a vetuftiffimis juxta ac nobi-liffimis familiis de Bourgchier, & Fitzwarren efflux t & jure hereditario, ac titulo cognationis afcita fibi infignia de Woodftock, Bohem, Say, Mandeville, Brufe, Baddlefmer, Clare, Montchefney, Comehill, Windfor, Peverell, Clifford, Giffard, Martin, Mohun, Tracy, Cogan, Dinham, Courtenay, Rivers, Stourton, Hangford, reliquarum celebris notæ familiarum arma natalitia cum propriis infignibus intertexta, ac circumfufa fcuto fuo gentilitia complectitur & pofteris marmore hoc infculpta exhibet fatis eft Lector. habes jam tandem compendiofam fuorum natalium feriem, ubi generis fplendorem, & profapiæ fua fublimitatem fpectes, fi vero virtutes, & animi fupel-lectilem luftraveris nomen fuum ære perennius marmore diuturnius, aut quovis elogio aut Epitaphio Confpectuis tandem aliquando confulas.

On the other fide:

Æternitati Sacrum.

Sifte viator, fub hoc tumulo. Sive *Ciſtro* Mamoreo
Depofuit exuvius carnis,
Henricus Comes Bathonienfis
Præfentis Sæculi Livor, & venturæ
Pofteritatis Luctus
Vir venerandis natalibus quam apprime infignis.

Et

OLD GATEWAY   TAWSTOCK.

Drawn & Engraved by T. Bonner.

This Plate is inscribed

To Sir Bourchier Wrey, Bart.

By his Obligd. Servant.

R. Polwhele?.

published by R. Polwhele April 17 1793.

INSTOW corruptly for *Johnſtow*, ſtands at the conflux of the Taw and the Torridge.*

FREMINGTON gives name to a hundred, having been a place of conſiderable conſequence, ſending members to parliament in the time of Edward the 3d.†

Et prolixa Nobiliſſimi ſtemmatis profapiâ
Non minus Conſpicuus.
Videas qua ſupellectile fortunae ſit ſtipatus,
Nec minus virtutum peculio grandis animus
Exuberavit.
Vaná folidioris Literaturæ limatura fuit
Exeultus,
Et tamen blando comtæ elegantiæ lenocinio
facilis & effuſus.
Egenis ſua inopia vacillantibus fuit præſidium
& Columen.
Academicis ingruente hujus temporis barbarie
pene fractis fulcrum & *ſtatumen.*
Amicis fuit diffuſæ urbanitatis, inimicis vero
Benignæ compenſationis Specimen.
In omnes alios pronus, & demiſſus, folum in
ſeipfum gravis.
Erga Regem erat infractæ, licet calamitofæ
Fidelitatis Symbolum.
Ac denuo erga Deum intemeratæ Pietatis
Aſſiduus Affecla.
Sed eheu dum tantos virtutum iconiſmos,
Umbratili ſtylo calamiſtramus,
plorantibus paſſim piis & ſtipantibus Angelis
A terreſtri hoc pulvere in cæleſte
Faſtigium evectus eſt,
in cujus memoriam
ne ſitu & ærugine
Tabeſceret,
Hoc monumentum affectus ſui teſſeram,
Rachel Comitiſſa Lugens poſuit.

At bottom :

Who was daughter to Francis Earl of Weſtmorland, Sone, & heir of Thoˢ. Fane by Mary his wife, daughter & heire of Henry Nevil Earl of Abergavenny. Her mother was Mary daughter & heir to Anth: Mildmay by Grace, daughter & coheir of Henry Shermeton Kᵗ: 1656.

North of this, on a round pedeſtal, is a ſtatue of white marble, and this inſcription :

Rachel
Comitiſſa Henrico digna, vix altera e ſexu
vel animo, vel virtute æquipollens,
Rebus domeſticis, civilibus, ſacris, ingenio
pluſquam virili at materno,
quo ſuo tempore vix majus dabatur in terris,
Eccleſiæ Anglicanæ filia humilis & devota,
Et iniquis temporibus ejectorum patrum Mater
Et hic pene unica Fautrix.
Unicum lugendum quod in ſe peniſſet nobile
Bourcherii nomen ni ſat illa habuit virtutum
vel illud immortale reddere,
Et licet improlis plus Mille Liberorum Parens
quos liberaliſſime educavit, dotavit,
Sacravit, nobilitavit,
adhuc vivit, & nuſquam moritura dum his
Regionibus Superfunt grata Pectora.

Arms Bourchier & Fane.

Monument on the South ſide, ſtatue couch. in white marble Lᵈ & Lady Bath, an Earl kneeling at yᵉ head :—on yᵉ N: wall pedigree and monument of Bold's of Upton in Cheſhire.

In the North Croſs Iſle monument of Sʳ Hen. Northcote ſon of Sʳ Arthur Northcote a Dʳ of Phyſick who died 1729. In one of yᵉ windows in painted glaſs A. Bp Bourchiers arms, 2 Bourchier & England, 3 England.—In another window 3 horſes heads bridled, and a coat of Bath arms.

* " Here Walter Clavell held lands by the Conqueror's gift. And in the time of Henry the 3d, John de St. John. Alexander St. John was lord of Inſtow in Edward the 2d's reign ; and Oliver St. John in that of Edward the 3d. Since Sir Richard Hankford, knight, inherited theſe lands." *Riſdon.*

† " *Fremington* in the Saxons time, *Fremanton*, as if one ſaid the Freeman's Town ; which, at the conqueſt, was the king's demeſne, but before was held by Algar an Engliſh-man, containing ſixteen villes, and guilded after 14*l*. 10*s*. *ad Penſam & Arſuram.* The Tracys, barons of Barnſtaple, were afterwards lords of this mannor ; from whom it came by the Martins, to the Lord Audleigh, who intailed the ſame to the crown. By which means Nicholas Lord Audleigh dying without iſſue, it came to King Richard the 2d, who gave it to his half brother John Holland Earl of Huntingdon, which reverted again to the crown. And King Edward the 6th granted the fee-farm thereof to Bernard-Hampton, who alienated the ſame to Hugh Sloly of Sloly ; whoſe great grand-child bearing the ſame name, now enjoyeth the ſame, with the honour of the hundred of Fremington, who married the daughter of Sir Lewis Pollard, baronet ; his father the daughter of Pollard of Langley ; his grandſire the daughter of Bellew ; ſecondly, the daughter of Pollard. At *Rokeſbear* in this pariſh, ſometime dwelt a knight of the family of the Frank Cheynies, whoſe eſtate came unto the name of Stanton." *Riſdon.—Fremington-Houſe*, once poſſeſſed by Richard Ackland, eſq. now belongs to William Barbor, eſq. ſheriff of Devon in 1793.

ARCHDEACONRY OF BARNSTAPLE.

DEANRY OF TORRINGTON.

IN the deanry of Torrington, we ſhall notice the pariſhes of Torrington, St. Giles, Little Torrington, Roborough, Beaford, Merton, Huiſh, Dolton, Aſhreigney, Winkleigh, Dowland, Ideford, Methe, Petrockſtow, Buckland-Filleigh, Shebbeare and Sheepwaſh, Newton St. Petrock, Peter-Merland, and Langtree.*

The approach to the town of Torrington,† the declivity on which it ſtands, the fine river Torridge, and the rich appearance of the oppoſite hills, are worthy mention. From the ‡ Caſtle-hill, the valley immediately below has a picture-reſque

* " *Benefices remaining in charge:*

First Fruits. £.	s.	d.		Yearly Tenths. £.	s.	d.
24	0	0	Aſhreigney, or Ring's Aſh R. [St. James] Rep. B. Proc. vis. viii*d*. Syn. iis. v*d*. A. D. Proc. vis. viii*d*. r. V. 170*l*. Patr. and R. John Toiſell Johnſon.	2	8	0
11	15	7½	Beaford R. [All Saints] Rep. B. Proc. vis. viii*d*. Syn. iis. v*d*. A. D. Proc. vis. viii*d*. r. V. 100*l*. - -	1	3	6¾
11	16	0½	Buckland-Filleigh R. [St. Mary] Rep. B. Proc. ivs, vi*d*. Syn. iis. v*d*. A. D. Proc. ivs. vi*d*. r. V. 100*l*. - Patr. Biſhop of Exeter.	1	3	7¼
20	16	8	Dowilton R. [St. Edmund] Rep. B. Proc. vis. viii*d*. Syn. iis. v*d*. A. D. Proc. vis. viii*d*. r. V. 140*l*. - - Patr. Clevland.	2	1	8
17	1	3	Edſleigh, or Idſleigh R. [St. James] Rep. B. Proc. vis. viii*d*. Syn. iis. v*d*. A. D. Proc. vis. viii*d*. r. V. 200*l*.	1	14	1
29	1	3	Langtree R. [Ded. unc.] Rep. B. Proc. vis. viii*d*. Syn. iis. v*d*. A. D. Proc. vis. viii*d*. r. V. 140*l*. - - Patr. Rolle.	2	18	1½
20	15	7½	Martin, or Merton R. [All Saints] Rep. B. Proc. vis. viii*d*. Syn. iis. v*d*. A. D. Proc. vis. viii*d*. r. V. 130*l*. - Patr. Lord Orford.	2	1	6¾
9	7	6	Methe R. [St. John Baptiſt] Rep. B. Proc. vis. viii*d*. Syn. iis. v*d*. A. D. Proc. vis. viii*d*. r. V. 100*l*. - - Patrs. The Daughters of Richard Blinch, eſq.	0	18	9
8	5	7½	Newton St. Petrock R. Rep. B. Proc. iis. ii*d*. ob. Syn. iis. v*d*. A. D. Proc. iis. ii*d*. ob. r. V. 80*l*. - -	0	16	4¾
10	8	9	Roborough R. [St. Peter] Rep. B. Proc. vis. viii*d*. Syn. iis. v*d*. A. D. Proc. vis. viii*d*. r. V. 120*l*. - - Patr. May.	1	0	10½
17	0	2½	Stow St. Petrock, alias Petrockſtow, alias Haynton R. Rep. B. Proc. vis. viii*d*. Syn. iis. v*d*. A. D. Proc. vis. viii*d*. r. V. 120*l*. - - - - - - - - - - - - Patr. Lord Orford.	1	14	0
20	0	0	Great Torrington C. [St. Michael] with Stow [St. Giles] made an Impr. ſince 1534. Rep. B. Proc. vis. viii*d*. Syn. iis. x*d*. A. D. Proc. vis. viii*d*. r. V. 90*l*. - - - - - - - - Patrs. Dean and Canons of Chriſt-Church.	2	0	0
14	18	11½	Little-Torrington R. [Ded. unc.] Rep. B. Proc. vis. viii*d*. Syn. iis. v*d*. A. D. Proc. vis. viii*d*. r. V. 120*l*. - Patr. Rolle.	1	19	10¾
21	8	9	Winkleigh V. [All Saints] Rep. B. Proc. vis. iv*d*. Syn. iis. v*d*. A. D. Proc. vis. viii*d*. r. V. 110*l*. - - Patrs. Dean and Chapter of Exeter.	2	2	10½

Diſcharged.

King's Books. £.	s.	d.		Certified Value. £.	s.	d.
			Dowland Imp. Rep. Syn. iis. v*d*. A. D. Proc. iiis. iv*d*. r. V. 40*l*. - - - - - - - Patr. Sir Stafford Northcote, bart.	20	0	0
8	0	0	Huiſh R. [St. James] Rep. B. Proc. iiis. iv*d*. Syn. iis. v*d*. A. D. Proc. iiis. iv*d*. r. V. 90*l*. - - - Patr. Mr. Thomas Dufty.	44	0	0
			Petermerland Cur. Rep. Syn. iis. v*d*. A. D. Proc. ivs. vi*d*. r. V. 40*l*. Patr. Lord Orford.			
11	8	4	Shebbear V. with the Chapel of Sheepwaſh [St. Laurence] Rep. B. Proc. vis. viii*d*. Syn. iis. v*d*. A. D. Proc. vis. viii*d*. r. V. 100*l*. - - - - - - - - - - - - - Patr. The KING.	49	5	0

† " Torrington a bigge market town. It ſtands on the brow of an hill, and hath 3 fair ſtreets in it, and a good market every week; and once a year, on St. Michael's day, the beſt fair in all theſe quarters." *Leland.*—" *Torrington*, alias *Chepin-Torrington*, an ancient burrough, and the river Touridges prime iſſue ſituate on the brow of a hill, lying in length a great way. For the word *Chepan* in the Saxon tongue, is as much as as to buy. This place guilded in the Conqueror's time, after one rod, one farthing, and ſeven carucates: It paid forty ſhillings *ad penſam*. Then Baldwin the Viſcount, Ralph Paynell, Anſgerius, and Odo the ſon of Gamalyn, held lands here. The king alſo had ſome in demeſne at the conqueſt; and Githa, the mother of Earl Harold, had her dowry in lands, in this tything." *Riſdon.* " The lands of the barony of William Fitz-Robert, Baron of Torrington, were diſperſed into diverſe families, by the five coheirs of the laſt baron, married unto Martin, Sully, Merton, Umfrevile and Bryon. This mannor in proceſs of time, came to the crown, and Queen Mary gave it to her ſervant, James Baſſet, whoſe ſon ſold the ſame unto Sir John Forteſcue, chancellor of the Dutchy of Lancaſter, and a privy councellor." *Riſdon.*

‡ " Towards the ſouth, the ruins of an old caſtle hath for many years hovered, which by extreme age is almoſt brought to its period, whereof there only remaineth a chapel within the ſcite, now converted to a ſchool-houſe. Of the honour of this caſtle, many knights fees were held, and very notable it hath been for a barony, which ſo continued from the Norman Conqueſt, to the time of K. Edward the 1ſt, whoſe barons bare for their armories, in a field *gules, two bars, and a lion in chief paſſ. or.*" *Riſdon.*

refque effect. The church is a large regular ftructure; at the fouth-fide of which ftands the tower.* Cardinal Wolfey, when he founded Chrift Church, appropriated this rectory to the College. It included St. Giles's; and a ftipend was allotted to the vicar or curate, with a fmall glebe, and the tythe of two or three fields.

In ST. GILES, *Stevenftone* has been a feat of the Rolle family, from the time of Henry the 8th.† The houfe lies at the bottom of a long eafy defcent: Its park is well wooded and watered.

In LITTLE TORRINGTON,‡ *Crofs* is pleafingly fituated. The courfe of the Torridge winding amidft the hills, and the fine maffes of foliage here and there overfhading the river, would not efcape the eye of the painter. Henry Stevens of Crofs, nephew to the late Denys Rolle, married Mifs Marwood of Somerfet.

ROBOROUGH lies about five miles to the fouth-eaft of Great Torrington.§

BEAFORD

---

* " The church of Torington is fpacioufly fair, and decently kept, whereunto a library belongeth; in which church are diverfe exquifite epitaphs, made to the memory of the deceafed. The largenefs of the lands of this parifh, and the far diftance from that church, caufed fome of the remoteft inhabitants to petition Walter, Bifhop of Exon, that, for their more eafe, they might found another church, anno 1309; which, with the confent of Sir Richard Merton, knight, the patron of Chepin-Torington, was by the bifhop granted; and the inhabitants purchafed a piece of land to build a church, which was confecrated to the honor of St. Giles, the holy hermit." *Rifdon.*—
" Margaret Countefs of Richmond, mother to King Henry the 7th, lived fome time here, who pitying the long path the paftor had from home to church, gave to him, and his fucceffors, the mannor-houfe here, with lands thereunto. In thefe parts, the charitable devotion of our forefathers founded alms-houfes for the poor; and, for their better relief, William Fitz-Robert, Baron of Torington, in King Richard the 1ft's reign, gave them a large wafte called the Common." *Rifdon.*

† " Not a mile eaft from Torington, is a hamlet called St. Giles, where George Rolles hath buildid a right fair houfe of bryke." *Leland.*
—" *Stevenftone* had anciently owners fo called. Michael de St. Stephens is the firft I find upon record; who granted the fame to Richard Baffet; whofe fon Elias poffeft it 27th Henry the 3d, who granted the demefnes thereof to Walter de la Lay or Ley. John de la Ley changed his name to Stevenftone, and fucceeded his father Walter; to whom Elias Baffet, Lord of Bepier in Wales, 3d of Edward the 3d, releafed all his right in Stevenfton. After him came John, Walter, and John de Stevenfton, fucceffively; the latter of whom had iffue Elizabeth his daughter and heirefs, married to Grant of Weftleigh—whofe daughters and coheireffes were married, the one to Monk of Potheridge; the other to Moyle. Moyle had Stevenfton for his part, where he refided. Here probably was born Sir Walter Moyle, knight, one of the juftices of the king's bench, under Henry the 6th. One of the Moyle's fold this eftate to George Rolle, efq." *Prince.*—" It hath ever fince been the dwelling of the Rolles, knights; where they have their warren for conies, and their park for deer. The now inheritor of a great eftate, married Margaret daughter of the Lord Pawlet, of Hinton St. George; his father Anne, the coheir of Sir Thomas Dennis, knight, his grandfire the daughter and heir of Watts; fecondly, the daughter of Fortefcue of Vallopit.—Within this tything you have *Bartons-Way* alias *Way*, which had inhabiters fo named in King John's time. This land Walter de la Way, the fon of William de la Way, granted unto Walter Pollard, in the reign of King Edward the 1ft, calling to witnefs, Sir Henry Sully, and Sir Thomas Merton, knights; from which ancient family, many notable branches are budded forth; but this barton is become the inheritance of Mr. Lewis Wellington.—
Winfcot was the long continued feat of that no lefs ancient family of the Barrys; iffuing from Robert Barry, a perfonage of great worth, who went into Ireland with his unkle Fitz-Stephen, in King Henry the 2d's time; and in the Conqueft thereof, received wounds; chufing rather among the firft to be chief in deed, than fo to feem: And the firft he was in Ireland, that mann'd and brought the hawk to hand: Whofe pofterity, by martial prowefs deferved to receive the title of Barons, Barry, of the Kings of England, and afterwards Vifcount Bonterant. And for their revenues, and great port they kept, got amongft the people, the firname of Barry the More; that is, Barry the Great; one of which family gave all his lands in England, to his fecond fon, as by evidence which I have, appeareth. Divers defcents of them dwelt in this houfe, and matched with many worthy families; whofe heir general (fays Rifdon) my fifter by one venter, dying without iffue, made me owner both of this manfion and manor." *Rifdon.*—Michael Barry, efq. by Joan his wife, daughter of Geo. Pollard of Langley, left iffue Thomafin, who married John Tripconey, of Gulvall, in Cornwall. Joan, the relict of Barry, had for her fecond hufband William Rifdon, 3d fon of Bableigh-houfe, by whom fhe had iffue Triftram and others. Thomafin, dying without iffue, left a fair demefne and a good manor to her brother Triftram Rifdon, whofe fon lived there in *Prince's* time.—" *Doddefcot.* Here lived Sir Thomas Hereward, in the days of Henry the 3d—Sir Hamlin, in thofe of Edward the 1ft—Sir William, in the reign of Edward the 2d; who by Dulcia his wife, fifter of Walter Stapledon, Bifhop of Exeter, had iffue Sir Wm. Hereward, knight, (whofe only daughter Joan, married to Sir Maurice Berkeley, died without iffue); Robert, archdeacon of Taunton; and Thomas, archdeacon of Totnes—whofe ecclefiaftical celibacy brought a period to their name and family in this place;—fo that the eftate was divided among their four fifters, married to Soore, Prodham, Denband, and Sir Thomas Molton, of Pinho." *Prince.*—In the little church of St. Giles is a tombftone on the floor of the north-fide of the chancel, having on a brafs plate an infcription, in memory of the mother of Triftram Rifdon the antiquary. See *Prince,* p. 548.

‡ " The Crewys family were lords of the manor for feveral ages. This inheritance came to the three coheirs of William Crewys—Nichola, wife of Richard Lucy; Egidia, wife of St. Clare; and the third daughter, married to Luccombe. From Lucy defcended Alice, the wife of John Davells:—And the Davells family, of late years (fays Rifdon) poffeft the lands in this parifh."

§ " A rill rifeth by *Roborough*, written in old evidences *Rougaburga.* Places of fuch termination, whereby our fore-fathers fenced in one fafhion or other, and thereby became burghs or burroughs.—The mannor of *Roborough* was the lands of Alexander Ceighney, in the reign of King Henry the 3d. Henry Barry, and Walter Pollard, were lords of thefe lands in King Edward the 1ft's time. Pollard conveighed his part to one of his younger fons, from whom iffued Sir Lewis Pollard the judge; and Barry gave his part to a younger fon, which dwelt at Combe, and was called after the name of this houfe; which land at length came to coheirs; Emma was wife of Coles of Northampton, fince of Somerfetfhire: Elizabeth was wedded to William Wollacombe, fometime of Wollacombe, in the parifh of Mort; but fince the match of that inheritrix, his pofterity made this place their manfion, who are allied to worthy families. The prefent poffeffor married the daughter of Fortefcue, his father the daughter of Coffin, his grandfire the daughter of Baffet.—Gotfceline held *Fedeven,* *Huwifch,* and *Lollard-Stone,* at the time of the Conqueft. Robert Ruffel was Lord of *Fellavin,* in the reign of King John. Nicholas Avenell, and William Swefta, held Fellavin, in King Edward the 2d's age: William Burnell, and Henry Suggaworth, in King Edward the 3d's days. In which hamlet, fince our remembrance, Anftice Steer lived, unto the age of a hundred and forty years. The riveret which rifeth by Roborough, emptieth itfelf into Touridge, over againft *Torrington-Parva.*" *Rifdon.*

BEAFORD borrows the latter fyllable of its name from a paffage thro' the river Torridge, "againft which it lieth out in length, indented with many retches."*

MERTON is fo named from its fcite by the merefide.†

HUISH is wafhed by a ftream that feeds the meers in the moors of Merland.‡

DOLTON is high ground; partly inclofed, partly common.§

ASHREIGNY

* " Beaford, or Beauford, (which is Norman) fignifies *Fairford.* The chief manor of Beauford was the land of the Lady Hawifia de Redvers, daughter to Baldwin, Earl of Devon. She gave Woodhoufe, in this parifh, to the abby of Hartland, in the life-time of her father, who confirmed her grant to the abbot. She gave *Down* to Thomas le Hopdown, the 22d year of Henry the 3d. She alfo gave lands for the maintenance of a clerk for ever, in this parifh." *Rifdon.*

† " *Merton* gave name to an ancient family of knight's degree, who lived in this place, and continued lords of this manor from the time of Henry the 2d, to the latter end of the reign of Edward the 3d. Then Eleanor, daughter of Sir Richard Merton, by her marriage with Sir Matthew Stawell, brought a fair eftate to that family; which have enjoyed this land ten defcents, fince Eleanor." *Rifdon.*—For the following account of the parifh, I am obliged to the Rev. Malachy Hitchins, of St. Hilary, in Cornwall. " This parifh, which is vulgarly called Martin, or Marton, is bounded on the eaft by the river Torridge, on the fouth by the parifh of Huifh, on the weft by Petrockftow and Merland, and on the north by Little Torrington. The church lies equidiftant from three market towns, being fix miles S. E. of Torrington, nearly N. of Hatherleigh, and N. E. of Sheepwafh. It is probable that the rivulet which bounds this parifh on the fouth, and partly on the weft fide, is properly called *Mere,* tho' the common people pronounce it Mure, or Meur. What ftrengthens this conjecture, is the ftagnation of its water, which, according to the Saxon original, feems rather like a pond or lake than a running ftream. This being admitted, there can be no doubt, that Merland, Little Merland, and Merton derived their names from this rivulet. Another thing which favours this opinion, is the conftant ufe of the name of this fmall rivulet by the people in the neighbourhood, *Meur* being as frequently mentioned by them as Torridge, or any other large river; a circumftance not often happening with refpect to the fmall waters of this county. Upon the whole, if it be confidered that this rivulet rifes from feveral fprings in the parifh of Merland, in its progrefs touches Little Merland, and laftly paffes juft under Merton church and village, it will feem pretty evident that its proper name is *Mere,* and that from hence thofe places received their name. In the N. E. part of this parifh lies the barton of Potheridge, remarkable for being the refidence of the family of *Monk* for many generations, and for giving the title of Baron to the Duke of Albemarle, the famous General Monk, who was the laft male defcendant of that ancient family. This place certainly took its name from its fituation *upon Torridge,* which was firft contracted to 'Pontorridge, and then corrupted to Potheridge; for the river Torridge, by a remarkable curvity, bounds the eftate on three fides, making the eaftern part, which was formerly the park, a kind of peninfula. About half of the dwelling-houfe is now * in ruins, and the remainder is inhabited by a farmer, who rents the eftate. Great part of the buildings has fallen down within a few years paft; but of the fteward's houfe, and many other edifices formerly there, fcarcely a ftone is now to be feen, the old materials having been carried off to build a large barn on the lower part of the barton in the year 1734. The chapel, now become ruinous, tho' the roof is yet ftanding, exhibits a fcene of beautiful confufion, and excites ideas of admiration and regret. It is 42 feet in length, including the antichapel, 24 feet in breadth, and near 30 feet in height, and was a ftructure of moft exquifite workmanfhip as to fculpture and plafter. On each fide it had four Corinthian columns, and two of the fame order at each end, befides a great profufion of other ornamental carved work. Over the altar on the cornice fat two angels, of both which only one hand, in which is a clafped book, remains on the fpot, but from the fallen parts it is evident that they were fine pieces of fculpture. There is fome painted glafs in the windows, having the family arms, &c. on it, which feems to have been done at a period when that art was but little underftood, being but poorly executed. The chapel ftands in a north and fouth direction, and, from an elegant gallery at the north end, communicated with one of the principal rooms of the houfe. There is in the chapel a very large piece of free-ftone, on which is a ducal coronet, and under it the letter A. and the date 1672, which probably was the year wherein the prefent dwelling-houfe and chapel were finifhed, as there appears the fame date on a large ftone dial on the front now ftanding.—The barton of Potheridge, upon the whole, is but coarfe land; for tho' it is reported to be feven miles in circumference, which however cannot be true, unlefs we follow the meanders of the river, the rent is lefs than £.200 *per annum.* It is faid that there is a *modus* for the tithes of this eftate, by which the occupier is obliged to pay three pounds a year to the rector, give him a Sunday's dinner, and keep his *grey mare,* throughout the year, of which conditions the firft only is now fulfilled. This is a great detriment to the rectory of Merton.—Adjoining to Potheridge on the weft, lies the barton of *Speccott,* formerly the refidence of a family of that name. The houfe now ftanding thereon was built in the year 1698, and is at fome diftance from the fite of the old buildings, which is now afcertained only from the culver-houfe and fome banks near it."

‡ Here in the reign of Henry the 2d, Philip Huifh held lands; which hereditarily defcended in that name to the latter end of Edward the 3d's reign. Many of this family were of knightly rank. Emma, the daughter of the laft of this line, was married to Sir Robert Trefilian, chief juftice of England; afterwards to Sir John Colfhill, knight. This land was purchafed by Leonard Yeo, a flourifhing branch of Heanton houfe; who built here a houfe for himfelf and his pofterity. He married Arminel, the daughter of Corbet, and relict of Beresford of London, and left iffue; who married the coheir of Smith, and had iffue Leonard; who married the daughter of Fortefcue, of Wear, and had iffue George; who by the daughter of Sir Robert Baffet, of Heanton Punchardon, knight, had iffue Leonard; who by one of the daughters of Colonel John Giffard of Brightley, left iffue.—This eftate was thus advertized in 1782: " To be fold, a very capital and valuable freehold eftate, defirably fituate in the parifh of Huifh, near the turnpike road leading from Torrington to Hatherleigh (two good market and poft towns), diftant from the latter about five, and from the former feven miles; of the yearly value of four hundred and feventy-fix pounds, exclufive of chief rents, confifting of the manor of Huifh, with manorial rights over the whole parifh of Huifh, a delightful fporting country, abounding with great plenty of game; together with 686 acres and upwards of rich arable and pafture land, in fine condition, within a ring fence, beautifully diverfified with hanging woods, wherein are growing many thoufands of very fine thriving timber trees and faplins, and nearly furrounded with the fine river Torridge, and fome lakes of a lefs denomination, all plenteoufly ftored with all kinds of frefh water fifh; with a very capital and large Manfion-houfe, fuited with proper offices, orchards, and gardens, and which for feveral centuries paft was the refidence of a very genteel family; together with the perpetual advowfon and next prefentation to the very improveable living of Huifh aforefaid, confifting of a very fine glebe, about 67 acres and upwards of very rich arable, meadow, and pafture land, which, with the rectorial tythes, is now about 84*l.* per annum, the prefent incumbent about 47, who hath lately erected an excellent dwelling-houfe, fitted up and finifhed in a very good ftile, at a confiderable expence."—The manor and advowfon of the living were foon after purchafed by Sir James Norcliffe Innes, a Scotch baronet, who built a new houfe on the premifes, called Innes-houfe.—" *Lovelfton,* in this parifh, were the lands of Robert Lovell, the 20th year of Henry the 3d. And Robert Lovell held the fame in the reigns of Edward the 1ft and 2d—the inheritance of which lately belonged to Leigh." *Rifdon.*—Lovelfton, or *Loviftone,* was late the property of John Cunningham Saunders, efq. a gentleman, who, for his reported oppreffion of Mr. Tafker, was called by the poet, " an unnatural brother-in-law !"—They are both gone !—And (as Mr. Hole fings in more melodious verfe), " the oppreffor and the oppreft are undiftinguifh'd clay." See Hole's admirable Ode to Melancholy; *Devon* and *Cornwall* Poets, vol. I. pp. 86, 94.

§ The Earls of Devon were lords of the manor. After whom, Ameredeth was feized of it. Since, Sir Thomas Monk, knight, had this manor given him in marriage, with the daughter of Sir George Smith, knight. From the Monks, I underftand, it came to the

Granville's;

* Anno 1770.

ASHREIGNY, or RINGSASH, feems to have been a royal demefne.*

WINCKLEIGH is a very large parifh, faid to contain about 6000 acres.† *Court,* the feat of Mr. Lethbridge, commands an extenfive profpect. It is fituated near the church. Winkleigh church is a fpacious old fabric, ftanding four miles S. S. W. from Ringfafh.

DOULAND is in ancient evidences *Duelland.*‡ It is reported that a part of the church of Douland was built by a wealthy potter, who fet up in a window three cups, as a badge of his occupation.§

IDDESLEIGH‖ is fituated on the banks of the Torridge, oppofite to Meeth.¶ It confifts of about 3000 acres, diverfified with hills and vales, enclofures and

VOL. III.   K   woods.

Granville's; and it was purchafed of the Granville family by John Clevland, efq. at the fame time that the manor of Bideford was alienated from that family, in the reign of Geo. the 2d.—" *Stoford.* Thomas Kellaway, the fon of William, gave Stoford to Philip his younger fon, together with Edrifcot, about the end of the reign of Henry the 3d. Thomas fucceeded Philip, and affumed the name of Stoford from his houfe. And the Stofords held this land many generations; till at length Robert Stoford left his only daughter his heirefs, who carried moft of his inheritance into the family of the Wifes." *Rifdon.—Halfton,* the feat of the Rev. Peter Wellington Furze, is a new-built houfe, in a crofs-road from Hatherleigh to Torrington. It was formerly a farm.

* " *Afhreigney* is moft commonly called *Ring's-Afh*: It is alfo called *Afhraignyt, Aifhreigney, King's Afh;* and I find in my title deeds *Effe-Regney* from the family of *Effe,* formerly fettled here, fo that the etymology becomes eafy. The parifh is about five miles in length, and two and half in breadth, and abuts on Burrington to the north, from which it is divided by a fmall brook called *Mellabrook,* which falls into the Taw at the eaftern extremity of the parifh. It borders on Chulmleigh to the eaft, from which it is feparated by the river Taw aforefaid, over which are two bridges, the one a ftone bridge of 3 arches, maintained by the commiffioners of the Barnftaple turnpike; the other is a wooden bridge, and *partly* fupported by the occupiers of lands of the Rev. Henry Hawkins Tremayne, within the parifh of Wembworthy, and *partly* by the tenants of Sir Jacob Wolf, bart. of Chulmleigh. This parifh abuts to the fouth on Winckleigh and Wembworthy, from which it is disjoined by a fmall rivulet called Hollacombe-Water, over which is a fmall wooden bridge, forming a communication with thofe parifhes. It borders on Dolton, Beaford, and Roborough to the weft. The parifh is well wooded with oak, and watered; and is inclofed with quickfet hedges, excepting about 800 acres of wafte or moor lands, which afford pafture for fheep and black cattle. The other parts are a due proportion of arable, meadow, and orchard. The foil is principally a ftiff clay. The fituation is high and healthy. The parfonage-houfe is a modern building, partly flated, partly thatched, about half a mile to the north-eaft of the church. The church is an ancient fabric, dedicated, according to Ecton, to St. James; tho' from the anniverfary revel or wake being held at Lammas, this is queftionable. The church is 53 feet and half in length, 28 in breadth, and 24 in heighth, and is partly divided from the chancel by the remains of a fort of fkreen or rood-loft. There is a veftry. The tower, confifting of a ring of four bells, is about 50 feet in height, and appears to have gone from it's perpendicular. The church and church-yard abut on the weftern extremity of the village, which is nearly in the center of the parifh. About a mile to the weft of the church is the village of *Piddlecomb* belonging to this parifh, where the veftige of an old chapel may be traced. But to return to the church; 5 plain wall ftones are affixed within it; two of which fimply record the memories of fo many female branches of the Melhuifh family; one is infcribed to Richard Babbage, a young man who died whilft educating at Oxford for the church. The other two belong to fome obfcure families. There are feveral floor-ftones in the chancel, as well as the church; in the former, near the communion table, we meet with a Latin infcription on the floor, denoting it to be the place of burial of a Mrs. Shortrudge, the relict of a former rector. There is alfo adjoining to the above a fimilar memorial in Englifh, of the Shepheard's, two of which family, father and fon, have been rectors of this church. There are a few head-ftones in the church-yard, but neither there nor in the church are there any infcriptions, which, I fhould fuppofe, can merit a literal tranfcription. I can at prefent trace five rectors that have preceded me; the firft was —— Slade, the next Hugh Shortrudge, then followed William Shepheard, who was fucceeded by his fon William Shepheard; then came John Cutcliffe, my immediate predeceffor. The prefent incumbent, the Rev. John Toffel Johnfon, is feized in fee of a moiety of the manor of Afhreigney, and alfo of the advowfon; the other moiety belongs to truftees for fome charitable ufes, and the reprefentatives of the late John Carew, efq. The rector is entitled to all forts of tythes in kind, according to law. I had nearly forgot to mention that we have feveral charitable inftitutions here. A fchool endowed by the truftees of the late Mrs. Gertrude Pyncombe, with fix pounds a year for the inftruction of boys in reading and writing; another by the fame munificent perfon, with four pounds a year for girls, &c. A widower derives forty fhillings annually from the fame charitable hand." Letter from the Rev. John Toffel Johnfon, 1790.

† " *Winckley,* fituate in a fomewhat cold foil, yet is the chief place of the honour of Gloucefter in this county, unto the fee whereof much land belongeth. The parifh is large, within the limits whereof the hundred is bounded. This was granted to the family of Keynes in King John's time, which continued their lands fifteen defcents, being patrons of the church; before one of them finding the parfon to mifcarry himfelf towards him, gave the fheaf to St. Peter's in Exon, whereunto it appertaineth. But fome fuppofe it rather, by reafon Thomas Keynes married Joan, the fifter of Walter Stapledon, bifhop of Exeter. Hiftory makes mention of one William Keynes, that took King Stephen upon Candlemas-day, in a battel at Lincoln the 6th year of his reign, and delivered him to Robert Duke of Gloucefter, who fent him prifoner to Briftol Caftle." *Rifdon.—Southcote.* The Southcotes flourifhed in this place from the days of Henry the 3d, in the 27th of whofe reign, Michael Southcote lived at Southcote; who was fucceeded by William, Michael William, Michael, and William. William Southcote of Southcote, by Alice his wife, daughter and heirefs of Philip Keyns, had iffue William; who had iffue Nicholas; who had iffue William; who had iffue Nicholas; who had iffue William, John, and William. William Southcote of Southcote, the eldeft fon, had iffue Elizabeth, who was married to John Callard, and brought Southcote into that family, in which it continued many generations. John, the fecond fon, was fettled at Indeho, in Bovey Tracey, where his pofterity flourifhed long in great honour—feveral of whom were knighted, as Sir Popham Southcote, of Indeho and Mohun Ottery; Sir Edward Southcote, one of the youngeft fons of Thomas Southcote of Santon, in the parifh of Braunton, who lived there in confequence of his marriage with the widow of Lutterel of that place; and Sir George Southcote of Shillingford, near Exeter, the eldeft fon of Thomas Southcote of Indeho, by his third wife, Elizabeth FitzWilliams. Of William, the third fon, John Southcote was the eldeft fon, one of the juftices of the king's bench in the time of Elizabeth.

‡ " *Douland* was in elder ages the inheritance of Ailward: Walter Claville fince owned it." *Rifdon.*

§ Douland alienated in the time of Henry the 8th, is an impropriated cure. It was many years in the patronage of the Staffords; one of whom a Northcote married: And its great and fmall tythes are now in the poffeffion of the Northcotes. The perpetual cure has lately been augmented by an eftate purchafed from Queen Anne's bounty.

‖ Iddefleigh is fpelt in the old valors *Edfleighe* and *Edifleigh*—originally perhaps *Edith's Leigh.*

¶ " Iddefleigh is notable for its ancient lords the Sullys, who dwelt there in the days of Richard the 1ft; having two fair parks, garnifhed with goodly woods, and ftored with game. Here lived, in the time of King John, Henry Sully, knight; from whom defcended

John

woods. Here were formerly two parks, called Eaft and Weft Park; in which the trees were once fo thick, that (as the neighbourhood tells) a fquirrel might leap from tree to tree over the whole extent of both.

METHE, or MEETH, ftands in " the trend of the Torridge, where the Ock falleth into its ftream." Its fituation is high, in general: It is enclofed and rather woody.* Its church is nearly central.

At PATRICKSTOW, *Heanton-houfe* will, for a moment, detain us. This man-fion is built in the form of the letter E.—whence it is referred to the days of Elizabeth. It occupies a large plot of ground; but prefents nothing remarkable in point of architecture. In Colonel Rolle's and Lord Orford's time, it was a place of great refort. A motto, carved in wood, in a dining parlour, † reminds us of thofe old convivial days.‡

BUCKLAND FILLEIGH " was the ancient inheritance of the Filleighs, knights, who held lands at Hartleigh, in the time of Edward the 1ft. From this family, by the daughter of Denfell, that wedded the heir of Wear, thefe lands came to

Martin

John Lord Sully, one of the barons that fubfcribed to a letter in anfwer to Pope Boniface's pretenfions to the realm of Scotland, in the reign of Edward the 1ft. Thefe were the pofterity of Raymond de Sully, one of the twelve knights who affifted Robert Fitz-Hamon of Normandy, in the conqueft of Glamorganfhire, in the reign of W. Rufus. Sir John de Sully, knight, the laft of this houfe, married one of the co-heireffes of the baron of Torrington. He was a man much renowned in the wars of the holy land againft the Saracens, where he remained many years; and in the end wounded, returned to this country; to whom, at his home coming, his officers brought ftore of coin; which laying on his cloak, that was cloth of gold, he faid, That for once he would tumble in gold and filver; of which he gave one-third part to his wife, another to his officers and fervants, and the remainder to the poor: And he gave his honor of Torrington to his coufin the Lord Fitzmartin. This Sir John Sully died of thefe holy wars wounds, and lieth buried in Crediton; but hath here a ceno-taph, and that after a martial manner, with his effigies crofs-legged cut thereon." *Rifdon.*—The tradition of the parifh is, that Sir John Sully long abfent in Paleftine, was never expected home—that his lady, in the mean time, was reduced to the greateft extremity—that, re-turning on horfeback, he met her at fome diftance from the town, meanly habited, and bearing a pitcher of water; and that he took her up behind him, and carried her in triumph to his manor, of which, on his claiming it, he regained the poffeffion. Sir John Sully left only one daughter, married to a knight in Somerfet, of the name of Vowel; from which faid Vowel, the moiety of the manor came to Smith, and from Smith to Sir Charles Bingham, an Irifh baronet, who fold it to Sir Stafford Northcote, baronet.

* " The Giffards were the ancient lords of this manor; which Matthew Giffard held with Stockley in the reign of Edward the 3d. This inheritance, after many defcents in that line, defcended to Dennys of Bradford: And by the daughter of Gilbert Dennys, to Giffard of Yeo.—*Hele* in this parifh, was the ancient lands of the Crockers. Here William Crocker lived in the days of Edward the 2d, and thence removed to Linham.—Another barton of the name of Hele, carries with it the adjunct of its ancient owners, the Fryes. The laft of this family had iffue Elizabeth, who was married to Parker of North Molton. And Frys-Hele is now poffeft by the Parkers.—*Walledon*, held by the Walledons, then the Snedalls." *Rifdon.*

† Over the chimney-piece: " He that fits down firft gives the leaft trouble."

‡ " *Patrickftow*, that is Patrick's Place, contractly *Padftow*, is feated high, and feareth no inundation; wherein you have *Hall*, a barton fometimes belonging to the abby of Buckfaftleigh, and *Heanton*, which hath the addition of Sackvile, fo denominated of the ancient owners thereof; where Hugh de Sachvile dwelt in the reign of King Richard the 1ft. A race of gentlemen, defcended of the Norman progeny, whom Henry Kelligrew, and Mauger his fon, fucceeded in this land. After whom, in the beginning of King Edward the 3d's reign, Nicholas Yeo, fon of William Yeo, had this place with a fair eftate, by Elizabeth his wife, daughter of Kelligrew; which patrimony, after it had paffed fome defcents in that name, Margaret the heir of that houfe, invefted Henry Rolle, the fon of John Rolle, of Stevenfton, with her heritage by marriage right; whofe fon married the daughter of Hele, his grandfon Sir Samuel, the coheir of Sir Edmond Strad-ling, knight. Secondly the daughter of Sir Thomas Wife, knight of the bath. Thirdly, the daughter of Carew." *Rifdon.*—It feems that Heanton-Sackville continued in the name of Sackville to the reign of Edward the 3d; when the heirefs of Sackville brought it to her huf-band, Nicholas Yeo, whofe pofterity continued here for about ten generations. We may collect from Sir William Pole and Weftcote, that Nicholas Yeo by his wife Elizabeth, had iffue John; who by Alice his wife, had iffue William; who by Joan, daughter and heirefs of John de Effe, had iffue Robert; who by Joan his wife, daughter and heirefs of William Pyne of Bradwell, had iffue John; who by Joan, daughter and coheir of William Jew of Cotebey, had iffue William; who by Ellen, daughter of William Grenville, had iffue Robert, Nicholas of Hatherley, and Edward of Hewifh. Robert Yeo of Heanton Sackville, by Alice, daughter of John Waldrond of Bradfield, had iffue Edward; who by Joan, daughter of Sir Thomas Fulford, had iffue Robert and Humphry. Robert, by Mary, daughter of Bar-tholomew Fortefcue of Filleigh, had iffue Margaret his fole daughter and heirefs, who brought a great eftate to her hufband, Henry Rolle, the third fon of John Rolle of Stevenfton, efq. Samuel Rolle, efq. poffeft this place and refided there in Prince's time. Margaret, the daughter and fole heirefs of Samuel Rolle, efq. was married in 1724, to Robert Walpole, the year before created Lord Walpole, Baron of Houghton. They had iffue George, on the death of his father, Earl of Orford, Vifcount and Baron Walpole, Baron of Houghton, and Baron Clinton and Say. On the death of this earl, the earldom, vifcounty, and barony of Walpole came to Horatio Walpole his uncle; but the baronies of Clinton and Say, together with Heanton and its appendages, to Trefufis, of Trefufis, in Cornwall.— *Merland*, a barton-houfe. Captain Henry Davils, the younger fon of William Davils of this place, is mentioned by Prince as a perfon of high military fpirit, who ferved in Ireland in the time of Elizabeth. His father, William Davils, was the fon of Lewis, who was the fon of John, the fon of Thomas Davils of Badefton, efq. who by Ifabel his wife, daughter and heirefs of Almeric Fitzwarren of Toteley, in the parifh of Black Torrington, became poffeft of Toteley and Merland. The refidence of this family was originally at Badefton, in the parifh of Peters Merland.

Martin Fortefcue, and by him and his wife were given to William their younger fon;" fays Rifdon.*

SHEBBEARE gives name to the hundred.†

In NEWTON-PETROCK; ‡ MERLAND, or *Peter-Merland*; § and LANGTREE, ‖ there is little worth obferving.

* A correfpondent thus anfwers my enquiries:—" Buckland-Filleigh, fo fpelt originally as fuppofed, being perhaps the regiftered land of *Filleigh*, the lord of the manor and founder of the church. The extent of the parifh from weft to eaft about three miles, from north to fouth about two and half; but from north-weft to fouth-eaft at leaft four miles. Inclofures of all kinds from one to twenty acres; well watered with various ftreams, and with the river Torridge on the fouth-eaft fide; well wooded, and indeed abounding with oak trees. On the barton there is a wood of oak, in general, of 157 acres, whofe underwood confifts of hollies, beautifully variegated in colour. In this wood are two woodcock roads: In the *eye* of the lower road is a delightful wood fcene, with a view over a large tract of land terminating in the eaftern part of Dartmoor, nearly 30 miles diftant; and in the *eye* of the higher road is a pleafing view of the high grounds and mountains of Cornwall. Scarce any trees but flourifh here, whether indigenous or exotic. Materials fufficient to make good roads.—The manfion-houfe of John Inglett Fortefcue, efq. lord of the manor of Buckland-Filleigh, built with ftone, in the fhape of a Roman F. and covered with flate, ftands nearly in the midft of the manor, adjoining to the church, on a rifing ground, declining on every fide, except to the weft, where the lands eafily afcend, but fo as to be a kind of fkreen to the manfion againft the weftern rains. On the eaft, meadows defcend to a large brook or river driving the manor mill, beyond which there are high downs guarding the houfe againft the cutting eafterly winds. On the north, after paffing a vale with a little purling ftream, there arife very high grounds, commanding a beautiful inland profpect, and defending great part of the barton from the northern ftorms. Before the fouth front of the manfion is an extenfive lawn of about 40 acres, bordered on the eaft and fouth by the wood before-mentioned. In the weftern part of the lawn there breaks out a ftream, which fupplies the fifh-ponds that cover the greateft part of the vale, below the church and the manfion, included in the lawn. There belong to the manor 29 meffuages, with farms or tenements, built partly with ftone and partly with mud walls. The greater part of the parifh belongs to this manor. The fpot being healthy, the inhabitants live in general to an advanced age, and, if not unworthy of notice, it may be remarked, of the two laft parifh-clerks that the one died aged 86, the other 87. The Fortefcue family has clearly been in the poffeffion of the manor for three hundred and twenty-four years, that is, from the year 1466, without any interruption but by John Spooner, efq. who having married the only daughter of the Right Hon. William Fortefcue, mafter of the rolls, held it by the courtefy of England during his life. The church is fituated as before faid, near the manor houfe, but in refpect of the whole parifh rather on the weftern part thereof, dedicated to St. Mary, built of ftone, the fouth roof being covered with fhingles made of heart-oak, and the north roof with flate; a fquare tower, not rifing high, with four bells. The length of the fouth-aifle of this church is 37 feet, breadth 14 feet, and height 19 feet. The chancel arranges from this aifle to the eaft, of the fame height, and is 17 feet long. The north-aifle is 37 feet long, 10 feet wide, and 19 feet high. In this aifle are two monuments of the Fortefcue family, and one alfo for the firft wife (a defcendant of the fame family) of John Spooner, efq. aforefaid. In the chancel there are alfo two monuments. The church yard contains about an acre of ground, or fomewhat more, in which are a few memorial ftones of the late inhabitants: And therein, not far diftant from the fouth-eaft corner of the chancel, ftands a venerable oak tree in a flourifhing and thriving ftate, not indeed to be noted for the length of its ftock, as that is but ten feet; but in circumference it is nine feet, and the branches thereof are fo remarkably extended, nearly in a circular form, as to cover 86 feet of ground in diameter. In the regifter-book of baptifms, there appear to be baptized eleven children, 5 fons and 6 daughters, of John Fortefcue, efq. and his wife Thomafin, from the year 1622 to the year 1639 inclufive.—The living is a rectory, the patron the Bifhop of Exeter for the time being—the prefent incumbent the Rev. William Walter, M. A. whofe immediate predeceffor was the Rev. William Jenkins, who held the living for five or fix years, and exchanged it for Up-ottery in this county; the Rev. James Silke, M. A. preceded him; and immediately before him was the Rev. Edward Bradford, M. A. The Rev. —— More ftands in tradition before him, and he fucceeded the reverend and noted Henry Wilfon, who was ejected in the grand rebellion, and whofe place was filled by Owen Williams, who came to the living in 1651, (vide Walker's Sufferings of the Clergy, page 392,) and continued upon the fame to the time of his death, which happened in the year 1755. He lies buried at the weft-end of the church, on the outfide of the belfry window, over which there is a piece of brafs, with thefe Welfh words, *Mia Goda Gida*—which fignify, Εγω αναϛησομαι ϛυν αλλοις.— The parfonage houfe ftands a little on the fouth-weft of the church, at the diftance of about a quarter of a mile—an old houfe, built very probably in the form it now is, by feveral incumbents, but upon the whole convenient within. There is nothing remarkable in the compofition for the tithe; and as to a modus, there is a paper in writing, but the validity of it feems to be dubious. However, as to Buckland Filleigh wood, the tenth part thereof is portioned out as tithe to the rector, lying on the fouth-weft fide of the wood, and always called the tithe coppice."

† " Immediately after the conqueft, Baldwin, Baron of Okehamton, held lands in this tything. Sir Ralph Neville, Earl of Weftmoreland, was fince lord of this manor. The 19th of Richard the 2d, John Alvethot held this manor by the following fervice: Johannes Alvethot tenet terram in Shebbeare de Domino rege, per Servitium tenend. Strepam Domini Regis, quoties cunque venerit ad manerium de Shebbeare. There is a monument in this church covered with feats, (fo much are fepultures neglected!) which, as tradition fays, was erected to the memory of the Lady Prandergift, fometime lady of Ladford and Beare, who built the fouth fide of the church, and covered it with lead." *Rifdon.*—" *Sheepwafh*, anciently *Sepewaffe*, fhall be next, being a daughter of Shebbear; of which lands Letitia de Pirro was lady before the date of deeds. In the reign of King Henry the 2d, William Fitz-reginald was lord of Sheepwafh, whofe daughter and heir was married to Sir Nicholas Avenell, with whom he had one knight's fee. Auguftine be Bathon held the fame after that; of which family Henry de Bathon was a judge in King Henry the 3d's days; who being appealed of falfhood by Sir Philip Darcy, fell fo highly into the king's difpleafure, that he gave liberty for any man to kill him: but his wife being of kindred to the Baffets and Samfords, (great men in thofe days) by their means, and the payment of 2000 marks, he was reconciled to the king. Sir Andrew Medfted was owner of this land, and dwelt here in the days of King Edward the 2d; by whofe daughter and heir Eleanor, it defcended to the Hollands, a family of noble birth." *Rifdon.*

‡ " *Newton St. Petrock* is a mile and a half long, and a mile broad. Its fituation is high, and it is feparated from the parifh of Milton Damarell by the river Torridge, over which there is a bridge called Woodford Bridge, built of ftone, and confifting of three arches. The inhabitants of Newton are at leaft a hundred and fifty. They are healthy, and in general long-lived. The farms are chiefly occupied by rackholders and leafeholders, and are well cultivated. The only place of any confequence in this parifh is Lane, formerly the feat of Sir Simon Leach, who died about the beginning of this century. His family is now extinct." 1791.

§ *Merland.* This church is dedicated to St. Peter. It was, fometime, a prebend to the priory of Frithelftoke.

‖ *Langtree* in the Conqueror's time was rated after 2 hides and 20 carucates, and paid £.7 5s. ad penfam et arfuram.—" The Earls of Gloucefter were anciently lords of this manor, which, after the death of Gilbert de Clare, defcended to the Spencers." *Rifdon.*—In Langtree *Browne's Marfh.* Here Sir Thomas Browne built a genteel houfe, with a park belonging to it. He was a younger brother to Brute Browne, who was killed at fea by the Spaniards, under Port Rico. Probably William Browne the poet, who was born at Taviftock in 1590, was from the Brownes' of this parifh, who had become extinct in Langtree long before *Prince.*

ARCHDEACONRY

ARCHDEACONRY OF BARNSTAPLE.

DEANRY of HERTLAND.

OUR view of the Archdeaconry of Barnftaple will clofe with the prefent deanry, which includes the parifhes of Hertland, Clovelly, Frithelftock, Welcombe, Woolfardifworthy, Parkham, Alwington, Abbotfham, Bideford, Northam, Lancras, Alfcot, Wear-Giffard, Littleham, Monkleigh, Buckland Brewer, Eaft-Putford, and Bulkworthy.*

Of HERTLAND I have related fo many particulars in the former part of the work, that little remains for obfervation. " The promontory of *Hercules* which braves the boifterous billows of the Severn, retaineth (fays Rifdon) fome fhadow of its antiquity to this day, being known by the name of Hertland Point." Not-withftanding the grant which the Dynants had made of the church and monaf-tery in Hertland, the barony of the place ftill remained in the hands of the Dynants till the reign of Henry the 7th, when the Baron Dinham, high trea-furer of England, dying without iffue, it defcended by his fifter to the Zouches, Fitzwarrens, Carews, and Arundels. Since that, it has been fold into other

hands;

First Fruits.		* " *Benefices remaining in charge:*	Yearly Tenths.

* " *Benefices remaining in charge:*

First Fruits.
£. s. d.

13 3 11½   Alwardifcot or Alfcot R. [All Saints] Rep. B. Proc. iiis. ivd.   Syn. iis. vd.   A. D. Proc. iiis. ivd.   r. V. 70l.   -   1 6 4¾
Patr. James Rowe, efq.

17 4 9½   Alwington R. [St. Andrew] Rep. B. Proc. vis. viiid.   Syn. iis. vd.   A. D. Proc. vis. viiid.   r. V. 130l. -   -   1 14 5¾
Patr. Coffin.

27 7 6   Bideford R. [St. Mary] Rep. B. Proc. vis. viiid.   Syn. iis. vd.   A. D. Proc. vis. viiid.   r. V. 300l.   -   - 2 14 9
Patr. Buck.

19 11 5½   Clavelleigh R. [All Saints] Rep. B. Proc. vis. viiid.   Syn. iis. vd.   A. D. Proc. vis. viiid.   r. V. 120l. -   - 1 19 1¾
Patr. Sir James Hamlyn, bart.

14 16 10½   Littleham R. [St. Swithin] Rep. B. Proc. iis. ivd.   Syn. iis. vd.   A. D. Proc. iis. iid. ob.   r. V. 90l. -   - 1 9 8¾
Patr. Baffet

12 14 7   Monkleigh V. [St. George] Rep. B. Proc. ivs. vid.   Syn. iis. vd.   A. D. Proc. ivs. vid.   r. V. 90l. -   - 1 5 5½
Patr. John Saltren, efq.

20 6 8   Parkham R. [St. James] Rep. B. Proc. vis. viiid.   Syn. iis. vd.   A. D. Proc. vis. viiid.   r. V. 270l. -   - 2 0 0
Patrs. John and Daniel Kay, efqrs.

13 5 0   Weare-Giffard R. [Holy Trinity] Rep. B. Proc. vis. viiid.   Syn. iis. vd.   A. D. Proc. iiis. ivd.   r. V. 80l. -   1 6 6
Patr. Earl Fortefcue.

Livings difcharged.

King's Books.   *Certified Value.*

16 4 7   Abbotfham V. [St. Helen] Rep. B. Proc. vis. viiid.   Syn. iis. vd.   A. D. Proc. vis. viiid.   r. V. 60l. -   - 46 0 0
Patr. The KING.

5 4 9½   { Buckland Brewer V. [St. Mary and St. Benedict] with the chapels of Eaft Putford and Bulkworthy. Rep. } 48 10 0
{ B. Proc. vis. viiid.   Syn. iis. xd.   A. D. Proc. vis. viiid.   r. V. 80l. - - - - }
Patr. The KING.

5 4 9½   Lancras R. [Holy Trinity] Rep. B. Proc. viid.   Syn.   A. D. Proc. viid.   r. V. 40l. - - - 15 0 0
Patr. Rolle.

10 10 0   Northam V. [St. Margaret] Rep. B. Proc. vis. viiid.   Syn. iis. vd.   Rep. B. Proc. vis. viiid.   r. V. 70l. - 30 0 6
Patrs. Dean and Chapter of Windfor.

Not in charge.

Hertland C. [St. Nectan] in the gift of the Charter-houfe, London. Rep. B. Proc. vis. viiid.   Syn. iis. vd. A. D. Proc. vis. viiid.

Welcombe Imp. [St. Nectan] Rep. none in charge - - - - - - 8 10 0
Patr. Lord Orford.

Frithelftock C. [St. Mary and St. Gregory] formerly a priory. Rep. B. Proc. vis. viiid.   Syn. iis. vd. A. D. } 14 0 0
Proc. yis. viiid. - - - - - - - - - }
Patr. and Cur. Gay.

Woolfardifworthy C. [Ded. unc.] Rep. B. Proc. vis. viiid.   Syn. is. vd.   A. D. Proc. vis. viiid. - 20 5 0
Patr. Rev. Potter Cole."

Thes. Eccles.

HARTLAND ABBEY.

The Seat of Paul Orchard Esq.r to whom this Plate is Inscribed

By his Obliged Servant R. Polwhele.

Painted by E. Garvey, R.A.

Engraved by T. Bonnor

Published by R. Polwhele, May 1.st 1791.

hands; and the chief part is at prefent the property of the family of *Orchard*. Mr. Orchard's feat is one of the moft pleafant in the county.* The parifh is rated at 4367l. 15s. and contains about 1200 inhabitants.†

CLOVELLY, (fays Prince), is a pleafant fummer feat, juft on the banks of the Severn fea, oppofite the Ifle of Lundy.‡ Clovelly was anciently the Giffards. Sir Roger Giffard held one knight's fee here in the reign of Henry the 3d; when paffing through the hands of Stanton, Mandeville, and Crewkerne, thefe lands were purchafed, in the time of Richard the 2d, by Sir John Cary the judge.§ Clovelly continued in the name of Cary till the year 1724, when the laft heir of this family died; and his fifters enjoyed the eftate. It is at prefent in the poffeffion of Sir James Hamlyn, baronet; whofe only fon, in 1798, took the name of Williams, in compliance with the will of his grandfather Thomas Williams, efq. of Carmarthenfhire.

FRITHELSTOKE,‖ WELCOMBE, and WOOLFARDISWORTHY,¶ will furnifh little, on which to remark.

The parifh of PARKHAM muft not be paffed in fo curfory a manner.*† The Giffards and the Rifdons were once families of note in Parkham. ‖‡

VOL. III.   L   Of

* A minute defcription of a fcene reprefented by a painter, would be fuperfluous. Stoke-Abbey, as it was in *Hervey*'s time, is defcribed by that writer. In a letter dated Stoke-Abbey, June 19, 1738, Hervey fays: " I write this in a pleafure-houfe of Mr. Orchard, fituate upon a high cliff, on the very edge of the fea. On one fide a vaft tract of land extends itfelf, finely diverfified by ftately trees, floating corn, and pafturage for cattle. On the other fide rolls the great and wide fea. I have been about 20 or 26 miles into Cornwall, and feen wonderous workmanfhip of the all-creating God—rugged rocks, roaring feas, frightful precipices, and dreadfully fteep hills. Mr. Orchard's houfe is fituate in a fine vale: It is an ancient ftructure, built for the ufe of religious reclufes, and has an antique, grave, and folemn afpect. Before it, is a neat fpot of ground, fet apart for the ufe of a garden, enriched with fruits, and beautified with flowers. This leads into a curious fort of artificial wildernefs made of elms and limes planted in rows, cut into form, and uniting their branches. In the midft is a fountain large enough to fwim in, and a little engine playing the waters. On each fide are arbors for fhade—in various parts, feats for reft. On the right hand, runs parallel to it a clear purling brook replenifhed with trout—on the left, a thick grove hanging from the fide of a hill. The one ferves for a watery mound; the other is a leafy fhelter from the north wind—and both, I think, greatly ornamental." See *Hervey*'s Letters.

† Within this parifh were formerly 12 chapels of eafe, all of which are now demolifhed.

‡ Within fix miles of Hertland Point, to the eaftward, ftands Clovelly, " where is a pile to refift the inrufhing of the fea's violent breach, that fhips and boats may with the more fafety harbour there, built by George Cary, efq. Here the cliffs are very fteep; and the way right down to the quay they call *Precipitate*—therefore beaten with winding retches from the one fide to the other, to make the defcent more eafy. Above the cliffs appear banks and motes rudely caft up, called Clovelly Dykes." This far *Rifdon*.

§ Robert Cary, efq. the fourth in defcent from the judge, who had fucceffively three wives, and iffue male by each of them, left Clovelly to Robert his eldeft fon by his third wife, daughter and heirefs to William Fulkroy of Dartmouth. He married and had iffue George, who had iffue William; who married firft Gertrude, the daughter of Richard Carew, efq. of Anthony. Secondly, he married Dorothy, daughter of Sir Edw. Gorge of Wraxhall, in Somerfet, by whom he left iffue Robert, George, and William. Robert was in great favor with Charles the 2d, who made him one of the gentlemen of his privy chamber, and afterwards conferred on him the honor of knighthood. Sir Robert Cary dying unmarried, Clovelly, with the other fair inheritance belonging to the family, fell to the fecond brother George, then Dean of Exeter; who by Anne his wife, daughter of William Hancock of Comb-Martin, efq. had a numerous offspring. His firft child was George Cary, knighted by Charles the 2d in the dean's lifetime, who married firft Elizabeth, one of the daughters and heirs of Peter Jenking, efq. of Trekening, in Cornwall, and had no iffue; fecondly, Martha, daughter and heirefs of William Davie, efq. of Canonteign, without iffue. His fecond fon was William Cary, in Prince's time poffeffor of Clovelly; who married firft Joan, the daughter of Sir William Wyndham, bart. of Orchard Wyndham, in the county of Somerfet, without iffue; fecondly, Mary, the daughter of Thomas Maunfel of Britton-Ferry, in Glamorganfhire, by whom he hath iffue, fays Prince. The dean's third fon was Nicholas, who died young; his fourth, Edward, rector of Silverton and fubdean of Exeter, at 26 years of age, who married the daughter of Thomas Pointington of Penicot, efq. and left iffue a daughter. His fifth, Robert, a major in the army. The dean had iffue, alfo, two daughters, Dorothy married to Counfellor Harris of Salifbury, who died before her father; and Judith married to Richard Hele of Fleet-Damerel, rector of St. Hellens, in Cornwall, by whom he left iffue Richard Hele of Fleet, efq. in Prince's time. To the memory of his father, Dean of Exeter, William Cary, efq. of Clovelly, erected in that church a ftately monument. In the fame chancel he raifed a monument alfo to his brother, Sir Robert Cary, with an epitaph in golden letters. *Prince*, pp. 216, 217.

‖ *Frithelftoke*, anciently *Frideleftock*. Rifdon fpeaks of the priory bells of Fridelftock, whofe tuneable ring much delighteth the hearers. Here, as we have feen, Sir Roger Beauchamp, knight, built a religious houfe for canons regular. The fcite and barton contained 1000 acres. Henry the 8th, on the diffolution, granted it, together with the manor, to Arthur Plantagenet, Vifcount Lifle; who by Elizabeth, fifter and heirefs to John Gray, Vifcount Lifle, left iffue Bridget, wife of Sir William Carden; Frances, married firft to John Baffett, fecondly to Thomas Monk; and Elizabeth, married to Sir Francis Jobfon, knight.

¶ *Woolfardifworthy* (which I have fo fpelt to diftinguifh it from *Wolfardifworthy*, in the hundred of Witheridge) is vulgarly called *Wolfworthy*. Rifdon intimates, that it might have been fo called from *Wulpher*, the Mercian king, who founded a monaftery at Northampton, to the honor of St. Peter, for the expiation of his crime in fhedding his fon's blood.

*† " The parifh of Parkham is bounded on the north partly by the fea, and partly by the parifh of Alwington on the north-eaft; eaft and fouth eaft by the parifhes of Littleham and Buckland-Brewer; and on the fouth-fouth-weft and weft, by the parifhes of Eaft-Putford, Weft-Putford, and Woolfardifworthy. Its length and breadth are very irregular—the longeft place, from north-eaft to fouth-weft, is about
fix

fix miles; and its broadeft place, from fouth-eaft to north-weft, is upwards of three miles, and contains about 5230 acres. The foil is various, interfperfed with hills, vallies, meadows, and woods, and fome champaign and moory ground. The whole may be divided into three claffes of different values, the north-weft; north and eaft, which is the beft, may be worth yearly com. ann. from 14 to 20 fhillings per acre. This clafs contains nearly one third of the parifh. The central clafs contains nearly half the parifh, and is worth from 10 to 15 fhillings per acre. The fouth and fouth-weft clafs confifts of a large tract of land, called Melbury, which, together with a moor belonging to the barton of Bableigh, (the ancient feat of Rifdon), and another belonging to the village, called Broad-Afh, containing in the whole about 1000 acres—is in its prefent ftate of little value, not more than from one to four fhillings per acre, but capable of great improvement, particularly Melbury, which by a moderate expence in building, dividing, and inclofing, might be made a very valuable eftate. The church ftands on an eminence, nearly in the centre of the parifh, is a handfome old Gothick ftructure, 75 feet in length and 47 ditto in breadth, and about 29 ditto in heighth. The tower is well built and handfome; the fquare of its bafe is 26 feet, and its height to the top of the pinnacles is near 90 feet: It has fix neat well-tuned bells in it, which was formerly but four, having been lately caft. The church is faid to be dedicated to St. James, and a wake or revel is held annually on Melbury Moor, in commemoration of that day. The cliffs adjoining the fea are remarkably high, craggy, and romantick. The higheft bears the marks of and is fuppofed to have been an ancient fortrefs, and ftill retains the name of Peppercombe Caftle. Another not far diftant from Peppercombe Caftle, is noted for a remarkable accident which happened there about half a century ago, which is this: Some of the ancient family of Gifford and others, on a party of pleafure, having feated themfelves on the top of this cliff, which commands an extenfive view of the fea, one of the Giffords (a young man) fitting carelefsly near the brink, and turning himfelf about haftily, fell backward over the precipice, upwards of one hundred and thirty feet perpendicular, and the floor at bottom covered with craggy rocks and large ftones, yet received no manner of hurt. Since which this place has borne the name of Gifford's Jump. The principal manure ufed in this parifh is Welfh lime, (the ftones being brought over and burnt at Bideford), and fea fand, which is taken up at ebb tide by perfons who earn their living by it, and laid up in large heaps at the foot of the cliff, where the farmers take it away with their teams, paying fo much per hundred horfe-loads, for the labour of landing as 'tis called.

Defponfati—in 1538.

May. Philip Ryfedon the fonne of Giles Ryfedon.——xxv.

1547.

In fefto St. Leonardi abbatis in Menfs Novemb. ⎫
Johanes, Filis et Heres—Thoma Gyfford ⎬—vi.
de Halsbery Armung baptifat   ⎭

1548.

May. Thomas the fonne of Thomas Gyffard Gent.——iv.

1551.

Febr. Egidius Filiu Egidii Ryfedon Gent.——xxv.

1639.   Heny. Bray, curate.

Roger the fonne of Thomas Gifford, Gent. was bapd. 22 March.

1660.

William the fonne of Giles Rifdon, Efq. Febr. 27.

1665.

Symone the fonne of Giles Rifdon, Efq. was bapd. 15th Octr.

Francs. Nation, Rector.

1689.

Giles the fonne of Giles Rifdon, Efq. and Anna his wife, bapd. Octr. 1ft.

Defponfati in 1716.

Thomas the fon of Thomas Saltren, Efq. and Mary his wife was bapd. Augft. 28th.

Will. Kingford, Rector.

1720.

William the fon of Thomas Saltren, Efq. and Mary his wife bapd. Octr. 11th.

1726.

John the fon of Thomas Saltren, Efq. and Mary his wife bapd. Octr. 18th.

1731.   Thoms. Bray, Curate.

1732.

Giles the fon of Giles Rifdon, Efq. and Anna his wife was bapd. April 2nd.

1733.

John the fon of Roger Gifford, Efq. and Eliz. his wife March 14th.

1739.   Humphrey Bawdon, Rector.
1777.   Thomas Swindale, Rector.
1781.   J. Barton, the prefent Rector.
                                        Jn. Sloley, Curate.

MARRIAGES.

1562.

Sepr. Thomas Ryfedon, Gent. and Wilmot Gifford——viii.

1573.

Januarii. John Gifford, Efq. and Alice Smith.——xxv.

1713.

Roger Gifford, Efq. and Agnes Kingford were married Sepr. 2nd.

1752.

Thomas Saltren, clerk, and Grace Buck, widow, May 27th.

Sepulti.

April. Thomas Gyfford of Halfberry, Efq. deceffed.——xix.

1596.

Sepr. Thomas the fonne of Giles Rifedon, Efq.——iii.

Decr. John Gifford, Efq. deceffed.——15th.

1624.

Julii. Johana uxor Johannis Rifdon Clerici fepulta fuit—xvi die Julii.

1628.

May 4th. John Rifdon, Rector of this Parifh.

1648.

Thomas Gifford, Efq. was buried Novr. 20th.

1678.

Giles Rifdon, Efq. was buried March 24th.

1692.

Thomas the fon of Gyles Rifdon, Efq. July 7th.

Of ALWINGTON, the late ingenious Hooper Morrifon has written a complete account.*

About

1697.
Gyles Rifdon of Bably, Efq. was buried Sepr. 24th.

1702.
Francis Nation, Clerk, was buried May 12th.

1724.
Roger Giffard, Efq. was buried Octr. 21^{ft}.

1739.
The Rev^d. Mr. William Kingford, Rector of this Parifh July 24th.

1753.
Thomas Saltren, Efq. buried Aug^{ft}. 8th.

1765.
Thomas Saltren, Clerk, Vicar of Monkleigh, and Rector of Dolton, buried Jany. 6th.

1769.
Mrs. Mary Saltren, widow of the late Thomas Saltren, Efq. of Stone, buried Jany. 6th.

1775.
The Rev^d. Mr. Humphrey Bawdon, Rector of Parkham, Decr. 23^d.

1780.
Thomas Swindale, Rector of this Parifh Decr. 3^d, 1780."

||‡ " Towards the eaft of Woolfardifworthy *Parkham* appeareth. It had the Belftones its ancient landlords, of whom three fucceffively were called Baldwin; the laft of them had iffue three daughters; Maude married to Sir Richard Speccot, Mariot unto William Fulford, and Joan unto John Chamberlain. Two parts of this mannor were fold unto Sir John Beamont; the third part defcended in the family of Fulford. John de Belfton, the grand-child of Sir Baldwin Speccot, that affumed his mother's name, granted lands in this mannor; Belfon, Lamford, and Marfh, unto Richard Beamont, and John his fon. Witneffed by John de Sully, Richard Merton, and Walter Woodland, knights. Dated at Marfh, xliij Edwardi III.—*Halfbery* was the ancient inheritance of Walter de Halfbery, in King Henry the 2d's time, whofe grand-child Peter, in King Edward the 1ft's time, had iffue a daughter called Joan, wife unto Bartholomew Giffard, a family that hath ever fince enjoyed thefe lands. The gentleman that now owneth it, married the daughter of Champernon of Dartington, his father the daughter of Tremain, his grandfire the daughter and heir of Smith."—The manor of Halfbury, late the Giffard's, was purchafed by John Davie of Orleigh, efq.—*Bableigh*, about fix miles from Bideford. The Rifdons defcended from Ralph Rifdon, lord of the manor of Rifdon in Gloucefterfhire, in the reign of Richard the 1ft, and long flourifhed at this feat of Bableigh; where Robert Rifdon lived in the 3d year of Edward the 1ft. Thomas Rifdon, a learned bencher of the inner temple in Elizabeth's reign, was a younger fon of Thomas Rifdon of Bableigh. He purchafed an eftate called Sandwell, in the parifh of Harberton, about three miles to the weft of Totnes, where he refided in the decline of life. He married a daughter of Hawkins. If he had any children, he had no iffue by her that furvived him. Dying at the age of near 100, he left his eftate, which was very confiderable, to Francis Rifdon of Bableigh, efq. his eldeft brother's fon by a fecond wife, Dorothea, a daughter of Blewet of Holcombe Rogus. In his pofterity it remains (fays Prince) the prefent poffeffor being Francis Rifdon, efq.—One of the Rifdons of Bableigh built the north-aifle of Parkham church.

* " *Alwington*, or *Allington*, is a parifh of about three miles in length, and as many in breadth, the northern part bordered by the fea. There is but one manor in it, which, with the patronage of the living, a rectory, belongs to the Coffins, and hath, according to Rifdon, been in that family from the conqueft :—" The antiquity of this family (he fays) appears by a boundary deed written in the Saxon language, (a copy of which deed Mr. Prince, in his hiftory, acquaints us was in his poffeffion) between Richard Coffin, lord of this manor and Cockementon, and the abbot of Taviftock, lord of the manor of Abbotfham, (the adjoining parifh), concerning the bounds of both their lands, which agreement was made with the confent of Galfride the fon of Baldwin, and Nicholas his heir, chief lord of the fee; whereunto were witneffes William Dacus, Richard de Bohecumba, Joel de Launcels, Henry de Aluco, Ralph de Lega, Hamlyn de Leigh, Fulk de veteri Ponte."—He adds, " of this family, from the time of King Henry the 1ft unto the King Edward the 2d, all were called Richard, of whom were divers knights."—The manor-houfe, called Portledge, is fituated near the fea, in a warm and fheltered vale, furrounded with woods. It is built of exceeding good ftone, dug from the neighbouring cliffs, equal to that of Portland, and very fimilar in color and appearance to it. The parifh church is faced with the fame; and the tower, which is a handfome and well proportioned one, being 81 feet high, including the pinacles, is entirely built with it. The church confifts of two ailes, the northern 71 and the fouthern 62 feet in length, their breadth 28. There is likewife a fmall aifle on the north belonging to and repaired by the barton of Yeo-Vale. The pillars of the church are remarkable, the fhaft of each is 8 feet high, exclufive of the bafe and capital, and confifts of one fingle ftone. There are only three monuments in the church, two in Yeo-vale aifle, one of which is much defaced, not the leaft trace or appearance of infcription remaining. Tradition fays that it was erected in memory of a Judge Gyffard. The other has the following infcription :

Underneath
is depofited the body of
Charlotte Morrifon,
Daughter of Paul Orchard, Efq.
Of Hertland Abbey & wife of
The Rev^d. Hooper Morrifon,
Of Yeo-vale in this Parifh—
For many Years
She bore fevere ficknefs
With the moft unrepining Refignation
And on the 30th of October, 1791,
In the 56th year of her age,
She departed hence
Dying with well grounded hopes
Of exchanging a Life of Suffering
For that happy State
Where Pain and Sorrow fhall be no more.
In the fame vault lies alfo the body of
Charlotte Morrifon
Her eldeft daughter, who in the bloom of Life
Was torn from her difconfolate Parents Septr. 18, 1788,
Aged 18.

The Gyffard's arms—fable, 3 fufils in fefs ermin; together with the Dennis's of Orleigh—azure 3 dane axes, or,—are painted on glafs in the window of the aifle.

The

The other monument is over the chancel door, with the following infcription :

M. S.

Richard Coffin, Efq. of Portledge, and Elizabeth his Wife, Daughter of Leonard Lovis of Ugbeare, in the County of Cornwall, Efq. Hee deceafed July 25th, An. Dom. 1617, Ætat. fuæ 48. She departed this Life May 3d, An. Dom. 1651, Ætat. fuæ 80.

> All here pourtray'd fhewes one joyn'd Coffin fent
> Through Heaven's Canopy & to Earth here lent
> Perfum'd with vertues & bedew'd with Grace
> T'adorne Them with a Progeny for a Space—
> One Man took Life from dead Elifha's bones
> Eight Martial Sons liv'd from this Coffin's Loynes—
> With Daughters feven that from this vine did fprout
> Like Olive Plants their Tables round about.
> Thrice happy fruitful Coffin may thy Buds fpring
> And to Eternity Hallelujahs fing—

There are fix'd againft the eaftern wall of the fouth-aifle, under the window, four large flabs of Portland, or a ftone very fimilar, with infcriptions in memory of the Coffins.

On fome marble flabs on the pavement are the following infcriptions :

H. S. E.

Richardus Coffin de Portledge Armiger
vir et Literis et fenio venerandus
Rarâ fide
et
Summâ vitæ
Morumque integritate præclarus.
Regi Patriæque fidelis Servus
Nec non
Ecclefiæ Anglicanæ filius pientiffimus.
Inimico carens vixit et
Omnibus ploratus cecidit.
Lentâ ætate confumpfit
Et tandem
Die nativitatis Domini Jefu Chrifti
Lubens animam
Deo refignavit—
Vixit annos 77—obiit Anno 1699.
Mors fola fatetur
Quantula fint hominum corpufcula—Juv. Sat. 10th.

———

Memoriæ Sacrum
Johannis Coffin de Portledge Armigeri
Qui
Cum Galliam Helvetiam et Italiam
Peragratus et
Aulas Subaudiæ Ducis, Regifque Chriftianiffimi
Magnificas
Nec non
Romam ipfam
Aulamque Pontificis fplendidiorem
Vidiffet
Plenus virtutibus
Rarifque animi dotibus ornatus
In natale Solum Se recipiebat
Proximis Cognatis non majus Solatium
Quam
Patriæ et decus et defiderium—
Habuit in Conjugio Catharinam
Filiam Johannis Kellond de Painsford Armigeri
Mortalitatem exuit
Eheu quam inopinate et fine Prole
Undecimo die Julii
Anno { Ætatis 25.
{ Salutis 1703.

———

Here lyeth interr'd
The Body of Ann the Relict of
Richard Coffin of Portledge, Efqr.
the Daughter of Edmond Prideaux
Of Padftow in the County of Cornwall, Efqr.
Who had Iffue
Bridget, John, Honour & Richard.
She was the melancholy Survivor
Of her 2 elder Children
And left behind her, her 2 younger
to bewail their Lofs
&
to imitate her virtue
She exchanged this Life for a better
the 10th Day of Auguft
In the 60th Year of her Age
& in the year of our Lord 1705.

Here

Here lieth In
terr'd the Body of
Bridget Widow of
Charles Kellond of Painsford
In this County Esqr—Daughter of
Richard Coffin of Portledge Esqr by Anne
His wife—Daughter of Edmond Prideaux
Of Padftow in the County of Cornwall Esq^t
Who departed this Life the 14th day of
March in the 21^ft Y^r of her Age & in the
Yeare of our Redemption 1696-7
leaving behind her Anna her only Child.

———

Subtus jacent
Mortales exuviæ Ricardi
Coffin de Portledge Armigeri
Supremum Diem obiit nono
Kalendas Decembris
Anno $\begin{cases} \text{Salutis 1766} \\ \text{Ætatis fuæ 83.} \end{cases}$

Within the communion rails are four infcriptions to the memory of 4 rectors of this parifh :

Here lieth the Body of John Pyne Gent late Rector of this Parifh who was buried the 20th Day of April 1655 Ætat. fuæ 64.

Relliquiæ Nathanaelis Haydon A. M. et hujus Ecclefiæ Rectoris, in Spem Refurrectionis hic repofitæ funt—obiit Junii 3^d 1668.

H. S. E.
Omne
quod fuit mortale
Rev^di Viri Thomæ Blake
Hujus Ecclefiæ Rectoris
Per Annos amplius triginta
Vixit cum præcipuâ
Benevolentiâ erga omnes
Mortem obiit aliorum
Damno non fuo
Anno Ætat. 64
Dom. 1713.

H. S. E.
Reverendus
Georgius Blake A. M.
Theologus confummatus
Filius et Succeffor
Reverendi Thomæ Blake
In Rectoria hujus Ecclefiæ
Olim Collegii Exonienfis
Apud Oxonienfes Socius
Integer vitæ, maturus Cœlo
Obiit Maii 29—Anno
Inftitutionis fuæ 50
Ætatis 81
Dom. 1763.

There are two or three infcriptions in memory of the family of the Brutons; this is one of them :

Hic Jacet
Spe lætæ Refurrectionis
Johannes Bruton de Yeo Gen:
Vir
Genuinæ $\begin{cases} \text{Pietatis} \\ \text{Humanitatis} \\ \text{Probitatis} \end{cases}$ erga $\begin{cases} \text{Deum} \\ \text{Amicos} \\ \text{Omnes} \end{cases}$
a terris in Cœlos migravit
Die Afcenfionis dominicæ
29 die Menfis Mayi An Dom 1701—Ætatis 44.

There are feveral other grave ftones in the church. On one affixed to the outfide of the eaftern wall is the following epitaph :

Near this Place lieth the Body of John Pine & Samuel his Son, and Mary his Son's wife & alfo John Pine their Son who died the 19th of February An: Dom: 1769—Aged 82.

I've travelled far by Sea and Land
Thro' Hardfhips Froft & Snow
In difmal woods beyond the Seas
I wander'd to & fro
Yet God with whom my Soul doth hope
To reft for evermore
Did by his Goodnefs bring me fafe
Home to my native Shore
Where with my Friends I liv'd & dyed
And here my Corps doth lie
Intombed in my Parents Grave
In hopes to rife with Joy.

In

About two miles to the north of Alwington, we come to ABBOTSHAM; the manor of which belongs to Auguftus Saltren Willett, efq. of Porthill, in the parifh of Northam.

BIDEFORD is pleafantly feated on both fides of the Torridge. Its latitude is 51° 6' N. and its longitude from London is 4° 16' W. About three parts of the town lie on the flope of a pretty fteep hill on the weftern fide of the river, and the other part at the bottom of an hill on the oppofite fide. In refpect to local advantages, few towns in England, and not one in the north of Devon, can challenge a fuperiority over this.* Nothing, perhaps, can be more picturefque than the view above the bridge. Near the fording place a pretty large wood rifes from the fide of the river to the fummit of a high hill of a fquare pyramidal form: and at the bottom of that fide, fronting the town, is a beautiful fmall meadow, which is a perfectly natural amphitheatre, and is verdant all the year round. This, with a large ancient houfe clofe by, gardens and fields in a high ftate of cultivation, forms a landfcape admirably worth the attention of the eye of tafte. The weftern part of the town ftands upon a rock, which has a bed of coarfe, black mould upon its furface: and this is the general characteriftic of the foil in the neighbourhood. The land is well cultivated, and the value of eftates has increafed, of late years, to a very great degree. Wheat, barley, and oats conftitute the chief articles of agricultural cultivation; but of the latter there is little raifed in the parifh itfelf, as it is a grain fuited to a worfe foil, and but indifferently anfwers the farmer's attention. Great quantities are, however, produced in the adjacent parifhes to the weftward, and are brought to Bideford for exportation to Briftol and London.† The church was, probably, built about the fame time with the bridge, which was in the fourteenth century. The form of the church was originally a proper crofs: but repeated alterations and additions, fince the Reformation, have confiderably changed its figure. It prefents but an indifferent appearance on the outfide; but within it is a neat, though by no means an elegant ftructure. A plain fquare tower rifes to the height of about feventy feet from its weft end, containing fix bells, which, as the church is fituated very near the river, have a very harmonious found. The church has two aifles, and three galleries, with two additional wings, which will con-

tain

In the eaftern part of the parifh is fituated Yeovale, anciently fpelt Yoe, which, fays Sir Wm. Pole, was the dwelling of a family fo called, of whom Thomas at Yoe, the laft dweller there of that name, had iffue Joan, wief of Geffry Gyffard, whofe dwelling was there and his pofterity after him. Thomazin, the only daughter of John Gyffard, the laft of that family, was firft married unto John Byry of Collaton, and from him divorced (propter frigiditatem); and after married unto Sir George Cary of Cockington, and had iffue George and two daughters, which all three died without iffue; and hee hath conveyed this land unto Sir Edward Cary his brother's fon, whofe now it is. Of the Carys it was purchafed by the Brutons, about the year 1683, in whofe poffeffion it remained till 1769, when it was by them fold to the Rev. Hooper Morrifon. Rifdon, in his Survey of Devon, fays it was a fair houfe, according to the building of thofe times. There was a fmall chapple adjoining, in which was a tombftone (which is ftill preferved) with the following infcription: Orate proanimâ Willielmi Giffard Arm: qui obiit 22 die Decembris Anno Domini 1400 cujus animæ propietur Deus.—Near Yeovale is the barton of Winfcott, the houfe is well fituated, and there are feveral very pleafing views from the eftate. This has been the refidence of the family of the Meddons for many years. The only charitable foundation in this parifh are three dwellings, with gardens, and fome land annex'd for three families who receive no affiftance or relief from the parifh, given by the Coffin family—each fhare reckoned worth thirty fhillings per annum. The parifh is rated to the poor £.708 15s.—To the church £.720—Pays to the land-tax £.116 10s. 11d. per annum.

* We find the name of this town written various ways in records and books, as *Bedeford, Byddyford, Bedyford, Bydeford, Bytheford, Biddeford,* but more properly BIDEFORD, which is compounded of the Saxon BI, *fituated,* and *ford, a fhallow place in a river that may eafily be paffed over.*

† The parifh of Bideford contains about fix miles. The number of tenanted houfes is 527, of which 15 are farms. That of the inhabitants is 2800 nearly. There is only one feat in the parifh, which is Daddon, on the weft of the town, at the diftance of a mile: it is a good modern houfe, belonging to the Buck family.

tain a confiderable number of perfons. Here is alfo a north-aifle, which was appropriated to the purpofe of a chapel or chantry, and, at the Reformation was divided into pews. About the year 1728, the church underwent a thorough repair, and received the ornament of an organ. In 1785, a wing was added to the north fide of the church, furnifhed with rifing pews beneath, and a large gallery over them.*

The manor of NORTHAM was given by the Conqueror to the church of St. Stephen in Caen, in Normandy.†

The little parifh of LANCRAS, (anciently *Langraffe*, from the plenty of its paftures) is peninfulated by the rivers, that nearly encircle it.‡

At WEAR-GIFFARD, lying on the eaft-fide of the Torridge, about three miles to the north of Great Torrington, lived Sir Walter Giffard 27th of Henry the 3d; whofe daughter and heirefs Emma became the wife of Sir Hugh de Widworthy.§

LITTLEHAM lies on the weft of the Torridge.‖

In

* Though the church be large enough to accommodate at leaft two thoufand perfons, yet, be it fpoken to the honour of the inhabitants of this town, in an age when the very *appearance of the religious charaƈter* is too generally contemned, there is feldom, if ever, any reafon to complain of the want of a large congregation every Sunday. Even the weekly prayer days, and the fafts and the feftivals of this church, are certain of being properly refpeƈted here; and on fuch occafions, there is frequently a much larger congregation than in fome churches is to be feen on a Sunday. In the facrilegious and rebellious period of the middle of the laft century, this church fuffered confiderable dilapidations, among which one was particularly remarkable. The pious, or rather impious reformers threw the baptifmal font out of the church as a relique of the Whore of Babylon's abominations; and one fchifmatic, to fhew his zeal the more confpicuoufly, appropriated it to the purpofe of a trough for his fwine to feed out of; and if he had had his deferts, he would have made one of their company. Many neceffary improvements have been made in the church fince 1783, (when the prefent reƈtor came to the poffeffion of the living), and thofe to the expenditure of more than two hundred pounds, exclufive of common repairs. The ereƈtion of a new veftry-room is to be reckoned as one of the beft. The original veftry was the record-room of the town, and as fuch it is ftyled in fome of the parifh books and regifters; but how it came to be given up to that ufe is now unknown. On the fcite of the old veftry-room, five new feats or pews have been ereƈted; and the new veftry-room was built upon a fpot of ground taken out of a convenient part of the church-yard, and is much more neat and commodious than the former. There are on fome of the walls and pew doors of the church, feveral armorial bearings of the Granville's: many of thefe are quartered with other coats, but the greateft number have the Granville arms alone. The only fepulchral monument which that family have in this church, is on the fouth-fide of the chancel near the altar. It is a free-ftone table, upon which lies extended, the ftatue of a man in armour, with a dog, not as is cuftomary at the feet, but, by his fide: over him is an arch with fcreen-work pretty high, the top of which is muriated. Round the arch is the following infcription:

𝔥𝔦𝔠 𝔦𝔞𝔠𝔢𝔱 𝕿𝔥𝔬𝔪𝔞𝔰 𝕲𝔯𝔞𝔲𝔫𝔱𝔟𝔦𝔩𝔡 𝔪𝔦𝔩𝔢𝔰 𝔭𝔞𝔱𝔯𝔬𝔫𝔲𝔰 𝔦𝔰𝔱𝔦𝔲𝔰 𝔢𝔠𝔠𝔩𝔢𝔰𝔦𝔢 𝔬𝔟𝔦𝔦𝔱 𝔯𝔳𝔦𝔦𝔦 𝔡𝔦𝔢 𝔪𝔢𝔫𝔰𝔦𝔰 𝔪𝔞𝔯𝔠𝔦𝔦 𝔞𝔫𝔫𝔬 𝔡𝔬𝔪𝔦𝔫𝔦 𝔪𝔟𝔯𝔦𝔦𝔦 𝔠𝔲𝔦𝔲𝔰 𝔞𝔫𝔦𝔪𝔢 𝔭𝔯𝔬𝔭𝔦𝔱𝔦𝔢𝔱𝔲𝔯 𝔡𝔢𝔲𝔰. 𝔞𝔪𝔢𝔫. i. e. " Here lieth Thomas Granville (or Grauntvild as it is here fpelt), Knight, patron of this " Church, who died the eighteenth day of the month of March, in the year of our Lord 1513. On whofe foul God have mercy, Amen."

Beneath this monument was the vault belonging to this noble family, in which was interred the Lady of Sir Richard Granville, the brave but unfortunate Admiral under Queen Elizabeth. The regifter of this Lady's burial is as follows: " The Ladie Mary Grenvile, " daughter unto the Right honourable Sir John St. Leger, Knight, deceafed, and wife to that famous Warriour Sir Richard Grenvile, " Knight, alfo deceafed, beinge in his life time the Spaniord's terrour; She was buried in the Grenvile's Ifle in the Church of Bediford, " the fifthe daie of November, Anno Domini 1623." See *Watkins's* Acct. of Bideford.

† " A place deferving refpeƈt for breeding, and, in part, furnifhing the royal navy with able mariners. Here the well-difpofed people have twice enlarged their church, in our remembrance, the tower whereof ferves for a mark for failors that bear with the bar." *Rifdon.*—*Burrow*, in this parifh, was poffeft by a family of this name, from whom it paffed by marriage to the Leighs, who held it for many defcents, till it came to the daughters and coheirs of Leigh, one of whom was married to colonel Baffet of Heanton-court; the other to Berry who fettled at this place, and had a fair progeny both of fons and daughters. His eldeft fon Sir Thomas Berry, knight, married one of the coheirs of Mr. Martin of Lindridge, but died without iffue. The other children died unmarried." *Prince.*

‡ " *Lancras*, in former times the inheritance of the Beaumonts. Elizabeth, the fifter and heirefs of Will. Beaumont, gave Lancras to Richard Beaumont and John his fon, with Afhford and other lands, the 38th of Edward the 3d. Since, the Baffets poffeft it. And one of this family gave it in frank marriage with his daughter to a Pomeroy (together with Ingfdon and Knighfton Beaumont)." *Rifdon.*

§ " Sir Walter Giffard, knight, lived in the time of King Henry the 3d, who left his lands to Emma his daughter, firft married to Sir Hugh Widworthy; fecondly, to Sir William Trewin; thirdly, to Sir Robert Dynham. She had iffue only by Trewin, that fucceeded in the Giffard's inheritance, whofe fon William was called Wear of his dwelling. William the laft of his line, which dyed in the beginning of King Henry the 5th, left iffue a daughter, married to Richard Denfell. And his fon Richard left one only daughter, firft married to Martin Fortefcue, fon of Sir John Fortefcue, chief juftice of England; fecondly, unto Richard Pomeroy. This lineage of the Fortefcue's, hath produced many notable perfons, both in letters and arms, whofe treatifes of the laws, and politick government of the common-wealth, are extant. This family hath flourifhed in this feat, fome nine defcents, and have matched in many eminent houfes. This gentleman married the daughter of Rolle of Heanton, efq. his father the daughter of Speccot, his grand-father the daughter of Sir John Chichefter." *Rifdon.*

‖ " This manor of *Littleham* was once Stapledon's. It hereditarily defcended to St. Leger from the Botelers, Earls of Ormond, by matching with an heirefs of Hankford. It was, in Rifdon's time, the inheritance of Leigh, by the marriage of one of the coheireffes of Boteler of Parkham; to whofe anceftors Sir John St. Leger fold it. Within this manor, Robert Boteler granted to Clement Boteler and Ifabel his wife, all his lands, called Holland, by a deed bearing date 31ft Edward the 1ft." *Rifdon.*—Littleham-manor, near *Bideford*, formerly belonging to Francis Baffet, efq. is now poffeffed by George Anthony, efq. of Southmolton, a defcendant from Gregory Anthony, M. A. who was ejeƈted from the living of Petrockftow.

In MONKLEIGH, we vifit *Annery*; anciently held by Ofbert, furnamed *de Annery*; after that by the *Stapledons*, then the *Hankfords*.*

BUCKLAND-BREWER is a large parifh;† exclufive of EAST-PUTFORD ‡ and BULKWORTHY,§ which are confidered as chapels appendant to it.

* *Annery* is a noble feat, on the weft-fide of the Torridge, over which it ftands, commanding a delightful profpect of that river. The houfe, now gone to decay, was heretofore ftately and magnificent. It was famous for a large upper gallery, in which might be placed 30 ftanding beds, fifteen on each fide, and yet not one to be feen there: nor could you from one bed fee another. For the gallery being long and wainfcotted, both to the right and left, there were feveral doors in it which led into little alcoves or apartments, large and convenient enough for private lodgings. Here the family of Stapledon continued for feveral defcents, till Thomafin brought it by marriage to Hankford. The name is local. It is taken from the original habitation of the Stapledons, at Stapledon, in the parifh of Cookberry. We meet with Sir Richard Stapledon, in the time of Edward the 1ft; whofe fon, of the fame name, it is believed, fucceeded him, in the reign of Edward the 2d. No lefs than four knights of the name of Stapledon came in fucceffion. Walter Stapledon, Bifhop of Exeter, was the younger fon of Sir Richard Stapledon, knight.—Judge Hankford left iffue two fons, Sir Richard of Annery and John of Lodeford, in the parifh of Shebbear. Sir Richard Hankford of Annery, married Thomafin the heir general of the knightly family of Stapledon; by whom he had iffue Sir Richard Hankford of Annery; who was twice married, firft to Elizabeth, fifter and heirefs of Fulk Lord Fitzwarren; by whom he had iffue Thomafin, wife of Will. Bourchier Lord Fitzwarren; from whom defcended the Earls of Bath of that name. Sir Richard Hankford's fecond wife was Anne, daughter of John Montacute, Earl of Salifbury; by whom he had iffue Anne, wife of Thomas Boteler, Earl of Ormond; who had iffue two daughters, Anne, wife of Sir James Seintleger, knight, and Margaret, wife of Sir Thomas Bulloin, knight, grandfather to Queen Elizabeth: whence it appears that Queen Elizabeth derived her original from the county of Devon. Annery, with the manor belonging to it, fell to the portion of Sir James St. Leger and Anne his wife. They had iffue Sir George St. Leger, who had iffue Sir John Saintleger of Annery, knight; who married Catherine, daughter of George Neville, Lord of Abergaveney, and had iffue—John and Dudley, both without iffue—Mary, married to Sir Richard Grenville, of Bideford, knight—Frances, married to John Stukeley of Affton, and Eulalia, firft married to Edmund Tremayne, efq. of Collacombe, fecondly to Triftram Arfcot, efq. to whom Sir John Saintleger, having no male iffue, fold Annery. The Arfcots poffeft it for two or three generations, and then fold it. The houfe is in ruins.—" In this church Sir William Hankford lieth honourably interred, having a fair monument erected to his memory, with this epitaph inlaid in brafs:

Hic jacet Willielmus Hankford, Miles, quondam Capital. Jufticiar. Domini regis de Banco qui obiit xx die menfis Decemb. Anno 1422. Cujus anime propitietur Deus. Amen.

He is pourtrayed kneeling in his robes. From the mouth of the figure proceeds this prayer:

Miferere mei Deus fecundum magnam mifericordiam Tuam.

On his head is this:

Beati qui cuftodiunt Judicium & faciunt jufticiam in omni tempore.

A book in his hand hath this:

Miferere mei Deus fecundum magnam jufticiam Divinam.

Near unto the former, is Sir Richard Hankford his fon's ftatue in armor kneeling, on whofe furcoat are his arms; then the pourtraiture of his mother, on whofe upper veftments Hankford and Stapleton's armories are curioufly cut in brafs. It is received for truth, that Sir Wm. Hankford, upon the death of King Henry the 4th, doubting of his fafety for the imprifoning of the late Prince, (then King Henry the 5th), as you have heretofore heard; and miftrufting the fequel of the matter, fent for the keeper of his park, and rebuked him for fuffering his game to go to fpoil; which he denied. Howbeit, his mafter threatened him, and gave him this charge, That in his night-walk, whomfoever he met, if he would not ftand and declare what he was, his keeper fhould kill him, and he would be his warrant. Not long after, the faid Sir William Hankford came into his park late in the night, whom the keeper meeting, called unto him; but he refufing to fpeak, was prefently fhot through by his keeper, of which wound this knight died. Which report is fo credible among the common fort of people, that they can fhew the tree yet growing where this fact was committed, known by the name of Hankford-Oak." *Rifdon.*

† " *Buckland-Brewer* continueth the memory of its ancient lords, the Brewers, Barons in King Richard the 1ft, King John, and King Henry the 3d's time; with whom William Brewer was in great favour, and of his privy council, whom he promoted to this bifhoprick, the tenth year of his reign, and put him in truft with the conveying of his fifter into Germany, to be married to the Emperor. William Lord Brewer the younger, married Joan, one of the daughters of the Earl of Devon, but dyed *fans* iffue; and his inheritance was divided among his five fifters. The portion of Margery the eldeft, being annexed to the honour of Lancafter.—*Orleigh* hath been the inheritance and dwelling of the Deniffes, for a long continuance, which Jollenus Dacus held in King Henry the 2d's reign. This ancient family hath enjoyed this land eighteen defcents, in lineal fucceffion. The gentleman that now enjoyeth it, married the daughter of Sir Thomas Wife: Secondly of Sir Bernard Grenvile, knight; his father, the coheir of Violl; his grand-father the daughter of Monk." Dennis fold Orleigh to an anceftor of Jofeph Davie, efq. its prefent poffeffor.—" *Vielfton* is the refidence of Rifdon, a branch budded out of Babley-houfe; the now poffeffor married one of the coheirs of Abbot; his father the daughter of Braddon, his fon the daughter of Molfworty.—*Holwill* in the mannor of Buckland, was held by John, the fon of Hailmer Vielfton, in the reign of King Edward the 2d, of Laurence at Week; for which land he payed yearly xl*s.* unto which deed were witneffes, Walter Pollard, Walter Winfcot, and Gilbert Wibberye.—*Winflate*, in the parifh of Buckland, was the ancient inheritance of that name. A family which for their great revenues, were dignified with the title of *White-Spurs*, by putting on their heels a pair of filver fpurs, and about their neck a filver collar of S's, by the kings of this land; a title only belonging to the eldeft fons. The laft inheritor of thefe lands, made claim to the Earl of Devon's lands, but loft all his own by attainder in the time of King Edward the 6th. Howbeit, Queen Mary reftored this barton to his eldeft fon." *Rifdon.*

‡ " *Eaft-Putford*, or *Poteford*, had lords of the fame name. From Milo-Poteford, who held it in the reign of Henry the 3d, it was a long time called Poteford Miles. In the time of Edward the 1ft, Sir Roger Poteford flourifhed in this place. He had iffue two daughters, his heireffes—Afcara, the wife of Robert Stockey, the other, of Joel Pollard. This family gave for their arms, a plain crofs fitchee, in a field argent." *Rifdon.*

§ " *Bulkworthy* had once inhabiters fo named. Laurence de Bulkworthy releafed to Robert de Stockley, the fervice of William of *Eaft-Hankford*, for land in *Eaft-Hankford*, in the prefence of Richard Coffin, Walter le Dennis, Edmond de Speccot, Bartholomew Giffard, Hugh le Moigne, fans date." *Rifdon.*—" At *Bulkworthy* is a chapel of eafe built by Sir William Hankford, knight of the Bath, at the coronation of King Henry the 4th, whofe arms in a window thereof was lately to be feen, with this, underwritten:—*Orate pro bono ftatu Willielmi Hankford qui iftam Capellam fieri fecit.* In this tything, he had a dwelling-houfe bearing his name. This is that deferving judge, that did juftice upon the king's fon, (afterwards King Henry the 5th), who, when he was yet prince, commanded him to free a fervant of his, arraigned for felony at the king's-bench bar; whereat the judge replied, he *would not.* Herewith the prince enraged, affayed himfelf to enlarge the prifoner; but the judge forbad. Infomuch, as the prince in fury ftept up to the bench, and gave the judge a blow on the face; who nothing therewith daunted, told him boldly, *If you will not obey your fovereign's laws, who fhall obey you, when you fhall be king? Wherefore, in the king's (your father's) name, I command you prifoner to the* king's-bench. Whereat the prince abafhed, departed to prifon. When King Henry the 4th his father was advertifed thereof, (as faft flieth fame) after he had examined the circumftances of the matter, he rejoiced to have a fon fo obedient to his laws, and a judge of fuch integrity, to adminifter juftice without fear or favour of the perfon; but withal difmiffed the prince from his place of prefident of the council, which he conferred on his fecond fon." *Rifdon.* See *Prince*, p. 364.

ARCHDEACONRY

ARCHDEACONRY

OF

TOTNES.

———✦———

DEANRIES

OF

HOLSWORTHY,
OKEHAMTON,
TAVISTOCK,
TAMERTON,
PLYMTON,
WOODLEIGH,
TOTTON,
IPPLEPEN,
MORETON.

ARCHDEACONRY of TOTNES.

GENERAL CHOROGRAPHICAL DESCRIPTION.

IN noticing the rife of the Torridge, I obferved that, as it ran along, it left on each fide a ftring of parifhes, where the land was good and well culti- vated. Thefe (among others) are Eaft and Weft Putford, Abbots Bickington, Milton-Damarel, Thornbury, and Bradford. Holfworthy, a fmall town, is fitu- ated between the Torridge and the Tamar, in the middle of a coarfe country, very deep in clay, and thinly inhabited. To the fouth-eaft of it, is an open moorifh country, almoft impaffable in winter, by the deepnefs of the clay: a great part of this being in the parifh of Clawton, is famous by the name of Claw- moor; concerning which they have this faying, That the Devil was claw'd in Clawmoor.

There are a few parifhes widely fpread between the river Torridge and Dart- moor. The country is in general coarfe and open: a great many downs and heaths, the foil in general clay, and its fituation on the north fide of Dart- moor make it very cold, and the harvefts late. In this diftrict are fituated the parifhes of Okehamton, Inwardleigh, Jacobftow, Afhbury, North Lew, Be- worthy, Holwell, Germanfweek, Virginftow, Afhwater, Bratton Clovelly, Sourton, Briddiftow, Lidford, and Brentorr.

The country from Okehamton towards Exeter, is more fertile. In the pa- rifhes of Belfton, Moreton, and others bordering on the moor northwards, is good grazing land.

The country between the Teign and Dart is very fertile, at leaft the fouthern part of it, from Newton and Afhburton to the fea, which is a red foil, lying on a limeftone, producing exceedingly good corn and grafs, and very good cyder. The parifh of Paignton is remarkable for the richnefs of its foil, and the warmth of its climate. This part of the country, tho' uneven, has not very high, nor fteep hills, and abounds with clear ftreams, iffuing out of the clifts of the lime- ftone rocks, which in fome part of this diftrict, as in the parifhes of King's Kerfwell, Torbryan, Tor-Mohun, Mary-Church, Marldon, and Berry Pome- roy, appear naked above the furface of the ground. From Newton and Afh- burton northward the country is coarfer, and rifes gradually into moors and commons, which adjoin Dartmoor. Amongft thefe hills, are the parifhes of

Buckland

Buckland in the Moor, Withecomb in the Moor, Ilfington, Manaton, and North Bovey.

The land on the weſt-ſide of the Dart is very much inferior to that on the eaſt-ſide. The latter is a rich red ſoil, abounding with limeſtone; the former a thin light flatey ſoil, without any depth or richneſs. Beſides which, the land is very high and bleak, expoſed to the cutting winds, that will not permit any fence to be made, except earthen banks, on the top of which grow ſome ſcrubbed buſhes; but no timber trees, or good hedge rows, except in the valleys, and where they are ſheltered from the weſt wind. The cyder here is not equal in ſtrength or flavour to that made in the pariſhes of Brixham, Paignton, and Stoke Gabriel.

The country between the Dart and the Aune, which contains the two hundreds of Colrige and Stanborough, is encloſed, and has hardly any coarſe land. It is chiefly on a ſhelf, except the pariſhes of Buckfaſtleigh, Dean Prior, Brent, and Dartington, which are on a limeſtone rock. The ſouthern parts, eſpecially thoſe between Salcomb Haven and the Aune, are fertile, and abound with corn, as moſt of this part of the country does. The pariſhes of Woodleigh, Morleigh, and Diptford are the coarſeſt part of this diſtrict.

The country between the Aune and Arme is good, and near Medbury and Ugborough very fertile, abounding in excellent paſture. That between the Arme, Yealme, and Plym, is pretty much of the ſame kind. There are fords at low water over the Aune and Arme, and a ferry over the Yealme, each at the mouth of their reſpective rivers; but the want of bridges over theſe rivers cuts off their communication very much from the neighbouring countries.

The banks of the Aune, the Arme, and Yealme, are generally ſteep, and covered with oak coppice wood: The Plym, near its ſource, and almoſt to Buckland Crabtree, ſeems to be more plentifully furniſhed with it.

There is a ſtrong deep clay which lies between the two roads from Aſhburton and Totnes to Plymouth. As we go northward we come to a coarſe country, conſiſting of moors and mountains, with narrow valleys running up to the ſources of the rivers, which deſcend from Dartmoor. The roots of theſe hills extend from Buckfaſtleigh to Brent, Ivy-bridge, Cornwood, Plymton, keeping for the moſt part the ſame courſe with the road from Aſhburton to Plymton. But here they turn northward to Shaugh, and go by Meavy, Walkhamton, Peter Tavy, Mary Tavy, Brentor, Lidford, Sourton, Okehamton. The ſoil between the Plym and the Tamar is but thin, but owes its great improvement to the plenty of manure which the two towns of Plymouth and Dock afford. There is little or no timber near Plymouth, hardly any in the hedge rows, but in the northern part of this diſtrict a great deal. The lands on the ſide of the Plym and Tamar are well cultivated; but about three miles from Plymouth riſes a ridge between theſe rivers, and forms a great down, called Roborough, which extends to a rivulet that falls into the Tavy, below Walkhamton. We have ſome encloſures there; but beyond it the country is again open, and conſiſts of

commons

commons quite to Lidford, excepting the valley we crofs on the Tavy, between Peter Tavy and Mary Tavy.

The country between the Tavy, northward, to the Tamar and Torridge, is pleafant and fruitful: the parts of it which lie on the Tamar, including the pa-rifhes of Lamerton, South Sydenham, Milton Abbot, Dunterton, Bradfton, Kelley, Curriton, Lifton, Stowford, Trenchard Lewe, Thruffelton, Bratton, and Bridiftow, are enclofed and improved, hilly, but bear good corn, and have feveral commons and open grounds belonging to them. North of this, to the Torridge, the land is coarfe, a ftrong clay, and full of moors.

Here again returned to the Torridge, I fhall purfue a directly oppofite courfe, as I particularize the parifhes in the nine deanries of Holfworthy, Okehamton, Taviftock, Tamerton, Plymton, Woodleigh, Totton, Ipplepen, and Moreton.

ARCHDEACONRY OF TOTNES.

DEANRY OF HOLSWORTHY.

THE parishes of Holsworthy, Bridgerule, Pyeworthy, Clawton, Tetcot, Luffincot, Ashwater, Holwell, Hollacombe, Black-Torrington, Cookbury, Bradford, Thornbury, Milton-Damarel, Sutcombe, Abbots-Bickington, Bradworthy, Pancras-week, and West-Putford, here present themselves to notice.*

The parish of HOLSWORTHY, (anciently *Hollesworthy*) is nearly eight miles from north to south, and three from east to west.† In an excursion of May, 1789,

* " *Benefices remaining in charge:*

First Fruits. £.	s.	d.		*Yearly Tenths.* £.	s.	d.
26	6	8	Ashwater R. [St. Peter] Rep. B. Proc. vis. viii*d.* Syn. iis. v*d.* A. D. Proc. vis. viii*d.* r. V. 170*l.* Patr. Mr. Melhuish.	2	12	8
22	8	9	Blacktorrington R. [St. Mary] Rep. B. Proc. vis. viii*d.* Syn. iis. vi*d.* A. D. Proc. vis. viii*d.* r. V. 180*l.* Patr. Sir Charles Warwick Bampfylde, bart.	2	4	10½
25	5	5	Bradworthy V. [St. John Baptist] Rep. B. Proc. vis. viii*d.* Syn. iis. v*d.* A. D. Proc. vis. viii*d.* r. V. with Pancras Wyke Ch. 100*l.* Patr. The KING.	2	10	6½
13	8	4	Bradford R. [All Saints] Rep. B. Proc. vs. Syn. iis. v*d.* A. D. Proc. vs. r. V. 90*l.* Patr. —— Cary, esq.	1	6	10
12	3	9	Halwill R. [Ded. unc.] Rep. B. Proc. vs. Syn. iis. v*d.* A. D. Proc. vs. r. V. 80*l.* Patr. The KING.	1	4	4½
32	0	5	Holsworthy R. [St. Peter and St. Paul] Rep. B. Proc. vis. viii*d.* Syn. iis. vi*d.* A. D. Proc. vis. viii*d.* r. V. 200*l.* Patr. Earl Stanhope.	3	4	0½
26	13	6½	Milton Damarel R. [Holy Trinity] with Cookburie Ch. [St. John Baptist] Rep. B. Proc. vis. viii*d.* Syn. iis. v*d.* A. D. Proc. vis. viii*d.* r. V. 160*l.* Patr. Lord Viscount Courtenay.	2	13	4½
27	8	4	Pyworthy R. [St. Swithin] Rep. B. Proc. vs. Syn. iis. v*d.* A. D. Proc. vs. r. V. 100*l.* Patr. and R. Mr. John Kingdon.	2	14	10
17	10	7½	Sutcombe R. [St. Andrew] Rep. B. Proc. vis. viii*d.* Syn. iis. x*d.* A. D. Proc. vs. r. V. 150*l.* Patr. Humphrey Morice, esq.	1	15	0¾
11	3	11½	Thornbury R. [St. Peter] Rep. B. Proc. vs. Syn. iis. v*d.* A. D. Proc. vs. r. V. 90*l.* Patr. W. Fry, esq.	1	2	4¾
9	11	0½	West-Putford R. Rep. B. Proc. vs. Syn. iis. v*d.* A. D. Proc. vs. r. V. 100*l.* Patr. Earl of Orford.	0	19	1¼

Discharged.

King's Books.				*Certified Value.*		
0	0	0	Abbots Bickington Imp. [St. James] Rep. Syn. ii*d.* r. V. 40*l.* Patr. Denys Rolle, esq.	14	0	0
14	0	0	Bridgerule V. Rep. B. Proc. vs. Syn. iis. v*d.* A. D. Proc. vs. r. V. 90*l.* Patr. and V. Mr. John Kingdon.	37	0	0
0	0	0	Clawton Imp. Rep. B. Proc. vs. Syn. iis. v*d.* A. D. Proc. vs. r. V. 30*l.*	20	0	0
4	0	0¾	Hollacombe R. [St. David] Rep. B. Proc. vs. Syn. is. v*d.* r. V. 30*l.* Patr. Miss Harris.	24	0	0
6	0	0	Luffingcot R. [St. James] Rep. Syn. ii*d.* r. V. 60*l.* Patr. Sir John St. Aubyn, bart.	30	0	0
13	16	8	Tetcot R. [Holy Cross] Rep. B. Proc. vs. Syn. is. x*d.* A. D. Proc. vs. r. V. 60*l.* Patr. John Arscott, esq."	45	0	0

Thes. Eccles.

† The river *Dere* rises near the north-west corner of the parish; and running round the western and partly the southern sides, separates this parish from Pyworthy, and empties itself into the Tamar at Tamerton bridge, in the parish of Tamerton. There are two bridges over the Dere, at the south-west corner of this parish, the one called *Deriton*, the other *Ridon*; the former with one arch, the latter two; built of stone, after a rude country fashion, and repaired by the joint parishes of Holsworthy and Pyworthy. This river (or rather rivulet) produces good trout, but of no great size.—" *Holdesworthy*, standing upon a branched Brooke, was sometime the Lord William Bruers, whose son dyeing issueless, his land descended to William de Feritate, son of one his sisters, and heirs, and so to the family of Chaworth, which the Lord Martin had of the house of Lancaster. From which family it came to the Lord Audley; and, for want of issue in that name, by means of an entail, to the crown, and was purchased by Prideaux of *Soldon*. Which Soldon had in former ages lords locally named; and these lands came, by purchase, to the family of Prideaux. The gentleman that is now lord thereof, married the daughter of Coriton; his father, the daughter of Fortescue; his grand father, Sir Nicholas, first the co-heir of Hengescot; secondly, the co-heir of Violl; thirdly, the heir of Kerswell. *Thorn* was the lands and dwelling of lords surnamed thereof, in the days of King John, of which name I find fourteen generations. A family that well increased their estate, by marrying Melior, the daughter and heir of Horton of Upcot, insomuch as their posterity have ever since made that place their mansion. *Manworthy*, within the parish of Holdesworthy, belonged in elder ages to some so named; which, Maude, the daughter and heir of William, brought unto Robert le Davis, son of Sir Alan by

1789, the deep fwamps on each fide of the road between Holfworthy and Ha-therley, had an appearance more than ufually dreary, from the continual rains. We faw only a folitary building on the extenfive downs; and on approching it, found it to be a windmill. Not a traveller did we meet on the road. A few fhaggy-coated horfes were grazing on the right: There was a lonely crow on the other fide. And two curlews paffed us, whiftling thro' the ftorm. Near Ha-therley the enclofures were pleafing; the hedges prefenting us with the white and black thorn, oak, and afh.

Of BRIDGERULE three fifths are in Devon, and two in Cornwall; divided by the Tamar.*

PYEWORTHY was anciently fpelt *Poworthy*.†

CLAWTON commonly called in old evidences *Claveton*, takes its name from the brook *Claw*.‡

TETCOTE is fituated near the turnpike road leading from Launcefton to Holf-worthy.§

Of the little parifh of HOLLACOMBE, the greater part belongs to Harris, Molefworth, and Trelawney.‖

In BLACK-TORRINGTON ¶ is *Coham*, the feat of the Rev. William *§ Holland Coham,

by her marriage; and after fome defcents in that family, Philip Boterford was invefted with this inheritance, by matching of Thomazin the heir-general, whofe daughter and heir was wife of Gibbs of Venton; in which name both Manworthy and Gidicot remained before William Gibbs fold the fame to Hurft of Exeter." *Rifdon.*—The family of the Prideauxs, (baronets), were the ancient poffeffors of the manor of Holfworthy. About 90 years ago the firft Lord London-derry (fon of Governor Pitt) purchafed it of Prideaux. His fon, the late Lord Londonderry poffeft it after his father; by whofe death that branch being extinct, it devolved to Philip Earl Stanhope.—*Soldon*—the capital feat of the manor of Holfworthy. *Simpfon*—a barton belonging to the Prideauxs, formerly a part of the manor of Holfworthy, and as fuch belonging to Earl Stanhope.

* *Bridgeruell.* So called, I prefume, from the bridge built at the expence of the two counties, which *governs* the boundaries of the two parifhes; each county repairing one arch. The bridge is a decent object, from the neighbouring villas and beautiful lawns adjacent. Bridgerule, in Devon, is comprehended by the manor of Bridgerule, the property of Sir William Molefworth, bart.; and the manor of Tatfon the property of John Kingdon, clerk. The foil is good. Moft of the principal farm-houfes are covered with flate. The inhabitants are chiefly leafeholders and rack-tenants, and are remarkable for their longevity. Some time fince, a perfon was there interred, ninety-nine years of age and nine months.—Tatfon is an ancient building, formerly the refidence of Capt. Piper; now the property of John Kingdon, clerk. There is a fchool in the church town, maintained at the expence of the parifh. The church is fituated in Bridgerule in Devon; is on an eminence, fronting the north, and appears to advantage in the road from Holfworthy to Stratton; is built with free-ftone, and covered with flate. The tower is of moor-ftone, and elegantly neat: The plantations around the church yard afford great advantage to the object. In one of the windows remains an entire defcription, in painted glafs, of St. Bridget, the tutelar faint. There are fome characters in the tower, which have attracted the notice of ftrangers, but are not fatisfactorily decyphered. The regifter of baptifms is upon a duplicate ratio with that of forty years fince. The parifh confifts of a vicarage and impropriation, both the free-hold property of John Kingdon, clerk, the prefent incumbent. The vicarage houfe is a modern-built brick houfe, covered with patent flate, is upon an eminence, and has a good appearance from the Launcefton road to Stratton. The prefent incumbent has made confiderable donations, which, with the bounty of Queen Anne, have much advanced the value of the vicarage, by the rent of the pur-chafed eftates.

† This is one of the many worthies in the hundred of Black-torrington. The manor of Pyworthy belongs to Sir Wm. Molefworth: The manor of Moor, in this parifh, to John Kingdon, clerk. The inhabitants of this parifh are amazingly increafed within twenty years; and chiefly compofed of yeomanry and leafeholders. This church is built with free-ftone, and covered with flate; is fituated high; and the tower being a mark at fea has been lowered. The rectory is the perpetual advowfon of John Kingdon, clerk, A. M. the prefent incumbent. The glebe being very extenfive, when properly improved will be one of the beft in the county. The parfonage is a decent new-built brick houfe, about quarter of a mile from the church.

‡ *Clawton* is a perpetual cure, which was in the prefentation of John Pitman Coffin Pitman, efq. who 1788 fold the fame, with the glebe tythes and barton, to the Rev. T. Melhuifh, for 1200 guineas. The clerk has not inftitution or indiction.

§ ALURED, in the time of the Saxons, is the firft poffeffor of Tetcote, that occurs; the laft, ARSCOT.

‖ " The hamlet of *Hollacombe* was long fince the lands of Wermond de Portu Mortuo; fince that ancient lineage of the Borrys inherited thefe lands. For John Mofefenne releafed all his right in this mannor to Henry Barry, calling to witnefs Robert Rifdon, Henry Bobick, Walter Corbyn, dated the 3d of Edward the 1ft. In the time of King Henry the 2d, the Lady Rofe, wife of Sir Henry Champernon, held Burgh and Southcot, and Oliver Champernon their fon after him enjoyed Burgh. But Michael de Southcot was Lord of Southcot, from whom iffued divers families; for he was the original of a great kindred in this county. John Callard married Elizabeth, the heir of this family, and had Southcot. Oliver Tracy held one fee in Winckley, in the reign of King Richard the 1ft. He gave Radford unto Robert de Bickley, the fon of Ralph Borne. The pofterity of which Robert, that made their dwelling in this place, affumed the name of Radford. From whence defcended Nicholas Radford, which in the time of King Henry the 6th, dwelt at Upcot in Cheriton parifh, unto whom Roger Prouz of Prouz was heir, and had his land." *Rifdon.*

¶ " *Black-Torrington* bordereth on the river, belike fo named of the waters blackifh colour. This parifh giveth name to one of the greateft hundreds this fhire hath, which is hemmed in, for the moft part, with the rivers of Touridge and Tamar. King Henry the 1ft gave this hundred and mannor unto Geofry de Main, in exchange for lands in Normandy; whofe fon Joel de Main granted the hundred, with the liberties thereof, unto Richard, the fon of Efbus of Black-Torrington, paying one mark of filver yearly at the feaft of St. Michael.

But

Coham, who married a daughter of the late George Bickford, efq. of Dunfland, in the parifh of Bradford.

Cookbury is a daughter church to Milton-Damerel.*

The deep clay roads in the parifh of Bradford † and its neighbourhood, were almoft impaffable in winter, till the improvements of the late George Bickford, efq. who much attended to the roads; particularly round his feat at Dunfland. This pleafant feat may be termed a garden in the wildernefs. The houfe was built in 1609. The hall and fuite of rooms are fuperior, in defign and execution, to thofe of moft houfes of the fame age. Dunfland came to Bickford by marriage with Arfcot. Its prefent poffeffor, Arfcot Bickford, fon of George

But for that the faid Joel revolted from the Englifh to the French, King John affumed the mannor into his own hands, and gave it unto Geofry de Lucy to hold the fame at will. King Henry the 3d gave this mannor unto Roger la Zouch, who beftowed it on William la Zouch his younger fon, whofe dwelling was at Totleigh in the fame parifh. Many worthy branches budded forth from this dry tree; for fo (as I take it) the name doth fignify, the heir-male of which name as yet endureth. Sir Almerick la Zouch left this land unto his only daughter and heir, married unto Walter Fitz-warren in King Edward the 1ft's time, whofe fon Almeric Fitz-warren dwelt likewife at Totleigh. And his fon Walter left this mannor to Ifabel his daughter, married unto Thomas Dorells. The heir-general of which family, that enjoyed this land fince King Henry the 4th's reign, brought the fame unto the houfe of the Harrifes in our remembrance.—*Wampford, Whitalegh,* and *Northcot,* the faid Joel de Main granted unto the forefaid Richard, the fon of Efbus, whofe pofterity took to name Wampford, being the principal place of their dwelling. Nicholas, the laft of that name, died in the reign of King Richard the 2d, and left iffue two daughters his heirs; Joan, the wife of John Keins, and Elizabeth married unto Durant. This hundred and land fell to the portion of Keyns, whofe grandchild Joan brought the fame by her marriage unto John Speake; by which family it was fold unto Hurft of Exeter; and now it is the inheritance of Sir Nicholas Martin, knight.—Walter Fitz-Warren gave a tenement in this tything, by thefe words: *Walterus filius Warini Dominus de Ponte dedit Benedicto de Bear unum Tenementum in Villa de Black Torrington in perpetuum. His Teftibus Thomas de Wampford, William de Stapledon, Walter Pollard, Henr. de la Wolley, Helio de Arvile tunc Bedallo. &c." Rifdon.*

*§ William Holland, efq. married Mary Fortefcue, in the 17th year of the reign of Charles the 1ft, by whom he had feveral daughters, and one fon only, named William, who married firft Elizabeth Venton, by whom he had iffue John, who married Rifdon, but died S. P.; and fecondly, Joan Stafford, in the 34th year of the reign of Charles the 2d, by whom he had iffue Mary and Margaret coheireffes. Mary was married to Stephen Coham, in the 5th year of the reign of Queen Anne, fon of Lewis Coham, (by Mary Arfcott, daughter of John Arfcott, efq. of Tetcott, Devon), of Coham, in the parifh of Black Torrington, and had iffue Lewis, William, Stephen, and Holland, befides feveral daughters; the three former fons died S. P. but Holland, who was a clergyman, married Chriftian, the daughter of the Rev. James Silke, of Buckland Filleigh, in the faid county, and left iffue by her Stephen, William Holland, and a daughter. Stephen died in the year 1786, S. P. *William Holland* was born in the year 1763. Margaret was married about the year 1712, to John Coham, (brother of the aforefaid Stephen) of Bovacott, in the parifh of Bradford, in the faid county, and had iffue Stephen, William, Arthur, Lewis, and Arfcott, and feveral daughters; all which fons had, or have, no iffue, except Arthur. William is ftill living, and Arthur is the prefent archdeacon of Wilts, who married Anne, daughter of William Woodroffe, efq. of Chifwick, in the county of Middlefex, and has iffue Arthur, now a ftudent in Oxford, William in the navy, and two daughters.

* " *Cookbury,* about two miles long and three-quarters broad. The chapel, built with ftone and covered with flate, is fituated on a level piece of ground, at the eaft-end of the parifh. Church-yard half an acre. The chapel confifts of two aifles, the north aifle 30 feet long, 11 broad, 20 high; the fouth 30 long, 8 wide, and 15 high. A wing fouth from the fouth aifle forms an handfome feat belonging to Dunfland, (the feat of George Bickford, efq.) and is the family feat. Altho' Dunfland is in Bradford parifh, the family attend Cookbury chapel, being much nearer than Bradford. The chancel is 20 feet high, 22 long, 17 broad. A filver flaggon, and a filver plate to collect the alms on facrament days, were given by Walter Elford, late rector; there is alfo a filver chalice. The fteeple contains three bells. A fmall rivulet, over which is one ftone bridge of one arch, (jointly maintained by Cookbury and Thornbury), divides the two parifhes on the north from Cookbury. The fouth is divided by a fmall rivulet from Bradford. The highway divides this and Holfworthy on the weft: and a fmall rivulet on the eaft, under the Church Town, divides it from Black Torrington. This parifh contains five villages, viz: Cookbury Church Town, containing twelve dwellings; Cookbury Week, fix dwellings; Halfdon, three dwellings; Upcott, five dwellings; and Stapledon, three. The parifh in general enclofed, notwithftanding every village has a common moor. Cultivation, not to be boafted, altho' a tolerably firm foil. Situation level, but low. A week before Whit-Sunday a wake is held at the Church Town. Every eftate is fituated weft from the chapel. Houfes of mud walls and thatched roofs. The parfonage-houfe a very fmall cot adjoining the church-yard, too poor to deferve the name of parfonage. No regifters worth notice, except thofe of Elizabeth, daughter of George Bickford, efq. and Mary his wife, baptized Oct. 14th, 1773; and Arfcott, fon of the above George, &c. born and baptized at Okehamton, and received into Chrift's church the fame day." Letter from the minifter, 1791.

† " *Bradford,* fo named, *de Vado Lato,* of a large paffage thro' the Touridge, by which river it lyeth; the inheritance of Edric in the Norman's infancy, fince of Dabernon's. Ingram de Abernon was lord thereof in King Henry the 3d's reign, who gave this mannor unto William his younger fon. From whom iffued John Dabernon, whofe daughter Joan was married to Dennys, whofe fon Walter Dennis, dwelt here. This man by Alice his firft wife, daughter of Bampfeild, had iffue Gilbert; and by Elizabeth his fecond wife, daughter of Robert Hatch, had iffue Thomas, from whom Sir Thomas Dennis defcended. Gilbert Dennis had iffue Redigond, his only daughter, that took to hufband Robert Giffard of Yeo, in which name thofe lands remained unto thefe late times. Wilmot, the only heir of that houfe, was firft married to John Bury of Collaton, and from him divorced. Secondly, unto Sir George Cary of Cockington, knight, whofe brother's fon, Sir Edward Cary, is now the lord of this land.—*Dunfland* lyeth in this parifh, the dwelling of Richard Cadiho, the 27th year of King Henry the 3d. After eight defcents in that family, Robert Cadiho, the laft that inhabited here, left thefe lands to Thomazin his daughter, wife of John Daubernon, one of whofe name, was well learned in the laws. He was warden of the ftannary, and of the fees of the dutchy of Cornwall, in King Edward the 3d's time. In the 30th year of which king's reign, he was chofen one of the knights for the fhire. From the heir of which houfe, by Philippa the daughter and heir of Humphry Batten, *Dunfland* defcended to the Arfcots. The now inheritor, Arthur Arfcot, married the daughter of Yeo of Petherwin, his father the daughter of Monk.—*Hengefcot* was the ancient inheritance of Cornu, of which place, a family that dwelt there diverfe defcents, took their name; even from Galfride de Hinfcot, in the beginning of King Henry the 3d's time, unto the reign of Queen Elizabeth. John, the fon of Triftram Hengfcot, left two daughters his heirs, Mary married to Sir Nicholas Prideaux, knight, and Elizabeth unto Pomery of Aukefdon.—*Gidcott* in this parifh, was the lands of Walter le Dennis, the fon of Sir Robert le Dennis, of Manaworthy, in the beginning of King Edward the 1ft's reign, which after fome defcents in that line, Thomazin the heir general brought to Philip Boterforde; by whofe daughter it defcended hereditarily unto Gibbs of Venton." *Rifdon.*

George Bickford, efq. is an officer in the army. In the parifh-church are feveral handfome monuments, with the coat armour of Arfcot and Bickford.*

In THORNBURY are the ruins of *Thornbury-Houfe*.† The upper part of the low tower at the parifh-church, is of cleft oak. Here are fome monuments of the family of Speccot.

In MILTON-DAMEREL are fome old ruins, fuppofed to be the feat of the Damerels.‡ The church-yard is fo full of fprings, that the water is generally dipt from the graves during the burial fervice.

ABBOTS-BICKINGTON, on the Torridge, before it joins the Ock, was once a cell to Hertland-abbey.

VOL. III.   P   BRADWORTHY

* " In memory of William Bickford of Dunfland, efq. who departed this life 3d Novemb. Ann. Dom. 1659. And alfo of Grace Bickford his wife, who was the fole daughter and heirefs of Arthur Arfcott of Dunfland, efq. who departed this life Jan. 9, 1686. Arthur Arfcott of Dunfland, efq. departed this life Oct. 18, 1664."

" Sacred to the memory of Arfcott Bickford, late of Dunfland, efq. who died Apr. 21, 1771, aged 59. Alfo of John Bickford his brother, lieut. of grenadiers of the 4th, or King's own regiment of foot, who died May 31, 1765, aged 28."

† " Walden watereth *Thornbury*, where Achard held lands, about the beginning of the Normans reign. Roger Cornutus, (for fo they then wrote) was lord of this mannor in King Henry the 2d's time, whom Nigell his fon fucceeded. Many defcents of this family followed, until the iffuelefs deceafe of William the laft, left thefe lands unto Margaret his coufin, and next heir, married into the family of the Speccots, knights, who made their chief dwelling there. It is averred by fome, that the Speccot's ancient name is Fitz-Barnard, and that they took name of their houfe fo called. Indeed from the conqueft, unto the time of King Edward the 1ft, the addition of Fitz was fo frequent with the Normans, that to avoid confufion in that kind, men were commanded to affume unto themfelves local names. And Sir Baldwin Speccot, a younger fon of Sir Richard Speccot, knight, by Maude, one of the coheirs of Sir Baldwin Belfton, relinquifhing his own name, was called Belfton after his mother, whofe part of heritage he enjoyed, with the portion of another of Belfton's coheirs, that dyed *fans* iffue, and his pofterity continued that name.—*Thorn* in this parifh, had for his ancient lord, Richard de Cadiho, which mannor, by an heir of Cadiho, came to Dabernon. An ancient freeholder of this land, called by the name of the place, was afterwards lord thereof. Sir Roger Giffard was chief lord of this mannor, the 19th of King Henry the 8th, unto whom Joan the wife of Parnacott, and Margaret Thorn, daughters of Robert Thorne, did homage for their lands in Thorn." *Rifdon*.

‡ " *Milton Damarell*; probably, anciently Mill Town, belonging to one Damarell, having at the foot of the hill, on the weft-fide of the church, a mill, at which all Milton Town, as well as all other of Earl Stanhope's tenants are by leafe bound to grind. This mill is driven by a very good trout ftream, which runs thro' the middle of the parifh; which ftream takes its name from the different parifhes thro' which it runs, and empties itfelf in the Torridge, about four miles down from the mill. The river Torridge divides this parifh on the north-eaft from Newton St. Petrock, on the eaft from Shebbear. The highway on the fouth-weft divides it from Holfworthy. The aforefaid trout ftream on the fouth-eaft divides it from Thornbury; the north-weft is bounded by a rivulet under Bickington; and the weft by another fmall rivulet adjoining Sutcombe. Length four miles, breadth in general about two. Over Torridge it maintains a moiety of two large ftone bridges, one named Woodford Bridge, of two large arches, (which ought to have been a county bridge), in the great road from Cornwall to Bideford, Torrington, Barnftaple, Molton, &c. &c. maintained jointly by this parifh and Newton St. Petrock; the other Gidcott Bridge, of two large arches, maintained by this parifh and Shebbear. Over the aforenamed trout ftream (Milton water) are three ftone bridges, one of which is called Thornbury Mill Bridge, of one arch, which divides Milton and Thornbury, and is jointly maintained by the two parifhes. The other two are maintained folely by Milton; one named Walden Bridge, of one arch, in the great road from Cornwall and Holfworthy to Bideford, Torrington, &c.; the other Milton Mill Bridge, of two arches. The parifh in general inclofed, and with hedges, except a few moors, namely, Milton Graddon, Whitbere Down, Gidcott Down, and Weft Wonford Moors. Rather an hilly fituation. The eaft-fide is well wooded with near three miles of wood, adjoining the Torridge, and belonging to different eftates, viz. Woodford, Walland Knotts Wood, Growleighs, and Gidcotts. A good public road made of common quarry ftone; private roads rather bad. On an eftate name Walland, adjoining Whitbere Down, grows a large birch tree, vifible thirty, and fome fay forty miles diftant. There are four villages, to wit, Milton Church Town, fituated in the middle of the parifh, containing eleven dwelling-houfes, with fmall eftates belonging to them of little value; in fome of thofe houfes are two poor families: About three quarters of a mile eaft is Whitbere, a village of feven dwelling-houfes of the above defcription: On the fouth-weft, rather more than a mile from the church, is Eaft Wonford, containing five dwellings: And on the weft from the church, a mile and half, is Weft Wonford, of five dwellings alfo, with fmall eftates belonging to them, as to Eaft Wonford. The village of Weft Wonford, except a fmall eftate under leafe to Thomas Allin, belonging to John Woollcombe, of Afhbury, efq. and another of Earl Stanhope's at yearly rent to Wm. Allin, belongs to Edmund John Glynn, of Glynn, in Cornwall. The lands of Eaft Wonford to Sir Wm. Molefworth and John Woollcombe, efq.; Whitbere to Henry Stephens, of Crofs, efq.; and Milton Town to Earl Stanhope. All the above houfes, and the houfes in general, have mud walls and thatched roofs. Dirworthy barton, belonging (the land) to John Tickell (lately to John Arfcott, efq. of Tetcott, deceafed), and rented by John Pedlar, is now the largeft eftate in this parifh, with a flated houfe, about a mile north-weft from the church. Gidcott, formerly an ancient chapel, now occupied by James Moore, tenant, under leafe to Sir Wm. Molefworth, (lately to above named John Arfcott, efq.) was the largeft barton in the parifh, till leafed out in fmall parcels or portions, each portion having on it a fmall houfe in proportion to its fize. All the above portions are known and called by the name of Gidcott, as in the fchedule annexed. Lord Courtenay, the patron of this and the daughter parifh, Cookbury, is lord of the manor. The Wanfords and Gidcott, (and Down belonging to Colonel Buck of Daddon), under leafe to Thomas and John May, and Crofs excepted, the forenamed Edmund John Glynn, of Glynn, in Cornwall, is high lord of the manor of Weft Wonford; Sir Wm. Molefworth of Gidcott and Crofs; and —— Harris of Hayne, efq. of Eaft Wonford. The church, fituate in the middle of the parifh, confifts of two aifles, neatly built, and of proportionable height, with a light fcreen between church and chancel: Built with ftone, and covered with flate: Rather a low tower, with three bells: Church-yard about an acre. The church is in length fixty feet, breadth thirty, height twenty-five; length of the chancel eighteen feet, fifteen broad, and twenty-three high; tower thirty-eight feet high, and twenty-one broad. In the north corner of the chancel is a neat veftry, fourteen feet by twelve, with a fire-place in it. This church is alfo furnifhed with very handfome plate, given by Walter Elford, late rector, viz. Two large flaggons of filver, very handfome; an handfome bafon for collecting the alms on facrament days; and a very large chalice. The pulpit cloth, firft given by aforefaid Elford, and fince fupplied by the parifh, is alfo handfome, with the glory on it of gold thread, inclofing the letters I.H.S. On the firft Sunday after Trinity a wake (rather revel in the country phrafe) is held at the Church Town, which day is called Revel Sunday. A good parfonage-houfe, according to the fituation of the country, irregularly built, partly with ftone and partly with mud, covered with flate, and about a mile from the church, with a walled garden. The poverty of the inhabitants caufes bad cultivation. The foil, which is in general firm, might undoubtedly be much improved by manure. Paupers, communibus annis, about thirty." From the minifter, in 1791.

BRADWORTHY (four miles long and four wide) is enclofed, but is fo deftitute of wood, that the chief fuel of the inhabitants is furze or turf.* The houfes are, in general, built of mud and ftraw, and thatched. The farms are fmall, and badly cultivated. In 1791, the inhabitants did not exceed 400. They are healthy, and live to a very advanced age. The church is fituated at one ex-tremity of the parifh; built with ftone, and covered with fhingles. The tower is a handfome ftructure.

PANCRAS-WEEK (or *Wic*) " the village of St. Pancras," was the moft ancient refidence of Dennis.† It lies high; about three miles in length, and the fame in breadth.‡

WEST-PUTFORD is fituated about fix miles below the fpring-head of the Torridge.§

* " In elder ages *Braworb*, the inheritance of William Lord Brewer, who gave lands in this manor to his abby of Torr. The refidue came to Reginald, Lord Mohun, by marriage of Alice, one of the daughters of the Lord Brewer. By a daughter of the Mohuns, it de-fcended to Lord Strange: And Lord Strange's daughter brought it to the houfe of the Stanleys, Earls of Derby.—*Hermandfworthy* was the property of Robert Flexbery, in Henry the 3d's time. In the time of Edward the 1ft it was the property of Robert de Bofco, who lived at Woode in this parifh, where, by licence of the abbot of Torr, he built a chapel. The family of Langford had alfo a manor in Bradwor-thy, which in the time of Henry the 3d was granted to Sir Gervaife de Horton, Lord of Upcot." *Rifdon.*

† " *Robertus le Dennis Dominus de Weeke Sancti Pancrafii falut. fciatis me in honorem Dei, Sancte Marie, & Sancti Pancrafii, que pertinet Ecclefie de Braworth pro falute Domine mee dediffe Abbat. de Torr Brewer unum domum fcilicet a la Burg in manerio meo de Wike Sancti Pancrafii & fex acras terre jacent. que fe extendunt in occidentale parte dicte domus & la Burg & pec. ter in parte boreali que jacet inter terram meam & la Burg——fans date——"*

‡ The river Tamar enters this parifh at the north-eaft corner, and after cutting off about a quarter of the parifh, leaves it at the fouth-weft corner. There are two bridges over the river, the one called Dexpur, the other Tamar ftone-bridge. The latter leads from Holf-worthy to Stratton, in Cornwall, and is a county bridge, confifting of two arches, built of brick. The former is no more than two large ftones laid acrofs for a church road, repaired by the parifh. The church, a daughter to Bradworthy, is fituated on a hill, in the fouth-eaft part of the parifh; it confifts of a nave, and one aifle about 40 feet long, including the chancel, and 20 feet wide; built of ftone, and co-vered with flate. The tower is a good ftrong fquare building, and contains five bells. The vicarage-houfe a miferably fmall cot, about half a mile from the church.

§ " In elder days Anfgerius held it, and guilded about thirty fhillings. Since, William de Morton, and the Carys. We find the Vigures in this parifh, whofe eftate was purchafed by Sir Nicholas Prideaux, knight, who built a good houfe on it, and left the inheri-tance to his lady, and her fon by her firft hufband, Dr. Morrice." *Rifdon.*

ARCHDEACONRY

ARCHDEACONRY OF TOTNES.

DEANRY of OKEHAMTON.

THIS deanry includes the parifhes of Okehamton, Belfton, Sampford-Court-enay, Jacobftow, Exbourne, Honichurch, Bradwoodkelly, Monk-Oke-hamton, Highamton, Hatherleigh, Inwardleigh, Afhbury, Northlew, Bewor-thy, Germanfweek, Bratton-Clovelly.*

OKEHAMTON, (on the Okement) is plentifully watered, and was formerly fur-rounded with woods. Okehamton is for nothing more remarkable than its having been once the Barony of Baldwin de Brioniis, in the days of the Con-queror. This barony was hereditary to his heirs male: And here he had his caftle, market, and park. Thus the Domefday: Baldwinus tenet de Rege Ochementon, & ibi fedet Caftellum, & habet ibi 4 Burgenfes et Mercatum. Richard Fitz-Baldwin held this honor after Baldwin, and was fheriff of Devon in the reign of Henry the 1ft; a man of the greateft revenue of any in the county. After his deceafe, the barony, for want of heirs male, defcended in another line. From this family, it came hereditarily to the Courtenays, Earls of Devon. At laft, the lands of the barony were by coheirs difperfed into divers families. And it continues to this day, fays Rifdon, the title of a Baron, con-

ferred

First Fruits.			* "Benefices remaining in charge:	Yearly Tenths.		
£.	s.	d.		£.	s.	d.
21	5	2½	Bratton Clovelly. Rep. B. Proc. vis. viiid. Syn. iis. vid. A. D, Proc. vis. viiid. r. V. 200l. - -	- 2	2	6¼
			Patr. Bifhop of Exeter.			
14	7	6	Broadwood Kelly R. Rep. B. Proc. ivs. Syn. iis. vd. A. D. Proc. vs. r. V. 80l. - - -	- 1	8	9
			Patr. Hole.			
27	11	8	Exbourne R. [St. Mary] Rep. B. Proc. vs. Syn. iis. vd. A. D. Proc. vs. r. V. 180l. - - -	- 2	15	2
			Patr. Alleyn Belfield, efq.			
20	0	0	Hatherleigh V. [St. John Baptift] Rep. B. Proc. vis. viiid. Syn. iis. vd. A. D. Proc. vis. viiid. r. V. 90l.	- 2	0	0
			Patr. George Notley, clerk.			
16	11	3	Inwardleigh R. [Ded. unc.] Rep. B. Proc. vs. Syn. iis. vd. A. D. Proc. vs.. r. V. 120l. - -	- 1	13	5
			Patr. William Moore, clerk.			
6	14	7	Monk Okehamton R. Rep. B. Proc. vis. viiid. Syn. iis. vd. A. D. Proc. ivs. r. V. 70l. - -	- 0	13	5½
			Patr. Sir Stafford Northcote, bart.			
27	8	9	Northlew R. [St. Thomas Becket] Rep. B. Proc. vis. viiid. Syn. iis. vd. A. D. Proc. vis. viiid. r. V. 140l. - 2	14	10½
			Patr. The KING.			
20	0	0	{ Okehamton V. [All Saints] with Okehamton Ch. in the Borough. Rep. B. Proc. vis. Syn. iis. vd. A. D.} { Proc. vs. r. V. 180l. - - - - - - - - - - } 2	0	0
			Patr. and V. Thomas Pearce Hockin, clerk.			
47	12	1	{ Sampford Courtenay R. [St. Andrew] with Brightleigh Chapel. Rep. B. Proc. vis. viiid. Syn. iis. vd. A. D.} { Proc. vis. viiid. r. V. 90l. - - - - - - - - - } 4	15	2½
			Patr. King's College, Cambridge.			
11	4	4½	Stow St. James alias Jacobftow R. Rep. B. Proc. vs. Syn. iis. vd. A. D. Proc. vs. r. V. 90l. -	- 1	2	5
			Patr. —— Burton, efq.			

King's Books.			*Difcharged.*	Certified Value.	
5	13	4	Afhbury R. [St. Mary] Rep. B. Proc. is. vd. A. D. Proc. is. vd. r. V. 45l. - - - -	- 37 11	0
			Patr. The KING.		
6	6	0½	Beworthy R. [St. Alban] Rep. B. Proc. vs. Syn. iis. vd. A. D. Proc. vs. r. V. 70l. - -	- 49 0	0
			Patr. Molefworth.		
8	9	4½	Highamton R. [Holy Crofs] Rep. B. Proc. vs. Syn. iiis. vd. A. D. Proc. ivs. r. V. 80l. - -	- 47 10	0
			Patr. John Woolcombe, efq.		
6	7	8½	Hony Church R. [St. James] Rep. B. Proc. iid. A. D. Proc. iid. r. V. 60l. - - - -	- 26 0	0
			Patrs. Executors of Mr. Richard Dunny.		
9	0	2½	Belfton. Rep. B. Proc. vs. Syn. iis. vd. A. D. Proc. vs. r. V. 80l. - - - - -	- 50 0	0
			Week St. German's Cur. Rep. Syn. iis. vd. A. D. Proc. iiis. ivd. - - - -	- 6 0	0
			Patr. Chapter of Briftol.		
			Okehamton Gh. in Burgo, [St. James]."		

Thes. Eccles.

ferred upon John Lord Mohun, who is defcended from one of thofe coheirs. Charles, Lord Mohun, quarrelling with the Duke of Hamilton about an eftate left by the Earl of Macclesfield, whofe niece he married, challenged him to a duel, in which he was himfelf killed, Nov. 15, 1712. He left no iffue: And fo the honor became extinct; though a principal branch of this family ftill remained in Cornwall. The Duke alfo died of his wounds.*

On the north-fide of the parifh of SAMPFORD-COURTENAY, the foil is a red loam; on the fouth, a dun-coloured clay. About two-thirds of the manor belong to King's-college; the other third to different owners.†

Of JACOBSTOW,‡ EXBOURNE,§ HONY-CHURCH, and BRADWOODKELLY,‖ I have fubjoined a few memoranda.

MONK-OKEHAMTON was a grange to Taviftock-abbey.¶

In

---

* The honor of Okehamton was held by the fervice of 93 knights.—" The park, which contains a large circuit of land, King Henry the 8th, by the perfuafion of Sir Richard Pollard, difparked and alienated." *Rifdon.*—" There are many hamlets and under tythings in this parifh. Here Richard Rifdon, an anceftor to Rifdon of Bableigh, held lands in the time of Edward the 3d. And Alford, an ancient family, held lands in this parifh. The hamlet of *Cadickbeer*, commonly *Keckbeer*, is in this parifh. It was once in the poffeffion of Wm. Littlewere; from whom, by an heir of Devyock, it defcended to Cary." *Rifdon.*—The parifh church is more than half a mile from the town, ftanding by itfelf on a hill. Here is a mean town-hall, with as mean a chapel of eafe; to which, in the reign of James the 1ft, one of the Trelawneys added a neat little tower, to give the whole a churchlike appearance.—Halftock chapel, on the manor of Halftock, (Vifcount Courtenay's) is quite demolifhed. In the time of Henry the 3d, it was called Huggleftock.

† " *Sampford-Courtenay* (fays Rifdon) was the ancient inheritance of the Courtenays, Earls of Devon, till the attainder of Henry, Marquis of Exeter, in 1538, when Henry the 8th gave it to King's-college, in Cambridge."—So faid Rifdon's authority, Sir William Pole: But the following account taken from the muniment-room of King's-college, will prove that Rifdon and Pole were miftaken.—" I fhall tranfcribe, (fays a correfpondent in 1792), the account I have lately received from the Burfar of King's-college, Cambridge, concerning the time when, and the manner how, the manor of Sampford Courtenay, together with the advowfon of the living, came into the poffeffion of the faid college:—It appears by indenture, dated 26th Dec. 12th Eliz[th]. between Philip Baker, D.D. provoft of the King"s-college of our bleffed Lady and St. Nicholas of Cambridge, and the fcholars of the fame college on the one part—and Sir Thos. Sackville, knight, Lord Buckehurft, on the other part—That the faid provoft and fcholars covenanted with Lord Buckehurft to grant to the Queen's Majefty, her heirs and fucceffors, all that their manor, called the Manor of Withiham, alias Monkon Court, in com. Suffex, and a penfion going out of the church of Withiham, and an annual rent of £.8 10s. going out of the manor of Blackenham, alias Blakeham, in com. Suffex; to the intent that the queen fhould regrant the fame to the faid Lord Buckehurft, his heirs and affigns for ever. In confideration whereof, Lord Buckehurft covenanted to convey to the queen, her heirs and fucceffors, the lordfhip or manor of Sampford Courtenay, in com. Devon, and the advowfon of the parfonage church of Sampford Courtenay aforefaid, which Sir John Paulet, knight, Lord St. John, and the Lady Winifred his wife, held for the life of the faid lady, Lord Buckehurft being entitled thereto after her death; to the intent that the queen fhould regrant the fame to the provoft and fcholars of the faid college, and their fucceffors for ever.—It appears again—by deed enrolled in chancery, dated 12th Jan. 12th Eliz. that Lord Buckehurft granted the manor of Sampford Courtenay, and the advowfon of the church there, to the queen; to the intent that fhe fhould regrant the fame to the provoft and fcholars of King's-college, and their fucceffors for ever.—It appears further—by indenture, dated 26th of Jan. 12th Eliz. that Lord Buckehurft granted to the college a yearly rent of £.28 payable out of all his manors, &c. for the life of Lady Winifred, in recompence of her life-eftate in the manor of Sampford Courtenay.—It appears laftly—that Queen Eliz. by grant, dated at Hampton-court, 4th of March, in the 12th year of her reign, granted the manor of Sampford Courtenay, and the advowfon of the church, to the provoft and fcholars of King's-college and their fucceffors, *whom God profper.*—In the parifh regifter, which commences from the firft of Eliz. 1558, there is a lift drawn up of the incumbents of the living, and one Roger Goftwyke is faid to have been the firft that King's-college prefented; but a mere catalogue of names, without any thing remarkable, you would not wifh to have. In the fame regifter it is faid, that the tower of the church was built later than the other part of it, as indeed now appears from the colour of the ftones.—In Ecton you will find it thus ftated, under the deanry of Okehamton—Sampford Courtenay, R. St. Andrew, with Brightleighe chapel. There is a chapel at a place called Stickle-path, in the road from Exeter to Falmouth, lying in the parifh of Sampford Courtenay, where divine fervice is performed twice a year; but it has never been called by that name within the memory of the oldeft perfon living; and yet, I fuppofe, that muft be the chapel meant. There is nothing faid about it in the parifh regifter."

‡ " The parfonage-houfe is covered with thatch, (as are the farm-houfes in the parifh), and is near the church. The parifh does not extend above a mile and half any way from the church. The river Okment runs thro' the parifh rapidly, on a rocky bottom, tho' the bulk of the parifh lies on a clay; the red loam ends on the glebe. The prefent lord of the manor, John Burton, efq.; the prefent rector of the parifh, George Bent, who in the year 1775 fucceeded John Benfon, D.L. who in 1758 fucceeded William Roberts, jun. who in 1741 fucceeded William Roberts his father, who in 1697 fucceeded a Mr. Turner, who in 1694 fucceeded John Lethbridge, who in 1680 fucceeded John Randalf, who in 1664 fucceeded James Lake, who in 1663 fucceeded Peter Ofborne, who in 1642 fucceeded Michael Porter, who in 1621 fucceeded Thomas Finney, who in 1617 fucceeded Richard St. Barbe, who was appointed rector of this parifh in 1598, from which period the regifter bears date." From the minifter, in 1792.

§ I take it in the ancient way of writing to be *St. Mary Ekefborne*. The parifh about two miles in length, lies rather high. An enclofed parifh, with hedges. The roads rather bad. The houfes all thatched. The parifh abounds with red land, and is in good cultivation.

‖ The name of the parifh *Broadwoodkelly*, fuppofed to be called fo from its extenfive coppices in ancient times, and from Kelly, the then patron and lord of the manor. No rivers, but only fome fmall brooks. Trees moftly oak. Roads bad. There is a fmall collection of houfes near the church, called the Church Town. The houfes are built of ftone and mud, and covered with thatch. The manor of the parifh belongs to Mr. John Cleave, an attorney, of Crediton: it formerly was the property of the Northmore family.

¶ " Its extent is not quite three miles. The church ftands at the weft-end of the parifh, near the river Okement, (which runs thro' the parifh) is ftone-built, covered with fhingle. The tower ftone-built, contains 4 bells: one of its pinnacles, a few years fince, was taken off by lightning, but it has fince been replaced. The parfonage-houfe mud walls, and covered with thatch. There are remains of a chapel about a quarter of a mile from the church. The parifh is inclofed with earth and wood fences. Both thefe parifhes appear to have once been very well wooded, which is not the prefent cafe." From the minifter.

In HIGH-HAMTON, HARTHERLEIGH,* (a large parifh, partly enclofed and partly open), INWARDLEIGH,† ASHBURY,‡ NORTHLEW, and BEWORTHY, I could difcover little to intereft or amufe.

BRATTON-CLOVELLY was anciently called Bracton.§

* " *Hatherlegh* is a market-town. This ftands on a red foil, and the mannor thereof did belong to Taviftoke-abby, who gave a great part of the wafte there, now called the Moor, unto the inhabitants of the borough, and the reft. unto Walter Medlande, and his heirs. After the furrender of religious houfes, this land was purchafed by Arfcott." *Rifdon.*—Hatherleigh is a borough, and governed by a port-reeve. The manor of Jacobftow, (called Brewford) pays 19½d. to that of Hatherleigh; and that of Norleigh, in the parifh of Inward-leigh, 9½d. There are two courts, befide the chief court, to which the aforefaid manors pay, as above. The manor of Hatherleigh, late Arfcots, now belongs to Molefworth.

† " *Inwardleigh*, vulgarly *Ingerley*, was anciently the inheritance of that no lefs ancient name of Coffin; which, in the latter end of King John's time, Henry Coffin held, whofe fon Elias Coffin held the fame, and in Weftcot after him. Their dwelling was near the church, where they had their park for deer. The very ruins of the houfe are vanifhed, time hath fo tyrannized thereon. This land con-tinued in that family unto the reign of King Edward the 3d, when it was diffevered among Diftaffs." *Rifdon.*

‡ Afhbury-houfe was lately belonging to John Morth Woollcombe, efq. whofe father, John Woollcombe, efq. was fheriff of Devon in 1751.

§ This appears from the following extract from an old deed, without date—*Sciant ... quod Ego Mabilia quondam uxor Baldw. Mallet Militis, in pura viduitate mea conceffi Thomæ de Tynworth et Luciæ uxori fuæ, Maner. meum de Bracton, in com. Devon.*—In the 23d of Edward the 3d, John de Bracton was witnefs to a deed of Adam de Smith de Stringfton, to Simon de Furneaux, of Rent in Stringfton.—" *Bratton-Clovelly*, which, with *Combe* and *Goudefcott*, Sir Hamlyn Deandon, Walter de Bathon, and Richard de Brett, held in King Henry the 3d's time. And Thomas Gonworth in King Edward the 1ft's reign, held this mannor of the grant of Mable Mallet, the widow of Sir Baldwin Mallet of Enmore, being the daughter and heir of the faid Sir Hamlyn.—*Burnby* hath been the dwelling of the Burnbeys many genera-tions; a name extracted even from the line of the Englifh Saxon nation, and continueth the inheritance of that name to this day, who are allied to worfhipful families; one of them married the daughter of Tothill, another the daughter of Pollard of Horwood." *Rifdon.*—The manor confifts of a very large barton or farm, containing upwards of 300 acres of arable, meadow, and pafture, and exceedingly well wa-tered; together with 12 other tenements. The whole being upwards of 1000 acres of arable, meadow, and pafture, all well watered, and lying contiguous to the barton, and having an extenfive royalty. Nine miles from Okehamton, 9 from Launcefton, and 11 from Taviftock.

DEANRY of TAVISTOCK.

WE are here invited to the furvey of Taviftock, Sydenham, Lamerton, Brentorr, Milton-abbot, Dunterton, Bradftone, Kelly, Maryftow, Thrufelton, Lifton, Stowford, Bradwoodwiger, Virginftow, Sourton, Brideftow, Lewtrenchard, Lidford, and Coryton.*

TAVISTOCK † lies on a bank of the river Tavy. I have vifited this town in fummer only; but never faw it, except thro' fhowers. Even in fummer, therefore,

fore,

* Benefices remaining in charge:

First Fruits. £. s. d.		Yearly Tenths. £. s. d.
32 17 11	{ Brideftowe R. [St. Bridget] with Sourton Chapel [St. Thomas Becket] Rep. B. Proc. vis. viiid. Syn. iis. vd. } { A. D. Proc. vis. viiid. r. V. 240l. - - - - - - - - } Patr. Bifhop of Exeter.	3 5 9½
8 3 4	{ Broadwood-wiger V. with Jarman's Wike Chapel. Rep. B. Proc. vis. viiid. Syn. iis. vd. A. D. Proc. vis. } { viiid. r. V. 52l. 10s. - - - - - - - - - }	0 16 4
8 13 9	Coryton R. [St. Andrew] Rep. B. Proc. iiis. Syn. iis. vd. A. D. Proc. iiis. r. V. 100l. - - - Patr. Tremayne.	0 17 4½
8 7 1	Dunterton R. [St. Peter] Rep. B. Proc. iiis. Syn. iis. vd. A. D. Proc. iiis. r. V. 80l. - - Patr. Nathaniel Noyfe, clerk.	0 16 8½
9 8 9	Kellie R. [St. Mary] Rep. B. Proc. iiis. Syn. iis. vd. A. D. Proc. iiis. r. V. 125l. - - - Patr. Kelly.	0 18 10½
13 2 1	Lamerton V. [St. Peter] Rep. B. Proc. vis. viiid. Syn. iis. vd. A. D. Proc. vis. viiid. r. V. 200l. - - Patr. Tremayne.	1 6 2½
9 13 9	Lewtrencharde R. [St. Peter] Rep. B. Proc. iiis. Syn. iis. vd. A. D. Proc. iiis. r. V. 120l. - Patr. Edward Gould, efq.	0 19 4½
15 13 9	Lidford R. [St. Petrock] Rep. B. Proc. iiis. Syn. iis. vd. A. D. Proc. iiis. - - - - Patr. The KING.	1 11 4½
31 2 11	Lifton R. [St. Mary] Rep. B. Proc. vis. viiid. Syn. iis. vd. A. D. Proc. vis. viiid. r. V. 160l. - Patr. William Arundel Harris, efq.	3 2 3½
12 16 0½	{ Mariftow V. [St. Mary] with Thrufelton Chapel [St. George] Rep. B. Proc. vis. viiid. Syn. iis. vd. A. D. } { Proc. vis. viiid. r. V. 120l. - - - - - - - - } Patr. Tremayne.	1 5 7¼
19 13 6½	{ Milton alias Milton Abbots V. [St. Conftantine] Rep. B. Proc. vis. viiid. Syn. iis. vd. A. D. Proc. vis. viiid. } { r. V. 160l. - - - - - - - - - } Patr. Duke of Bedford.	1 19 4½
10 6 8	Sydenham Damarell R. [St. Mary] Rep. B. Proc. viid. A. D. Proc. viid. r. V. 140l. - - - Patr. Tremayne.	1 0 8
11 12 6	Stowford R. [Ded. unc.] Rep. B. Proc. ivs. Syn. iis. vd. A. D. Proc. ivs. r. V. 130l. - - Patr. William Arundel Harris, efq.	1 3 3

Difcharged.

King's Books. £. s. d.		Certified Value. £. s. d.
6 7 6	Bradftone R. [St. Nun] Rep. B. Proc. iiis. Syn. iis. vd. A. D. Proc. iiis. r. V. 80l. - - Patr. Bifhop of Exeter.	49 0 0
10 17 6	Taviftoke V. [St. Euftache] Rep. B. Proc. viid. A. D. Proc. vid. r. V. 100l. - - Patr. Duke of Bedford.	11 0 0
5 6 8	Virginftow R. [St. Bridget] Rep. B. Proc. is. ivd. A. D. Proc. iis. vid. r. V. 40l. - - Patr. The KING.	30 0 0
	Brent-torr Chapel, [St. Michael]."	*Thes. Eccles.*

† " The parifh of *Taviftoke*, fo named from the town, fituated upon the river Tavy, is of great extent and irregular form. Its extreme points are faid to be about fourteen miles diftant; but it muft be obferved, that the parifh to the eaft is divided by the intervention of the parifhes of Maritavy and Petertavy, for about the fpace of a mile: Its breadth is likewife very unequal. The contents of the parifh, however, are tolerably afcertained by actual furvey. Exclufive of the houfes and gardens of the borough of Taviftock, and all the high roads, the parifh comprehends the fcite of the abby,

	Acres.	R.	P.
	172	0	33
Arable and pafture - - - - -	9,505	3	20
Coppice wood and timber - - - -	1,177	1	21
Commons - - - - -	3,122	1	38

In all 21 fquare miles and 547 acres, 3 R. 32 P. or, 13,987 3 32

It is fituated high, pleafant, and healthy, and is beautifully diverfified with hills and vales, and abounds with rivulets and fprings of excellent water. The foil is in general rich and fruitful. The river Tavy runs thro' the parifh, over which are three good bridges of freeftone, the firft of three arches, where it enters the town; fhe fecond of two, near the abby ruins; and the third at the weftern extremity of the borough, of three arches: The firft is repaired by the commiffioners of the turnpike roads, the two laft by the county. The parifh

MONUMENT OF JUDGE GLANVILLE
IN TAVISTOCK CHURCH.

Published by R.Polwhele, June 7th 1793.

Drawn and Engraved by T.Bonnor.

fore, its moorftone buildings appeared cold and damp, and its mouldering abbey-walls " breathed a browner horror." Taviftock, however, is delight-fully fituated. " Pleafant (fays William of Malmefbury) is the abbey, amidft the woods that ftand fo conveniently around it." In this parifh, an abbot of Tavi-ftock had a hunting feat at Morwell-houfe, near Morwell Down, adjoining the river Tamar. The houfe is built quite in the abbey ftile; a great part of it yet ftanding. Among the reft, is what they call the chapel; but it has more the appearance of a hall. The chapel feems to have been long ago deftroyed. The cieling of the gateway is entirely of ftone, curioufly arched, and pretty entire; over which is the porter's lodge. In a wood at a few fields diftance from the houfe, we fuddenly emerge from a gloomy path, upon a rock called *Morwell Rock*, projecting almoft perpendicularly over the Tamar, and exhibiting at once fo romantic a fcene, as in the opinion of good travelled judges is not to be equalled even in Europe. The fcene is tremendous, and yet beautiful—feveral hundred yards under our feet. There is a beautiful monument in the church of Taviftock, erected to the memory of Judge Glanville. His figure is well re-prefented in his fcarlet robes, and his countenance is fo expreffive and animated, that fpectators have been often furprifed at firft fight, fuppofing it a living per-fon. The old woman who fhewed me the monument, averred, in a manner

which

is in general enclofed with hedges of ftone, or earth, well planted. The weftern part abounds with wood: The oak is moft common. The roads are made for the moft part of a hard fpar, and are in general good. On the banks of the Tamar (which divides this parifh from Cornwall) are feveral enchanting picturefque views. That river is in Cornwall, and navigable to fhips of 200 tons, within four miles of the town of Taviftock. The Duke of Bedford hath five manors here, which comprehend almoft the whole parifh : The manor of Tavi-ftock—of Hurdwick—of Morvell—of Ogbear—of Parfwell—and Blanch Down Chafe. There are very good quarries of excellent flate in this parifh.—The town of Taviftock is fituated near the fouth extremity of the parifh, on the river Tavy, in a very fruitful vale in that part almoft triangular; it is furrounded with hills, and is in the manor of Taviftock. The houfes are built of ftone, and covered with 'flate—near the centre of the town are many very decent buildings, but in general they are old and indifferent—large ftreams of water run thro' the ftreets, and contribute to the health of the inhabitants by purifying the air. It is a borough by prefcription of very great anti-quity, and confifts of a portreeve and freeholders, having lands of inheritance, and refiding within the borough. A confiderable number of villages and farm-houfes are difperfed thro' the parifh, but none in any particular remarkable—they are in general built with ftone; the beft are covered with flate, but the reft with thatch. The farms are fmall, tho' there are a few large ones: Gardens and good orchards belong to the greater part, and they are in a very good ftate of culture.—The greater part of this parifh belongs to the Duke of Bedford, confequently the freeholders and leafeholders are not fo numerous as might be expected; but the number of rackholders is very confidera-able. The woollen is the chief manufacture of this place, in which upward of 800 perfons are employed; the other manufactures are not numerous. The day labourers are 114. The average of paupers for the laft 7 years 188—and the whole number of the inhabitants 3117. —The feats formerly inhabited by gentlemen have been purchafed by the Duke of Bedford, and belong to his grace. They do not merit defcription.—At the weft-end of the borough ftood a lazar hofpital, the chapel of which is converted into a dwelling for poor people. A grammar fchool, endowed by the Duke of Bedford, ftands in the church-yard. The abby refectory is ufed as a prefbyterian meeting-houfe; and the people, who call themfelves methodifts, have a meeting-houfe in the town.—Mr. Theophilus Edward is minifter of the prefbyterians, who are about 200.—The church is fituated near the abby ruins, where the three principal ftreets of the town meet: It is dedicated to St. Euftachius, is built of free-ftone, and covered with flate; is 113 feet long, 62½ broad, and 34 high in the clear. The altar piece is neat, and the cover of the font curious. Befides Glanville's monument, Prince mentions an honorary one to Q. Eliz. which has been long fince erafed. Another monument againft the north wall, oppofite to Glanville's, without an epitaph,—from that circumftance, the ftyle of the building, and the arms, was probably erected by their only child Mary, to the memory of Sir John Fitz of Fitz Ford, in this parifh, (who is faid to have died a violent death,) and Gertrude his wife, daughter of Sir William Courtenay of Powderham-caftle. The tower is 106 feet high, is 27 fquare, with buttreffes near the angles; is built on four arches, of excellent free-ftone, and contains eight very mufical bells. The church-yard is 189 feet long, and 187 feet broad. The charitable donations to this church and parifh have been very great; a confiderable part of which was, about 20 years ago, vefted by an act of parliament, in the late Duke of Bedford and his heirs for ever, in confideration of the fum of £.120 to be paid by them annually for ever, to truftees appointed by the faid act, who are to diftribute the money according to the direction of the faid act. Sir John Glanville, knight, fergeant at law, gave by deed, bearing date 29th March, 1749, a meffuage in Brentor (now worth £.15 15s. per ann.) to truftees, for the better maintenance of a boy at the free-fchool of Taviftock, and alfo at one of the univerfities.—Feb. 17, 1674, Nicholas Watts, late of Taviftock, mercer, deceafed, gave to certain truftees, by will, feveral tenements and houfes of confiderable value, which are all (except two) leafed for lives—the con. rent amounts to £.11 6s. 4d. and the rack rent of thefe two to £.21 5s. 7d.; in all £.32 11s. 11d.—which, with the fines on letting leafes, is to be difpofed of as directed by the faid will.—The Courtenay family, of Powderham-caftle, have likewife given an houfe to four poor widows for ever, and fettled on them and their fucceffors forty fhillings a year each. The widows are named by the family. There are feveral other houfes in the town which have been given for the ufe of the poor, which are inhabited by them, and repaired at the expence of the parifh.—Average of the regifter for the laft feven years: Baptifms 108—Marriages 28—Burials 77.—The Duke of Bedford is patron of the vicarage. The prefent incumbent is John Jago, A. M. who fucceeded Dr. Thos. Salmon, on his being confecrated Bifhop of Leighlin and Ferns in 1758—who fucceeded Mr. W. Brown, who refigned in 1748—who fucceeded Mr. Nathaniel Beard in 1730—who fucceeded Mr. Jafper Cann in 1689—who fucceeded Mr. Thos. Glanvil in 1673—who fucceeded Mr. Triftram Cleake in 1638. There is no vicarage houfe. The tythes are the property of the Duke of Bedford, and due in kind." John Jago, V. 1792.

which difcovered as ftrange a credulity as ever marked the tales of other days, that the eyes of the judge have been feveral times obferved to move; and fhe had a confufed idea of fomething ominous in the occafion of it. This monument is fallen much to decay, which Mr. Prince indeed long ago lamented.*

In SOUTH SYDENHAM † and LAMERTON are eftates of Tremayne. In Lamerton, we ftill recognize, by the fide of a fmall brook, in a retired rural fpot, the roof that gave birth to the elegant and gentle Rowe. It is a fweet fcene, that feems a picture of the poet, whofe tendernefs, like Otway's, is the tendernefs of nature.‡

About three miles N. W. of Taviftock, BRENT-TORR is to be feen. It is a rock that rifes in the midft of an elevated down, to a very great height. Upon the very top of the rock, within a few feet of the edge, on its abrupteft fide, and upon a bafe of very little more extent than the building, ftands the church

—in

---

* On three marble tables, however, thefe infcriptions are ftill legible. In the middle towards the top, this:

Honoratæ facrum Memoriæ
Johanis Glanvill, unius quondam
Jufticiariorum de communi
Banco: Qui merito factus Judex
Summo cum labore adminiftravit
Juftitiam; Juftitiâ confervavit
Pacem, Pace expectavit Mortem—
Et Morte invenit Requiem 27
Die Julii, Anno Dom. 1600.

Underneath, on one fide:

Statutum erat hoc monumentum
Anno Dom. 1615. Impenfis
Dominæ Aliciæ Godolphin viduæ
Prius Uxoris ejufdam Johanis Glanville,
Renuptæ vero Francifco Godolphin
Militi, jam etiam defuncto: Quæ
Peperit fidem Johani viro fuo 7 Liberos
Quorum nomina et connubia
Proximâ Tabulâ fuo ordine
Continentur.

Underneath, on the other:

1. Maria defuncta nupta Edwardus
Eftcourt Arm: poftea militi. 2. Francifcus
Qui duxit in uxorem Elizabetham
Filiam Willmi Crymes Ar: 3.
Dionifia nupta Thomæ Polwheile Ar:
4. Johannes, qui duxit in uxorem
Winnifredam filiam Willmi Burchier
Ar: 5. Alicia defuncta innupta
6. Johanna nupta Sampfoni
Hele Arm: 7. Thomas.

† " Sydenham hath his adjunct South of its fcite, and of fome Sidenham-Damerell from his ancient owners; in old records, Sidreham; of which mannor, John Damarell was lord, and of North-Huifh, in King Edward the 1ft's time; he alfo held Wagefen, with Tavy, in which tything, Sir Herbert Maryes was fometime feated, who married Ifabel the daughter of Tracy, of Woollacombe.—The barton of Paunfton is in this parifh, tho' many miles diftant from the church, which in elder ages was the inheritance of Pafwore, and Thomas de Paunfton held it in King Edward the 3d's time, in which name it continued unto the latter end of King Henry the 6th's reign. Now, and for divers defcents, it is the dwelling of Carwitham, ever fince John, the fon of Thomas Carwitham, took to wife, Joan, daughter of Robert Paunfton. For the tythe of which large demefne, the lord is evermore to pay yearly 14s. to the parfon; and by his ancient evidence, he and his wife, attended by a man and a maid fervant, is to hunt one week yearly, with five couple of hounds, and a white greyhound, at the parfon's houfe, upon his charge." Rifdon.

‡ In Lamerton, is Collacombe, a genteel feat a few miles diftant from Taviftock. Here live the Tremaynes, a family of Cornifh original—the firft of which upon record was Perys, lord of the manor of Tremayne near Penryn, in Cornwall; who married Opre Trefkewys, and had iffue John; who died without iffue. Secondly, Perys married Onera Trevartea, and had iffue Richard; who had iffue Thomas. Thomas married Ifabella, daughter and heirefs of Trenchard of Collacombe, efq.; in confequence of which, this family went into Devon, and fettled at Collacombe. This gentleman, by Ifabella, had iffue Nicholas, Thomas, rector of Aveton Giffard, and canon of the Cathedral Church of Exeter, and others. Ifabella furviving her hufband Thomas, was married to Sir John Damarell, knight, who gave her and her heirs by Tremain, (having none of his own), North-Huifh, Siddenham-Dammarel, and Whitchurch, and made her executrix by his will, dated Friday before the feaft of Simon and Jude, 1392. Nicholas, fon and heir of Thomas, married Joan, and had iffue Thomas, who married Elizabeth, daughter of Carew, to whom Edmund Lacye, bifhop of Exeter, granted licenfe in 1448, that per idoneos prefbyteros, they might have divine fervice celebrated in their prefence, within their manfion of Collacombe. They had iffue John; who by a daughter of Warr had iffue John; who had iffue Thomas; who by Philippa, the eldeft daughter of Roger Granville, of Stowe, efq. had iffue Roger, Edmund, Degory, and many others. Upon the death of Roger and Edmund, and their male iffue, Degory, the third fon of Thomas, fucceeded; who had iffue Arthur, that married Mary the daughter of Sir Richard Granville of Stowe; by whom he had iffue Edmund, Degory, John, Richard, Roger, Eulalia, wife of Thomas Lower of Trelafk, efq. Elizabeth, wife of Baldwin Ackland of Hawkridge, efq. with four other daughters, well married. Arthur died in 1634. Edmund Tremain of Collacombe, efq. married Bridget, the daughter of Sir John Cooper of Dorfetfhire, and had iffue John, Thomas, John, Edmund, and Arthur. The firft two died unmarried: The third married Elizabeth the daughter of John Courtenay of Molland, efq. and died without iffue before his father, who died in 1664, having fuffered much for his loyalty. Edmund, the fourth fon, dying unmarried in 1667, the eftate came to Colonel Arthur Tremain of Collacombe; who by Bridget, daughter of Nicholas Hatherleigh of Lamerton, had iffue Edmund; who by Arabella his wife, daughter and fole heirefs of Sir Edw. Wife of Siddenham, knight of the bath, and Arabella his wife, one of the daughters and heirs of Oliver Lord Saint John, had iffue Arthur, Edward Wife, Arabella, and Bridget. See Prince.—Of Nicholas and Andrew Tremain, the celebrated twins, we have feen a furprifing ftory.

—in which is infcribed, appofitely enough, from fcripture: "Upon this rock will I build my church: And the gates of hell fhall not prevail againft it."*

The parifh of MILTON-ABBOT is very beautifully diverfified by a continued feries of hill and vale.†

In DUNTERTON are fome romantic views.‡

In the parifh of KELLY,§ the Kellys have been feated for ages. Kelly is a modern-built compact houfe, fituated on a tongue of land in the midft of the

VOL. III.   R   domain,

* It has been fhrewdly faid of the inhabitants of this parifh, that they make weekly atonement for their fins: For they can never go to church without the previous penance of climbing up this fteep, which they are fo often obliged to attempt with the wearieft induftry, and in the lowlieft attitude. In windy or rainy weather, the worthy paftor himfelf is frequently obliged to humble himfelf upon all fours, preparatory to his being exalted in the pulpit.—" My parifh of Brent-Torr is very fmall, confifting only of eighteen houfes. There are no gentlemen's feats in the parifh, and the inhabitants are chiefly rackholders. The houfes are built with ftone, and in general flated. It is a perpetual curacy: Patron, the Duke of Bedford. It appears by the regifter, which goes no farther back than 1720, that Thomas Gotham was appointed to the curacy in 1731—John Tindall fucceeded him in 1736; he died in 1764, and was fucceeded by Thomas Rof-killy, who refigned it in 1771, when the prefent curate, Richard Sleeman, was appointed. There is no monument in the church, but a ftone fixed on the north wall, with the following infcription, which is tranfcribed *verbatim et literatim.*

" Heare under this Stone Lyeth the Bodie of John Cole, Junr: of Litton who departed this Life the 23^d of Novem^{br}. 1694: Ætas 22. Alfo: Johan: His Sifter who was Buried the 1^{ft} of Februa^y: 1694: Ætas 11.

If thou be ferious (Friend) perufe this Stone;
If thou be not foe: pray: let it alone.
Againft Deaths Poifon Vertues the beft Art:
When Good Men feeme to die they but depart.
Live well: then at the laft with us thoult feele
Bare dying makes not Death but dying ill."

On the fouth-fide of the church, directly oppofite the porch door, are fixed up on a little tablet thefe words—" Upon this rock will I build my church,"—which is certainly very applicable, as it is literally founded upon a rock. There is only one aifle in it. The church is covered with lead.

						Feet.	Inches.
Height of the tower	-	-	-	-	-	32	0
Ditto Pinnacles	-	-	-	-	-	1	6
Height of the church on the infide	-	-	-	13	0
Length of ditto in the clear	-	-	-	-	37	2
Breadth of ditto in ditto	-	-	-	-	14	6
Length of the church-yard	-	-	-	-	90	0
Breadth of ditto	-	-	-	-	-	60	0

The above is the meafure of the church-yard, including the ground on which the church and tower ftand, being in the middle of the church-yard." R. S. 1791.

† " The parifh of *Milton-Abbot* is fituated in the lower extremity of this county, being bounded on the fouth-weft by the river Tamar. It was originally called *Middleton-Abbot,* becaufe the church-town is nearly midway between Launcefton and Taviftock—from its connection with the abby of the latter, it received the adjunctive part of its name. It is about eight miles in length, and three in breadth. It abounds in fprings and wells of the pureft water. Of fmall ftreams there are an infinite number, every valley having one or more to re-frefh it; but there are no rivers, and confequently no bridges worthy to mention. Excepting the commons, of which there are feveral, the parifh is divided into moderately-fized inclofures. The fences are made fometimes of ftone, and fometimes of fod, according to the fituation—in both inftances they are planted. There is very little timber, and no hedge-rows; not, I conceive, fo much from any inap-titude in the foil to produce both, as from a difinclination of the farmer to fuffer them to grow, as it is notorious that trees materially in-jure all pafture grounds. After mentioning this circumftance, it is needlefs to add that we cannot boaft much of picturefque views; for tho' the furface of the country is admirably broken, and varied; yet one of the moft beautiful features in rural landfcape is ftill wanting. From this general obfervation the banks of the Tamar afford a pleafing exception, which prefent a view complete in all its parts, abound-ing in wood, water, and every natural embellifhment which the moft faftidious eye can require. The roads are in general firm and good, being made for the moft part of a hard friable fpar, which we call white-acre. The houfes in general are built of free-ftone, many of them flated, but the greater part are covered with thatch: Several of them are remarkably neat and compact—there are few, if any, with-out gardens. The farms are on the whole rather fmall, but for the moft part in a high ftate of cultivation. Thro' the greateft part of the parifh there is very little tillage, as the land is remarkable for pafture. The number of bullocks fed here annually is almoft incredible. Of orchards there are but few, which may be accounted for by the more certain return of a field of grafs, which is fubject to no blight, and the trifling demand there is for liquor in a country where the families are fmall; very few hands being required to manage a grazing eftate. The parifh particularly abounds in watered meadows; I mean fuch as are artificially floated (from the month of October to March when the operation ceafes), by ftreams of water diffufed on the furface. The value of fuch ground is very great, as it not only produces the earlieft grafs, but affords a plentiful fupply of hay, and never requires manure. The church is fituated nearly in the centre of the pa-rifh, and is dedicated to St. Conftantine. There is no date or tradition to afcertain when it was built. The walls are of free-ftone, 18 feet high—the roof of flate. The tower is 66 feet 6 inches high, exclufive of the pinnacles, which meafure 10 feet 6 inches—it is a fquare building, with a projection for the ftair-cafe, and buttreffes at the angles—it contains a mufical peal of fix bells. The church confifts of three aifles, and is 70 feet 10 inches long, and 49 feet 10 inches wide. It is a plain, decent edifice, but contains nothing worthy of par-ticular defcription. The only remaining painted glafs, is the arms of the Edgcumbe family. The church-yard is about half an acre." From the vicar, in 1792.

‡ " By Tamar's courfe, is *Dunterton* drench'd, which was the lands of Sir Roger Trelafke, knight, in King Henry the 3d's time, whom his fon Sir Andrew, fucceeded, whofe daughter and heir, was married to Mules, in King Edward the 1ft's time, who had with her one knight's fee in Aukefton and Hughton, from whence it defcended to the Lord Mules. Mariell, one of the coheirs of John, the fon of John Lord Mules, by her marriage brought this unto Sir Thomas Courtney, knight; by whofe daughter Mariell, this inheritance de-fcended to the Dynhams, and from that family to the Bourchier's, Earls of Bath." *Rifdon.*

§ " The parifh of *Kelly* is fmall, and barren of fubjects worthy of publication; however, the little information that I can collect, I fhall very readily give you. *Kelly,* its ancient fpelling, *Kelleigh,* is about two miles long, and near two miles broad, fituated high on the fide of an hill, enclofed with hedges, moderately wooded with oak trees, the roads rather indifferent, the views extenfive; towards the weft domain, which is three miles in length from north to fouth, and two and half from eaft to weft. The fituation is fine, floping every way. On its left, is a narrow valley, with a ftreamlet, on the oppofite fide of which are enclofures terminated by Ramfdown, one of the higheft hills in the country. In front, it prefents three diftances; the firft, the lawn gently finking to the vale, and fringed at the bottom with tall trees; the fecond, a gentle rifing terminated on the fummit by the tower of Bradftone church, which clofes an afcent of arable land between two hanging woods; the third, the pinnacles of the weftern mountains at a fufficient diftance to give the full effect of the aerial tint to the boundary. On the right of the houfe, is a vaft extent of well cultivated land, rendered picturefque by the winding of the Tamar, the park and plantations of Werington, and the town and caftle of Launcefton.

In MARYSTOW, is *Sydenham,* the feat of Tremayne.*

In

Bradftone church and tower, an hanging wood, and the Cornifh hills, form a fine landfcape; towards the north a well cultivated vale of fix miles, interfected by the river Tamar, extends beyond the town of Launcefton; and the antient romantic caftle of Launcefton, and the beautiful feat and park of Werington, belonging to the Duke of Northumberland, produce a pleafing fcene to the eye. Here is only one village, called Meadwell, fituated towards the eaft; the farms in general are well cultivated, and the grounds are cloathed with verdure and richnefs of herbage, not much tilled, but moftly kept for pafturage. The houfes in general thatched. Number of inhabitants about two hundred, chiefly rackholders. The air is falubrious. The church is fituated in the fouthern part of the parifh, dedicated to St. Mary, built of ftone, the roof framed with oak, and covered with flate. The church is 53 feet long, 38 broad, and 12 feet high in walls. The tower fquare, between 60 and 70 feet high, and contains fix mufical bells, lately caft. There is fome painted glafs in the church, arms of families that have intermarried with the Kelly family, and portraits not diftinguifhable on account of the fractures in the glafs. One fmall monument is erected to the memory of a former rector. The infcription, on the top, " *Hujus cancelli Parietes a fundamentis extruxit et tribus ab integro ornavit feneftris Richardus Edgcombe hujus Ecclefiæ Rector."*—Beneath on a marble tablet: " *Hic fubter Jacet prædictus Richardus Edgcumb e gente generofa de Edgcumb in Parochia de Milton Abbot, Fratrum natu tertius oriundus annos plus minus viginti & duos hujus Ecclefiæ Rector; Cujus beneficiorum diutius meminerint Succeffores grati, Cælebs obiit 9º die Jun: Anno Xii. 1724. Æt: fuæ 48. Monumentum hoc Sepulchrale fubjecerunt Fratres Quatuor et foror una Superftites."* The church-yard is 165 feet long, and 129 feet broad. This is a rectory; the name of the prefent patron, Arthur Kelly, efq. The Kelly family have been patrons for a great number of years. Incumbents: One Hill; Arthur Kelly, 1662, Peter Nicholl; 1702, Richard Edgcombe; 1725, Jofeph Hedges; 1769, John Darke, prefent incumbent. The parfonage-houfe lies on the north-eaft fide of the church, at a fmall diftance, and is an old building." From the minifter, in 1791.

* " The parifh of *Maryftow* is about three miles in length, from eaft to weft; and nearly of the fame breadth from north to fouth. Some parts of it are high, and others low. The river Lyd runs from eaft to weft through the parifh, over which are two ftone bridges, about a quarter of a mile diftant from each other, of one arch each, repaired by the county. The parifh is enclofed by hedges of earth, planted with plants of various kinds of wood, which in general thrive well, and produce a good quantity of fuel. The trees that flourifh moft are the oak and afh; that is, thefe are the forts moft propagated; but the beech, limes, poplars, fycamores, and even elms, where planted, grow remarkably well. The roads in general are rather bad, the materials of many of them being a kind of rotten flate, which foon turns to mud. The only view worth notice are the venerable woods near Sydenham. There is no town, village, or even farm-houfe of any note: moft of the houfes confift of mud-walls and thatch coverings, and make but a mean appearance. There is generally an orchard belonging to every farm, but the parifh is not remarkable either for the quantity or quality of its cyder: The farms are, for the moft part, fmall, and in no very high ftate of cultivation.—There is no trade carried on in the parifh, yet it is much burthened with poor: Almoft all the eftates are held by leafes for three lives, or for certain terms of years; and nearly all the inhabitants confift of farmers and day-labourers. The number of families are about 44 or 45. There is no wake, or any thing peculiar. There is but one gentleman's feat in the parifh, Sydenham, in the manor of the fame name: It is a venerable old manfion, built of ftone, and covered with flate, but has nothing peculiar, or remarkable in its ftructure. Its fituation is low, yet not unhealthy. Very near the houfe, on the north-fide, runs the river Lyd, and at a very little diftance beyond it, there is a noble hanging wood of large oak timber. The above-named feat belonged formerly to the honorable family of Wife; but for a century paft has been in that of Tremayne.—We have no public buildings, meeting-houfes, &c. &c. nor any diffenters in this parifh.—The church, (which ftands due eaft and weft), is fituated on an eminence, at the fouth-eaft extremity of the parifh, and is dedicated to the Virgin Mary: It is built with ftone, and covered with flate; its length within, in the clear, is 61 feet, and its breadth 27 feet: It has two ailfes, arched, and plaftered overhead, and the height from the floor to the ceiling is about 20 feet. The roof is fupported by a row of large fluted pillars, compofed of ftone. The tower is alfo built of ftone; its height is 52 feet—and its bafe, on the outfide, is 18 feet by 16. It has five tolerable good bells. At the north-eaft end of the chancel there is a fpace inclofed, of 19 feet by 12, for the cemetery of the honorable family of *Wife,* (formerly of Sydenham, as has been before obferved), wherein ftands a very handfome monument, with a Latin infcription on it, which, as well as I can make it out, (for fome of the words are pretty much defaced), is as follows: " *Hic jacet humatus Vir verè illuftris Thomas Wife de Sydenham, prænobilis Ordinis Balnei Miles, qui obiit Mortem 21 Febry. An: Dom: 1629."*—The pinnacles of the tower were thrown down by thunder and lightning on the 19th day of October, 1729, and have never been replaced; both church and tower received fo much damage by that ftorm, that the repairs were eftimated at nearly £.200.—There is a very ancient donation of an eftate of land, called Thorn, lying in this parifh, (now let for £.25 per annum, and given, as tradition fays), by one John de Thorne, for the purpofe of keeping this church in good repair. When the original grant was made, cannot now be afcertained; but, by a memorandum ftill remaining in the parifh-cheft, it can be traced back for more than 340 years. The extent of the church-yard is a little more than half an acre, inclofed by a common hedge. On the eaft-fide of the path leading up to the fouth door, and at a little diftance from the porch, ftands a tomb erected to the memory of Thomas Rofe, a former vicar of this parifh, which has the following infcription on it: " Here lieth the body of Thomas Rofe, vicar of this parifh, born at Foye, in the county of Cornwall; and buried Jan. 18th, 1696—

" Here

In LIFTON, *Whiteleigh* is an eſtate of the Harris's:* And in the pariſh-church of Lifton, there is a handſome monument to the memory of Serjeant Harris of Hayne.

STOWFORD means " the place at the ford."†

" The Ock, (ſays Riſdon) which fetcheth its fountain, from the high and hanging hills of Dartmoor, comes rumbling down the rocks, not far from SOURTON."‡

BRIDESTOW, ſignifies " the Place of the Bridge," or " St. Bridget."§

From

" Here lies a Chain of Gold,
A Pearl in Duſt;
A Stock of Roſes, which
In Heaven muſt,
Garniſh the Diſh, when
  God ſhall feaſt the Juſt.
This Flower broken, fades away;
So doth the Life of Man decay."

The oldeſt regiſter I have ſeen, belonging to this pariſh, goes no farther back than the year 1654; in which I find the baptiſm of one of Sir Edward Wiſe's children enter'd, as follows: " Thomas, the Sonne of the Honble. Sir Edward Wiſe of the noble Order of the Bath Knight, & Lady Arrabella his Wife was baptized the 13th Day of Aprill Annoq. Dom. 1667."—In the ſame regiſter is the following entry: " Arthur, the Son of Arthur Tremayne, Eſqr. (High-Sheriffe of the County) and Anne his Wife, was born the twenty-third Day of Febry. 1700, & baptized the 6th of March following." This gentleman is the preſent poſſeſſor of Sydenham, patron of the living; and proprietor of nearly all the lands in the pariſh; which came into his family, by one of his anceſtors marrying a Wife.—There is a good, neat, modern-built, vicarage-houſe, at a ſmall diſtance from the church, which fronts towards the ſouth, and is pleaſantly ſituated on the ſide of a hill, with a ſloping garden before it; it commands an agreeable, tho' not a very extenſive proſpect. It is built chiefly with ſtone, and covered with ſlate.—This pariſh is partly a rectory, and partly a vicarage; to explain which, I ſhall here give you a copy of a memorandum left by the Rev. John Teaſdale, (a former vicar), relative to the tythes of this pariſh, and alſo thoſe of Thruſelton, a daughter pariſh. " The great and ſmall tythes of all the pariſh are due in kind to the vicar, except the ſheaf on the north-ſide of the river Lyd, that runs eaſt and weſt thro' the pariſh, which belongs to Arthur Tremayne, eſq. the patron. The ſheaf alſo of the cha-pelry of Thruſelton belongs to the aforeſaid Arthur Tremayne; but all other tythes are due *there* in kind to the vicar of Maryſtow. There are no preſcriptions, cuſtoms, or modus in the pariſh, excepting two tenements at Allerford, another at Dippertown, and another called Twelve-Acres, which pay only half-ſheaf to Mr. Tremayne, and the other half to the rector of South-Sydenham; but all other tythes iſſu-ing from thence are due in kind to the vicar of Maryſtow." From the vicar in 1791.—THRUSELTON, (a daughter-pariſh to Maryſtow) is about four miles long from eaſt to weſt, and about three miles wide from north to ſouth; it is bounded on the eaſt by Brideſtow, on the weſt by Stowford, on the north by Bratton-Clovelly, and on the ſouth by Maryſtow. It is rather hilly, and the ſoil in general but coarſe. The poor are very numerous and burthenſome in both pariſhes, (in proportion to the number of inhabitants); and I have heard on good authority, that, within the laſt fifty years, the poor-rate is increaſed fifty-fold. The church, or rather *chapel*, (for ſo it is named in the preſentation and inſtitution), is ſituated on a riſing ground pretty nearly in the centre of the pariſh; ſtands due eaſt and weſt; is 46 feet long, and 29 wide in the clear, and is dedicated to St. George; built of ſtone, and covered with ſlate. The tower is about 40 feet high, and has five muſical little bells. The church-yard is about half an acre, incloſed by a common hedge. The number of families in the pariſh are about 60. There is no village, gentleman's ſeat, or even farm-houſe, worthy of note.

  * " Of *Liſton*, (now uſually *Lifton*), which ſome would have to be called *Lidſtown*, the whole hundred hath name: When Goodwin held here before the conqueſt, this was known by the name of *Lyſiſton*. Since it became the lands of Sir Galfride de Chauceaux, knight, whoſe ſon, Sir Giles, ſucceeded, who was buried in the abby of Newenham. John de Chauceaux yielded up this mannor, with the hundred, and the advowſon of the church, unto King Edward the 1ſt, the Friday next after the feaſt of the apoſtles St. Simon and Jude, the 13th year of his reign; which that king gave to Thomas Woodſtock, his ſon by his laſt wife, the King of France his daughter. From whom, by the Hollands, Earls of Kent, it deſcended to the Nevils, Earls of Weſtmorland, and was purchaſed by John Harris, ſerjeant at law, being the inheritance of John Harris his great grand-child." *Riſdon.*—" The arms of Aſhleigh, of *Aſhlegh*, were, *a pheon or.* Nicholas de Aſhlegh held Aſhlegh, in the pariſh of Lifton, 27th of Henry the 3d. After him, Sir John, his ſon; then John; then Richard Aſhlegh, ſon of John. In the 19th of Edward the 3d, Joan Tirrell poſſeſt this eſtate; probably the daughter and heireſs of Aſhlegh—ſince which time I have not met with an Aſhlegh of eminence in this county." *Prince.*

  † " Between the riverets of Lyde and Thruſhell, ſtands *Stowford*, which the Conqueror beſtowed on Anſgerius; which William de Huiſh, together with Bomlande, held in King John's time, whoſe ſon Sir William ſucceeded, and him four knights by the name of Richard. Emma, the daughter and heir of the laſt of that line, was wife of Sir Robert Trefilian, chief juſtice of England in King Richard the 2d's reign, who was attainted by parliament, and put to death, leaving his only daughter married unto John Hawly of Dartmouth, whoſe daughter was wife to John Copleſtone of Copleſtone.—In this pariſh you have *Hayne*, the long poſſeſſed place of a tribe ſo named, until Thomazin, the daughter of Walter Hayne, inveſted William Harris with that eſtate, and by her happy iſſue increaſed that family of the Harriſes, who had formerly married the daughter and heir of Stone, where their dwelling was in the time of King Henry the 6th. From whom iſſued John Harris, ſerjeant at law; the preſent poſſeſſor thereof, who married the daughter of —— Windham; ſecondly, the daughter of the Lord Mohun; his father, the heir of Davils; his grandſire, the daughter of Sir Fulk Grevill of Beauchamps-Court in Warwickſhire." *Riſdon.*—" John Harris, a younger brother of John Harris of Radford, in the pariſh of Plymſtock, married the daughter and heireſs of Stone of Stone, in this pariſh. His ſon William Harris of Stone, married Thomaſin his wife, daughter aod heireſs of Walter Hayne of Hayne. John Harris, the ſon of William Harris, and ſerjeant at law to Henry the 8th, rebuilt the houſe at Hayne, and made a commodious dwelling for himſelf and his poſterity. To his own fair inheritance, Serjeant Harris added the manor, hundred, and ad-vowſon of Lifton, adjoining to Hayne, which he purchaſed of Neville, Earl of Weſtmoreland." *Prince,* pp. 377, 378.

  ‡ " *Sourton*, in the Conqueror's time, belonged to the biſhop of this dioceſe. In this pariſh, Will. Talbot held inheritance in the time of Henry the 2d: And his lineage poſſeſt this land and North Ruſſell to the reign of Richard the 2d, about nine deſcents; when the heir general was married to Kelly of Kelly." *Riſdon.*

  § " Length three miles and half; breadth nearly the ſame. Low ſituation. A ſtone bridge at the extremity of the pariſh, of one arch; repaired by the county. There is an old ſeat belonging to the Calmady family, but now inhabited by a tenant; it is a compleat quad-rangle, tho' ſmall, and antiently built. The church ſituated at the N. E. end of the pariſh, dedicated to St. Bridget—ſtone—roof of ſlate Height of the church 40 feet—tower 70—6 bells. Length 80 feet—breadth 32. Church-yard 2 acres. Rectory—patron, Biſhop—In-

From Lew-Trenchard,* we pafs to Lidford. The greater part of the fo-reft + of Dartmoor lying in the parifh of Lidford, renders it the largeft parifh in the county, if not in the kingdom.‡

Five miles S. W. of Lidford lies Coryton; whence the Corytons of Corn-wall.§

cumbents, Coryndon Luxmoore, 1786; Thos. Heberden, 1779; Peter Burneford, 1730; Wm. Stuart, 1710; Edward Drewe, 1690; Wm. Hullen, 1669; Wm. Knapman, 1653; Edward Cotton, 1623. Parfonage-houfe modern built, in 1781, very excellent houfe, about two hundred yards from the church." From the minifter, 1791.

* " *Lew-Trenchard.* Roger de Mules, together with Wadrelefcot, held Lew in the 20th year of the Conqueror—a name that continued in honourable rank many generations : And a branch of that family remained unto our days. Sir Jn. Mules, about the conclufion of the reign of Henry the 3d, gave this land to the Trenchards. This was the moft ancient dwelling of the Trenchards in Devonfhire." *Rifdon.*— Lew-Houfe, in Lew-Trenchard, belongs to William Baring Gould, efq. to whom it was given in 1795, by his grand-mother, Margaret Gould, widow of William Drake Gould, efq. daughter of John Belfield, efq. ferjeant at law. Mr. Gould left two children, Edward, who, in 1788, died a bachelor, aged 45; and Margaret, wife of Charles Baring, efq. whofe eldeft fon, in confequence of this legacy, has taken the name of Gould.—" Orchard lies in this parifh, the lands of John Arundel in the time of Henry the 3d, which John Trelafke held in the time of Edward the 1ft. And the 19th of Edward the 3d, John Poding was lord thereof; fince whom it hath been the lands of the family of Wood." *Rifdon.*

† In *Prynne*'s Hift. (vol. iii. p. 95), we are told, that the tythe of the whole herbage of Dartmoor foreft was granted by King Edward the 1ft to the chaplain of Lidford.

‡ The large limits of this parifh, and the diftance of fome of its villages from the church, occafioned a petition from feveral of the pa-rifhioners to Walter, bifhop of Exeter, dated 13th of Sept. 1260. In this petition they reprefented the inconvenience of their attending divine fervice. In confequence of which, the bifhop ordered, with the confent of the patrons, that the inhabitants of *Balbery* and *Pufhill,* two villages on the moor, on account of their diftance from Lidford, their mother church, " being 8 miles in fair, and 15 in foul wea-ther," fhould refort to Withecombe church; and for fuch their privileges, fhould pay their tithe lambs, and three parts of their offerings, to the parfon of Withecombe, and all other tythes to their mother church.

§ " *Coryton* has given name to a family of great antiquity, now living in Cornwall, ever fince they matched the daughter and heirefs of Ferrers. This land from Geoffry de Coriton, in the time of Henry the 3d, hath continued in that name 14 defcents." *Rifdon.*—It now belongs to Tremayne.

ARCHDEACONRY

Drawn by W. Payne.

Engraved by T. Bonnor.

WARLEGH - HOUSE.

The Seat of Walt.ᵣ Radcliffe Esqᵣ. to whom this Plate is Inscribed

By his Obliged Servant. R. Polwhele.

ARCHDEACONRY OF TOTNES.

DEANRY OF TAMERTON.*

UNDER this head, we have Tamerton-foliot, (with Martinſtow-Chapel), Bereferrers, Buckland-Monachorum, Whitechurch, Petertavy, Mary-tavy, Sampford-Spiney, Walkhamton, Meavy, Sheepſtorr, Bickleigh, Eggbuckland, and Stoke-Damarel.†

The pariſh of TAMERTON-FOLIOT is hilly, with narrow vales inclining from the eaſt to the river Tavy: and ſome part of Roborough-down is within it; and hath been often the ſcite of encampments, and is a very commanding ſpot, well ſuited for the purpoſe.‡ It appears from Domeſday, that Tamerton was the king's demeſne in the time of Edward the Confeſſor. Warleigh-Houſe is ſituated in this pariſh, near the conflux of the Tavy and Tamar, and was the reſidence of Sampſon Foliot, (in King Stephen's time), who likewiſe poſſeſſed the manors of Warleigh and Tamerton. This property was never alienated till the year 1741, but paſſed by the female line from the family of Foliot to that of Gorges; from Gorges (whoſe reputed deſcendant lately ſuffered in France) to Bonvill; from Bonvill to Copleſton; from Copleſton to Bampfylde. In 1741,

* In the viſitation books of the archdeaconry of Totnes, the deanries of Tamerton and Taviſtock are put together, under the title of the deanry of Taviſtock.

† "*Benefices remaining in charge:*

Firſt Fruits. £.	s.	d.		*Yearly Tenths.* £.	s.	d.
24	1	0½	Bereferrers R. [St. Andrew] Rep. B. Proc. vis. viii*d*. Syn. iis. vi*d*. A. D. Proc. vis. viii*d*. Dean and Chapter of Exeter xxs. r. V. 300*l*. - - - - - - - - - Patr. Earl of Buckinghamſhire.	2	8	1¼
11	4	7	Bickleigh V. with Shipſtorr Ch. Rep. B. Proc. ivs. Syn. iis. v*d*. A. D. Proc. ivs. r. V. 120*l*. - -	1	2	5¼
19	8	9	Buckland Monachorum V. [Holy Trinity] Rep. B. Proc. vis. viii*d*. Syn. iis. v*d*. A. D. Proc. vis. viii*d*. r. V. 120*l*. Patr. and V. Charles Barter.	1	18	10½
8	4	8½	Eggbuckland V. Rep. B. Proc. vs. Syn. iis. v*d*. A. D. Proc. vs. r. V. 100*l*. - - - - - Patr. The KING.	0	16	5¼
17	1	8	Peters-Tavy R. [St. Peter] Rep. B. Proc. vs. Syn. iis. v*d*. A. D. Proc. vs.. r. V. 120*l*. - - - Patr. Biſhop of Exeter.	1	14	2
18	18	9	Stoke Damerell R. Rep. B. Proc. ivs. Syn. iis. v*d*. A. D. Proc. ivs. r. V. 400*l*. - - - - Patr. Sir John St. Aubyn.	1	17	10¼
14	5	7½	Tavey St. Mary R. Rep. B. Proc. vs. Syn. iis. v*d*. A. D. Proc. vs. r. V. 100*l*. - - - Patr. John Buller, eſq.	1	8	6¾
12	7	8½	Tamerton alias Tamerton Foliot, [St. Mary] with Martin-ſtow Chapel. Rep. B. Proc. vs. Syn. iis. v*d*. A. D. Proc. vs. r. V. 90*l*. - - - - - - - - - - Patr. The KING.	1	4	9¼
9	14	7	Walkhamton V. [Ded. unc.] Rep. B. Proc. vs. Syn. iis. v*d*. A. D. Proc. vs. r. V. 80*l*. - - -	0	19	5½
16	5	5	Whitechurch V. [St. Andrew] Rep. B. Proc. vis. viii*d*. Syn. iis. v*d*. A. D. Proc. vis. viii*d*. r. V. 90*l*. - Patr. Henry Pengelly, eſq.	1	12	3¼
6	0	0	Cantar. Tamerton Foliot. - - - - - - - - - - -	0	12	0
			Diſcharged.			
King's Books.				*Certified Value.*		
13	5	0	Meavy R. [St. Peter] Rep. B. Proc. vis. viii*d*. Syn. iis. v*d*. A. D. Proc. vis. r. V. 80*l*. - - - Patr. The KING.	48	0	0
			Sampford Spiny Imp. Rep. none in charge. - - - - - - - - - Patr. Dean and Canons of Windſor."	13	6	8

Thes. Eccles.

‡ The ſoil of this pariſh is chiefly a loam, on a ſtratum of ſlate, and ſome free-ſtone or dun-ſtone, and very healthy. It is beſt ſuited for corn and ſheep. Here is but little dairy land, but a conſiderable quantity of furze and wood land, owing to the high price fuel bears in Dock and Plymouth market. The extent of the pariſh, from eaſt to weſt, may be computed at about four miles, and from north to ſouth ſomewhat leſs. The pariſh church ſtands with the church-yard on a commanding knowl, ſurrounded with a verge of ſtately trees, above which the lofty well-built tower rears its head, in a very picturesque manner. The church is in dimenſion as follows: The inſide in length 67 feet in the clear; the body 17 feet 8 inches wide; the ſouth aiſle 11 feet 8 inches wide; the north aiſle 11 feet 8 inches. In the roof of this aiſle are painted the arms of Foliot, Gorges, Copleſton, with numerous others of the families they intermarried with.

Warleigh-houfe, with the manors of Warleigh and Tamerton-Foliot, with the borough of Tamerton, came by purchafe into the poffeffion of Walter Radcliffe, efq. who married Admonition Baftard, (daughter of William Baftard of Gorfton, in this county, efq.) who by the female line was lineally defcended from Gertrude Coplefton, one of the two coheireffes of John Coplefton, the laft of the male branch of Warleigh. This family of Radcliffe is a younger branch from the old ftem of the Radcliffes in Lancafhire. *Maryftow*, in this parifh, is a moft romantic place.* There is a peculiar greatnefs in the genius of the fcene. The rocks here boldly projecting, or there breaking thro' maffes of foliage, the river opening in the diftant valley, the extenfive fweep of foreft trees along the heights, and the gloom of the woods where the hills mingle with the blue horizon, have, altogether, a grandeur beyond defcription.

The parifh of BEREFERRERS is incircled with the Tamar and the Tavy.†

The manor of BUCKLAND-MONACHORUM was, in Rifdon's time, poffeft by " *Crimes* of London;" and long fince by the family of Crimes, now reduced. In this parifh, we note as moft diftinguifhed, the family of Drake, formerly; at prefent that of Elford.‡ The church at Buckland is a light elegant building. The fhafts of the pillars fupporting it, are one entire ftone, from Roborough-down.

WHITECHURCH,

* *Mariftow*, (called in the old deeds *Martinftow*), was given by William de Pin and Sibilla his daughter, who married Gilbert de Ferrers of Beer, by the name of " the chapel of St. Martin, with the fifhery and pafture, to the canons of Plymton refiding at St. Martin's," about the latter end of the 13th century. At the diffolution of monafteries, Henry the 8th, by letters patent, Ann. 1544, granted the manor of Martinftow, alias Mariftow, to Sir Philip and Arthur Champernowne; who in 1550 fold it to John Slanning of Shaugh, great grandfather to Sir Nicholas Slanning of Bickleigh, who was governor of Pendennis Caftle during the great rebellion, and afterwards flain at the fiege of Briftol. It became the feat of the family after his death; and devolved upon James Modyford Heywood, efq. by the marriage of Peter Heywood, efq. of Heywood-hall, in Lancafhire, with the daughter of Sir James Modyford, bart. and grand-daughter to the above-mentioned Sir Nicholas Slanning.

† " *Beare*, in the tax-book of England *Bire*, was beftowed by William the Conqueror on a branch budded out of the houfe of Alenfon in France, corruptly continuing the name to this day *Berealfton*, which hath privileges above fome other places of more note, in that it fendeth burgeffes to the parliament. Henry Ferrers held this honour in King Henry the 2d's time, and had his caftle here, whom many knights of that family followed. Martin Ferrers, the laft of this houfe, a principal man in the government of this fhire, was put in fpecial truft, with others, for the defence of the fea-coafts againft the invafion of the French in King Edward the 3d's time. He left iffue three daughters, from whom Sir Fulk Grevill, Copleftone of Warleigh, Bellew, and Dillon are defcended; viz. Grevill, by his anceftors the Lord Brooke and Champernon; Copleftone, by his anceftors Bonvile and Poinings of Bafing; and Dillon and Bellew by Fleming.—In this parifh lieth *Ley*, the ancient poffeffion of a family fo called, whence the name took his honour; for from hence Sir James Ley, knight, lord chief juftice of England and high treafurer, created afterward Earl of Marlburgh, was defcended: A law-giver in the chief place of juftice, and a preferver of venerable antiquity, whofe noble thoughts were fo fixed on vertue, and his difcourfes embellifhed with wifdom, and his heart with integrity, that his words did never bite, nor his actions wrong any man, to give him juft caufe of complaint." *Rifdon.*—Sir Richard Champernowne, of Modbury, had two wives—firft, Alice, daughter of Thomas Lord Aftleigh, by whom he had iffue Alexander, who fettled at Beerferrers; fecondly, Catherine, the daughter of Sir Giles Dawbeney, by whom he had iffue Richard of Modbury, and John of Infwork. This eftate came to Sir Alexander Champernowne by his match with Joan, daughter and heirefs to Martin Ferrers, the laft of this name, who was Lord of Beerferrers. His fon's daughter and heirefs, Blanch Champernowne, brought this inheritance to the noble family of Willoughby Lord Brooke.

‡ Amicia, wife of Baldwin de Rivers, Earl of Devon, daughter of Gilbert de Clare, gave this manor, with other lands and advowfons, to the foundation of a monaftery; which fhe dedicated to St. Mary and St. Benedict: Hence the adjunct Monachorum. The fcite and demefne of this abbey, at the furrender, was purchafed by Sir Rich. Greenvile, knight. Here he built a good houfe, and afterwards fold it to Sir Francis Drake, the famous navigator, who lived here. Sir Francis dying iffuelefs, left his lands to his brother Sir Thomas Drake, whofe fon Sir Francis Drake, baronet, (who married the daughter of Sir W. Strode), poffeft this place in Rifdon's time.—" The famous Sir Francis Drake left his eftates to the iffue of Mr. Thomas Drake, his younger brother; whofe pofterity yet flourifhes (fays *Prince*) in the degree of a baronet, (fo created by James the 1ft, May 16th, 1622), at Buckland Monachorum. And this hero's name furvives in the prefent Colonel Sir Francis Drake, of Buckland, baronet." *Prince.*—The family of Elford, now refident at Bickham, in this parifh, are of Cornifh extraction; it appearing by a record in the Court of Exchequer, that Robert de Elford was fheriff of that county in the 30th of Edward the 1ft, 1302. Towards the latter end of that century fome of the family fettled in the parifh of Sheepftor, in the neighbourhood of Plymouth: and the manfion-houfe of Longftone there, after having been in their poffeffion upwards of 200 years, paffed into another name about 40 years ago, on the death of the laft furvivor of the eldeft branch of the family. In the year 1517, John Elford, of Longftone, married the fole heirefs of the family of Scudamore. Roger Elford, his eldeft fon, having no male iffue, the family was continued thro' Walter the fecond; who married into the family of Langsford: whofe fon married a St. Aubyn; whofe fon Walter married a Crocker of Lyneham, by whom he had four fons and five daughters. His eldeft fon John had four wives—Elizabeth, daughter and coheirefs of Copleftone of Warleigh—Ann, daughter of Northcote of Hayne—Mary, daughter of Gale of Crediton—and Sarah, daughter of Woollocombe, of Coombe. By the firft he had four daughters, the eldeft of whom died unmarried; the fecond married a Woollocombe; and the two youngeft married refpectively, Fortefcue of London, and Fortefcue of Weare. By the third and fourth wives he had many children, moft of whom died unmarried, and all without iffue. But by Mifs Northcote, his fecond wife, he had three fons, Walter, Jonathan, and William, and two daughters; which two latter married Yonge of Puflinch, and Silly of Helligan, in Cornwall. Walter, the

WHITECHURCH, was fo called, a *colore*, Rifdon fays.*

In the centre of the parifh of PETER-TAVY, Coxton-hill commands the rich vale in which Taviftock lies, and overlooks the whole country from Plymouth-harbour—an extenfive and beautiful profpect.†

The clufter of parifhes noticed below, fcarcely require a diftinct furvey.‡

The

the eldeft fon, married Admonition, daughter of Prideaux of Padftow, by whom he had two fons and four daughters, all of whom dying without iffue, the eldeft branch of the family became extinct. Jonathan, the fecond fon, fettled at Bickham, which eftate had for fome time been in the family, and married Amy, the daughter and coheirefs of Hals of Keynedon, (whofe fifter married Sir Harry Trelawny of Trelawny, bart.) by whom he had many children. Jonathan, the eldeft, married the daughter and heirefs of Sir Thomas Neville, of Neville-Holt, in Leicefterfhire, bart. and died without iffue. All his brothers and fifters died unmarried, except Catherine, who married Ilbert of Bowringfleigh, and died without iffue. William, the youngeft fon of the before-mentioned John Elford and Ann Northcote, married a Tollard of Cornwall, (which family have fince taken the name of Trefry), by whom he had one daughter and two fons—the former died unmarried: William, the fecond, a captain in the navy, married Mifs Haviland, and left one fon, who died unmarried. John, the eldeft, married a Cramphorn, and had thirteen children. All the fons died unmarried, except Lancelot the fifth, who fucceeded to the eftate on the extinction of the other branch, and whofe eldeft fon William, the prefent poffeffor, (now Sir William, baronet), and his brother and fifter, are the furvivors of the family.—Almoft the whole parifh of Sheepftor, together with confiderable eftates in many neighbouring parifhes, were formerly poffeffed by this family, and many of them now bear its name, as Elfordleigh, Elfordtown, &c. &c. but a great part of thofe paffed to other poffeffors, before, and at the deceafe of the elder branch. There is in the neighbourhood of Longftone, a large cave, under a very high rock, into which the poffeffor had retired to avoid the adverfe party during the wars in Charles the 1ft's time; in which, during his feclufion, he amufed himfelf by making awkward fculptures and drawings, which remain to this day.

* " *Whitechurch*, the ancient inheritance of Sir Robert Giffard, whom Gervaife his fon fucceeded in King Richard the 1ft's reign. And Walter his fon, that had iffue a daughter, called Emma, wife of Sir Hugh Widworthy, knight. And fecondly, of Sir Robert Dinham, knight, that was lord of Whitechurch, the 24th of King Edward the 1ft: fince, the Tremains." *Rifdon.*—Moretown was the feat of the Morwens or Moorins, anciently *de Mora*. The fheriff of this county, in the reign of King John, whom Ifacke and others call *Morin*, is named Ralph de Mora in Sir Wm. Pole's catalogue of fheriffs. In the time of Edw. the 6th, *John Morwen*, of this family, was known as a man of learning. Moretown is now the property of John Ridout, efq.—*Halwell-boufe* in this parifh, not far from Taviftock, was the ancient dwelling of the Glanville family; having been in the name for more than 300 years, and fo continuing in *Prince's* time. At *Walreden*, flourifhed a branch of the Courtenays. *Greenofen* belongs to John Moore Knighton, efq.—In the north-wall of the chancel is en-arched, (fays Prince), a fair monument of freeftone, with coats of arms, in memory of Alice, the wife of Anthony Moorin, gent. buried in 1639, and four of his children; Gertrude, buried 1617; John, 1620; Anthony, 1627; and Mary, 1632.

† " *Peterftavie* takes its name from the faint to whom the church is dedicated and the river Tavy, which bounds it to the north-weft. Its length is three miles and half, and breadth one and half, exclufive of the barton of Sortridge; containing 138 acres, which (tho' two miles and three quarters diftant, and feparated from it by the parifh of Whitchurch), is part of this parifh. Its fituation is high, pleafant, and healthy: it abounds with rivulets and fprings of excellent water, but there are no bridges worth notice. The weftern part of the parifh is inclofed with hedges of ftone or earth well planted, and is in general well wooded with oak, afh, or fycamore: The eaftern part is open adjoining to Dartmoor. The roads are made of a friable hard fpar. The parifh is divided into two manors, Petertavy and Huntington, both belonging to the Duke of Bedford.—Wilfworthy hamlet, a part of this parifh, is fituated at the diftance of a mile and half to the north, and is three miles in length, and the fame in breadth. The greater part is open, nineteen tenements only being inclofed, which contain very good land, but very little wood. This hamlet is in the manor of Wilfworthy, the property of Arthur Tremayne, of Sydenham, efq. The houfes in general, both in the parifh and this hamlet, are built of ftone and thatched, are not remarkable for neatnefs or otherwife; have gardens, but very few orchards. The farms are in general fmall, but in good condition, the land being naturally good, and feldom tilled. In the parifh and hamlet are 47 dwelling-houfes, which contain 49 families, viz. 8 freeholders, 6 leafeholders, 20 rackholders, 10 day-labourers, 3 blackfmiths, 2 carpenters, 1 taylor, and 12 paupers, with their families. The number of inhabitants is 230. Peat is the common fuel of the inhabitants, and is dug in Dartmoor. The annual wake is on the Sunday after St. Peter's day.— Sortridge, belonging to the Pengelly family, is the only gentleman's feat in the parifh. It is built with ftone, and covered with flate, and let at a rack rent.—A chapel in Wilfworthy hamlet has been for time immemorial converted into a cow-houfe.—The church is pleafantly fituated about half a mile from the north-weft extremity of the parifh, is dedicated to St. Peter, built of ftone, and covered with flate; is 20 feet high, 59 long, 26 broad, with a crofs ifle of 12½ feet by 11½. The tower is an elegant ftructure, 17 feet fquare, with buttreffes near the angles, and finifhed above with four turrets: It is built of moor ftone, is 63½ feet high to the top of the parapet, and 16 from thence to the fummit of the pinnacles: It contains five bells. Within the communion rails, on the fouth-fide, is a neat monument, with this infcription :

In memory of the Revᵈ. Mr. Thomas Pocock
who was Rector of this Parifh near 40 Years
He was the Son of the moft Learned Dʳ. Pocock
and Dyed December yᵉ 15ᵗʰ, 1722.

The church-yard is 265½ feet by 200½: It is well planted with limes. Average of the regifter for the laft feven years: Baptifms 9—Marriages 2—Burials 7. The Bifhop of Exeter is patron of the rectory. The prefent rector is John Jago, A. M. he fucceeded the Right Rev. Dr. John Gilbert, on his tranflation from Llandaff to Salifbury in 1748—who fucceeded Mr. Thomas Pocock in 1722—who fucceeded Mr. Andrew Gove in 1686—who fucceeded Mr. Richard Evelegh.—The parfonage-houfe is about a furlong diftant from the church: It is a modern building, erected by Dr. Gilbert, when rector of this parifh." From the rector.

‡ " At *Harrowbridge*, the river *Store* ftreameth along, after it hath water'd *Sampford-Spine*, which adjunct, if the place happily had of the ftore of thorns there, fometime growing, his ancient lord left it to the land. For Robert de Spinet held it in the beginning of King Henry the 2d's time, whom Gerard fucceeded; and Walter and Herbert Spinet, to hold the fame in the reign of King Edward the 1ft. Now Sir Francis Drake, baronet, is feiz'd of lands in this tything."—*Walkhamton*, which I conceive to be the place which the Countefs Amicia gave with other lands to the abbey of Buckland, was fold after the furrender to the family of Slanning.—*Mevy-Church*, in which tything Turgis held half a hide of land; and Robert le Baftard, in the Conqueror's time. A family, fo named, fince inherited here. Sir Wm. Stroude, knight, had a manfion-houfe here, in Rifdon's time.—*Sheepftor*, the old inheritance of Herbert Combe; where Eliford (I fuppofe Elford) now enjoyeth lands; fays *Rifdon.*—*Bickleigh.* Here, the parifh-church is about three miles eaft of Tamerton-Foliot, and within a mile of the river Plym. The manor, with other lands, was given to the abbey of Buckland in 1278; and, after the furrender, was fold to the anceftors of Sir Nicholas Slanning, knight.—" John Giffard was Lord of *Egbuckland* in King Edward the 1ft's reign, together with Compton. Sir Robert Brandon held it in the 8th year of King Edward the 2d, and Joan his wife, which was Nicholas Halton's daughter and heir. The 19th of King Edward the 3d, by Margaret, daughter and heir of Robert Brandon, this land became parcel of Roger Whitleigh's poffeffions in marriage-right; which Whitleigh dwelt at *Efford* within the fame parifh, and fo it was

joined

The greater part of the parifh of STOKE-DAMEREL* belongs, at prefent, to Sir John St. Aubyn, bart. of Clowance, in Cornwall. Under the aufpices of this gentleman, *Plymouth-Dock*, in this parifh, hath fprung up into a town of elegance. Its ftreets are fpacious, and its buildings more ample and commodious than thofe of moft other towns in the weft of England.†

joined to Efford, which in fome records is written *Ebbingford*, of a paffage thro' the river Plym, by which it lieth. This Efford was the firft dwelling of an ancient family in Devonfhire, called le Baftard, planted here in the Conqueror's time; for in the 20th year of William the Conqueror's reign, Robert le Baftard had this land, Bachefton, Haroldfhore, Blacheard, Stonehoufe, Bitchford, and Mevye. Of this family were divers knights; they continued lords of this land, and inhabited here unto the time of King Edward the 3d, when Whitleigh was intitled therewith, whofe co-heirs were married to Greenvile and Halfe, to whofe portion Efford was allotted.—*Wefton*, the ancient inheritance of the Peverells of Ermington, which Sir John, the laft Peverell of that houfe, gave with Amicia his fifter unto Sir Nicholas Carew, knight, who was fhe firft of that family that dwelt in Devonfhire, having at that time Carew-caftle in Pembrokefhire, and Molesford in Berkfhire." *Rifdon.*—*Roborough Down*, in Egg-Buckland, belongs to James Modyford Heywood, efq. Widey, in that parifh, belongs to Philip Morfhead, efq. The Rev. Humfrey Julian, M. A. rector of Egg-Buckland, (a man of large fortune), married a Mifs Wife, of Kingfton. He owns, or did own lately, the manor of Kingfton.

  * *Stoke*, feparated from *Stonehoufe* by a fmall creek, bears the adjunct of the Damarells—its hereditary lords from the conqueft to Edw. the 2d. This family was connected with many diftinguifhed houfes, fuch as Woodbery, Middleton, Gidley, and North-Huifh. In the time of Edward the 1ft, John Kemyel held lands in this parifh. And in the 19th of Edward the 3d, Richard Branfcombe, whom the Britts, perhaps of Britifh origin, fucceeded. The property of the Britt family, (thro' a daughter and heir of Britt), was brought to the anceftors of the Wifes. Here Sir Thomas Wife built Mount-Wife.—In Stoke-Damerel is *Swilley*, the refidence of Furneaux.

  † The number of houfes in Dock is about 2400. Thefe were wholly erected by the inhabitants, to whom the lords of the manor granted leafes for ninety-nine years, determinable by the deaths of three lives of the builders' nomination, and fubject to a certain annual quit-rent, of probably from three fhillings to fourteen, according to the fpace of ground occupied; with a heriot, double the quit-rent, on the death of each life. The original leafes were renewable on the dropping of a life, on paying a fine to the lord of the manor, equal to about three years' value of the premifes. In the year 1791, a plan of perpetual renewal, at a fine certain, was prefented to the inhabitants by Sir John St. Aubyn; the bafis of which was, that the tenant fhould conftantly keep his premifes full lived, by nominating fome frefh perfon within a year after the dropping of any one of the then exifting lives; and paying for this privilege, a fmall addition of yearly conventionary rent, and a fine of about two years clear value of the premifes. Thefe terms, not being fo favourable as thofe held out by Lord Mount Edgcumbe for buildings at Stonehoufe, and by R. P. Carew, efq. at Torpoint, on the Cornifh fide of the Tamar, met at firft with many opponents: but latterly the inhabitants appeared fenfible of the advantages attending them; and all the houfes which by the dropping off of lives, on the original plan, came into the lord's hands, were leafed accordingly. At prefent, however, Sir John declines granting any more leafes on thefe terms, or even on the old mode of holding for three lives: the houfes which now fall into his hands, as well as the lands of the manor, are let at a yearly rent, for feven years only. The prefent annual income is confidered as amounting to about £.6000, but whenever the whole of the lands and houfes of the manor, not on perpetual renewal, fhall revert to the proprietor, little doubt can be entertained, that the rental will increafe to upwards of £.80,000 per annum.—The town of Dock, and the dockyard, are defended by ftrong fortifications. The firft act for this purpofe was paffed in the thirty-firft of George the 2d; but the works have been much improved under an act made in the twenty-firft of his prefent Majefty. On the north-eaft and fouth fides, the town is bounded by a wall about twelve feet high, called the King's interior boundary wall, which was begun to be built in the year 1787, under the direction of the Duke of Richmond: the weftern fide is fkirted by the Dock-yard and Gun-wharf. Without the wall is a line, or breaft-work, with a ditch from twelve to eighteen and twenty feet deep, excavated from the folid flate and lime-ftone rock. Thefe lines were planned by a Mr. Smelt, who belonged to the engineer department, and were begun about the year 1756. The ground lying between the King's interior boundary wall, and the front of the glacis of the lines,* includes about 195 acres, and was purchafed by government in the year 1758. This fpace is partly occupied by the governor's houfe; a handfome building, completed about the year 1795, (before which the feat of government was within the citadel at Plymouth); and fix fquares of barracks, of one ftory high only. In thefe fquares, which were begun in the year 1757, and originally intended for two battalions only, the troops garrifoning the place are lodged. In the lines are three barrier gates: the North Barrier, which leads to the new paffage acrofs the Tamar; the Stoke Barrier, leading towards Taviftock; and the Stonehoufe Barrier, conducting towards Stonehoufe, Plymouth, &c. Of the other fortifications, the principal are a battery on Mount Wife, (where the ancient feat of the *Wifes*, formerly lords of the manor, ftood); another at the Obelifk Hill, near Mount Edgcumbe; and the Redoubt and Block-houfe on Mount Pleafant, which commands the capitol of the lines.

  * Shortly after the alarm fpread through the weftern coafts by the appearance of the combined fleets of France and Spain, off Plymouth, in the year 1779, directions were given by the Ordnance Board for the repair of thefe works, which were then, from the fhallownefs of the ditch, and other caufes, incapable of much defence; and for the conftruction of other works of defence in the vicinity. The late General Dixon, then commanding engineer, not able to obtain a fufficient number of men, was powerfully affifted by Francis Baffett, efq. of Tehidy, (now Lord de Dunftanville), who brought up from Cornwall about 1000 miners, in an incredibly fhort fpace of time. By them, the works were immediately begun, and completed in the beginning of 1783.

ARCHDEACONRY

ARCHDEACONRY OF TOTNES.

DEANRY OF PLYMTON.

THE deanry of Plymton* includes Plymton-Earl, Plymton St. Mary, Plymouth, Wembury, Newton-ferrers, Revelftoke, Holberton, Yealmton, Brixton, Plymftoke, Shaugh-Prior, Cornwood, Harford, Ugborough, North-Hewifh, Ermington, Kingfton, and Modbury.†

The parifh of PLYMTON ST. MARY, is, for the moft part, enclofed with very high earth hedges, and well planted with quickfet and hazel.‡

VOL. III. T Of

* The hundred of Ermington, befides containing the parifhes of Ermington, Modbury, Ugborough, Hartford, Cornwood, Aveton-Gifford, Bigbury, Kingfton, Ringmore, Holbeton, and Newton-Ferrers, comprizes alfo the tithings of Dunftone, in the parifh of Yealmton, and Lupridge, Painfton, and Butterford, in the parifh of North Huifh.

† "*Benefices remaining in charge:*

First Fruits. £.	s.	d.		*Yearly Tenths.* £.	s.	d.
12	15	5	Charles Church V. in Plymouth [King Charles the Martyr] Rep. B. Proc. iis. vi*d*. A. D. Proc. ivs. ii*d*. r. V. 200*l*. Patrs. Mayor and Commonalty of Plymouth.	1	3	6½
33	4	7	Cornewood V. [St. Michael] Rep. B. Proc. vis. viii*d*. Syn. iis. v*d*. A. D. Proc. vis. viii*d*. r. V. 120*l*. Patr. Bifhop of Exeter.	3	6	5½
33	11	3	Ermington V. [St. Peter] Rep. B. Proc. vis. viii*d*. Syn. iiis. viii*d*. A. D. Proc. vis. viii*d*. r. V. 150*l*. Patr. The KING.	3	7	1½
24	0	0	Ermington Mediety R. [St. Peter] Rep. none in charge. r. V. 200*l*. Patr. William Cholwich, efq.	2	8	0
11	14	4½	Herford R. Rep. B. Proc. ivs. Syn. iis. iv*d*. ob. A. D. Proc. svs. r. V. 80*l*. Patr. Jofeph Williams, efq.	1	3	5½
29	18	11½	Hewifh alias North Hewifh R. Rep. B. Proc. vis. viii*d*. Syn. iiis. v*d*. A. D. Proc. ivs. r. V. 80*l*. Patr. Tremayne.	2	19	10¾
24	1	8	Holbeton V. [All Saints] Rep. B. Proc. vis. viii*d*. Syn. iis. x*d*. A. D. Proc. vis. viii*d*. r. V. 120*l*. Patr. The KING.	2	8	2
19	11	0½	Modbury V. [St. George] Rep. B. Proc. vis. viii*d*. Syn. iis. x*d*. A. D. Proc. vis. viii*d*. r. V. 160*l*. Patr. Eton College.	1	19	1¼
45	12	1	Newton-Ferrers R. [Holy Crofs] Rep. B. Proc. vis. viii*d* Syn. iis. x*d*. A. D. Proc. vis. viii*d*. r. V. 300*l*. Patr. Mr. Yonge.	4	11	2¼
25	10	10	Plymouth V. [St. Andrew] with the Chapels of Stone-Houfe, Budock, and St. Pancras. Rep. B. Proc. iis. vi*d*. A. D. Proc. ivs. ii*d*. r. V. 300*l*. Patr. Mayor and Burgeffes thereof.	2	11	1
35	19	4½	Yalmeton V. [St. Bartholomew] with Revelftoke Chapel. Rep. B. Proc. vis. viii*d*. Syn. iis. x*d*. A. D. Proc. vis. viii*d*. r. V. 100*l*. Patr. Preb. of King's Teignton, in the church of Sarum.	3	11	11¼

Difcharged.

King's Books.				*Certified Value.*		
20	0	0	Ugborough V. [Ded. unc.] Rep. B. Proc. vis. viii*d*. Syn. iis. x*d*. A. D. Proc. vis. viii*d*. r. V. 70*l*. Patr. —— Savery, efq.	24	10	6

Not in charge.

Brixton Imp. [Ded. unc.] Rep. none in charge. Patrs. Dean and Canons of Windfor.	35	15	0
Kingfton Ch. to Ermington.			
Plymton St. Maurice Imp. Rep. none in charge. Patrs. the fame.	17	0	0
Plymton St. Mary Imp. Rep. none in charge. Patrs. the fame.	39	13	4
Plymftock Imp. [St. Mary and All Saints] Rep. none in charge. Patrs. the fame.	42	0	0
Wenbury Imp. [St. Werburgh] Rep. none in charge. Patrs. the fame.	28	13	4
Shaugh Imp. [Ded. unc.] Rep. none in charge. Patrs. the fame."	25	0	0

Thes. Eccles.

‡ The parifh of Plymton St. Mary takes its name from the church, being dedicated to the Virgin Mary, and is one of the moft extenfive of any in the county, being near fix miles long from fouth-weft to north-eaft, and above five from fouth-eaft to north-weft. It is bounded on the fouth by part of Plymftock and Brixton; on the eaft by part of Brixton and Ermington; on the north by part of Cornwood; and on the weft by part of Shaugh, part of Bickleigh, and part of Eggbuckland. Some part of the north fide of the parifh is very highly fituated, and affords very fine and grand views of the fea, and many gentlemen's feats; but there is an apparent fcarcity of wood and timber, altho' there is no want of either in the valleys and lower fituations. There are three pretty large villages in the parifh, fituated

ated near the church, called Underwood, Colebrook, and Ridgway, moftly built of ftone and flated, and inhabited by labourers and poorer fort of people. The farms are in general fmall, and in a good ftate of cultivation, and moftly let to rackholders. The parifh is populous, and contains about 2000 inhabitants; it is a very healthy parifh, the people living to old age. The paupers amount comm. annis to 60, of whom about 50 are maintained and fupported in a houfe built at the parifh expence about 16 years fince, under the management of the overfeers of the poor, and conduct of a governefs, who fuperintends and provides the poor with neceffaries, and gives them their ftipulated allowance of food, which is of the beft kinds, beef, pork, peafe, oatmeal, milk, and wheaten houfehold bread. The rates amount to £.400 per annum. The poor-houfe is built on the fcite of a very ancient hofpital for the reception of Lazars, which was governed by the oldeft inhabitant according to furvivorfhip, who was for feveral generations of the name of Taverner. It had a bell and a chapel, and was endowed with an eftate to the amount of £.30 per ann. which is now in poffeffion of the parifh, and of which the income goes in aid of the poor rate. The roads thro' the parifh are in general good. The turnpike road from Plymouth to Exeter paffes for above five miles thro' it. In the weftern part of the parifh is fituated the feat of Boringdon, which gives title to the prefent owner; and has been in poffeffion of feven of the name of Parker, the firft of whom, Edmund, from North-Molton, in this county, married Frances Mayow, daughter of Jeronomy Mayow. The houfe is built of moor-ftone, but is in a ruinous ftate, and inhabited only by the farmer who rents the eftate. The park is extenfive, being about 300 acres, and fome part of it abounds with remarkably fine oak trees. The fituation is fine and bold, and commands very extenfive and beautiful views.—On the fouthern extremity of the parifh is Saltram, the refidence of the Lord Boringdon. This houfe was formerly in poffeffion of Sir James Baggs, bart. afterwards of a Walfingham, who fold it to George Parker, efq. the great grandfather of the prefent Lord Boringdon. This feat is generally efteemed one of the moft beautiful in the weft of England. The houfe ftands in a lawn of 300 acres. The plantations are extenfive and thriving. The houfe is a noble, large, fquare building, handfomely finifhed, and adorned at a very great expence; the faloon is a double cube, being 50 feet long, and 25 in breadth and height, and is faid to have coft at leaft £.10,000, including the pictures.—Newnham-Park, the feat of the Strodes, is now in poffeffion of Wm. Strode. This houfe is very handfome, and modern-built, at a fmall diftance from the old feat. It ftands in the middle of the park, which is well ftocked with deer, well wooded, and having the river Torey running thro' it, and contains about 200 acres. The views from this place are very fine and extenfive.*—Goodamoor, a very neat, compact houfe, the feat and refidence of Paul Treby Treby, efq. great grandfon of the Lord Chief Juftice Treby, is fituate on the fide of a hill, and commands a very large and extenfive view to the fouth-eaft.—Chaddlewood is a modern-built houfe, and is pleafantly fituated. This feat formerly belonged to the Snellings, and is now in the poffeffion of the executors of the late Elford Sparke, efq.—In the northern part of the parifh there are feveral large downs, the foil of which is very like that of Dartmoor, and fcarcely capable of any improvement. In the lower grounds of thefe downs or moors, and in feveral of the valleys, there are marks of ftream works for tin, and in fome places there are fhafts dug.—The parifh-church is a handfome building. The great aifle is 141 feet long, the other two 108 feet; the fouth fhort aifle 59 feet; the north fhort aifle 43 feet. In this aifle, on the fouth fide, is Sir William Strode's monument. The breadth of it is 87 feet, including the fmaller aifles. Its fituation is fo very low, that during land floods the graves are nearly filled with water. The church-yard is of the extent of four acres. The collegiate church of Windfor is now in poffeffion of the tithes of this parifh: The prefent Lord Boringdon is the leffee of them, under a leafe of 21 years, renewable at every feven, at a ftipulated fum. The tithes are worth at leaft £.700 per ann. The minifters of this parifh are but poorly provided for, there being no more, per annum, than £.39 13s. 4d. fettled on them, which probably at the time of the diffolution was equal to the amount of the fmall tithes, but is now very inadequate to the care of fo large a parifh: nor is there any houfe whatever for the refidence of the minifter.

The monument of Sir William Strode, in the church of Plymton St. Mary:

Cubiculum

Gulielmi Strode, Equitis Aurati,

et in ifto ordine tandem antiquiffimi:

Familiâ fatis clari,

Sed Religione, Integritate Morum, Confilio, Juftitiâ publicâ,

Generofa Hofpitalitate, Rebus probé et feliciter geftis,

Longe clarioris.

Qui et feptem filiarum (quinque nuptarum Equitibus) nexu jugali,

Et arctiori nexu plurium virtutum,

Devoniæ fuæ gluten, et oraculum diu fubftitit.

Is, duarum uxorum unanimi fretus confortio

Mariæ ac Dionyfiæ,

Quarum ex alterâ decem fufcepit liberos, ex alterâ fenii folamen,

Dierum et operum fatur obdormuit;

In gremio Terræ Matris,

Cum forore Vermiculâ, et ultimâ propinquitate naturæ de cumbens,

Conquerentibus amicis.

In te occidit

Spes omnis et Fortuna noftri nominis;

Donec nominis generifq difcrimen

Communi gloriâ Refurrectionis, et folius affinitate Chrifti

Evanefcat.

Occidit Junii 27. 1637. Ætat: fuæ 76.

Patri Gulielmo, Matri Mariæ, et Dionyfiæ quafi Matri,

Monumentum hoc pofuit Gulielmus Strode.

It is a handfome monument, and contains three figures—the knight, kneeling between his two wives: over that on his right hand is this infcription:

Mary, incarnate vertue, foule and fkin

Both pure, whom death, not life convinc'd of fin,

Had daughters like feaven Pleiades, but fhee

Was a prime ftar of greateft claritie.

Over the knight:

Treade foft, for if you wake this Knight alone,

You rayfe an hoaft, Religion's champion,

His country's ftaff, Right's bold diftributer,

His neighbour's guard, the poor man's almoner.

Who dies with workes about him, as did hee,

Shall rife attended moft triumphantlie.

Over

---

* The family of Strode is very ancient, and derives itfelf directly from Adam (fays Prince) who took upon him, or at leaft his anceftor did fo, the name of Strode, from his habitation fo called in the parifh of Ermington, near Modbury; it had he refided in the days of Henry the 3d. And when a number of Devonfhire gentlemen were fummoned by Edward the 1ft to attend him on his expedition into Scotland againft King Baliol, his herald returned, among others, Adam Strode of Strode, efq. as appears from the rolls in the tower. Sir W. Pole tells us, that Adam Strode was fucceeded by Roger, Richard, William, John, Reginald, who by Florence his wife, had iffue John, that married Melior the daughter and heirefs of Newnham. See *Prince*, p. 564.

Of Plymouth, we have already feen a variety of views, from its origin to its prefent ftate.*

EAST-

Over Dionyfia, on his left hand:
Dewnes hath merited no vulgar prayfe,
In that fhee well fupplied the former's dayes;
Conceave how good fhee was, whofe very worft
Unto her knight was this, that fhee died firft.

On a plain marble monument, to the memory of the late Lord Boringdon's elder brother:
*Under this monument lies interred
The body of George Parker, Eldeft Son of
John Parker, Efq^r. and the Right Honble. Lady Catherine his Wife:
he died after nine Months illnefs
on the 23^d of May, 1740,
Aged twelve Years, nine months, and fix days, to the great grief of his
Afflicted Parents.
He was educated under the care of the Mafters of Weftminfter fchool,
of which for his age he was a fhining ornament.
Few living gave proof of more amiable qualities,
& none dying ever fhew'd more refignation.

* " Between Tamer and Plym, is fituate that town fometime called *Sutton*, of its foutherly fcite, and feems to confift of two parts; for there is mention made of Sutton Prior, and Sutton Vaultort, whofe lord left this name to the one, and Plympton Priory (to which it appertain'd) an adjunct to the other. In the Saxons heptarchy, this harbour was called *Tamerworth*, (as is to be read in the life of St. Indractus,) if St. Nicholas Ifland be not meant thereby. For Weorth in Saxon, is a River-ifland: But be the Tamer (as it is) famous formerly, yet Plym hath now preheminence here, for baptizing of this bay fo far renown'd, whofe commendation Drayton fetteth forth in thefe verfes.

Plym chriftneth that town which bears her noble name;
Upon the *Britifh* coaft, what fhip yet ever came,
That not of *Plymouth* hears, where thofe brave navies lie
From cannons thund'ring flote, that all the world defy;
Which to invafive fpoil, when th' *Englifh* lift to draw,
Have check'd *Hyberia*'s pride, and kept her ftill in awe.
Oft furnifhing our dames with *India*'s rare devices,
And lent us gold and pearl, with filks and dainty fpices."   *Rifdon.*

St. Andrew's Church is a fpacious building—has a very high handfome tower at the weft end, adorned with pinnacles, and containing fix large bells. The body of the church is large and beautiful; as are, alfo, the fide aifles —*Charles's Church*, fo called from the dedication of it to the memory of Charles the 1ft, is a good building, with an handfome fpire, covered with lead. Colonel Jory gave fix good bells to Charles's church, valued at £.500.

Plymouth Old Ch.—Epitaphs:

To | the pious memory | of John Sparke Efq. | late of this Towne and Deborah his Wife Daughter | to John Rafhleighe of | Fowy Efq. | who departed this Life in expectation | of a joyfull refurrection. Hee March 17th | 1640 aged 66. She Novemb. ye 1ft, 1638 aged 57. |

A father Mother & two Daughters deere
In filent earth are fweetly lodged heere
Two full of age & two in infancye
Denote to all both olde & yong muft dye
A vertuous life they liv'd made Chriftian end
And crowns of glory now for them attend

This infcription is on a mural monument, ornamented with figures of the deceafed, and their arms—againft the N. wall of the chancel —and is the firft in order, counting weftward from the N. E. angle clofe to which it is placed.

Here lieth the Body of Judeth late | the wife of Mr. Moyfes Goodyeare—Merchant Daughter of Mr. Abraham | Jennens Merchant aged 24 yeares | who died in Childbirth of a fonne | dead-borne 21ft of October 1642 | Here is alfo interred their fonne Abraham | Goodyeare aged .... yeares who died the 30th of September 1641. |

I being deliver'd of a dead-borne fonne
My foules deliver'd & my labour donne
His Birth day wrought my death; to fweeten this
Death is to me the Birth day of my bliffe.

natalis æternitatis.

To the precious memory of that truely | vertuous gentillwoman Mrs. Mary Sparke | Daughter of Jonathan Sparke of this towne | Efq. who departed this life the xxx day | of December. Anno Domini 1665.

Life's but a fparke a weake uncertain breathe
No fooner kindled but puft out by death.
Such was my name my frame my fate yet I
Am ftill a livinge Sparke tho' thus I die
And fhine in heaven's orb a ftar moft bright
Tho' death on Earth fo foone eclipft my light.

In the church-yard (Plym. Old Ch.) is this curious infcription, on a child that was killed by a horfe:

My Parents dear, weep not for me, I pray,
The Thing by which I caught my Death, I met upon the Quay.

The tything of *Wefton Peverell* lies in the parifh of St. Andrew, Plymouth, and the chapel there, called Pennycrofs, is fubject to that church. A principal houfe in the tything is called Ham, fituated on a branch of Hamoaze. A younger fon of the ancient and refpectable family of Trelawny in Cornwall, came to Plymouth about the latter end of Queen Elizabeth, and fettled himfelf there in the mercantile way. The family foon became opulent, and made confiderable purchafes in Plymouth and the tything of Wefton Peverell. Robt. Trelawny of Ham, had a patent from Charles the 1ft, for a large allotment of land in Maffachufet's Bay, North America, which, through negligence of the family, treachery of agents, and the fubfequent independence of the colony, is in danger of being loft. This Robert Trelawny,

* This monument is placed in the chancel on the fouth-fide, in the fouth window.

EAST-STONEHOUSE, fituated on the eaft fide of the Tamar, " from a private houfe became a convenient town well inhabited," fays Prince. It was the dwelling of Joel de Stonehoufe 27th of Henry the 3d.

WEMBERY, that belonged to Plymton Priory, was purchafed, at the diffolution, by Mr. Rider, and by his grandchild fold to Sir John Hele. *Wembery-houfe*, about four miles eaft of Plymouth, was a magnificent ftru&ure.*

In NEWTON-FERRERS, the land is moftly arable, and enclofed. It is a hilly parifh, and well watered.†

In

Trelawny, and fome of his fucceffors, reprefented the borough of Plymouth in parliament for many years. And Samuel Trelawny of Ham, was member for Bofiney, in Cornwall, in the reign of Charles the 2d. The laft male heir of this eftate was Samuel Pollexfen Trelawny, who left an only child, Mary Trelawny his heirefs, now the wife of George Collins, efq. (fon of General Collins), and mother of feveral children.

* Here, the famous Sir John Hele, ferjeant at law in the reign of Elizabeth, built a noble manfion-houfe, exceeding in magnificence all other ftru&ures of the kind in Devonfhire. The expence of building it, could not be fo little, Mr. Prince fays, as £.20,000. The gate-houfe, leading into it, was fit to entertain a large and genteel family. " This houfe," to borrow Mr. Prince's words, " was a fightly feat for fhow, for receipt fpacious, for coft fumptuous, for fituation falubrious—near the fea, upon an advanced ground, with all the houfes of office under it, having a delightfome profpe& both of fea and land; round which lay a noble park, well ftocked with fallow deer, whofe refle&ion, as they were grazing, might be feen in the marble clavels, through the cafements, of the chamber chimnies. In the dining-room was a rich and curious chimney-piece, valued at no lefs than £.500, containing the reprefentation of two armies drawn up in battalion, all in polifhed marble, done after the life with fuch exa&nefs, that nothing could exceed it : The very nails in the horfe-fhoes were not omitted. From the lower gate, which ftood at a confiderable diftance, you might have feen to the upper end of the great hall—to which the afcent was by fteps, diftinguifhed into feveral uniform plats, adorned with rails and balifters. Omitting other curiofities, there might you have beheld a large and profitable pond, ftrongly walled and gated—which gate, upon the flood, opened itfelf; and the tide ftored it, in its feafon, with fea-fifh of divers forts, as bafs, mullet, foal, falmon, plaife, and the like : And the ebb would of its own accord fhut the gate upon them again, and keep them all in, for the fervice of the houfe—a very profitable as well as ingenious contrivance."— Sir John Hele married Margaret, one of the daughters and heireffes of Ellis Warwick of Batfborow, by whom he had a numerous iffue, eight fons—Sir Warwick, John who died without iffue, Sir Francis, Nicholas, Walter, Ellis, Benjamin, Thomas; and one daughter married to Sir Reginald Mohun of Hall, in Cornwall. Sir Warwick Hele of Wembury, married firft Mary, daughter of Halfe of Efford, reli& of William Hawkins of Plymouth; and fecondly, Margaret, a daughter of Sir Will. Courtenay of Powderham, and died 1625, without iffue. Sir Francis Hele, brother of Sir Warwick, married Jane, daughter of Rogers of Cannington, in Somerfet, and had iffue John, and one daughter. John married, and left iffue a daughter and heirefs, married to Sir Edw. Hungerford, knight of the bath, to whom fhe brought a vaft fortune. *Wemberry* became the purchafe of George Duke of Albemarle; whofe fon Chriftopher, Duke of Albemarle, difpofed of it to Mr. Pollexfen, an eminent merchant, and younger brother to the Lord Chief Juftice Pollexfen. Mr. Pollexfen made great alterations in the houfe, though it is faid not to its difadvantage. See *Prince.*—A few years fince was advertized, " to be fold, the fee-fimple and inheritance of the capital manfion-houfe, meffuages, bartons, farms, park, warren, and demefne lands, of *Wembury*, in the county of Devon, containing in the whole about 500 acres of fine arable, meadow, and pafture ground (exclufive of the manfion-houfe and garden, and about 50 acres of coppice wood, part of which may be fell'd every year) ; together with the manor of *Wembury*, confifting of feveral tenements, fome let at rack rent, and other parts thereof to feveral tenants on leafes for years, determinable on one, two, or three lives, under referved conventionary rents : And alfo the royalty, fifhery, and oyfterage of and in the harbour of Yealm; with the anchorage and ferry thereto belonging. All the above premifes lie contiguous, and are within the parifh of Wembury, in the faid county of Devon, about 3 miles from Plymouth, 4 from Plympton, 8 from Modbury, and 15 from Taviftoke, all confiderable market towns, at each of which feveral fairs are yearly held for cattle, &c."—Wembury houfe may be now faid to be entirely deftroyed. A few years ago the materials of the houfe, as it ftood, were fold for £.800 : every thing, therefore, that was faleable, was ftript away, even to the Portland ftone that faced the walls all around. Mr. Pollexfen added confiderably to the eaft-end of it; and fuch was its magnificence, that a few years a~o the outfide wood-work of the fafh frames had the gilding remaining ftrong upon them. After Pollexfen it came to the Molefworth family, by purchafe : the only daughter and heirefs of that family, married Mr. Pratt, a fon of Lord Camden, now Earl.—" In 1802, T. Lockyer, efq. of Plymouth, purchafed from Earl Camden, the beautiful lordfhip, royalty, and manor of Wembury, for £.26,500, befides £.1,500 for the timber growing thereon. It is a very compa&, improveable eftate, and confidered as a cheap purchafe. The profpe&s from the high-lands are uncommonly beautiful and pi&urefque." From a correfpondent.—In Wembury is *Stottefcombe.* " Here," fays Prince, " I find a family of great antiquity, named *Britte*, fuppofed to have proceeded from the Britifh race." Sir Richard Brit was a Devonfhire knight, in the time of Henry the 2d. This family had once the name of Halgwell, which they changed into Brite, from a place of this name in their poffeffion. Guy de Britte held Stottefcombe, Halgwell, Walford, and Stodden, 27th of Henry the 3d. Four generations of the name of Guy followed one another : Three more fucceeded, of whom was Ralph Britte, fheriff of Devon in the time of Edward the 3d. Whether Walter Britte, the author, in the time of Richard the 2d, was of this family or not, it may be difficult to fay. A daughter and heirefs of Britte brought this inheritance to the family of Wife of Sydenham, whofe iffue male (fays Prince) became lately extin& in that ingenious gentleman, Sir Edw. Wife, knight of the bath.—Serjeant Hele, who died on the 4th of June, 1608, in his 66th year, lies interred in the church of Wembury. Here is a noble monument, reprefenting himfelf and his children. See *Prince,* p. 401.

† " Parifh of *Newton-Ferrers*, between three and four miles from S. W. to N. E. between two and three from S. E. to N. W. The Yealm river is the north boundary, and divides it from the parifh of Yealmton ; with which it communicates by two ftone bridges, repaired by the county : Torr-bridge above, and Puflinch-bridge below ; the former confifting of two arches ; the latter, by reafon of a meadow which it croffes, has three. All the enclofures are earthen mounds, planted with quick. Oak and afh are the trees that feem moft fuited to the foil, but none worthy particular notice. Roads moderately good, of ftone, rubble, or river gravel. Towns are Newton, Higher and Lower Town, on the fouth-weft ; near the church, Bridge-end, fouth-eaft. Villages of Higher and Lower Torr, on the north. Farm-houfes of note, exclufive of thofe in the villages, are : Creber, Brownfton, and Prefton, on the north-eaft fide ; Gnaton and Collaton about the middle ; Clannacombe fouth-eaft ; Newton Downs weft ; Old Puflinch north. The parifh is divided into two manors, of Puflinch on the north, and Newton on the fouth. All the farm-houfes I have mentioned, and Newton towns, are, I believe, within the jurifdi&ion of the manor of Newton. There are only the villages of Torr and fome inconfiderable farm-houfes in the manor of Puflinch. The houfes are all built of ftone, and moftly roofed with flate, and of ancient date. Gnaton, formerly the head of the Hele family in this parifh, is now in the poffeffion of Mr. Henry Roe, who has lately rebuilt a confiderable part of it in a very neat and fubftantial manner, and inhabits it himfelf. Collaton, formerly in the poffeffion of Pomeroys, and from them to Yeos, was lately fold by Mr. Yeo to a farmer of this

parifh,

parifh, of the name of Algar: it held a confiderable rank among the houfes of this parifh, but not fuitable to the comforts of modern days: it has lately been much altered, and fitted up by the fon of the man who bought it. Brownfton, too, is inhabited by Mr. Samuel Roe, its owner; all the reft are fet to, and inhabited by different tenants at rack rents.—Old Puflinch was inhabited by the family of Uptons, or Uppetons, as fometimes fpelt, for feveral centuries, till at the beginning of this century it fell to the joint poffeffion of two daughters, Elizabeth and Mary; the latter of whom, early in this century, married James Yonge, furgeon of Plymouth, by which means, and by purchafe of the other fifter's moiety, he became poffeffed of the whole, and it has fince continued in his family. This gentleman was grandfather of the Rev. James Yonge, and was fon of James Yonge, alfo furgeon and phyfician at the fame place, by which practice he made a pretty confiderable fortune for thofe times, and whofe father appears to have had fome concerns or eftates in Ireland, and, perhaps, was originally from that country, tho' he appears to have been fettled in Plymouth in the year 1640. The above-mentioned James Yonge, on his marriage with Mary Upton, built the houfe, which is now called Puflinch: It is a large well-built brick houfe, on which was expended about 9000 or 10,000: It has been completed between fixty and feventy years. He purchafed alfo the manor of Puflinch, and the perpetuity of the rectory of Newton, of the Duke of Leeds. Puflinch-houfe ftands on the northern border of the parifh, overlooking the river, about a hundred yards to the eaftward of the old houfe, and on a rifing ground, and feems about midway from the eaft and weft extreme of the parifh. A little detached from the old houfe, ftood a chapel of confiderable fize, as a private chapel: It had been, time immemorial, ufed as an out-houfe for the farm; it was very indifferently built, and was fo much injured by a large tree falling acrofs it, that it has lately been entirely removed. In all probability a field in the midft of Puflinch eftate, and another in that of Collaton, containing about twenty acres, were appropriated to the maintenance of this fervice, one being called Parfon's Hendon, and the other Parfon's Park, far diftant from the glebe, which is in other refpects remarkably compact around the parfonage-houfe. The Heles had two feats in this parifh; Gnaton, which was the moft confiderable, and Brownfton. About the beginning of this century all the Hele eftate, in this parifh, remained with two daughters of Hele, of Gnaton, one of whom married with Lord Carmarthen, afterward Duke of Leeds; and the other with Mr. Treby, now remembered by the name of Secretary Treby, with whofe family, in the female part of it, there were intermarriages with Ourry, Hayes of Holwell, and Drew of Exeter. The Hele family, in different branches, were alfo poffeffed of Wembury, in the parifh of Wembury; Fardle and Widfham, commonly called *Wifdom*, in the parifh of Cornwood; and Fleet in Holbeton. The eftate of Hele, of Fleet, was entailed after a long fucceffion upon the family of the prefent poffeffor, John Bulteel, efq. who is faid to be one of the moft ancient families in this country, and was formerly of the neighbourhood of Taviftock. The family of the Heles, who were once fo numerous and refpectable for the high-fheriff of the county to be able to collect a grand jury out of his own family, feems now, thro' the ftrange chances and changes of this life, to be nearly extinct. The name, indeed, is ftill known among the labourers of this neighbourhood; and there is a family who are well known as clever fellows in the repair of highways, but I believe they can hardly make out their relationfhip with this numerous and wealthy family; and it is generally now faid, there is not a remainder of the family with a freehold poffeffion, except it be one of the name of Solomon Hele, of the parifh of Dipford.—The family of Holberton is alfo of one of the moft ancient in this parifh: They here lived upon and farmed their own eftate at the village of Higher Torr, in a good farm-houfe, in that kind of rank which is hereabout diftinguifhed by the appellation of gentlemen farmers. By different intermarriages and deaths, a pretty confiderable eftate is nearly centered now in one man, who is owner of one moiety of the manor of Newton; Mr. Roe, before-mentioned, holding the other. The prefent Mr. Holberton is a worthy refpectable character, and has made a confiderable improvement to his houfe, by pulling down a large part at the weft end, and raifing a good handfome ftone front, which now, tho' plain and unaffuming, makes a confiderable figure above the houfes of the village.

Family of Hele, from the regifter of Newton Ferrers:

Marriages.	*Baptized.*
1604 John Snelling, gent. & Frances Hele.	1630 Elizabeth Dr. of Sampfon Hele, gent. & Elizabeth,
12 Edward Brown & Joan Hele.	31 Jane Dr. of Sampfon and Joane Hele.
18 Thomas Ifaac, gent. & Sufan Hele.	33 Thomas Son of Sampfon and Elizabeth Hele.
23 { Hugh Brown & Judith Hele.	Arthur Son of Sampf. Hele, efq. of Gnaton, and Joane.
{ Wm. Pearfe & Sufan Hele.	64 Walter Son Walter Hele, gent. and Sufannah.
30 John Davie, efq. & Ifabel Hele.	65 Joan Dr. of do.
31 Thomas Hele, gent. & Mrs. Agnes Hele.	67 Mathew Son of do.
45 Richd. Hele, efq. & Mary Hillerfdon.	69 Elizabeth Dr. of do.
99 Daniel Sheath of Stokingham & Petronel Hele.	70 Nicholas Son of Francis Hele, gent. & Philippa.
Walter Neeld of Totnefs & Sara Hele.	72 Sarah Dr. of do.
Baptized.	75 Mathew Son of do.
1601 Sufan Dr. of Geo. Hele.	Ifabel Dr. of Walter & Sufanna Hele.
3 Bridget Dr. of Geo. Hele.	78 Sarah Dr. of do.
12 Alice Dr. of Sampfon Hele, efq. & Joane.	81 Petronel Dr. of Francis & Philippa Hele.
14 Elizabeth Dr. of do.	*Buried.*
15 Mathew Son of do.	1602 Jane Dr. of Walter Hele, efq.
18 Joane Dr. of do.	9 Walter Hele, efq.
19 John Son of do.	12 Alice Dr. of Sampfon Hele, efq.
21 Sampfon Son of do.	22 George Hele, gent.
21 Sarah Dr. of do.	23 George Son of Sampfon Hele, efq.
23 Geo. Son of Sampfon Hele, gent. & Elizabeth.	24 Sufanna Dr. of Sampfon & Joane Hele.
Walter Son of Sampfon Hele & Joane.	26 Elizabeth Dr. of Walter & Eliz. Hele.
24 Sufannah Dr. of Sampfon Hele & Joane.	32 Elizabeth Hele of Gnaton, widow.
Wilmot, of Sampfon & Eliz. Hele.	Jhane Dr. of Sampfon & Joane Hele of Gnaton.
27 Sampfon, of do.	77 Sarah Dr. of Francis Hele, gent. & Philippa.
27 Francis Son of Sampfon Hele, efq. & Joane.	94 Margery wife of Mathew Hele, gent.
29 Alfe Dr. of do.	1702 Walter Hele, gent.
30 William Son of do.	17 Philippi Hele.

John Atkyns, Rector of Newton Ferrers, was buried May 1600, in the chancel.
John Sprot, appears Rector 1600, Subdean & Canon of St. Peters, buried March 1631.
Edward Elliott, appears as Rector 1632, buried May 1644,
Daniel Morton, appears Rector in 1646,
John Hill, do.   1651,
Anthony Clifford, do.   1661, buried Jany. 1685,
Francis Hingfton, do.   1685, buried July 1725.
William Williams, do.   1725.
John Yonge, do.   1751, buried June 1767.
Richard Doidge, do.   1767, refigned   1770.
John Yonge, do.   1770, buried June 1772.
Richard Doidge, do.   1772, refigned   1774.
James Yonge, do.   1774.

About

In HOLBERTON, *Fleet* is, perhaps, the fineft fituation in Devonfhire. On a rifing ground, it commands the rich and winding vale of Erme, almoft to the fea. Great improvements * have been lately made both in the houfe and grounds. And the houfe carrying fourteen windows in front, makes a very ftriking appearance at a confiderable diftance. By an entail from Hele, Fleet came to Bulteel.†

In the parifh of YEALMTON, ‡ *Kitley* is the principal place. Rifdon calls it (in one word only) the inheritance of Pollexfen. It is now the elegant feat of John Pollexfen Baftard, efq. a gentleman to whom his country cannot be too grateful, for his fpirited and patriotic exertions in its defence. The houfe, of limeftone,

About the year 1734, the advowfon of the rectory was purchafed of the Duke of Leeds, by James Yonge, efq. of Puflinch, in the faid parifh, whofe defcendants have been patrons and incumbents from that time. The parfonage-houfe is a very ancient building, and much of it in a ruinous ftate. Formerly a large hall, upwards of thirty feet long, twenty wide, and five and twenty high, to the timber of the roof, occupied the centre part of the houfe; this has been turned into a kitchen, hall, and bed-rooms, by fome of the latter incumbents. The houfe ftands nearly on the top of a hill, and the church about 150 or 200 yards below it. The length of the middle aifle of the church, including the belfry and the chancel, is about 120 feet: The clear breadth within, taking in the north and fouth aifle, is 51 feet 6 inches. The height to the cieling of the middle aifle, is about 24 feet. The height of the tower is 72 feet 9 inches to the battlements, and the pinnacles are 14 feet above, of moorftone, cramped with iron, and terminated each by a crofs of the fame ftone." From Mr. *Yonge*, of Puflinch, in 1792.

* " Fleet-houfe (faid a tourift fome years ago), is fituated on an afcent; the front confifts of eleven windows, three ftories, baluftrades, with a heavy pediment at each end. The only objects from the houfe are Modbury and Ermington fteeples. A pretty view might be made of the river, between two hanging woods, by cutting down an orchard."

† " In this parifh is *Mothecombe*, a handfome well-built ftone houfe, built by Mr. Pollexfen about 80 years fince, and is one of the moft refpectable houfes in this country. The old dwelling is now converted to a farm-houfe, and is adjoining to the prefent manfion; tho' within a quarter of mile of fea, it is fo fnugly retired in a little valley, that you can fufpect nothing of your fituation by any thing you fee from the houfe, tho' a very pleafant walk brings to a little beach at the mouth of the Erm. This houfe and lands were purchafed by the late Warwick Calmady, a captain in the navy, who dying a few years ago, gave it to a gentleman of the name of Robinfon, who married his natural daughter. For many years paft it has been rented by different familes; Mr. John Pering's family is the fifth that I remember to have inhabited it.—At *Membland* is a well-built brick houfe, with offices on each fide, connected to the main body of the houfe by a kind of arched way. Champernon fold it to —— Stert, efq. who built the prefent houfe about the year 23. By his will, I believe, it came to his relation, Mr. Jofeph May: He fold it about the year 57, to John Bulteel, efq. who about the year 80 fold it to Peter Pering, efq. who now refides there. He entirely deftroyed the old houfe, which had been ufed as a farm-houfe, ever fince the new one had been built, and was at a confiderable expence in new modelling the grounds about it. An old woman is now living in my parifh, who has worked as a weaver, &c. at the place, in the time of all the above proprietors, and affifted in making bricks for building the houfe: She is now in her 92 year, and has conftantly worked there, by the kindnefs of Mr. Pering for her fixpence a day, till this winter, tho' fhe lives a mile from the houfe." Mr. *Yonge*.

‡ " The mannor of *Yampton* anciently appertained unto Matthew Fitz-Herbert, a noble foldier, who was one of the magnates or barons, at the making of Magna Charta; and was alfo one of thofe potent noblemen for the King, that made the accord between King John and the barons, at Running-Mead; his fon, called Herbert Fitz-Matthew, is the fourth baron that is mentioned in the roll of the parliament at Tewkfberry. Matthew Fitz-John, the laft of this family, lord of this mannor, was called a baron to the parliament in King Edward the 1ft's reign, whofe only daughter was married to Sir Ralph Mounthermer, and the inheritrix of Thomas Mounthermer, was wife unto John Mountacute, from which family this land defcended unto the Haftings, Earls of Huntingdon." *Rifdon*.—In Yealmton, the village is one of the moft beautifully fituated of any in the county, on the fide of a long falling ground, on the fouth-fide of the parifh, and overlooking the river. The manor and lordfhip of Yealmton belong to Mr. Baftard of Kitley. It is a fertile good parifh, and that fouthern part of it which is bounded by the river, and in which the village of Yealmton ftands, is remarkable for the number and fine growth of elms, which were planted by one of his anceftors, Edward Pollexfen, commonly called Counfellor Pollexfen.—" By the river's bank, (fays Rifdon) lyeth *Lynam*, the inheritance of John fo furnamed; in whofe lineage it continued unto the time of King Edward the 3d. Then Robert Topcliff, and his pofterity dwelt there, unto the days of King Edward the 4th. After that John Crocker, fon of John Crocker, of Hele, made this his manfion-place, whofe offspring have inhabited here ever fince, moft of them being called John. Amongft whom Sir John Crocker, knight, was cup-bearer to King Edward the 4th, and as an emblem of his office had a golden cup given him for his creft; who in the reign of King Henry the 7th, behaved himfelf courageoufly againft Perkin Warbeck, that imaginary Duke of York. This gentleman married the daughter of Champernon, his father the daughter and heir of Bonvile; his grandfire Servington's coheir." *Rifdon*.—" *Lineham*, a pleafant feat (fays Prince) by the fide of the Yealm, about fix miles to the S. E. of Plymouth. It was the inheritance of John Lineham, in the time of King John, in which name it continued to the reign of Edward the 3d, when Topcliffe poffeft it, and his fon after him. In the beginning of the reign of Henry the 4th, John Crocker lived at Lineham; where his pofterity have flourifhed (fays Prince) near 300 years. Crocker's Hele belonged to the Crockers; and Crockern-well was, we are told, the primitive inheritance of Crocker. And Crockern-Torr, poffibly, derived its name from this family. Courtenay Crocker, efq. fon of John, by his wife, fifter to Sir Courtenay Pole of Shute, bart. married firft the daughter and coheir of Richard Hillard, fon of Membland, efq. by whom he had iffue one daughter; fecondly, he married Sarah, daughter and coheir of John Tucker of Exeter, gentleman." *Prince*.—I apprehend this eftate paffed from Crocker to Bulteel, by an intermarriage. The laft poffeffor was Courtenay Bulteel, efq. and on his death it came to the poffeffion of his uncle, John Bulteel, of Fleet, whofe fecond fon now inhabits it. It is a handfome, well-built, fquare houfe, raifed with feveral others of this neighbourhood, about the beginning of this century: It is, I believe, built of brick within, and faced with moor-ftone. The old houfe and out-offices ftill remain, and ferve for a farm-houfe and other out-offices. A good deal has been lately done in improving the grounds about it: The park has been deftroyed, and one made at Fleet in lieu of it.—" *Bowden*, in this parifh of Yampton, was the dwelling and original of a family fo named; whofe daughter Bafilia brought the fame unto Richard Collande, her hufband: From which name, by an heir of Stone, that had married Matilde, the inheritrix of Lawtram, thefe poffeffions were tranfplanted into the name of Copleftone; a branch budded forth from the houfe of the great Copleftones, and hath been there dwelling divers defcents." *Rifdon*.—Bowden was bought, I believe, by the late Mr. Baftard of Kitley—now only a farm-houfe, tho' both the name of Copleftone, and the prefent appearances, fpeak its former days to have been much more honorable.

Drawn by W. Payne.

Engraved by J. Bonnor.

FLEET HOUSE.

The Seat of John Bulteel Esq.

to whom this Plate is Inscribed

By his Obliged

Servant R. Polwhele.

Published by R. Polwhele, June 1st 1796.

Painted by S. Garvey, R.A.

Engraved by I. Bonner.

K I T L E Y.

The Seat of John Pollexfen Bastard Esq.ʳ to whom this Plate is Inscribed

By his Obliged Servant, R.ᵈ Polwhele.

Published by P. Polwhele April 1.ˢᵗ 1793.

limeftone, has three fronts, eleven windows in each, and confifts of three ftories and garrets. It is agreeably fituated near an arm of the fea.

In BRIXTON, *Coffleet* ftands on a height; but has no profpect, from the intervention of another hill directly in front of it.*

PLYMSTOCK is a fmall parifh, lying on the eaft-fide of the Plym, near the mouth of the river; oppofite the town of Plymouth. Orefton, in this parifh, is a large village, containing about 100 houfes, chiefly the property of the Duke of Bedford.†

In CORNWOOD,‡ *Blachford*, the feat of Rogers, baronet, well merits particular attention. Its fituation is rather too low, and water too near the houfe; but its extenfive lawn, and the groupes of trees, have a pleafing effect. *South-hele*, and *Choldich* or *Cholwich*, were the ancient feats of the Heles and the Cholwiches.§ The church is near the centre of the habitable part of the parifh, on a gentle afcent from every quarter. ‖

The famous Dr. John Prideaux, Bifhop of Worcefter, who was a native of *Stowford*, in the parifh of HARFORD, erected in the fouth-wall a monument to the memory of his parents. ¶

UGBOROUGH

* " *Coffleet* (fays a correfpondent) the feat of Thomas Lane, efq. feems to ftand within the limits of this parifh, tho' I believe it properly belongs to Yealmton. It was formerly inhabited by Mr. Stert, a clergyman, and on his going to decay was bought between thirty and forty years fince by Mr. Veale, an attorney of Plymouth, who, on his death, gave it to his nephew, the prefent inhabitant."

† The Childes, of Plymftock, were an ancient family—the laft of whom, in the time of Edward the 3d, is faid to have directed in his will, " that wherever he fhould happen to be buried, to that church fhould his lands belong."

‡ The parifh of *Cornwood*, in the hundred of Ermington, extends in length, from north to fouth, about feven miles; its greateft breadth is about three miles. It is bounded on the fouth by the parifh of Ermington; on the fouth-weft by Plymton St. Mary; on the weft by Shaugh; on the north it joins the foreft of Dartmoor, which is part of the parifh of Lydford; on the eaft it is bounded by the river Erme, and the parifh of Harford; on the fouth-eaft it touches the parifh of Ugborough in a point, the bridge called Ivy-bridge having its four corners in four different parifhes. Cornwood is divided into two parts, nearly equal, by the river Yealm. The northern part of Cornwood is rough and uncultivated, abounding with peat-mofs and rocks of granite. The fouthern part is diverfified by paftures, meadows, hills, and dales, *corn*-fields and *woods*; and, probably, from the two laft articles takes its name. Indeed there is reafon to believe that the whole parifh (except the bleak fummits of the hills) was formerly a wood.

§ " *South-Hele.* John de la Hele lived here in the reign of Henry the 3d; and William de la Hele his fon, 2d of Edward the 1ft. William Hele of South-Hele, (fays Weftcote) had iffue five fons, John, Hugh, Nicholas, Baldwin, and William. Of the laft two I find nothing. John, the eldeft, had iffue Walter Hele of South-Hele, whofe pofterity refides there. Hugh, the fecond fon of William, had iffue Thomas Hele, whofe feat in this parifh was called *Wifdom.* John Hele, efq. having no iffue, fold it, with other demefnes, to Sir John Rogers, of Plymouth, baronet. Nicholas, the third fon of William Hele of South-Hele, had two wives, and iffue by both His firft wife was the daughter of Walter Woodley of Tedburn St. Mary; by whom he had iffue, firft, William, fecondly John; from whom defcended the Heles of Holwel, near Kingfbridge. His fecond wife was Margery, daughter of Richard Down of Holfworthy. By her he had iffue five fons—firft, Thomas, from whom defcended the Heles of Fleet, near Modbury; fecondly, Hugh, from whom came Hele, of Newton-Ferrers, of which family was John Hele, efq. reader of the Inner Temple, in the time of James the 1ft; thirdly, Walter, whence were the Heles of Brixton, of whom the famous Elizæus Hele, who gave his eftate to pious ufes, fhould be gratefully remembered; fourthly, Sir John Hele, ferjeant at law, in the time of Elizabeth, who was the founder of the houfe at Wembury; fifthly, William, without iffue.—*Choldich.* William Cholditch of Cholditch, efq. married, in Prince's time, Frances, the eldeft fifter of Colonel Sebaftian Ifaac.

‖ " It is a regular neat building, and contains a few monuments: Of thefe, the moft ancient, without any infcription, is in the fouth chancel; and (as appears from fome remains of the arms and from tradition) belongs to the family of Cole. They were once poffeffors of Slade, a confiderable eftate and antient manfion. From them it came to the Saverys, and is now the property of John S. Pode, efq. Near to this is the monument of a child, whofe mother was the laft of the family of Drake, of Ivy-bridge: She was married firft to Hele of Wifdom (or Widefham), afterwards to Savery, by whom fhe had this child, and afterwards to —— Saffure. There is alfo in the chancel, a marble tomb, placed over " the Body of the Lady Jane Rolle, daughter of John Fortefcue, efq. and wife, firft of Richard Hals, afterwards of Sir Henry Rolle, knight. She died June 9th, 1634, aged 82."—In the middle chancel (which is the property of the vicar) is a monument of the Bellmaines, who owned the manor of Cornwood and the antient manfion (now in ruins) of Delamore. From the Bellmaines this property came to the Maynards, who fold it to George Treby, efq. (fon of Lord Chief Juftice Treby), and is now the property of Benjamin Hays, efq. who married one of his daughters and coheireffes.—The north chancel belongs to the barton of Fardle, formerly the refidence of Sir Walter Raleigh; fince that of the Heles; and now the property of Sir Robert Palk.—In the body of the church are feveral neat monuments belonging to the family of Sir Frederick Leman Rogers, who has a large eftate in this parifh, purchafed chiefly from the Heles. Another monument is erected to " Benjamin Burell, a captain in the army of Charles the 1ft, who died Mar. 16, 1715." And another to the laft of the name of Fortefcue, that owned Hangher, who died Jan. 3d, 1770.—In this parifh alfo is Cholwich, the original feat of the family of that name; and Hele, the origin of the Heles.—Befides the parifh church, another place of worfhip has lately been erected at Ivy-bridge, for the convenience of the inhabitants of that pleafant flourifhing village.—The fheaf of this parifh belongs to the prieft-vicars of Exeter cathedral. The vicarage (endowed with the fmall tithes, including every thing except corn), is in the patronage of the Bifhop of Exeter." From the late vicar.

¶ See *Prince*, p. 513.—The firft place the river Arme embraceth, is *Harford*, which long fince belonged to the Peverells of Ermington. After which family, it was the inheritance of John, baron of Torrington, who was lord both of Eaft and Weft Harford; fince Hugh de Harfton held the fame; of latter times the Coles; which mannor confifteth moft of freeholders.—*Stowford* in this parifh, was fometime

the

UGBOROUGH adjoins to Modbury, a parifh remarkable for its combes—as Fowelfcombe, Bolterfcombe, Smithfcombe, Spridlefcombe, Bawcombe.*

In NORTH-HEWISH, † the only feats of note are *Butterford* and *Blackhall*. Butterford was built by Preftwood. It was confiderably improved by its late poffeffor,

the poffeffion of Matthew of Ivy-bridge, whofe daughter Margaret, married to William Dymock, brought it unto three of Dymock's fons fucceffively, all which died without iffue. By means whereof, the Lord Bonvile by a deed in taile got this land; which upon the attainder of the Duke of Suffolk, came to the crown; and was bought by Adam Williams, anceftor of Thomas Williams, a man of rare gifts, and excellently learned in the laws, and fpeaker of the parliament in the reign of Queen Elizabeth, whofe grand-child Thomas, by his fon John, lately enjoyed this land. Here by the river's courfe is crown'd with a bridge, whofe chiefeft tapeftry is ivy, whereof it took name, and gave it again to the ancient inhabitants thereof, a place that admits a great thorow-fair; which lands Sir Hugh Peverell, Lord of Ermington, gave unto Alfred de Ponte Hedera, and Sir John Peverell confirmed his father's grant in Edward the 1ft's age. This Alfred had iffue Matthew de Ivy-bridge, whofe daughter Ifabel was wife of William Dymock, all whofe iffue, both by this wife, and by his fecond the daughter and heir of Ralph le Roufe of Little Modbury, died iffuelefs. By means whereof, by an entail wherein the Lord Bonvile was in remainder, this with all Dymock's other lands came unto him; and he gave it unto John Bonvile his natural fon, which he had by Elizabeth Kerkby." *Rifdon.*

* " It appears by the regifter, that the word *Ugborough* hath been fpelt as at this day, ever fince the year 1535. Not the leaft hint whence deriv'd. The mean breadth of the parifh is about 5 miles from eaft to weft, and its length 9 miles from north to fouth. The fituation is high, and confequently the rivers fmall, and eafily croffed by bridges of one arch, which are moftly built of moor-ftone, or flate. The fields are inclofed by hedges, which are banks of earth five or fix feet thick at the bottom, and about three feet over on the top; five feet high, and fortified with fuch fhrubs and plants as will moft quickly form a fence. The turnpike roads thro' Totnes and Afhburton, from Exeter to Plymouth, meet in this parifh; and thefe, with the reft, are duely and regularly repaired with excellent materials, commonly found near or on the fpot.—There are in the whole parifh 82 cotts, moftly in a woeful plight; 2 mills, 5 public and 74 farm-houfes (in all 81) of which about a fcore or fo are tolerably neat and compact; the reft make but a paltry figure. The dwellings are generally flated; the out houfes thatcht. Paupers between 60 and 70. Farms fome large, fome fmall, as everywhere: All in high cultivation, or the rackholder could not live. Manufactures none. Inhabitants in what they call the Church-town, upwards of 400, thro' the parifh between 5 and 600, in all about 1000; and of thefe not one diffenter.—About a mile S. E. of the church, lies Fowels-coomb, the ancient feat of the Fowels, of whom Sir Edmund had children John, Margaret, and Elizabeth. John married and fettled at Wafhburton, in the parifh of Afhprinton (now Lord Boringdon's); and dying before his father, left a fon, named alfo John, whom his grandfather feems to have made tenant for life, fettling the lands on his iffue, and in default thereof on his two daughters in joint-tenancy, and died in the year 1674. In the year 1676, Sir John, the laft male of the family, alfo died, and without iffue, and was buried in the north wing of Ugborough church, his family vault. His two aunts being married, Margaret to —— Champernown of Dartington, efq. and Elizabeth to —— Parker of Boringdon, efq. agreed to a partition, on which this, the principal feat, fell to the lot of Margaret, the eldeft fifter; from whom (dying in March 1729) it defcended to her fon Henry, who fold it to —— Herbert, efq. and he to Mr. Th. King, who is daily improving both the venerable manfion, and its valuable appurtenances. Half an hour's pleafant walk brings us hence to Marridge: This was once a religious houfe, of what order I can't fay. The regifter, for feveral generations, reprefents it as the feat of the Stears, or Steurs. It hath been rebuilt by (the Taylors) the family now in poffeffion, and under the eye of the prefent occupier is become a moft commodious and elegant habitation.—The church is fituated a little to the S. W. of the middle of the parifh; uncertain to what faint dedicated. It was probably built in the reign of Edward the 1ft, when Plympton Abbey was founded, of which it feems to have been a principal member. The walls are moor-ftone, and the roof is covered with flate. The height of the tower is about 100 feet to the battlements; and at each angle it is adorned with a well-proportioned pinnacle, 12 feet higher. It is exactly fquare, a very regular, and beautiful ftructure, and furnifhed with a ring or peal of fix bells. Dimenfions of the church, viz. Weft-wall of the tower (thick) 6 feet; belfry (fquare) 21 feet; nave or mid-aifle 135 feet; eaft-wall of the chancel 3 or 4 feet. Whole length 165 feet. Length of north and fouth aifles 124 feet. Breadth of ch. 42 feet; of mid-aifle 18 feet; of north and fouth aifles 12 feet each. North and fouth wings 16 by 11 feet each. Height of ch. upwards of 30 feet. Church-yard out of all proportion to either the ch. or parifh, fmall.—Vicarage forfooth, endowed with a ftipend of £.20 per ann. for doing the duty of a (church) living worth £.1000 per ann. The houfe old, perhaps as the church, the poor remains of once-ftately, and fpacious buildings, preferved as a fhelter (good-enough) for the curate. Patrons the worfhipful the Grocers' Company, London. No modus or peculiarity as to the compofition for tythes." From the vicar in 1792.

† " John de Albamara was lord of the manor of *North-Hewifh* in Richard the 1ft's reign; many of that name fucceeded him. It defcended by an heir of Trenchard to Tremain, aud is the lands of that family.—In this parifh is *Norreys*, the lands of Laurence de Norreys long fince, which continued in that name to the reign of King Edward the 3d. Then William Norreys had iffue by a daughter of Roger Colaton, a daughter married to Sir John Fortefcue of Shepham, captain of Meaux, by whom fhe had Henry Fortefcue of Wood, Sir John Fortefcue, chief juftice and lord chancellor of England, and Richard Fortefcue, from whom are iffued the Fortefcues in the eaft-part of England. This land now belongs to Francis Fortefcue of Wood, defcended from Henry aforefaid.—*Boterford* was the dwelling of Philip Boterford in King Edward the 1ft's reign; in which line, when this land had remained divers defcents by the heir-general of that tribe, Gibbs was invefted therewith. And William Gibbs of Fenton fold the fame to *Thomas Preftwood* of Exon, that deriveth his defcent from a family in Worcefterfhire, and is allied to ancient houfes in this county." *Rifdon.*—" The parifh of *North-Hewifh* is about three miles long, and not two in breadth. It is well inclofed, and in general of an high fituation. Through it runs the river Aune, over which is a county-bridge of two arches. This river, together with the neighbouring woods, hills, and well-cultivated lands, interfperfed with cottages, farm-houfes, &c. forms a variety of picturefque and diverfified views.—*Butterford*, fifty years ago, was in poffeffion of the Preftwoods: fince which time, to the year 1788, it belonged to William Strode, efq. and his fon Richard, deceafed. This feat and extenfive eftate was purchafed about three years fince by its prefent poffeffor, Thomas Palk, efq. nephew to Sir Robert Palk, bart. of Haldown-houfe, in this county. The family of the Strodes is very ancient and honourable, having flourifhed at leaft 500 years, and having been remarkable for its public fervices and reputable connections. Of this we may fee a long account in Prince's Worthies.—It is but juftice to the memory of the late poffeffor of Butterford, Richard Strode, efq. who died in the laft year, to fay, that his good character, as a private gentleman, was of the moft diftinguifhed eminence. In him we faw happily blended, moft of thofe qualities which can adorn humanity. Whether we confider his perfonal, chriftian, or focial virtues, we fhall be equally at a lofs which moft to admire. The univerfal refpect fhown him when alive, and the general and unaffected grief caufed by his untimely death, is a fufficient teftimony that this panegyric by no means exceeds the bounds of ftricteft truth.—The prefent *Blackhall* was built by William Fowell, who married a daughter of Sir Thos. Glanville of Taviftocke. Fowellfcombe, the original feat of the Fowells, was loft to the family in about the year 1695, for want of male iffue in Sir John Fowell, who left two daughters, one of whom was married to George Parker, efq. of Boringdon; and the other to —— Champernoune, efq. who had the houfe and part of the eftate. The family divided fometime before the year 1600, when the younger branch fettled in North-Hewifh, and built the prefent Blackhall. This feat is chiefly a modern, handfome building, fituated in a very eligible fituation. This modern part has been entirely added, and the grounds without greatly improved by the prefent poffeffor, John Fowell, efq. This gentleman was an officer in the army, and ferved in the war before the laft in Germany. He married Mifs Mary Digby, a lady of a

moft

poffeffor, Richard Strode, efq. and fince elegantly completed by its prefent proprietor, Thomas Palk, efq. The pleafure-grounds are now laid out with
VOL. III.   X   ftriking

moft refpectable family in Lincolnfhire. His family is mentioned under, though not in any regular order. The principal houfe in the
parifh of Diptford is Crabaton, formerly the feat of the Newtons; but now belongs to the Fowells: John Fowell, efq. of Blackhall, in
1729, marrying Elizabeth, fole heirefs of John Newton, efq. the laft poffeffor.—Regifter of the principal families.

Baptifms of the Preftwoods.

1677, May 29. Frances, daughter of George Preftwood, efq. and Mary his wife.
Sept. 3. Elizabeth, daughter of George Preftwood, efq.
1679. Julian, daughter of George Preftwood, November 26.
1696. Elizabeth, daughter of Thomas Preftwood, and Honora his wife, April 20
1698, Nov. 6. Mary, daughter of Thomas Preftwood and Honora.
1699, Jan. 4. Julian, daughter of Thomas Preftwood and Honora.
1702, Sept. 6. George, fon of George Preftwood and Joan his wife.
1711, June 22. Mary Anne, daughter of Thomas Preftwood, efq. and Anne.
1712, Oct. 24. Judith, daughter of Thomas Preftwood, efq. and Anne.

Marriages of the Preftwoods.

1691. Wm. Huckmore, efq. and Mary Preftwood, daughter of George Preftwood, efq.
1703. Mr. Ambrofe Rhodes of Modbury, and Mrs. Elizabeth Preftwood, Jan. 20.
1729. Mr. Humphrey Jutfham and Mrs. Mary Preftwood, Dec. 31.
1732. Mr. William Moore and Mrs. Judith Preftwood, Dec. 21.
1739. Mr. Evans Cove and Mrs. Catharine Preftwood, May 28.
June 13. Mr. John Lufcombe and Mrs. Elizabeth Preftwood.

Burials of the Preftwoods.

1676. Thomas Preftwood, efq. January 13.
1682. George Preftwood, March 22.
Sept. 25. Mary, wife of George Preftwood, efq.
1701. George Preftwood, fon of Thomas Preftwood, gent. Feb. 5.
1703. George Preftwood, efq. July 16.
1707. Honor, wife of Thomas Preftwood, efq. Feb. 3.
1708. John Preftwood, June 30.
1735. Mrs. Honor Preftwood, April 12.
June 20. Thomas Preftwood, efq.

===

Baptifms of the Fowells.

1661. Honoria, daughter of Richard Fowell, and Elizabeth his wife, Dec. 13.
1689. William, fon of Wm. Fowell, gent. and Sufanna, Jan. 30.
1692. Sufanna, daughter of Wm. Fowell, efq. and Sufanna, June 26.
1693. Elizabeth, daughter of Wm Fowell, and Sufanna, Mar. 4.
1695. Richard, fon of Wm. Fowell, and Sufanna his wife, Nov. 13.
1701. Anne, daughter of Wm Fowell, efq and Sufanna, May 17.
1703. Edmond, fon of Wm. Fowell, gent. and Sufanna, May 28.
1732. Elizabeth, daughter of John Fowell, efq. and Elizabeth, Sept. 9.
Dec. 2. John, fon of John Fowell, efq and Elizabeth.
1737. Urania, daughter of John Fowell, efq. and Elizabeth, April 27.
1739. Richard, fon of John Fowell, efq. and Elizabeth, June 5.
1742. Francis, fon of John Fowell, efq. and Elizabeth, Jan. 5.
1745. George, fon of John Fowell, efq. and Elizabeth, Dec. 4.
1765. John Digby, fon of John Fowell, efq. and Mary, Auguft 15.
1773. James Digby Fowell, fon of John Fowell, efq. and Mary, Auguft 27.
N. B. John Digby Fowell privately bap[d]. Jan. 20, 1765.
Newton Fowell privately bap[d]. July 30, 1768, admitted into the congregation Nov. 23.

Marriage of the Fowells.

1767. Philip Goodridge and Urania Fowell, both of North Hewifh, March 14.

===

Baptifms of the Strodes.

1737. William, fon of William Strode and Mary Anne, July 13.
1742. William George, fon of William Strode, efq and Mary Anne, Auguft 19.
1750 Richard, fon of William Strode, efq. and Mary Anne, June 22.
1761. Grace Strode, Dec 11.
1774. Mary Anne, daughter of Richard Strode, and Admonition his wife, Sept. 2.
1777. William, fon of Richard Strode, efq. and Admonition, Sept 4.
1780. Richard Strode and George, fons of Richard Strode, and Admonition, Sept. 13.
1782. Admonition, daughter of Richard Strode, and Admonition, Aug. 20.
1787. Thomas Lear, fon of Richard Strode, and Admonition, Oct. 23.

Burials of the Strodes.

1735. William George Strode, Jan 14.
1748. William George Strode, Nov. 14.
1764. William Strode, efq. Jan. 23.
1776. Mary Anne Strode, widow of William Strode, efq. April 9.
1786. Thomas Lear Strode, a child, May 2.
1790. Richard Strode, efq. April 22.

This is all, of the families above, that the bad condition of the regifter books will permit me to make out.—The church, fituated in the
north part of the parifh, is 90 feet long, and 32 broad in the clear. It is plain and neat, with little ornament, and without a monument.
The tower is of a conical fhape, containing 4 bells. Perhaps it may not deferve notice, that on the night of the 12th of laft month this

tower

ftriking tafte—with as much, indeed, as the place itfelf will poffibly admit. Blackhall was built in 1641, by Will. Fowell, efq. and has been in the family fix generations.*

ARMINGTON, or ERMINGTON, on the river Arme, or Erme, gives name to a hundred, and has been fucceffively in poffeffion of the Peverells, Carews, Fitz-ftephens's, Benfteds, Stovers, and Roufes.† Thefe ancient families are, for the moft part, extinct; and their poffeffions divided among people of no confideration. A part of Ivy-bridge (which ftands as before obferved at the extremities of four different parifhes) is in Armington. It confifts of houfes compactly built, and neatly roofed with flate. The fcene at Ivy-bridge is particularly picturefque; the bridge over a rapid ftream being mantled with ivy, and the hills and rocks about the village making a romantic appearance. There are good accommodations at the London Inn; behind which a garden rifes with a gradual afcent, and at its head (where is a well of excellent water) commands a rich and extenfive profpect. A little detached from the village of Ivy-bridge, and within the parifh of Armington, is *Cleery*; an elegant feat built by William Webber, efq.‡

From KINGSTON,§ we haften to Modbury.

The parifh of MODBURY, about fix miles from eaft to weft, and three from north to fouth, is, in general, very fertile, except a little in the eaftern part.

It

---

tower was flightly damaged by lightning. It is covered on the outfide with lime mixed with fand; under which it is flated. Thefe two coverings were violently torn off, the length of about 6 yards, and in breadth a foot and half: not altogether in a direct perpendicular line, but fomewhat in a zigzag manner. The flates were not in general torn off whole, but moft of them cut into two pieces (one of which now remains upon the tower) at the edge of the narrow way cut by the electrical fluid —The patronage belonged laft to the family of the Tremaines, in Cornwall. The prefent rector and patron is the Rev. Henry Holdfworth: Before him, William Cowell; Rev. —— Crofs; Benjamin Spurway, who died March 22, 1704; John Edgecombe, buried Nov. 6, 1666.—The parfonage-houfe, a neat modern building, is about a quarter of a mile weft of the church." From Mr. John Pering, in 1791.

　* The original feat of the Fowells was Fowellfcombe, about three miles from Blackhall, in the parifh of Ugborough.

　† " *Armington*, a name framed from the river, was long fince the principal place upon that ftream, both for the Saxons impofing of names in like fort, and for that the whole hundred hath its nomination thereof.—Hugh Peverell was lord of this manner and hundred in King Henry's the 1ft's time. This family of Peverell was anciently diftinguifhed from another of the fame name in this fhire and time, by their dwelling and armories; this family's feal being an eagle difplayed, that of Samford 3 fheaves and a chief. Amicia, the fifter of Sir John Peverell the laft of this place, was wife of Sir Nicholas Carew of Carew, in Pembrokefhire, who had with her Wofton, Mamhed, Galmeton, with other lands. But Sir Gilbert Fitz-Stephens of Norton, had this manner and hundred, who granted the fame unto John de Benfted in King Edward the 1ft's reign, and John de Stover held the fame the 19th of King Edward the 3d, in which race it remained, until Sir Edmund Stover fold it unto the Roufes, in which family the inheritance now is.—*Stretchleigh* ftands in this parifh, a dwelling that gave name to an ancient family lately extinct; of which William was the firft, and William was the laft. Between whom being twelve defcents, Chriftian his only daughter wedded to Chriftopher Chidleigh, this inheritance came to that houfe, in which it remaineth.—*Stroude* hath given name to a family of good eminency, his inhabiters, being the dwelling of Adam Stroude in King Henry the 3d's time; which ancient inheritance is in that name unto this day, whofe eftate is much advanced by the match of the heirs of many worthy houfes.—At *Langford* lived Sir Galfride de Leftre in King Richard the 1ft's reign, whom fucceeded William de Leftre his fon. Since, about the time of King Edward the 1ft, John Lord Mules held this inheritance, from whom by Botreaux and Hungerford, it defcended to the Haftings, Earls of Huntingdon, who fold it unto Sir John Popham, chief juftice of the King's Bench." *Rifdon*.

　‡ " The parifh of *Ermington* is from eaft to weft about feven miles long, and from north to fouth about three miles broad, bounded on the eaft by the parifhes of Modbury and Ugburrow, on the weft by the river Yalm, on the north by the parifh of Cornwood, and on the fouth by the river Erme. The parifh has, befides the church-town, (which has annually two fairs), four villages, i. e. Ivy-bridge, Cadley, Weftlake, and Woodland: It has likewife five manors, i. e. Ermington, Strowde, Worthele, Woodland, and Beach or Chapel-Lee. It is inclofed by hedges, well wooded. The houfes are chiefly built with ftone and mud, and are moftly thatched. The inhabitants are healthy, and live to a tolerable age. The paupers, communibus annis, are about thirty. The foil is remarkably good, lying chiefly on dunftone and flate. The church is pleafantly fituated on the decline of a hill, facing the fouth-eaft, at an agreeable diftance from the river. It is built with excellent ftone, in the fhape of a crofs, and is in the clear a hundred feet long, and fifty wide. It has three aifles. Its roof, which is upwards of thirty feet high, is fupported by moorftone fluted pillars. It hath a fteeple about 120 feet high, containing five beautiful bells. The church, if well feated, would be as elegant as any in the county. The vicarage-houfe, which is about a quarter of a mile from the church, is a fmall mud cot houfe, and is thatched. The parfonage, which is near the church, is a fmall new ftone-built houfe, and is flated. The tythes are divided into three parts, the fmall or vicarial tythe belong to the Rev. G. Townfend, the prefent vicar. The great tythes are divided into two medieties, and belong to the Rev. G. Rhodes and John Bulteel, efq." From a letter, dated 1791.

　§ " The parifh of *Kingfton* is from eaft to weft about four miles long, and from north to fouth about three miles wide. It is bounded on the eaft by Bigbury, on the weft by the river Arm, on the north by Modbury, and on the fouth by Bigbury Bay. Its fituation is partly high and partly low. It hath but two villages, and is but one manor, belonging to the Rev. Humphrey Julian. Its inhabitants, buildings, inclofures, &c. &c. are much the fame as at Ermington. The paupers are, communibus annis, about twenty. The church, which is a daughter church to Ermington, is a fmall ftone building, being in the clear about 50 feet long, and 25 feet wide: It hath a low tower, containing four poor bells. The tythes belong, and are divided the fame as Ermington."

It is, for the moft, bare of timber.* In his account of Modbury, Rifdon is unufually diffufe. He defcribes Modbury, Shilfton, Orcharton, Delaport, Brownfton, Wimpfton, Leigh-Challons, Yarnecombe, and Edmefton.† The town of Modbury lies about a mile to the weftward ‡ of the central part of the parifh, and contains about 200 houfes. It confifts principally of four ftreets, which meet at right angles in the market-place. In thefe ftreets are four large conduits, three of which are of moorftone. The largeft was the gift of Adrian

Swete,

* " Its weftern extremity (Orcheton Point) divides into two branches an arm of the fea, called Mothecombe Harbour, formed by the mouth of the river Erme; and fome have formerly thought it practicable to have water carriage, by a canal, within one field of the town. It appears to have been anciently divided into two parts, called Great and Little Modbury; the latter of which diftinctions ftill remains; but the former, tho' a manor, is now little known in common fpeech. Its yearly value, as rated to the poor, is £.3973 13s. 4d.; but, by a more particular eftimate, the real value of the parifh (including houfes, in the town and elfewhere, moft of which are not rated) muft be near, if not full £.6000. The living is in the gift of the college of Eton: It is a vicarage, endowed with one-third part of the great and fmall tithes; which, with the glebe, are worth near £.200 a year. The other two-thirds of the tithe belong to the college; but in the village of Penquit, (detached from the reft of the parifh, to the north) they are entitled to the whole tithes; as, on the contrary, in a village called Weft Leigh, the whole tithe belong to the vicar. The yearly land-tax, at 4s. in the pound, is £.340 9s. 4d."

† " Modbury, a place for multiplicity of ancient houfes and fertility of foil, inferior to few in this county—it hath been diftinguifhed into Great and Little Modbury. The chief manor was the Vaultorts, Barons of Huberton, which Roger de Vaultort, among other lands, conveyed to Sir Alexander Okefton, knight, who had married Joan the widow of Ralph Vaultort. By which woman, he had iffue Sir James Okefton, that died without iffue, who, by commandment of King Edward the 2d, conveyed Modbery and all his lands (formerly granted) unto Sir Richard Champernon, knight, defcended from Joan before mentioned, whom Edmund Earl of Cornwal calleth by the name of fifter, in a grant made by him to the faid Richard and Joan of the affize of bread and ale Ann. 12, Edward the 1ft. This name of Champernon hath been very numerous, and have planted themfelves at divers places, as Bear, Umberley, Infworke, Ilfarcombe, Dartington, Bigbery, Tawton, this place, &c. who in ancient evidences are written de Campo Arnulphi. The inheritor of thefe lands married the daughter of Sir Anthony Cope in Oxfordfhire, knight, his father Sir Arthur, a worthy commander in the wars, the daughter and heir of Crewkern, his grandfire, the daughter and heir of Sir Richard Edgcombe, knight.—Henricus Lapiflode concef. Manerium de Modbury Jacobo de Oxton & Idæ Uxori ejus conditione poft deceffum remaneat Ricardo de Campo Arnulphi fecundum cartam Domini Regis & fecundum cartam dicti Jacobi per vim Chartæ Domini Regis mihi Concef. Teftibus Will. de Prouz, Job. Bigbery, Jo. de Ferrariis. Dat. 9 Edw. fil. Edwardi.—This burrough hath a Thurfday's market, and fairs on the days of St. George and St. James, being furnifhed with neceffaries, is well frequented, and fomewhat the more, for that the town is noted for nappy ale. Of which liquor, Henry of Auranches, an arch poet, in King Henry the 3d's time, wrote thus:

Of this ftrong drink, much like to *Stygian* Lake,
Moft term it *Ale*, I know not what to make,
Folk drink it thick, and pifs it out full thin,
Much dregs therefore muft needs remain within.

Shilvefton, now *Shilfton*, was in King Henry the 3d's time the lands and dwelling of John de Shilvefton, whofe daughter Eleanor was firft married to Sir Richard Banchem, fecondly to John de Afhleigh. The faid Richard had iffue, Joan married unto Sir Richard Huyfh, whofe fon Sir Richard in King Edward the 1ft's time, did contend with the faid John Afhleigh for the faid land. Afterwards, Robert Hill the judge fettled his dwelling here, and his pofterity have continued the fame even to thefe our days.—*Orcharton* was held by Jordan de la Warre in King John's time. Gilbert Prideaux held this land in King Henry the 3d's reign: He was a younger fon of Geoffry, fon of Sir Roger Prideaux of Prideaux-Caftle, in Cornwall, whom divers knights of that tribe fucceeded. Sir John Prideaux loft much of his land by killing of Sir William Bigbery, knight; yet he left Orcharton and Allington unto his fon, which continued in his pofterity unto our remembrance; and this name planted elfewhere, flourifheth in degree of knight and baronet. They held Orcharton 13 defcents.—John de la Port the laft, by Hilaria his wife, had iffue three daughters, Alice wife of Thomas Heanton. unto whom *Old Port* fell for her portion; from whom by Joan their daughter and heir married to Richard Malduit, called Somafter, this land defcended in that line.—*Bromfton* was given by Reginald de Valletort, Lord of Modbury, unto Ralph de Morvile.—I may not pafs *Wimondefham*, now *Wimpfton*, unremembred, which King John beftowed on John Fortefcue, a foldier in arms, the 10th year of his reign. Many feveral families of this name are branched abroad, which have produced many worthy perfonages, whofe names (as Holingfhed hath) is deduced from the ftrength of their fhield, and their motto is, — *Forte fcutum falus Ducum.*—Of this tribe have been famous men, both in honour of arms and feats of juftice. To particularize a few of many, Sir Henry Fortefcue, knight, was a worthy commander under that illuftrious Prince, King Henry the 5th, who made him governor of Meaux in Berry. Another Sir Henry was Lord Chief Juftice in Ireland, a man of great efteem for his vertue and fincerity in fo high a calling. Sir John was Lord Chief Juftice of England, from the 10th of King Henry the 6th, to the end of his reign; who in that laborious place mifpent not his time, but penned a learned difcourfe of the laws of this realm, commending it to the hopeful prince. Befides it, he wrote a prayer-book, which favoured much of the times we live in. What fhall I fpeak of Polefborn in Hartfordfhire, Fulborn in Effex, Souldon in Buckinghamfhire, where Sir John Fortefcue, a right honourable knight, built a goodly houfe, who, for his deep learning and approved wifdom, was Chancellor of the Exchecquer and Dutchy of Lancafter, and of the Privy Council of Queen Elizabeth? I will engage no farther, for Wimondefham is alienated.—*Leigh Challons* took that adjunct of its ancient owners; the firft of which name I find was Harwinus, the fon of the Earl of Challons, who married the Lady Florence de Leigh, the lady of this land, of which family were divers knights. This land, after eleven defcents in that line fell away to females. Katherine the wife of Sir John St. Albin, was the daughter of the laft Sir Robert Challons, and fhe had iffue two daughters, Joan wife of William Dennis, of Combraleigh; and Margaret wife of Reinald Trethurfe. Henry Challons of this houfe made a voyage for the difcovery of Virginia and New England in our time, wherein he was taken by the Spaniards, and inhumanely handled.—*Hart*, anciently *De la Hart*, hath his habitation at *Yarnacombe*, in this parifh. Thus we have paffed Great Modbury, let us make fome mention of *Little Modbury*, the dwelling of Sir Ralph le Roufe, in King Henry the 3d's time. The laft of this place had iffue Elizabeth, firft married to Peverel, fecondly to Dymock, and thirdly to Walter Cornu, fon of Alan Cornu, fhe had iffue only by Dymock.—*Edmerfton* had lords long fince fo firnamed, the laft of which family had iffue Alice, married unto William le Roufe, the fon of Robert, fecond fon of Ralph le Roufe of Little Modbury. Of this race I read of Sir Robert Roufe, a valiant warrior, who was captain in Chierburgh, in the reign of King Richard the 2d, and this ancient name inheriteth this land to this day: The gentleman that now is, married the daughter of the Baron of Truro, his father the daughter of Ofborn, his grandfire, Sir Anthony, the daughter of Southcot, by an heir of Barnhoufe." *Rifdon.*

‡ " Modbury (faid a gentleman of the author's acquaintance) is a ftrange folitary town in a dell, between green hills, without trees and without water."—This is, in fome degree, characteriftic of the place. There is, certainly, little wood in the parifh, tho' it be " green" and fruitful.

Swete, efq. and the next of Nicholas Trift, efq. (lord of the borough) both in the year 1708. There appears to have been a manor in the parifh, called the Manor of the Priory. Divers lands in the parifh, which are ftill called Priory-lands, are rated at 96l. but now let for about 150l. a year. Thefe all belong to the college of Eton, (by grant from Hen. the 8th), as alfo do other lands, diftinguifhed by the name of Provoft-lands: and thefe ecclefiaftical lands (as may naturally be fuppofed) are fome of the beft in the parifh. *Shilfton*, which a little before Rifdon, was the property of the Hills, was in 1614 purchafed by the elder branch of the Saverys, a family of confiderable antiquity and eminence, in whofe heir it ftill remains; having been the principal family refidence for about 170 years: till the prefent owner, John Savery, efq. purchafed and removed to another feat, called Butcombe Court, near Briftol.* *Orcharton* is an ancient farm-houfe, and faid to be a manor, and formerly the refidence of fome confiderable families. It now belongs to John Bulteel, efq. of Fleet. *Delaport*, now called *Oldaport*, is alfo a farm, the property of Lord Afhburton. *Brownfton* is a village (about three miles eaft of the town) containing feveral farms and houfes, belonging to different perfons. It appears, from old writings, to have been antiently a manor, the royalty of which feems to be now loft. *Wimpfton* is a confiderable farm, and alfo a manor. After the Fortefcues, it appears to have belonged to the Champernownes; and fince to the Ourrys. It is now the property of Paul Treby Treby, efq. (of Goodamore, in Plymton St. Mary) who affumed the furname of Treby, inftead of Ourry. The villages of *Eaft* and *Weft Leigh* are nearly contiguous, and confift of farms and tenements, belonging to different proprietors. *Yarnacombe* continued in the family of the Harts till about thirty or forty years ago, when it was fold by Samuel Hart, efq. to William Mackworth Praed, efq. Mr. Hart had an only child, a daughter, now living, and unmarried; at whofe deceafe the family will be extinct. *Edmefton* about 30 years fince was the feat of John Froude, efq. afterwards of his fon Robert Froude, efq. whofe widow now enjoys it. *Little Modbury* is now the common name of feveral farms, which lie contiguous to each other a little fouth of the town, and belong to divers perfons. There are feveral

other

* " The family of the Saverys, about the beginning of the fixteenth century, were merchants in Totnes, and appear to have been poffeffed of confiderable property. Sir Chriftopher Savery was made a knight banneret, in the time of Queen Eliz. by virtue of which the family are entitled to *one* fupporter to their arms; called by heralds a *defender*. He married a defcendant (and then fole heirefs to the lands) of William Servington, efq. who was fheriff of Devon in the 40th of Edward the 3d. In 1614, his fon, Chriftopher Savery, efq. purchafed Shilfton, in Modbury, of Robert Hill, efq. and Edward his fon; and it has ever fince been the chief refidence of the Saverys, till the prefent owner, John Savery, efq. purchafed and removed to another feat, called Butcombe Court, in Somerfet, near Briftol. The fame Chr. Savery was fheriff of Devon in the 18th of James the 1ft, (1620). His fon, Chr. Savery, was colonel of a regiment of foot in the parliament's army, in the time of Charles the 1ft; and at that time paid, as his quota, out of his eftates in Devonfhire, towards maintaining the forces in the neighbourhood of Plymouth, £.50 per month, as appears by receipts now in being. He married a daughter of Colonel Clobery; and King Charles the 2d, on his reftoration, granted a pardon to him and his fon Servington Savery. In James the 2d's time a warrant was iffued by the lord lieutenant, to the fheriff, (but never executed), for apprehending faid Servington Savery and his fon Chriftopher, and conveying them to the fort of Plymouth, as perfons difaffected to the government. They appear to have been very active in bringing about the revolution; and Chriftopher was fheriff of Devon in the time of William and Mary, (1693). His fon, Servington, (who in 1691 married a daughter of Judge Hale), was a very ingenious mathematician and mechanic; being the inventor of artificial magnets, the diagonal barometer, &c. as is well known among men of fcience. His fon, Chriftopher, in 1717, married Sarah, daughter of Sir John Davie of Creedy, bart. by whom he had John, the father of the prefent John Savery, efq. above-mentioned, and of two other fons, and three daughters.—The arms are, *Gules, a feffe verry, between three unicorn's heads, coped, argent.* On the dexter fide, a defender, viz. *A man in compleat armour, having the creft of the arms on his fhield, and two lances in his right hand.* The creft is, *An eagle's head erafed, between two wings, fable, with a fprig in his mouth, vert.* Motto, *Aut Vita libera, aut Mors gloriofa.*—About the fame time that Shilfton was purchafed by the elder branch of the family, a younger branch fettled at Slade, in Cornwood; which continued in the name till about 1780, when Waltham Savery, efq. fold it to Mr. Spurrel." From Andrews, 1790.

perfons. There are feveral other confiderable farms and bartons within the parifh, particularly *Trayne*, the feat of the Swete family, who acquired it in the time of either Hen. the 8th, or Edw. the 6th, by defcent from a family called Scoos, whofe name became then extinct. After feveral defcents (not eafy at this diftance of time to trace with certainty) it appears, in 1624, to have been in the poffeffion of Adrian Swete, efq. who married Judeth, daughter of John Mayne of Prefton, in Ermington, and died in 1647, when it came to his fon, Maine Swete, efq. who married Judith, daughter of Hele of Fleet. He dying in 1682, was fucceeded by his brother, John Swete, then vicar of St. Keverne, in Cornwall; a man of moft confummate learning and application, as appears by a great many fermons and other manufcripts of his, ftill preferved in the family. On his death, in 1695, it came to his fon Adrian, who was fheriff of Devon in 1724, and dying without iffue in 1733, left it to his brother Maine Swete. On his death, in 1735, it became the property of his fon, Adrian John Swete, then very young. He dying in 1755, by will left Trayne and all the reft of his lands to his mother, Mrs. Efther Swete; who dying in 1771, left the fame entailed on her relation, the Rev. Mr. John Tripe, (now John Swete), fon of Nicholas Tripe, efq. of Afhburton, by Rebecca, a daughter of Mr. Yarde. Trayne-houfe is pleafantly fituated, very near the town; of which, and the adjacent country, it would command a delightful profpect, if laid open in the modern tafte, under the direction of the prefent proprietor: But his refidence is at Oxton-houfe, in Kenton.* The church is a large and handfome, tho' plain building: the fpire in particular, (which was probably new-built about 1621) is confidered as a mafter-piece of good work. The church is remarkable for a very fine marble font, and three large and commodious galleries, erected in 1716.†

* The Swete family have been confiderable benefactors to the town and parifh of Modbury. In 1684, John Swete, efq. gave a piece of land, whereon the alms-houfe is built: And in 1708, Adrian Swete, efq. built the beft of the four conduits, to which the principal fupply of water (then lately purchafed) is conveyed.—The fame gentleman, by his will, bequeathed £.40 to buy a large and handfome filver flagon, gilt, which is now conftantly ufed at the communion. The Swetes, before their acquifition of Trayne, appear to have lived at Uppeton, in South Milton, where they can be traced as far back as 1438. They have fince been connected with the Heles, Saverys, Champernownes, and Archers of Cornwall.

† It is rather bare of monumental decorations: The only one which has any degree of elegance was erected to the memory of one of the Swete family, who died in 1690, a batchelor of 25. From feveral niches, however, and mutilated remains of ftatues, (efpecially one of the Champernownes family, in compleat armour) which appear to have lain there in ftate, it is evident that the church was once more pompoufly ornamented than it is at prefent.

Extracted from the Register at Modbury:

Sir Richard Champernowne, died 28 June,	1622
Alexander Champernowne, fon of Henry & Winefrid his wife, 22 Septr. baptized,	1637
Lady Elizabeth Champernowne, buried 7 March. I fuppofe fhe was a daughter of Sir John Popham.	1637
Philip Champernowne, fon of Henry Champernowne, efq. and Mrs. Margaret, bap. 8th, [Q. of what month ?]	1648
Warwick Champernowne, fon of Philip Champernowne, efq. & Margaret his wife, - 22 Augt. bapt.	1650
Henry, fon of do. - 24 bapt.	1651
Margaret, dr. of do. - 14 May, bapt.	1653
Henry Champernowne - 2 Decr. buried	1644
Mr. John Champernowne - 21 Jany. buried	1647
Henry Champernowne, fon of Philip Champernowne, efq. buried 26 April	1652
Honor Champernowne, daur. of Philip & Margaret, 3d October, born	1655
Mary, daughter of Philip & Mrs. Margt. Champernowne. - 12 Aug. [Q. whether born or buried?]	1661
Philip Champernowne, efq. buried 30 July	1670
Arthur Champernowne, fon to Philip & Elizabeth, 12 Jany. bapt.	1671
Henry Champernowne, fon of Philip & Elizabeth, 17 Mar. bapt.	1673
Mrs. Amy Champernowne, buried 17 Septr.	1680
Margaret Champernowne, dr. of Philip & Sarah, 4 Jan. bapt.	1683
Philip Champernowne, buried 22d July. (N. B. Churchwarden 1681)	1684
Mrs. Sarah Champernowne, 20 July, buried	1717

DEANRY of WOODLEIGH.

WE have, here, before us, Woodleigh, Morleigh, Lodefwell and Buck-land-tout-faints, Aveton-Giffard, Bigbury, Ringmore, Eaft-Allington, Churftow and Kingfbridge, Thurlefton, W. Alwington, South-Milton, S. Hewifh, Malborough, Portlemouth, Chivelftone, S. Pole, Charlton, Dod-brooke, Stokenham, Sherford, Slapton.*

Though Woodleigh † give name to the deanry, yet it prefents very little to detain us. The fame obfervation may be applied to the four fucceeding parifhes.‡

BIGBURY

" Benefices remaining in charge:

First Fruits. £. s. d.		Yearly Tenths. £. s. d.
62 16 10½	{ Alvington alias Weft-Allington V. [All Saints] with Malbroke, Milton, and Hewifh Chapel.—Rep. Vicars } of the Cathedral of Exon, Penf. ii/. xiiis. 4d. B. Proc. vis. viiid. Syn. iis. vd. A.D. Proc. vis. viiid. } r. V. 160/. - - - - - - - - - - - Patrs. Dean and Chapter of Sarum.	6 5 8¼
38 1 8	Aveton Gifford R. [St. Andrew] Rep. B. Proc. vis. viiid. Syn. iis. xd. A.D. Proc. vis. viiid. r. V. 250/. Patrs. Heirs of Mr. Lane.	- 3 16 2
28 17 11	Bigburie R. [St. Laurence] Rep. B. Proc. vis. viiid. Syn. iiis. iiid. A.D. Proc. vis. viiid. r. V. 240/. Patr. Duke of Bolton.	- 2 16 9½
31 8 4	Charleton R. [St. Mary] Rep. B. Proc. vs. Syn. iis. vd. A.D. Proc. vs. r. V. 200/. - - Patr. John Parker, efq.	- 3 2 10
32 2 1	Eaft Allington R. [St. Andrew] Rep. B. Proc. vis. viiid. Syn. iis. vd. A.D. Proc. vis. viiid. r. V. 200/. Patr. —— Fortefcue, efq.	- 2 8 2
26 0 2½	Loddefwill V. [St. Michael] Rep. B. Proc. vis. viiid. Syn. iiis. iiid. A.D. Proc. vis. viiid. r. V. 140/. Patr. Lord Arundel, Ca.	- 2 12 0¼
22 16 5½	Pole alias South-Pole R. [St. Cæcilia] Rep. B. Proc. vs. Syn. is. viiid. A.D. Proc. vs. r.V. 160/. - Patr. Benjamin Hayes, efq.	- 2 5 7¼
29 18 4	Portlemouth R. [St. Onelaus] Rep. B. Proc. vs. Syn. iis. vd. A.D. Proc. vs. r. V. 140/. - - Patr. Duke of Bolton.	- 2 19 10
19 10 7½	Ringmore alias Rinmore R. [Ded. unc.] Rep. B. Proc. ivs. Syn. iiis. xd. A.D. Proc. ivs. r. V. 150/. Patr. Heirs of Francis Kirkham, efq.	- 1 19 0¾
43 7 8¼	{ Stockingham alias Stokenham V. [St. Barnabas] with Shirford [St. Martin] and Chivelftone [St. Silvefter] } { Chapels.—Rep. B. Proc. vis. viiid. Syn. iis. xd. A.D. Proc. vis. viiid. r. V. 200/. - - } Patr. The KING.	4 16 9¼
25 10 0	Thurlfton R. [Ded. unc.] Rep. B. Proc. vs. Syn. iis. vd. A.D. Proc. vs. r. V. 160/. - - Patr. Giles Yarde, efq.	- 2 11 0
22 8 4	Woodleigh R. [St. Mary] Rep. B. Proc. vs. Syn. iis. vd. A.D. Proc. vs. r. V. 140/. - - Patr. —— Lavers, efq.	- 2 4 10

Difcharged.

King's Books.		Certified Value.
16 17 3	Churftow V. [St. Mary] with Kingfbridge Ch. [St. Edmund] Rep. B. Proc. vs. A.D. Proc. viiis. viiid. r.V. 80/. 26 0 0 Patrs. Mayor and Chamber of Exeter.	
8 11 3	Dodbrooke R. [St. Thomas Becket] Rep. B. Proc. vis. viiid. Syn. iid. A.D. Proc. vs. r. V. 80/. - Patr. John H. Southcote, efq.	- 44 8 0
9 8 1½	Moreleigh R. [St. Mary Magdalen] Rep. B. Proc. vs. Syn. viid. A.D. Proc. iiis. r. V. 70/. - - Patr. John Seale, efq.	- 48 19 5
	Slapton Cur. [St. Mary] Rep. B. Proc. vs. Syn. iis. vd. A.D. Proc. vis. viiid. r. V. 60/. - - Patr. Lord Petre, Ca. held by Seq ieftration.	- 15 0 0
	Buckland Tout Saints Ch. to Loddifwell.	

This chapel which had long lain in ruins, was rebuilt at a little diftance from the antient fite, by John Henry Southcote, efq. in a ftyle and manner which does honor to the tafte and benevolence of that gentleman. It was confecrated in 1779."

Thes. Eccles.

* " In *Woodleigh* is *Wood*, the long-continued dwelling of the flourifhing family of the Fortefcues. —— Fortefcue married the daugh-ter of Sir John Speccot. The chief manor was the property of the Damarells, knights. By Rofe, the daughter of Damarell, it came to Roger Rofant, Lord of Dodbroke, and defcended (with Dodbroke) to the Champernowns, knights." *Rifdon.*

† MORELEIGH *Church-town* is half-way between Totnes and Kingfbridge, fix miles from each; and half-way between Dartmouth and Modbury, eight miles from each.—In Edward the Ift's age, Sir Peter Fifhacre, knight, held lands in Morleigh—who, (as we have it by tradition, fays *Rifdon*), had his dwelling " in this hamlet then belonging to the parifh of Woodleigh—whereupon, fome controverfy arifing between him and the parfon of Woodleigh touching tythes, the matter grew to that height that in his fury the parfon was flain—which fact was fo eagerly followed againft the knight, that he was conftrained to anfwer the fame at Rome, and could not be difmiffed before the Pope enjoined him for his penance to build the church of Morleigh, where he lieth buried in the wall arched over."—Parifh of LOD-DESWELL, in length about 5 miles, in breadth a mile and half. Situation high, well watered with fprings and wells. Bounded on the

weft

BIGBURY imparted its name, according to Sir W. Pole, to a very ancient family, which continued here for nine defcents, from the conqueft down to the reign of Edward the 3d, when the two daughters and heireffes of William Bigbury brought this inheritance to their hufbands, Champernowne of Beerferrers, and Dernford of Stonehoufe. Of the Bigburys, five were knights in fucceffion. The Duke of Bolton is the prefent lord of the manor of Bigbury.*

RINGMORE (anciently Ridmore) fcarcely deferves our notice.†

EAST-ALLINGTON, in the hundred of Stanborough,‡ is enclofed with quickfet hedges, and divided into fmall farms.§

In

weft by Yanfton brook, which falls into the river Avon, at a place called Smithland; on the north, eaft, and fouth by the faid river, which winds about 5 miles, and has 3 bridges on it—the firft, Topfham-bridge, with one arch; fecond, Loddefwell-bridge, two arches; third, Hatch-bridge, two arches, all built with ftone, and repaired by the county. An inclofed parifh, divided with hedges, well planted with brufh-wood. Oak and afh flourifh, elm not plenty. Roads and materials good. Views extenfive, both of fea and land.—There is a church-town; two villages, about 50 farm-houfes, built chiefly with ftone, and covered with flate and thatch; compact and neat, with gardens and orchards belonging to them, and well cultivated.—Number of inhabitants within the parifh, confifting of farmers, woollen-manufacturers, day labourers, and paupers, about 500.—Woolfton, a handfome modern building, fituated about a mile from the town, the refidence of George Furlong Wife, efq.—There are three manors, Loddefwell, Stanton, and Webbiton; and moft of the eftates pay a chief rent to the Duke of Somerfet.—The church is fituated at the fouth-end of the parifh. The tower has five bells; and there is an alms-houfe and two writing fchools not endowed. There are two charitable donations of £.18 a year each, given by Mr. Richard Phillips, one towards the repairs of the church, the other for the benefit of the poor. Loddefwell is an endowed vicarage, having the chapel of Buckland Tout Saints, otherwife Tout Zants, annexed to it. Francis Freke, efq. patron. Nicholas Thomas Freke, prefent incumbent, inftituted 1778; Thomas Freke, inftituted in 1744; Francis Freke, inftituted in 1685; John Freke, inftituted in 1680. The vicarage-houfe, a modern building, fituated about a mile from the church.—BUCKLAND TOUT SAINTS, otherwife Tout Zants, fituated about 4 miles from the parifh of Loddefwell: In length a mile and half, in breadth half a mile. Situation high, well watered with fprings and wells. Inclofed, and divided with hedges, well wooded. Oak, afh, elm, and fir flourifh. Roads and materials good. Buckland-houfe, within the manor of Buckland, a handfome fpacious manfion, built of ftone, with extenfive gardens and plantations of foreft trees: Prefent poffeffor, John Henry Southcote, efq. Bearfcombe, otherwife Woodmafon, an ancient family manfion, the property of the late Thomas Chefter, efq. but now of Mr. Philip Cookworthy, by purchafe. There are two large farms belonging to the above. There is a chapel annexed to the church of Loddefwell, where the vicar officiates monthly one part of the day." From the minifter in 1791.

* " The parifh of *Bigbury* is bounded on the fouth-weft by the fea, to which it gives the name of Bigbury Bay; on the fouth and fouth-eaft by the river Avon or Aune: This river divides the parifh from Thurlefton, and part of Aveton-Gifford. On the eaft it is bounded by Aveton-Gifford; on the north by the parifhes of Modbury, Kingfton, and Rinmore. Bigbury contains fixty-eight farthings of land, each farthing confifting of 20 acres, befides an ifland called St. Michael's, but more commonly known by the name of Borough-Ifland; it contains about ten acres moft excellent fheep pafture, which, however, has often been tilled to great advantage. The fands that join it to the main land are paffable at half tide. It is the property of the lord of the manor.—Bigbury is a rectory in the gift of the Duke of Bolton. The glebe confifts of four farthings. The parfonage is a very bad old houfe.—Bigbury contains two manors, befides feveral free-hold independent bartons. The manor of Bigbury belongs to the Duke of Bolton, and has been in that family ever fince the time of Henry the 8th: It has a court-leet and court-baron. The eftates are leafed out on lives, as is generally the cafe in this part of Devonfhire. It has likewife the royalty of the river Aune, as far as the manor extends, in conjunction with Lord Vifcount Courtenay, who poffeffes the manor of Thurlefton, on the oppofite bank. One circumftance is peculiar, that the falmon never makes its appearance in this river, till they are generally efteemed out of feafon in the other rivers on the fouthern part of Devonfhire. The other manor is Houghton, lately fold by the executors of the late Wm. Ilbert, efq. to a Mr. Langmead, a brewer of Plymouth. This manor pays a chief rent to the lord of the manor of Bigbury. There is no houfe in this parifh of any the leaft note. The foil of the whole parifh, on the hills is light on flate, in the vallies exceedingly rich and well watered: It abounds in orchards, and is particularly famous for fine fheep and barley. The courfe of hufbandry is fimilar to the neighbouring parifhes, only that lately they have ufed more lime for manure, and have neglected the fea fand. The culm for the kilns comes from Wales, the lime-ftone from Cat-down, near Plymouth. The church is fituated nearly in the centre of the parifh. It is a very neat ftructure, with a handfome tower, and fpire at the weft-end. The length from eaft to weft is 50 feet; its breadth 30 feet and one inch. I do not know when built. There are fome remains of painting in the windows of armorial bearings, but none perfect, except of the Champernownes and Drakes. The tower, as well as the church, is of ftone, and is 27 feet high, which is the height of the roof, and from the tower rifes a fpire of the fame height. The laft rector was Mr. Powlet; his predeceffor Mr. ——— De Vifme, who was ambaffador to feveral courts, and gained this preferment, (it is faid), as a fee for marrying the Duke of Bolton to the famous Polly Peach'em. The number of inhabitants about 370. No manufactures but the fpinning of wool for ferges. Poor-rates very high, from four to five fhillings in the pound. The village of Bigbury contains moft of the cottages of the poor, but there are feveral others difperfed at hamlets, moft of which are called Combe, with the addition of Higher, Lower, &c. There are two grift-mills." From the minifter in 1791.

† " The parifh of *Rinmore* is adjacent to Kingftone, and is much the fame in foil, buildings, inclofures, &c. &c. It hath two manors, the one belonging to Henry Roe, efq. the other to John Wife, efq. The church is a fmall ftone building, confifting only of one aifle, with a low fteeple, with three miferable bells. The parfonage is about a quarter of a mile from the church.

‡ " Having lately had Sir John Wm. de la Pole's publication of his anceftor's collections, refpecting this county, in my hands for about ten minutes only, I was induced to fee in what hundred he placed the parifh of Eaft Allington, and found it *Coleridge*. Now as I have many reafons for thinking that you may be induced to do the fame, and I am well convinced it is in the hundred of Stanborough, I think it right to lay before you fuch circumftances refpecting it as have come to my knowlege. In the county rates Eaft Allington has always been fet down as in the hundred of Stanborough, and inhabitants of that parifh are often chofen to do the office of high conftable for the laft-mentioned divifion of the county. In 1756-7, however, an accident happening at Fallpit (the ancient feat of the Fortefcues) in this parifh, whereby a deodand became forfeited to the lord of the manor, it was claimed by the high lord of the hundred of Coleridge, who, if I miftake not, was at that time the prefent Judge Heath. The late Mr. George Prideaux of Kingfbridge (father of the prefent gentleman of that name and place) being at that period attorney for the Fallapit family, wrote to the Rev. Robert Walker of Criftowe, for elucidations; and his letter in reply is now before me, wherein he makes the following obfervations and quotations from a copy of Domefday in his poffeffion:

" But

" But as to your queftion I find that ano. 31°. Edw. 1. this Allington is rated as within the hundred of Coleridge.

" Hurber—Stancomb Crifpin di. fe. Gilb. Crifpin tenet Aylington Crifpin 1 fe. Jdem Gilb. Crifpin tenet.

* " The interpretation of which is this; Gilb. Crifpin holds Aylington of the honour of Hurberton (now Harberton) as " one knights' fee.

" Hurberton was the barony of the Valetorts temp. Hen. 1. & after fix defcents in that name fell to the heirs general— " Pomery & Corbet.

" Eaft Allington lieth within the hundred of Coleridge—27 Hen. 3—Gilbt Crifpin held it, & 24° Ed. 1 f 8°. Ed. 2 Sr Nichs " Dauney—& after him Sr John Dauney—whofe daughter Emma brought it to Sr Edward Courtenay 2d fon unto Hugh " Courtenay & Earl of Dev. whofe fon Edwd. Courtenay gave it to Sir H. Courtenay of Haccombe his brother 2° Hen. 5.

" Weft Allington lieth within the hundred of Stanborough; & 31 Ed. 1. is rated thus;—Cardinham——† Allington D: " Fe: 9d hered. Walt. Treverbin ten. i. e. The heirs of Walter Treverbin hold Allington of the honour of Cardinham in the " county of Cornwall as half a knights fee.

" From Treverbin it defcended by ‡ Elizabeth dr of Hugh Treverbin unto Peter Prideaux the father of Sir Roger Prideaux " of Orcherton whofe defcendt. Robert Prideaux the laft of the name of the houfe of Orcherton fold it."

Mr. Walker further fays—" I find in my manufcript of Devon by Rifdon—both Eaft and Weft Allington fet down in the " rates as within the hundd. of Stanborough; which I impute to fome collector of the rates prior to his time."

That Mr. Geo. Prideaux was in the right, in confidering what Mr. Walker here calls *Weft* Allington to be *Eaft* Allington, the event proved; and, if my memory does not much fail me, the manor of Eaft Allington came to the Fortefcues from the Prideauxes. Be that as it may, the old gentleman gained his caufe, and not only proved by ancient papers that Eaft Allington was in the hundred of Stanborough, but brought old people of the parifh to make oath that they had formerly ferved on juries in the hundred court of Moreleigh in Stanborough. *Weft* Allington (or as it is now written Weftalvington) is alfo in the hundred of Stanborough. But you will poffibly now afk—where is Allington in the hundred of Coleridge? In the parifh of Chivelftone there is a hamlet called *South* Allington, and this I take to be the one mentioned in that hundred. I am, reverend fir, your moft obedient fervant,

Alfton, near Kingfbridge, 30th Nov. 1791.   ABRM. HAWKINS."

§ *Eaft-Allington*, otherwife *Alvington*, otherwife *Alwinftan*, and by fome old deeds *Eaft* and *North Allington*, or *Alvington*, or *Alwinftan*, Is bounded on the eaft by Slapton; on the fouth-weft by Sherford and Buckland Tout-Saints; on the north by Holwell and Moreleigh; and on the fouth by Stokenham and Sherford: Is 5 miles in length, in breadth 2. On the north fide of it, on the farm of Cuttery, belonging to Mr. John Prideaux, arifes a fmall rivulet, which takes a foutherly direction, and about 4 miles from its fource empties itfelf into the Salcombe river, at Bowcombe. This rivulet, tho' extremely narrow, not more in general than 10 or 12 feet wide, abounds with trout; and its banks, through fome parts of this parifh and Buckland Tout-Saints, are well adorned with fome beautiful hanging woods. This parifh contains three manors, Eaft-Allington, belonging to Edmund Nathaniel William Fortefcue of Fallapit, a minor, which confifts of about 20 fmall farms; Colehanger, confifting of one farm only, belonging to Lord Vifcount Boringdon; and Harleftone, confifting of three farms, belonging to Mr. Philip Cookworthy. For the manor of Eaft-Allington there is a court-leet and baron held here annually, at lady-day and michaelmas, for the receipt of rents, &c. &c. The other two manors hold but one court-baron annually for their rents, &c. In this parifh are five villages, Eaft-Allington, adjoining the church, fituated about the centre of the parifh, confifting of 22 houfes, and containing about 130 inhabitants; Coombe, fituated about half a mile eaft of the church, confifting of 6 houfes, and containing about 50 inhabitants; Harleftone, 3 miles fouth of the church, confifting of 9 houfes, and containing about 50 inhabitants; Yetfon, one mile north of the church, confifting of 4 houfes, and containing 20 inhabitants; and Rimfton, 2 miles fouth-weft of the church, confifting of 4 houfes, and containing about 20 inhabitants. The houfes in thofe villages are chiefly built with mud walls, and thatched. The inhabitants are moftly day-labourers, and healthy. In number in the whole parifh about 400. Poor communibus annis about 20. This parifh is on a clay and flate foil, chiefly the former, and tho' it lies cold, produces, in general, good wheat, barley, and oats; is manured with lime and fea-fand, which, from the diftance from Kingfbridge, being 4 miles, is brought here at no fmall expence. On Flear farm, in this parifh, belonging to Mr. Cornifh, is a quarry, which produces good blue flate, and which is exported from Kingfbridge to Holland. The farms are chiefly let to tenants at rack rent, tho' there are leafe and freeholders in the parifh. In the north of this parifh, about half a mile from the church, ftands Fallapit, otherwife Vallopit, the antient feat of the Fortefcues, from whom the prefent proprietor, Edmund Nathaniel William, a minor, is defcended. The Fortefcues of this houfe have had for nearly 400 years uninterrupted poffeffion of this houfe, with the manor of Eaft Allington, &c. and are lineally defcended from Sir Richard le Forte. Sir Adam, fon of Sir Richard, eftablifhed a noble family at Winfton. From Winfton the Fortefcues branched not only to Norreis, to Wood, to Fallapit, to Spurleftone, in this part of the county; to Buckland-Filleigh, to Caftle-hill, to Wear-Gifford, in the north of it; but to divers other places in other counties; among many others, to Punfborn in Hertfordfhire, to Fulborn in Effex, to Soulden in Buckinghamfhire; and have produced men eminently illuftrious, whofe fervices to their fovereigns in the cabinet, field, and fenate, are confpicuoufly and honourably recorded by different authors who have written on the fubject. Sir Henry Fortefcue, knight, one of the defcendants of the above, chief juftice of the common pleas in Ireland, (eldeft fon of Sir John, governor of Meaux) in the reign of Henry the 6th, was the founder of this houfe, and Wood, in the adjoining parifh of Woodleigh—Wood, by his firft wife Joan, daughter to Wood of Wood, by whom he had defcendants; and this houfe by his fecond marriage with the heirefs to this family, of Fallapit of Fallapit, whofe defcendants have to this time enjoyed, and are now in poffeffion of it.—The church is fituated about the centre of the parifh, on the fouth, adjoining the village of Eaft Allington, is built of hewn ftone, covered with flate, dedicated to St. Andrew, contains three aifles, and is fupported by eight Gothic pillars. It is in length in the clear 93 feet, in breadth 43, in height 22. The tower is likewife built of hewn ftone, contains five bells, and is 65 feet high. The church-yard is about 140 feet fquare. The pulpit and fcreen bear the appearance of great antiquity: The former indeed is handfomely adorned with carved work, and bears the arms and blazoning of the Fortefcues, and many refpectable families who have intermarried with them. In the chancel lie feveral of the Fortefcues, over whofe graves are infcriptions of their ages, burials, &c. &c. Among the reft, lie buried here, Edmund Fortefcue, one of the fheriffs of the county, of this branch of the family, who was buried 21ft May, 1624, and Elizabeth his wife, over whofe grave is this infcription:

> Here lieth a wight
> Of worthy defcent,
> Whofe loffe for her worth
> The people lament;
> The Rich for her love
> And kind affabillitie,
> The Poor for her alms
> Deeds and Hofpitallitie.
> obt: 28 Jan: 1611.

Within

* In the margin is a note thus, in Mr. Geo. Prideaux's hand writing: " *This is certainly a miftake, it cannot be Eaft Allington.*"
† Note by Mr. Geo. Prideaux in the margin: " *This muft be Eaft Allington.*"
‡ Note by Mr. George Prideaux in the margin; " *Ralph Prideaux Kt. married Eliz. the daur. of Walter Treverbin. Roger was the fon of Ralph.*"

Within the rails of the communion table, on the fouth wall, is erected a neat marble monument, with the underwritten infcription:

Sacred
to the memory
of
The Rev^d: Nathaniel Wells,
late Rector of this Parifh,
and of
Catharine
his Wife,
eldeft Daughter of Thomas Bury, Efq^r: of Exeter.

* * * * * * * * *

They lived univerfally beloved
and died as generally lamented,
The former
departed this life on the 28th of Sep^r: 1762
aged 48 years.
The latter
On the 10th day of July 1770 aged 43.
and had iffue eleven Children.
Namely
Alice, Catharine, Elizabeth, Edmund,
Dorothy, Mary, William, Nathaniel,
Samuel, Elizabeth Fortefcue, and Thomas.
who
have erected this monument,
in grateful refpect
to deceafed worth,
and
as a teftimony
of their affection and filial Piety
to their beloved and honoured
Parents.

* * * * * * * * *

Fame's boaftful Chiffel, Fortune's filver Plume,
Mark but the mouldering Urn, or deck the Tomb,
How lov'd how honour'd once avails you not,
To whom related or by whom begot;
A heap of Duft remains of you alone
'Tis now your fate, and foon muft be our own.

On a pillar on the north fide of the chancel, on a plain marble flab, is the following infcription:

In memory of the Rev^d. John Eveleigh M. A. Vicar
of Winkley; and in memory of Martha his Wife,
Daughter of John Scobell Gent. of Nutcombe
in this Parifh.
They had feven Children Martha, John, George,
Melloney, Thomas, William, & Henry: to whom
they approved themfelves excellent parents.
He died on Sunday Nov^r: 11 1770 aged 56:
And with his Daughter Melloney (whom he furvived)
lies buried near a ftone fimilar to this in
Winkley church.
She died 11 years after on Sunday Nov^r: 11
1781 aged 61 having furvived two of her
Children Melloney and Thomas: fhe lies buried
near her own Relations and near this ftone:
Both died in the fincere Faith of Chrift.
Reader thou alfo fhalt die.

The above John and Martha Eveleigh were father and mother to Doctor Eveleigh, provoft of Oriel College, Oxford.

On the eaft part of the fouth-aifle, called the Fallapit aifle, lie the greater part of the Fortefcues, who were buried here. Among them lies Sir Edmund Fortefcue, knight and baronet, fon of Sir Edmund, knight.

Alfo Sir Sandys Fortefcue, fon of Sir Edmund, knight and baronet, who died Oct^r: 27, 1683, aged 23, and Elizabeth his lady, who died Jany. 19, 1682.

On the eaft wall of this aifle is a handfome monument erected to the memory of a later part of this family, with the infcription under:

Here Lye the Bodies of
Edmund Fortefcue Efq^r: of Fallapit and Mary his Wife the Daughter of Mr Sampfon Wyfe of Ditifham,
She died on the 18th: day of Auguft 1722 in the 63 year of her age. He on the 9th of Jan^y: 1733-4 in the 74 year of his age.
And alfo of fix of their Children.
Peter, Mary, Edmund, Sarah, Dorothy, and Grace
Edmund dyed on the 24th day of Jan^y: 1693-4 in the 2^d year of his age:
Sarah dyed on the 22^d day of November 1701 in the 5th year of her age:
Peter dyed on the 10th day of January 1707 in the 21^{ft} year of his age
Mary was married to William Fortefcue Efq^r: of Buckland Filleigh, now
Mafter of the Rolls, by whom fhe had iffue Mary their only Child, foon after
whofe birth fhe died on the 1^{ft} day of Auguft 1710 in the 21^{ft} year of her age:
Dorothy was married to Thomas Bury Efq^r: of the City of Exeter, by whom fhe had iffue
Catharine and Dorothy, and died on the 12th day of July 1733 in the 34th year of her age:

Grace

In CHURSTOW, the grounds are all enclofed with hedges, planted with hazel, thorns, and various underwood. The foil is, in general, excellent, it being neither too ftiff nor too loofe, and rather inclined to red than black.*

KINGSBRIDGE

Grace died unmarried, at the Rolls in London, on the 8th day of March 1743-4 in the
43 year of her age, and by her direction in her laft will was here buried
They reft in the humble hope of a happy Refurrection, while to us remains the example
of their Piety, Benevolence and Innocence.
To their moft Beloved and ever Honoured Memory
The above mentioned William Fortefcue (Executor and Teftamentary Heir of Edmund)
and Elizabeth Fortefcue (the only furviving Child of Edmund and Mary)
Have caufed this monument to be erected
1745.

The late William Fortefcue, Mafter of the Rolls, who, with Elizabeth, erected the above monument, lies buried at the Rolls Chapel, in London, where is this infcription :

In this Chapel lyeth buried The Rt: Honble:
William Fortefcue
Of Buckland Filleigh and Fallapit in the County of
Devon Efqr: who having been one of the Barons of
the Court of Exchequer and afterwards one of the Juftices
of the Court of Common Pleas, was made Mafter of the
Rolls the 5th day of Novr 1741 and dyed the 16 day of
Decr: 1749 in the 63 year of his age.

In the north aifle, on two marble flabs, are the infcriptions under :

To the Memory of Elizabeth lately the Pious	In Memory
Wife of Rich: Wood Gent fhe died Jany 11. 1662.	Of John Scobell of Nutcombe Gent.
Elifa's foule a Graffe divine,	And Mellony his Wife, deceafed Parents
With clay was faftened unto Wood	Of John, Aaron Melloney, Martha, George, Elizabeth,
The Tree did fuddenly decline	Mary, Elizabeth, William and John Scobell,
The Fruit was blafted in the Bud,	the Survivors of which Children are
The Clay which death brake off lies here: the Wife	Martha, George, Elizabeth (the younger) and
Is now engrafted on the Tree of life.	John (the younger) who reflect with the
Reader expect not longe to hold thy breath	greateft pleafure on the lives of their
For heart of Oake, thou feeft cutt off by death.	Parents and fifter Melloney and Mary,
	The other four of the deceafed Children
	died young.

The earlieft entry in the regifter is in the year 1554, fince which time too the regifter has been very regularly kept. The prefent patron is Edmund Nathaniel William Fortefcue, a minor, the heir of Fallapit, whofe predeceffors have been patrons fince their poffeffion of this eftate. The lift of incumbents, as far as they can be traced, are as under :

The Rev. Edm. Elys,	- - - - -	from 1638 to 1677
———— Elias Thomas,	- - - -	——— 1690 — 1717
———— Jo. Egerton,	- - - - -	——— 1717 — 1730
———— Thomas Hurrell,	- - - -	——— 1730 — 1737
———— ——— Gregory,	- - -	——— 1737 — 1746
———— Nathaniel Wells,	- - -	——— 1746 — 1762
———— Thomas Adams,	- - - -	——— 1762 — 1780
———— William Wells,	- - - -	——— 1780 the prefent rector.

The parfonage-houfe, to which there are about 100 acres of arable, orchard, and meadow ground, is about a quarter of a mile foutheaft of the church, is rather a modern building, and pleafantly fituated."

* " The name of this parifh is derived from the high fituation of the church, the word ftow fignifying high. It is fituate on the northweft fide of the hundred of Stanborough, and is of an irregular, oblong fhape. Its greateft length, meafured from the fouth-weft extremity of the barton of Newton, belonging to Abraham Hawkins, efq. on the weft, to the eaft corner of a meadow now held by John Hawkins, efq. for a term of years, determinable on lives, under the lords of the manor of Churftow, called Townmeadow (clofe to a road known by the appellation of Darkey-lane) on the eaft, is two miles and half, and nine hundred feet ; and its greateft breadth, taken from the northern extremity of the barton of Lee, belonging to Benjamin Hayes, efq. on the north, to the fouth-weft corner of a brake called Windmill-brake, on a tenement named Downintown, belonging to Mrs. Elizabeth Hawkins, (clofe and adjoining to one of Bowringfleigh gates, commonly called Piers, belonging to the Rev. Roope Ilbert, in the parifh of Weftalvington) on the fouth, is one mile and half. It is bounded on the eaft by the parifh of Kingfbridge, which tradition fays was originally a part of Churftow ; on the north-eaft by a detached and infulated part of the parifh of Weftalvington ; on the north by the parifh of Loddifwell ; on the north-weft by the parifh of Aveton-Gifford (which is in the hundred of Ermington) ; on the weft and fouth-weft by the parifhes of Thurlfton and South-Milton ; and on the north by the parifh of Weftalvington. The tenants of the manor are bound by their leafes to grind their corn at Kingfbridge, thefe two manors, till very lately, belonging to the fame lord. The roads are not in the beft repair, though thefe are very expenfive here on account of the great road from Kingfbridge, to Modbury and Plymouth, paffing through Churftow. Here are no towns, and only three villages. Thefe are, firft, Churftow-town, on the fouth-fide of the church, confifting of 20 houfes, moftly built of mud-walls, and fcattered about in an irregular manner. Secondly, Ven, fituate on the north-weft fide of the parifh, and juft fuch another place as the former, having 12 houfes and 47 inhabitants. The village of Churftow-town has 132 inhabitants. Thirdly, Merrifield, fituate about three quarters of a mile north-weft of the church, and confifting of 6 poor-houfes and 31 inhabitants. Here is only one manor, viz. the manor of Churftow, and thofe who hold fee eftates within the limits pay a chief rent to the lord or lords thereof. It has a court-leet and courtbaron, and, till very recently, belonged to the Right Honourable Lord Petre, who fold it to Mr. Peter Tonkin of Plymouth, and Mr. Chriftopher Savery of Modbury, two attorneys and brothers-in-law, who give out that they mean to keep it ; but the better opinion feems to be, that the purchafe is made with a land-jobbing view, thefe limbs of the law having often an eye to the fweets of conveyancing in fuch purchafes as may be advantageoufly divided into lots, and difpofed of to the different tenants.—The church ftands on the north fide of the parifh, and one fide of the cemetry is almoft clofe to a part of the parifh of Loddifwell, which feems juft at this fpot to incroach very confiderably on what might naturally be fuppofed to be the proper limits of Churftow. It is built of good hewn ftone ; its length (exclufive of the tower, which is at the weft end, about 19 feet fquare, and of a proportionable height) is 82 feet on the outfide ; its breadth 30

feet ;

KINGSBRIDGE, (fays Rifdon), " fo called from the *Bridge* between that and Dodbroke, was long fince the lands of the Earl of Devon, until by the attainder of the Marquefs of Exeter it came to the crown, and was purchafed by Sir Will. Petre, knight, now the Lord Petre's inheritance." In 1793, the manor was fold by Lord Petre to Mr. John Scoble, attorney at law. The town of Kingfbridge is twelve miles from Dartmouth. It lies four miles from Salcombe harbour, and four miles and half from the main fea. A few years fince, the feoffees, the truftees of the town lands, were at the expence of new paving the ftreets. They added proper footways on each fide; removed the conduits; and built a refervoir at the upper end of the town, whence the water is diftributed by pipes into the feveral quarters. And Mr. Scoble, the lord of the manor, granted a leafe of the markets and butchery, upon condition of the latter being taken down, and another erected on the fcite of the corn market.*

WEST-

feet; and the height of the walls 12 feet. The building on the infide appears to be in the form of a T. The top of the letter, if I may be allowed fo to exprefs myfelf, confifts of two aifles, running from eaft to weft, and at the eaft end of thefe is the chancel, divided into two parts by the fame kind of wood-work as feparates it from the nave. In the northern divifion of this chancel (which is repaired by the owners of the tithes) is the communion table, between the front railing of which, and the door of one of the pews belonging to Norton, is the following infcription on a black flab:

" Here lies the body of John Hawkins of Norton, Efquire,
" who died the 16th day of September 1764. Aged 56 years."

The other part of the chancel (I mean that on the fouth fide) is repaired by Benjamin Hayes of Halwell, efq. as owner of the barton of Lee, in this parifh, and, with the faid barton, feems likely to have formerly belonged to the family of Ryder, fome of them now lying buried here, as appears by a marble tomb (placed on that fide which is next the communion table), on which is the following infcription:

" Near to this place lyes intered the body of Sam-
" uel Ryder, Armig. who departed this life the
" 13th day of April 1727. Aged 35 years. Likewife
" the body of Martyn Ryder, Armiger, who depar-
" ted this life the 30th day of Auguft 1723, Aged 80 years."

The fmall aifle on the north, which is 20 feet long and 12 feet broad, I confider as the ftem of the letter T; and, from four out of the five pews therein at prefent belonging to eftates which were formerly the property of the Ofbornes of Newton in this parifh, it is very likely that this aifle might be built by fome of that family. In the tower is a ring of 4 bad bells. The prefent vicar is the Rev. John Wilcocks, A. B. formerly of Merton college, Oxford, and now the erudite mafter of the free grammar fchool at Kingfbridge (prefented in 1779). Mr. Wilcocks's predeceffor was the Rev. Edward Michell, who fucceeded the Rev. Doctor Andrews, who was preceded by the Rev. Richard Jones (buried the 19th December, 1762), who was the fucceffor of the Rev. —— Baron, whofe predeceffor was the Rev. —— Freke, who fucceeded the Rev. Nathaniel Seaman, who was prefented in 1695, and died in 1723. This vicarage (of which Kingf-bridge is a part, or more likely only a chapel of eafe, as it is faid that that parifh was formerly taken out of this), according to a work publifhed fome time ago, the title of which I do not exactly recollect, but which gives a particular account of the different livings within the diocefe of Exeter, is faid to be in the prefentation of the Chamber of Exeter; and yet it is a certain fact that both the prefent incumbent and his predeceffor were prefented by the lord chancellor. The tithes are the property of the Exeter corporation or chamber, who let them in leafe. Thefe formerly belonged to the Abbey of Buckfaft. The regifter of this parifh commences the 18th day of Auguft, 1695, and the average of births for the laft ten years is from ten to eleven; the average of deaths during the fame period is from five to fix. The following is a table of the baptifms and burials from 1781 to 1790, both years inclufive.

Baptifms.		Burials.	
Date.	No. of Baptifms.	Date.	No. of Burials.
1781	6	1781	3
1782	11	1782	5
1783	10	1783	16
1784	16	1784	4
1785	4	1785	5
1786	12	1786	2
1687	14	1787	6
1788	11	1788	7
1789	11	1789	2
1790	13	1790	1
Total No. of births in ten years	108	Total No. of burials in ten years	51

The total number of inhabitants in this parifh the 8th day of April, 1791, was 283. Not only this parifh, but all the neighbourhood, abounds with orchards, which produce abundance of cyder. The cultivation of apple-trees has been much attended to here of late years, the merchants of London having fent agents to buy up large quantities of cyder, and fhip off for the capital, which has raifed the price confiderably, and, of courfe, rendered it an article more worthy of attention. Of gentlemen's feats there is now but one left, viz. Norton, the feat of John Hawkins, efq. This is fituate on the eaft fide of the parifh, on the barton of Norton (held by leafe, determinable on lives, under the lords of the manor of Churftow), and is about half a mile from the town of Kingfbridge. It is a plain ftone edifice, without any thing to recommend it worth noticing.

* " *Kingfbridge* and *Churftow* now form one vicarage. A deed granted by the rector of Churftow, proves that they were once a rectory, unappropriated. It is probable, however, that they were appropriated to the abbey of Buckfaft before the 7th of Edward the 3d, (1333), as a deed of that date has been feen in the cuftody of Lord Petre, by which it appears that the manors of Churftow and Kingfbridge then

belonged

WEST-ALLINGTON is fix miles in length, and about three in breadth. Some parts of this parish are flate; others, clay: And towards Malborough, there is a red loam. The whole is enclofed with quickfet hedges, and is in a good ftate of cultivation. The ufual courfe of hufbandry, is wheat, two crops of barley, and clover fucceffively, once in feven years; and the manures are lime, dung, and

belonged to that abbey. After the abbot and monks had got the rectory into their hands, they appropriated the great and fmall tithes of both parifhes to themfelves, allowing the fecular clergyman only £.20 per ann. for ferving the cure; and this is all that the vicar is entitled to from the rectory, except the glebe worth about £.9 a year. At what period the impropriation was difpofed of by the crown does not appear; but it was given many years ago by one Acland to the Chamber of Exeter, for charitable ufes. The ftipend of the vicar has been augmented with an annuity of fix pounds per annum, bequeathed for that purpofe fome years ago by the Rev. Francis Hingfton, rector of Newton-ferrers, payable out of a freehold eftate in the parifh of Malborough; and alfo by what is commonly termed *Queen Anne's bounty.* The vicar ferves thefe two parifhes each once every Sunday. The prefent incumbent is the Rev. John Wilcocks, A. B. prefented in 1779. His predeceffor was the Rev. Edward Michell, who fucceeded the Rev. Doctor —— Andrews, who was preceded by the Rev. Richard Jones (buried the 19th Dec. 1762), who was the fucceffor of the Rev. —— Baron, whofe predeceffor was the Rev. —— Freke, who fucceeded the Rev. Nathaniel Seaman, prefented in 1695, and buried in 1723. For the keeping of the church in repair, lands in feveral parifhes have been charitably given, which at prefent are vefted in feoffees in truft. They are now chiefly leafed out for a term of 99 years, determinable on lives, and, were they all in demefne, it is faid would let for the clear rent of £.200 per annum. The profits, by the prefent feoffment deeds, are directed to be applied " to the maintenance of the church of Kingfbridge, and for fuch other good and pious purpofes as the major or *chiefeft* part of the inhabitants may direct." By the ancient deeds it appears that a fmall portion of the revenue of thefe lands was originally defigned for the benefit of the poor; but they are now all claffed together, and the income is expended about the church, and in keeping the pipes which fupply the town with water in repair, which on an average does not exceed £.50 a year. By the original deed, now extant, dated the 1ft of April, in the 8th year of King Henry the 8th, one John Gye grants to certain feoffees therein named, a clofe of land near Wallingford, in the parifh of Dodbrooke, in truft, to pay part of the profits to the churchwardens of Kingfbridge to buy cakes, wine, and ale,* &c. &c.

In Kingfbridge church, the following infcription is pleafing from its piety and tendernefs:

In memoriam piam Georgii Geffery | Artium. Magiftri
vigilantiffimi | Domini noftri Jefu Chrifti | Evangelii
nuper in hac—Ecclefiâ miniftri.

Hic Geofride jaces, dulci cum prole fepultus;
    Tu terræ gremio, filia chara tuo.
Tu vigilans paftor, tua proles agna tenella;
    Cælicolûm grati Paftor et agna gregi.
Nomine, Tu famæ columen, mage marmore firmum:
    Filiolæ laus eft ampla, fuiffe tuam.

Here in th' Earth's bofome gently clafped is
Learn'd Jeffery, & his fweete Childe in his:
A painfull Sheepeheard He, She a bleft lambe:
Both to Heaven's crowned flock thrice welcom came:
    His name is his perpetual monument
    His daughter's Epitaph is her defcent.
Obiit 12° die Maii
Anno Dn̄ni 1611, Ætatis fuæ 35.

The infcription is cut in capital letters, gilt, on a black ftone, fet in a fquare black frame of wood, with gilt edges, and placed againft the north pier of the nave of the church, clofe to the pulpit on its right hand.

The regifter of the eftablifhed church commences the 19th day of June, 1636. A variety of religious opinions has long pervaded the town of Kingfbridge; and though the number of inhabitants, including all ages, as has already been feen, falls fhort of a thoufand, yet here are no lefs than three diffenting meeting-houfes, all which have been erected in the prefent century. One of thefe is fituate a little above the lower conduit, on the weft-fide of Fore-ftreet, behind a dwelling-houfe, adjoining a lane which leads to the weft backlet. This belongs to the anabaptifts, though teachers of various other perfuafions have at times been permitted to preach therein. It is a decent ftone edifice, 36 feet long, 24 feet broad, and 20 feet high, and was built in 1702. It has a burying-ground at Ven, in the parifh of Churftow, and, befides the dwelling-houfe adjoining the meeting, is endowed with an annuity of 20 fhillings, given by a Mr. Robert Hammick of Moreton Hampftead, as alfo with the intereft of £.40, the bequeft of the late Mr. David Trathen of Kingfbridge. No regular regifter was kept by the anabaptifts till 1785. About a hundred yards further up, on the fame fide of the ftreet, in a cemetery, ftands the quaker's meeting-houfe. This is a plain, decent, ftone edifice, fuitable to the fimple manners of its vifitors. It is 30 feet fquare, and 18 feet high; and was built by fubfcription in 1701-2, at the expence of £.167. Here the FRIENDS of the weftern divifion hold their autumnal quarterly meeting. The regifter of this fociety begins in 1659. The prefbyterians, formerly, had their meeting-houfe behind a dwelling now belonging to a Mr. Oxenham, fituate in Fore-ftreet, a little below Sugar-lane, and on the oppofite fide; but it being in wretched repair, they were lately induced to pull it down; and, having difpofed of the fite to the owner of the houfe in front, who has converted it into a garden, they purchafed a fpot of land behind a houfe on the eaft fide of the fame ftreet, a little below the butter-market, where, in 1790, they erected by fubfcription a neat ftone edifice, fafhed, ceiled, and otherwife properly accommodated for a religious affembly, 44 feet long, 24 feet broad, and 20 feet high. Behind, on the eaft, is a fmall burying-ground. This meeting is endowed only with an annuity of 20 fhillings, the bequeft of a Mrs. Weymouth, payable out of a leafehold eftate which now hangs on a fingle life. The regifter of baptifms at the prefbyterian meeting-houfe commences the 22d day of Dec. 1774, but they had no cemetery till 1790, and only two perfons have yet been buried therein. The only manufacture carried on in Kingfbridge is the woollen, and of that but little; and though the place is fo well fituate for trade, yet the fole exports are corn (of which there is more fhipped from hence, poffibly, than from any other port in Devonfhire); flates (which are brought from two neighbouring quarries, the one in the parifh of Weft-Alvington, called Century, and the other in the parifh of Buckland Tout Saints); and cyder, with which the South-hams fo much abound. The average of births for ten years, viz. from 1762 to 1771, both years inclufive, as taken from the church regifter and beft account to be had from the diffenters, is 17. The average of deaths during the fame period is 14.

A

* As the inhabitants of Kingfbridge have time immemorial made ufe of a liquor called *white-ale*, known only in their own neighbourhood, and give the name of beer to what is elfewhere called *ale*, it is natural to conclude that old Gye meant the beverage peculiar to his native place. This malt liquor has more the appearance of mulled wine than any thing elfe, and is never fine. A principal ingredient made ufe of in the brewing, called *grout*, is a fecret compofition known only to a few people who make and fell it to the alehoufe-holders.

and fea-fand, which produce great quantities of corn: And the Kingſbridge cornfactors buy it on commiſſion for the London, Briſtol, Liverpool, and Plymouth maltſters, brewers, and merchants. The cyder, of which ſome years there is a great quantity, is generally bought for the London market. Wood and timber are ſcarce in this pariſh. Situated towards the ſouth, on the brow of a hill, one mile weſt of Kingſbridge, in the road leading to Malborough, is the pleaſant village of Weſt-Allington. In 1791, it contained (in 52 families) 228 inhabitants, chiefly huſbandmen and artificers.* The pariſh church is a

Vol. III.   2 A   neat

A table of the births and burials in Kingſbridge, from 1762 to 1771, both years incluſive

Date.	Ch. of Eng.		Anabapt.		Quakers.		Preſbyt.		Total.	
	Bo.	Bu.	Bo.	Bu.	Bo.	Bu.	Bo.	Bu.	Bo.	Bu.
1762	22	19	0	0	2	0	0	0	24	19
1763	16	12	1	0	0	1	0	0	17	13
1764	23	15	1	0	1	0	1	0	26	15
1765	9	8	1	0	0	0	0	0	10	8
1766	14	13	1	0	1	0	1	0	17	13
1767	12	14	1	0	1	0	0	0	14	14
1768	14	15	1	0	0	1	0	0	15	16
1769	15	14	3	0	2	4	0	0	20	18
1770	13	9	2	0	0	0	0	0	15	9
1771	19	15	2	0	0	0	0	0	21	15
	C. 157	C. 134	13	0	7	6	2	0	179	140
	A. 13	A. 0								
	Q. 7	Q. 6								
	P. 2	P. 0								

Total No. of births in ten years - - } 179   140 Total No. of buryings in ten years.

A table of births and burials in Kingſbridge, from 1781 to 1790, both years incluſive.

Date.	Ch. of Eng.		Anabapt.		Quakers.		Preſbyt.	
	Bo.	Bu.	Bo.	Bu.	Bo.	Bu.	Bo.	Bu.
1781	21	10	2		0	1	3	0
1782	14	21	4	about 20	2	0	2	0
1783	26	13	3		1	1	4	0
1784	23	10	2		1	2	8	0
1785	18	14	1	2	1	0	0	0
1786	17	12	3	0	2	0	4	0
1787	26	12	9	2	2	0	5	0
1788	19	14	1	3	3	3	4	0
1789	18	11	7	1	2	1	6	0
1790	16	11	3	0	1	2	3	0
	C. 198	C. 128	35	28	15	10	39	0
	A. 35	A. 28						
	Q. 15	Q. 10						
	P. 39	P. 0						

Total No. of births the laſt ten years } 287   166 Total No. of buryings the laſt ten years.

The average of births the laſt ten years is 28; the average of burials during the ſame period is 16. By this it appears the proportion of births has greatly encreaſed, but the burials continued much the ſame." From Mr. *Hawkins*, in 1791.

* Going through the pariſh of Weſt-Alvington, on the road leading from Kingſbridge to Salcombe, we paſs over four ſmall bridges, thrown over places where the tide comes up at highwater, viz. Gallons Bridge, (repaired by Kingſbridge and Weſt-Alvington), Tacket Wood Bridge, Colopit Bridge, and Blanks Mill Bridge, where Weſt-Alvington ends: the three laſt-mentioned bridges are repaired by the county. The pariſhioners have been at a great expence in widening and hardening the roads, as good materials are very ſcarce: They are obliged to fetch a great part of their ſtone in barges, below Salcombe, and carry it afterward a mile or more by land carriage, which makes the roads very expenſive. Notwithſtanding, moſt of the roads in this pariſh are in good repair, and of ſufficient breadth for any carriage to travel. In the beginning of the year 1791, there were ſix hundred and fifty-four inhabitants in this pariſh, and forty-ſix farm-houſes. By the regiſter, it appears, that in the ten years preceding that date, viz. from 1781 to 1790, both incluſive, there were 44 marriages, 157 baptiſms, and 105 burials; which gives four and four tenths, fifteen and ſeven tenths, and ten and five tenths, for the yearly average of marriages, baptiſms, and burials reſpectively. Between the town of Kingſbridge and the village of Weſt-Allington, is the manor of Nordon, belonging to Lord Boringdon. This manor has only two farm houſes and four cottages. The whole is rated in £.103 9s. per ann. according to the poor's rate. Adjoining the manor of Nordon, on the ſouth, is the manor of Woodhouſe, by the ſide of Salcombe river, belonging to Bickford of Dunſland. In former years this was the principal manor of the pariſh, many eſtates belonging to it being ſold off, reſerving only a chief rent. There is only one farm-houſe on this manor, the other parts are overlands, and the whole is rated in eighty-two pounds eighteen ſhillings and four-pence a year. On the ſouth-weſt, adjoining the pariſh of Malborough, lies the manor of Woolſon, belonging to his Grace the Duke of Bolton, conſiſting of nine farm-houſes, moſt of them in the village of Woolſon; the other parts are overlands, and the whole is rated in two hundred ſeventy-three pounds ſeventeen ſhillings and one penny a year. On the weſt lies the manor of Bagton, belonging to Elizabeth Wells Sturgeon, daughter of the late Edmund Forteſcue of Fallapit, eſq. This manor conſiſts of two farm-houſes, the other parts are overlands, and the whole is rated in one hundred thirteen pounds ſixteen ſhillings and eight-pence per year. In the north diviſion, adjoining the pariſhes of Churſtow and Loddiſwell, is the manor of Rake and Sorely. The barton of Rake lies by the river Avon, or Aun, which parts it from Loddiſwell. Sorely village conſiſts of four farm-houſes, and one cottage. The whole manor is rated in two hundred ſixty-five pounds ſixteen ſhillings and eight-pence per year. It belonged to the late Robert Lake, eſq. whoſe daughters, coheireſſes, ſold it to Samuel Holditch Hayne, eſq. of Kingſbridge. In the eaſt diviſion lies a great part of the manor of Dodbrooke, belonging to John Henry Southcote of Buckland Tout Saints, eſq. conſiſting of nineteen ſmall tenements. There are only two farm-houſes on this part of the manor, the reſt are overlands, and rated at one hundred thirty-ſix pounds and ten-

pence

neat building, covered with flate. It has two rows of handfome pillars, and three aifles, and is decently feated.*

SOUTH-

pence per year.—In this parifh is "*Bowringfleigh*, the ancient dwelling of Bowring, the laft of which name, in King Edward the 4th's time, left a daughter, Alice, married to Pike of Somerfetfhire, whofe pofterity paffed away this land unto the family of Webber," otherwife Gilbert, for I find by the regifter that this family of Webber changed their name to that of Gilbert, in the days of Queen Elizabeth, and in this family it continued till the reign of King William the 3d, when it was fold to William Ilbert, efq. of Rill, in the parifh of Buckfaftleigh; fince which time it has been the inheritance of that family, and is now in the poffeffion of the Rev. Roope Ilbert, the great grandfon of the purchafer. Near Salcombe river, in this parifh, is Garfton, an old decayed manfion of the family of Baftard. How long it has been in that family I know not; I fee by the regifter that they were fettled there in the days of Queen Elizabeth, and the family has continued there many generations; our prefent reprefentative for the county, John Pollexfen Baftard, efq. of Kitley, is the owner thereof. And by the river Avon, or Aun, on the north, is the barton of " Rake, the ancient dwelling of John Rake, in King Henry's the 3d's time, and Sir Adam de Rake lived there in King Edward the 3d's time, fince which it has been in the family of Tremain for feveral generations;" and not long fince it was fold to the late Robert Lake, efq. of Scobbahull, otherwife Scoble, in South Pool, whofe daughters as coheirs now enjoy the fame. The old feat has been deftroyed, and there remains now only a farm-houfe on the fame.—In the north divifion is fituated Cumbe Royal, where a branch of the Gilbert family formerly lived, who fold it to the family of Lufcombe. This is a modern-built houfe, and was the feat of the late John Lufcombe, efq.; and John Lufcombe Manning, efq. his nephew, is the prefent proprietor thereof. Quay-houfe, near Kingfbridge, is the feat of Lieut.-colonel Ilbert.

* Meafuring in the whole fixty feet, by thirty-three and one half in the clear. The tower is fixty-feven feet high; built of good hewn ftone, with four large pinnacles.

MONUMENTAL INSCRIPTIONS.

In the floor of the chancel, clofe to the N. wall—on a brafs plate—infcription in *capitals roman.*

Heere lyeth interred the Bodye of | William
Baftard of Garfton Efquier | whoe departed
this life. the 10th of | March 1638. Beinge the 89th
yeare of his Age | Hee that raifed up the Lord 𝕵𝖊𝖘𝖚𝖘
fhall raife me allfo by 𝕵𝖊𝖘𝖚𝖘

Note—Another plate has been removed from the fame ftone, (probably the figure of the deceafed) the veftiges of which remain.

Another fimilar ftone, blue flate, is placed on its edge againft the N. wall, upon which is the following:

Hic jacet Corpus Gulielmi | Baftard de Garfton |
Equitis Aurati qui obiit | 30tio Junii Ano: Dom:
1690 | et ætatis fuæ 54.

Above this is a mural monument of white marble, in the centre of which is a fquare tablet, within a frame of foliage, feftoons of rofes dependant from cherub's heads; on each fide are two Corinthian pillars of black marble, raifed on truffes, and fupporting an entablature crowned with a femicircular pediment, open in the centre, upon each angle of which is placed an urn. Two angels, with trumpets, recline one on each fide of the pediment, in the opening of which are the arms of Baftard, viz.—Or, a chevron azure. on.which is an efcutcheon of pretence, viz. quarterly 1 & 4. *Argent*, a *lion* rampant, *gules*. 2 & 3 azure.—On a cap and mantling creft, viz. Iffuing from a wreath of his colours a dexter arm, in armour, holding a drawn dagger.

Beneath this, on the entablature, is another coat, viz. Baftard empaled with—Or, on a bend dexter gules 3 ftars of five points, argent.

Upon the fquare tablet above-mentioned, is the following infcription:

In memory of | William Baftard Efq: | fon and
heir of Sir William | Baftard Knight, who
having | his full hope in God which | raifeth
the dead departed | this life, in the thirty
fixth year | of his age, and was here | interred
The fixteenth day of Febry. MDCCIII.

At the foot of this infcription is another efcutcheon, with the arms of Baftard; and beneath the whole upon an oval tablet, the length being placed horizontally, this infcription:

Here are alfo | depofited the Remains | of Mrs.
Anne Baftard | eldeft Daughter of William |
Baftard Efq: who was interred | December
the 25th. 1706. | having liv'd twelve yeares |
of fuch is the kingdom of God.

On a head-ftone at the eaft end of the church-yard:

Here lyeth the Body of
Daniel Jeffery the Son of Mich-
ael Jeffery and Joan his Wife he
Was buried ye 2 day of September
1746 and in ye 18th year of his Age.
This youth When In his Sicknefs lay
did or the minifter Send ✸ that he would
Come and With him Pray ✸ But he would not atend
But When this young man Buried was
the minifter did him admit ✸ he Should be
Caried into Church ✸ that he might money geet.
By this you See what man will dwo ✸ to geet
money if he can ✸ who did Refufe to come
and pray ✸ by the Forefaid young man.

The above is tranfcribed *verbatim* et *literatim*, as a curiofity in its way. It may not be amifs to add, that upon fetting up this ftone, the church-wardens immediately waited on their minifter, reprefenting to him the offence which the epitaph had given themfelves and his parifhioners in general, from the fcandalous falfehoods it contained, and the ftigma intended to be fixed by it on his character; for they knew that the deceafed had died of a virulent fmall-pox, and that fo fuddenly, that there was fcarce time for giving notice of his illnefs before his death confirmed it. They therefore beg'd the epitaph might be obliterated, and that they might be fupported by his concurrence in doing it. But he having gratified the church-wardens indignation and his own curiofity, by looking at the infcription, beg'd it might be permitted to remain; for he could not allow himfelf to have a fhare in the deftruction of fuch poetry, of which probably he chofe

to

SOUTH-HUISH is enclofed with hedges planted with thorns, &c. except towards the fea, where the fences are of ftone.*

The

to be the *fubject rather than the compofer.* This minifter was the Rev. and learned Mr. Pyle, the prefent worthy incumbent of the parifh, fon
of Mr. Pyle, formerly of Lynne Regis, in Norfolk, well known for his " Paraphrafe on St. Paul's Epiftles, in the manner of S. Clarke's on
the Gofpels."

Here is a good vicarage-houfe, about a quarter of a mile from the church, the ground belonging to it about two acres. The re-
gifter of this parifh commenced in the year 1558, by which I difcovered the names of the vicars fince that time to be Theophilus Jones,
Chriftopher Elgar, Edward Elliott, Philip Lavers, Francis Bernard, George Pitt, Francis Fullwood, John Tomkin, Samuel Northcote,
Aaron Baker, Francis Barry, Hugh Trevanion, and the Rev. Thomas Pyle, the prefent vicar, who is alfo prebendary of the church of
Winchefter. This vicarage, confifting of Weft-Alvington and the three daughter churches, viz. Malborough, South Milton, and South
Huifh, is in the gift of the church of Salifbury. The great tithes are leafed by the Chapter to the Rev. Roope Ilbert of Bowringfleigh.

* This parifh is in the fouth-weft part of the hundred of Stanborough, and is fo regular in its fhape, as to be a more perfect parallelo-
gram, poffibly, than any other parifh in the kingdom. Its greateft length, taken from a rock on the fea coaft in Bigbury Bay on the weft,
called the *Woolman,* to the eaftern extremity of a tenement called *Rugwell,* now held by a farmer called Thomas Jarvis, for a term of
years, determinable on lives, under Lord Vifcount Courtenay, on the eaft, is two miles, fixteen perch, and fixty-four feet; and its breadth,
meafured from a rivulet in the highway at a place called *Bale's Bridge* on the north, to the fouth hedge of a field called *Higher-Jumping-
field,* now held by a farmer named William Jarvis, for a leafe, determinable on lives, under Lord Vifcount Courtenay, on the fouth, is
five thoufand two hundred feet, or 80 feet lefs than a mile. It is bounded on the north by the parifh of South Milton; on the eaft by the
parifh of Weft-Alvington; on the fouth by the parifh of Malborough; and on the weft by Bigbury Bay. The roads are narrow, and
being but little ufed may naturally be expected to be in much the fame repair now as they have been for thefe hundred years. The annual
value of the parifh, computed by the land-tax, is £.395 15s. 0d. Here are three little villages, viz. firft, *South-Huifh,* fituate a little to
the weft of the church, confifting of 12 ill-built houfes, (fome of which are farms), and 69 inhabitants. Secondly, *Galmpton,* which is on
the fouth fide of the parifh, and about half a mile eaft of Bigbury-Bay, confifting of 20 cottages, and the number of the inhabitants is
100. Thirdly, *Outer-Hope,* a little fifhing cove in Bigbury-Bay, (and juft by Inner-Hope, in the parifh of Malborough). This is at the
weft-end of the parifh, and confifts of 11 houfes and 51 inhabitants. The only manors in this parifh, are thofe of South-Huifh and
Galmpton, both which belong to Lord Vifcount Courtenay. The tenements are occupied by leffees for lives, and his lordfhip has a court-
baron in each manor. There is very little freehold in this parifh, but what belongs to his lordfhip; and thofe two or three tenements which
are not his property, pay him a chief rent. The foil is in general good, and rather inclined to red. On the eaft-fide of this parifh, in
fome fields called the Dolts, and which are part of a freehold eftate named Burley, belonging to a farmer called Jofeph Lindon, about half
a mile north of Malborough church, on the declivity of a hill, but very near the fummit, facing the north, and commanding a view of the
principal road leading from Plymouth, Modbury, and Kingfbridge, towards Malborough and Fort Charles, is an entrenchment much in
the fhape of an egg: Its length from E. to W. is 36 perch, and its breadth from N. to S. is 22 perch. The north and weft parts of the
entrenchment are 30 feet broad at the top, and 5 or 6 feet deep; the eaft and fouth from 3 to 4 perch broad, and from 10 to 15 feet deep.*
About two years ago a filver coin of Charles the Ift, was ploughed up, from which it is natural to conclude this entrenchment was made
during that prince's unhappy wars; and yet it is no lefs fingular than true, that not the fmalleft traditionary account of it, is to be met
with in the neighbourhood. On the north-fide of the parifh, about half a mile eaft of Bigbury-Bay, ftands the church. It is built of
ftone, and is in the form of a T; that is to fay, it has two aifles, which run parallel from eaft to weft, and a north aifle. Its length,
exclufive of the tower, is 59 feet on the infide, and its breadth 36 feet. The north aifle is 17 feet long, and 14 feet broad. The walls
are 13 feet high, and the tower (which is low, and of a ftone fo foft as to be fretted in holes by the fpray of the fea from the Bay), is
about 20 feet fquare; in it are four bad bells. The chancel, in the eaft-end, is feparated from the nave by the rood loft. Here is nothing
within worth noticing; but in the cemetry, on the eaft-fide, and juft without the communion table, is a handfome free-ftone tomb of
about 6 feet long and 3 feet and half high, covered with a black ftone flab, on which is the following infcription :

      " Beneath this tomb is depofited the body of William
      " Clark late of Plymouth, Efqr. a native of this
      " parifh, who departed this life the Ift day of November
      " 1786. Aged 55 years."

With refpect to the vicar and curate of this parifh, as alfo in whofe gift the living is,—fee the account of the parifh of Malborough.
The great tithes belong to the dean and chapter of Sarum, who grant them in leafe with thofe of Weft-Alvington, South-Milton, and
Malborough. The regifter of this parifh commences in 1672; and the average of baptifms for the laft ten years, (viz. from 1781 to 1790,
both years inclufive), is from 3 to 4. The average of burials during the fame period is from 2 to 3. The following is a table of the
births and burials during the faid period.

Births.			Burials.		
Date.		No.	Date.		No.
1781	———	0	1781	———	3
1782	———	5	1782	———	1
1783	———	0	1783	———	5
1784	———	4	1784	———	1
1785	———	0	1785	———	1
1786	———	5	1786	———	3
1787	———	6	1787	———	1
1788	———	4	1788	———	3
1789	———	8	1789	———	4
1790	———	3	1790	———	2
Total No. of baptifms in 10 years ...... }		35	Total No. of births in 10 years .... }		24

A *fafhion* prevails among the inhabitants of this parifh of being buried at Malborough, and alfo (but not to fo great a degree) of having
their children baptized there. The total number of inhabitants in this parifh, on the 11th of March, 1791, was 224. Here are no
gentlemen's feats.‡

* The farmer has planted the entrenchment on the fouth-weft, between S. and W. with apple trees.
‡ Clofe to the north-fide of this parifh, but within that of South-Milton, is Holwell, the feat of Henry Abraham Gilbert, efq. the only one of the male line of that
ancient family, I believe, which now retains any landed property in this county. This is an ancient manfion, but has nothing particular to recommend it further than
its having been for a long time the refidence of a younger branch of the Gilberts, formerly of Greenway, Compton, and Sandridge. The prefent owner is about 21
years of age, and now at Oriel college, Oxford, being intended for holy orders. I am not equal to the tafk of tracing his defcent very far, but the following particulars
may be depended on.—William Gilbert of Holwell, had two fons, Thomas and Abraham. Thomas died unmarried; and Abraham, when about 50 years of age,
wedded Margaret, eldeft daughter, and one of the coheireffes of John Ofborne of Newton, in the parifh of Churftow, efq. by whom he had four fons and one daughter,
viz. John, William, Abraham, Thomas, and Elizabeth. John and Abraham died without iffue; William married Mifs Elizabeth Peard, by whom he had one
daughter, Margaret, who married Thomas I'Ans of Ilfracombe, gent. by whom fhe has feveral children; Thomas married Mifs Jane Harrifon, and by her had iffue a
fon, Henry Gilbert, who entered into holy orders, and who married Mifs Mary Cove, by whom he had one fon, Henry Abraham Gilbert, the prefent owner of Holwell. Elizabeth became the fecond wife of John Hawkins of Norton, efq. by whom fhe had a fon, the prefent Abraham Hawkins of Alfton, efq.

The parifh of MALBOROUGH is very fimilar to the adjacent parifhes, in its general afpeĉt. I fhould obferve, indeed, that the foil in Malborough is remarkably red. Lord Courtenay has eight manors in Malborough, viz. 1ft, Malborough; 2d, Salcombe; 3d, Ilton; 4th, Eaft-Sewer; 5th, Bolberry-Allen; 6th, Bolberry-Beacham; 7th, Hope; and 8th, Collaton. And about half a mile fouth of the church is a manor called Pottlemouth, belonging to William Fry, efq.*

The

* With refpeĉt to the etymology of the name of this parifh, I have little or nothing to offer; poffibly it may be fo denominated from the French *mal*, bad, and borough, which together will very well exprefs the appearance of the village of that name, where the church ftands. This parifh, which is at the extremity of the hundred of Stanborough, is in fhape very much like an ox's tongue. Its length, meafured from a point on the eaft, juft over Salcombe Bar, called the Bolt-head, to another point of land on the weft, called the Bolt-tail, is five miles and 400 feet; and its breadth, taken from the church, (which ftands on the very borders of two other parifhes), and meafured fouth to a rock on the fea-coaft of the Warren, called Goat-rock, is two miles, three quarters, and 190 feet. It is bounded on the eaft by the navigable river, or rather inlet of the fea, which goes up to the town of Kingfbridge, from the little fea-port of Salcombe, (which is in this parifh), and thereby feparated from the feveral parifhes of Eaft-Portlemouth, South-Pool, and Charleton. On the north it is bounded by Weft-Alvington; on the north-weft by South-Huifh; and on the fouth and fouth-weft by the fea. There is one bridge in this parifh, repaired by the county; it is of ftone, and at the head of an inlet of the fea which branches off from that which goes up to Kingfbridge before-mentioned; this bridge and creek are both called after Blank's-mills, a fet of mills of that name that are clofe to this bridge. It is 130 feet long, 8 high, and 14 broad, with a railing on each fide, and was in great part rebuilt about the year 1768. The mill-ftream is the only water which paffes under it, except at the flood of the tide. The north-end of this bridge is in Weft-Allington. Of the mills in this parifh there are four fets, viz. Blank's (or Alfton) mills before-mentioned; Hanger-mills; Souther-mills; and Bolberry-mills. Thefe are all worked by water and over-fhot. The firft are now held by Henry Thorning, under a leafe determinable on lives, of Abraham Hawkins, efq. and are part of the manor of Alfton, which lies juft above thefe mills. The fecond, Hanger-mills, are rented by John Cole, of John Pollexfen Baftard, of Kitley, efq. and are part of the manor of Batfon, in this parifh. They lie in a vale, about a mile to the weft of Salcombe, and are a little above a cove called North-fands. The third, Souther-mills, are held by the aforementioned Henry Thorning, under a leafe for lives, of William Fry, efq. and lie in a vale a little to the weft of Hanger-mills, juft above a cove called South-fand. And the fourth, Bolberry-mills, are rented by —— Prowfe, of Mr. John Adams of South-down, in this parifh, who holds them, under a leafe determinable on lives, of Lord Vifcount Courtenay, and are part of the manor of Bolberry-Beacham. The grounds are moftly inclofed with hedges, planted with thorns, hazel, &c. Thofe near the fea are fenced with ftone walls. The roads in general are rather narrow, but thofe which are moft ufed are in good repair. As to the valuation of the parifh, I know no way of computing it, unlefs it be by the land-tax, and then it will amount to £.1335 per annum. Of the towns and villages, to begin with that which bears the name of the parifh, Malborough, and which is clofe to the church; it confifts of two ftreets of miferable mud-wall houfes, but one fide of one of thefe ftreets is in the parifh of Weft-Alvington. The number of thefe houfes (exclufive of thofe which are in the parifh of Weft-Alvington, and which are about a dozen), is 38, and the inhabitants are reckoned to be 144. This is in the manor or borough of Malborough, belonging to Lord Vifcount Courtenay, whofe fteward holds a court-leet and court-baron here, and appoints a portreeve, conftables, &c. The number of inhabitants in this parifh, in the month of July, 1790, was 831. The gentlemen's feats here are as follow: Firft, Alfton-houfe, belonging to Abraham Hawkins, efq. (a captain in the fecond, or north regiment of Devonfhire militia, and one of his majefty's deputy-lieutenants and juftices of the peace for this county). It is fituate in the manor of Alfton, belonging to this gentleman, on the north-eaft fide of the parifh, and commands a beautiful view, not only of the creek called Blank's-mills, which approaches within a fhort diftance of the houfe, but alfo of a place, called Wide-gates, in the inlet or branch of the fea which goes up from Salcombe to Kingfbridge (before-mentioned), and where feven different creeks form a junĉtion. The houfe is a modern, fafhed building, done over white. Alfton pays no chief rent to any other manor.—On the fouth of Alfton is Yarde-houfe, late the feat of Samuel Savery, efq. deceafed, but now of his fifter Mrs. Dorothy Gillard. This is on the barton of Yarde, and was formerly the refidence of the Devonfhire family of that name, to whom, according to Prince, it belonged for twenty generations. It then came to the Dyers, in whofe family it remained till the males became extinĉt. In 1765, the before-mentioned Samuel Savery fucceeded to it, (with many other valuable lands), in right of his great-great-grandmother, Mifs Joan Dyer, the wife of his great-great-grandfather, John Savery of Rattery, in this county, efquire, an ancient and refpeĉtable family. This John Savery and Joan Dyer his wife had a fon, John Savery of Rattery, who had a fon John Savery of Rattery, who had a fon Samuel Savery of Bickington, in this county, father of the before-mentioned Samuel Savery of Yarde, efquire, who dying the 21ft March, 1790, unmarried, bequeathed all his eftates to his fifter, Mrs. Dorothy Gillard. This lady has a daughter, Mifs Dorothy Savery Gillard. It is a neat houfe, built of hewn ftone.—" On the banks of the river that defcends from Dodbrook, and falls into Salcombe, ftood Ilton-caftle, the chief feat of Sir John Chiverfton, who married Joan, the daughter of Hugh Courtenay, fecond of that name, Earl of Devon; and in cafe of failure of iffue, fettled his eftate upon his father-in-law. He died without iffue; and the Earl of Devon poffeffing thefe lands, gave them all to his fon Sir Peter, who refided at Ilton-caftle. The parifh of Malborough, together with the caftle, came afterwards to Richard Courtenay, bifhop of Norwich; as alfo Thurlefton, and Chiverfton, and other eftates that had been in poffeffion of Chiverfton." *Cleaveland.*—It is on the barton of Ilton, within the manor of that name, and now belongs to a Mr. Nicholas Adams, who has a leafe of three lives in it, under Lord Vifcount Courtenay.—A little below the village of Batfon, about half a mile north-eaft of Salcombe, is Snapes-houfe, one of the feats of William Elford Ilbert, efq. (lieutenant-colonel of the fouth regiment of Devonfhire militia, and one of his majefty's deputy-lieutenants for this county). This is on the barton of Snapes, belonging to that gentleman. The houfe was rebuilt by the owner about the year 1786, and is a neat little box, fituate clofe to and commanding a view of part of the harbour of Salcombe.—About three quarters of a mile to the fouth-weft of Salcombe, and a quarter of a mile beyond Fort Charles, on a fpot projeĉting a little into the fea, and exaĉtly facing the bar of the harbour, is a delightful retreat, called Moult, belonging to Samuel Strode, efq. It commands an extenfive fea profpeĉt, and is fo happily fheltered from moft winds, that it feems to enjoy perpetual fummer.—Lord Vifcount Courtenay has eight manors in this parifh, and thofe who hold fee eftates within the limits, pay him chief rents, and owe fuit to court. In his right courts leet and baron are held, and a portreeve and other proper officers fworn. Differences arifing within his jurifdiĉtion are fettled by a jury. He holds a court of admiralty, a royal privilege granted by the crown to his anceftors, which extends itfelf from a rock on the eaft, called Saltftone, (lying in the creek or inlet of the fea which goes up from Salcombe to Kingfbridge, before-mentioned), to a place called Shagg-rock, in the river Aune, on the weft, including the fea-coaft between thofe limits, *as far off as a man on borfeback on the bills can fee an umber barrel*; and, by a jury of thirteen refpeĉtable men, fettles matters refpeĉting falvage; pays the fame, and preferves the property for the owners till claimed, when the fame is delivered over, deduĉting only what has been paid the falvors. Formerly his lordfhip's anceftors were at the expence of keeping boats, anchors, and cables, for the affiftance of fhips in diftrefs; and as it often happened that after veffels had been faved by thefe means from being dafhed on the rocks, the crews would take advantage of a change of wind to withdraw the fhip, without making fatisfaĉtion for the rifk of lives, labour, and fervice, in giving them affiftance; to prevent fuch behaviour in future, a cable, anchor, or fome neceffary

material

The parifh of PORTLEMOUTH is enclofed with quickfet hedges.*

VOL. III.   2 B   In

material was detained by way of depofit until fatisfaction was made.—The church is fituate on the north fide of the parifh, fo near the parifhes of Weft-Alvington and South-Huifh, that the north-eaft fide of the cemetery is bounded by the former, and the weft-fide (to within a few perch) by the latter. It is built of large hewn ftone; its length 120 feet, its breadth 60 feet, and the heights of the walls about 24 feet. There are three aifles in the body of the church, and as the building is an oblong fquare, thefe continue the fame thro' the chancel, which is feparated from the nave by the rood-loft. The fpire is rather lofty for a country church, and from the high ground on which it is built may be viewed at a great diftance. I remember myfelf to have feen it in a clear day from the Rame-head, in Cornwall. There is a ring of fix bells, much efteemed by thofe who are fond of fuch dingdong founds. The church has a vaulted roof, which was plaftered for the firft time in the year 1786.* This, with the churches of South-Huifh and South-Milton, are daughter churches to Weft-Alvington vicarage; Malborough and South-Huifh are ferved by a curate, each once every Sunday, and the other two parifhes no better. The prefent curate of the two firft-mentioned parifhes is the Reverend Roope Ilbert, A. B. and the prefent vicar the reverend and learned Thomas Pyle, A. M. prebendary of Winchefter. Mr. Pyle's predeceffor was the Rev. Hugh Trevannion, who was preceded by the Rev. —— Barry, who fucceeded the Rev. Aaron Baker, grandfather to the prefent phyfician to the King, Sir George Baker, bart. The vicarage is in the prefentation of the dean and chapter of the cathedral church of the bleffed Virgin Mary at Sarum, and the four churches are dedicated to All Saints. It feems there were formerly two vicarage or parfonage-houfes, the one at Weft-Alvington and the other at Malborough; but, at prefent, only the former remains. The latter ftood on the fouth fide of the higher ftreet in Malborough town; not a veftige of it, however, is now to be feen, and its ancient fcite forms part of a field belonging to the glebe. The laft incumbent, the Rev. Hugh Trevannion, a little before his demife, had begun rebuilding this houfe, and the walls were raifed fufficiently high to take the beams, when the death of that gentleman put a ftop to the work, and his fucceffor, the prefent vicar, not thinking proper to continue it, the little which had been done foon came to the ground. It appears from the regifter (which commenced in September 1557), that the average of births during the laft ten years is from thirty-two to thirty-three, and the average of deaths during the fame period is from twenty-one to twenty-two. The following is a table of the baptifms and burials, from 1781 to 1790, both years inclufive.

Baptifms.			*Burials.*	
Date.	No. in each year.		Date.	No. in each year.
1781	21		1781	23
1782	26		1782	25
1783	30		1783	27
1784	31		1784	22
1785	35		1785	25
1786	27		1786	12
1787	44		1787	15
1788	32		1788	21
1789	45		1789	22
1790	34		1790	24
Total number of baptifms in ten years .... }	325		Total number of burials in ten years .... }	216."

From Mr. *Hawkins*, in 1791.

* " This parifh, which may be called the moft fouthern in the county, is in the hundred of Coleridge, and is bounded on the eaft by Chivelftone, on the weft by Salcombe harbour, on the north by South-Pool, and on the fouth by the fea, between the Prawl Head and Salcombe harbour. The parifh is three miles in length, and two and a half in breadth; is inclofed with quickfet hedges, and divided into farms, belonging chiefly to his Grace the Duke of Bolton, and the truftees of Blundell's fchool in Tiverton. The former's property is, by far, the moft extenfive, lies on the weft fide of the parifh, and confifts of fixteen farms. The property belonging to Blundell's fchool confifts of 4 farms only, 3 of which, viz. Prawl, Moor, and Highhoufe, are the moft confiderable in the parifh. The whole of this parifh is let for leafe on lives, except the farm of Moor, which is let at rack rent. The parifh is on a clay foil, confifts of meadow, orchard, but chiefly of arable land, produces for the moft part brown, or what is here called red wheat; is manured at a fmall expence, from its fituation, by dung and lime, but chiefly by fea-fand, which is taken up in large quantities on Salcombe Bar, for the ufe of this neighbourhood. In this parifh are four villages. Portlemouth, fituated on the weft, on almoft the top of a hill, commands one of the moft extenfive, beautiful, and picturefque views in the county, taking in the harbour of Salcombe, the town of Kingfbridge, with different branches of the river, and a moft extenfive and well cultivated tract of land around. This village confifts of 18 houfes, and contains about 140 inhabitants. Rickham, the fecond village, lies on the fouth, confifts of 8 houfes, and contains about 50 inhabitants. Houlfet, the third village, lies in the centre of the parifh, confifts of 6 houfes, and contains about 50 inhabitants. Good-fhelter, the fourth village, lies on the north-eaft of the church, on the banks of Salcombe river, confifts of 4 houfes, and contains about 20 inhabitants. Thefe villages belong to the Duke of Bolton. The houfes are built chiefly with mud walls, and thatched. The inhabitants are moftly labourers, are in general very healthy, and in this and the neighbouring parifhes remarkable for longevity—inftances of many living near a century. The number of inhabitants in the whole parifh is about 350. Paupers, communibus annis, about 30. Within the prefent century there was a large mullet fifhery is this parifh, but it is now not much attended to. The Duke of Bolton holds a court-baron here annually, for the receipt of his rents: likewife the truftees of Blundell's fchool hold annually the fame court for their rents. Adjoining the village of Portlemouth, on the eaft fide, ftands the church, dedicated to St. Onelaus, built in the form of a crofs, of hewn ftone, with a flated roof. It is in length in the clear 62 feet; in breadth 34. The chancel is 14 feet by 15. The two aifles which form the crofs are 8 feet by 11. The church contains three aifles, and is fupported by eight Gothic pillars. The fcreen bears the appearance of great antiquity. The tower is likewife built of hewn ftone, 14 feet by 11, and 58 feet high, and contains 3 bells only. The church-yard is 120 feet by 90. The oldeft regifter is dated in 1563, and appears to be regularly kept, fince which time there are others which are not quite connected. From the date of the prefent one 1792, it has been very regularly kept. The patronage of the church, which is a rectory, belongs to his Grace the Duke of Bolton. The lift of incumbents, as far as they can be traced, is as under:

The Rev. Richard Cleland, who died 1618.	The Rev. John Rumbelow, who died 1729.
——— Doctor Robert Cary, who died 1688.	———— James Grantham, who died 1791.
——— William Cornifh, afterwards rector of Bigbury.	———— Samuel Wells, the prefent incumbent.

The parfonage-houfe, to which there is a glebe of about 25 acres of good orchard, meadow, and arable lands, is fituated about half a mile from the church, on the banks of Salcombe river, and is a very antient ftructure. There are the ruins of an old building on the glebe, which tradition fays was formerly a chapel: Indeed the ground on which it now ftands, and is a garden, takes its name from it; and adjoining this there are the remains of fome cottages, which tradition likewife fays were inhabited by fifhermen, who carried on a fifhery here." From the minifter in 1791.

* In the chancel, on the fouth fide, is the following infcription on a ftone of the pavement :
In memory of Samuel Savery, of Yarde, in this parifh, efquire, who died the 21ft day of March, 1790, aged 45 years.
In the cemetery, on the north fide of the church, is a neat tomb of hewn ftone, covered with a granite flab, on which is the following infcription :
In memory of Mrs. Bridget Finney, widow of the reverend Thomas Finney, & daughter of the honourable George Hamilton (fon of James VI. earl of Abercorn, &c. and fome time Member of Parliament for the city of Wells), who died at Alfton, in this parifh, while on a vifit to her niece, the 2d day of April, 1789, aged 66 years.

In CHIVELSTONE * is the village of South-Allington, where refide a number of refpectable people; particularly three farmers, worth between forty and fifty thoufand pounds.

SOUTH-POOL† is faid to have been formerly a part of the parifh of Stokenham. A farthing of land, value about 25l. per ann. part of the manor of Halwell, ftill pays tythes and rates and taxes to that parifh.

In CHARLTON,‡ the farms are in a high ftate of cultivation: And almoft every cottager can boaft of an orchard and herbary. §

DODBROOK

* " Here Nigel held half a hide and one farthing of land, in the Conqueror's days." *Rifdon.*

† " *South-Pool* was the lands of Lord Nicholas de Pola, in the time of King Henry the 1ft, whofe fon, the Lord William, went with King Richard the 1ft, into the Holy Land; after whom Maurice de Pola held this land, whofe two coheirs were married to Pipard and Clavell. In this tything Sir Thomas Cirencefter held lands the 8th year of King Edward the 2d, from whom it came to Sir Thomas Courtney, and by his daughter married unto Sir Thomas Peverel, defcended by Hungerford to the Earl of Huntingdon." *Rifdon.*—Weftcote fays, that the moft ancient of the Chichefters was Cirencefter, whofe moft ancient habitation was South-Pool, not far from Kingfbridge; once the poffeffion of de Pola. Walleran de Cirencefter is faid to have defcended from a brother of Robert de Chichefter, bifhop of Exeter. He married, and had iffue, John de Cirencefter, who had iffue Sir John; who had iffue Sir Thomas, who by his wife, Alicia de Rotomago, had the manor of Mary-church, in the time of Henry the 3d. Sir Thomas had iffue William; who had iffue John de Cirencefter; who had iffue Richard. Richard, who took up the name of Chichefter, had iffue John; whofe fon Sir John married Thomafin, the fole daughter and heirefs of Sir William Raleigh of Raleigh, near Barnftaple. His pofterity were allied to many honourable houfes, as Kains of Winkley-Kains, Powlet of Hinton St. George, Bourchier Earl of Bath, Courtenay, and Dennis. Sir John Chichefter of Raleigh, knight, by the daughter of Sir Robert Dennis, had iffue Sir Robert Chichefter of Raleigh, knight; whofe firft wife was one of the coheirs of Lord Harrington of Exton, in Rutland, by whom he had iffue Anne, heirefs to her mother, and the wife of Thomas Lord Bruce, baron of Kinloffe. Sir Robert, by a fecond wife, a daughter of Hill of Shilfton, had iffue Sir John Chichefter, baronet; whofe fon Sir Arthur Chichefter lived at Youlfton, in Prince's time.—" *Chivelfton* was the moft ancient inheritance of Scobbahull: And from Robert, in the reign of Henry the 3d, to Robert, in Henry the 4th's time, it remained in that family. The hamlet of North-Pole was at one time in poffeffion of John de Punchardon, whofe heir fold it to the Earl of Devon, Hugh Courtenay, the firft of that family.—As early as the conqueft, Ocheline inherited the hamlet of *Praul*. In other ages, Sir Roger and Sir William Praul, knights, poffeft it.—*Halwell.* The laft of the Heles of this place, were heireffes, two daughters; one of whom married George Treby, efq. fecretary at war to George the 2d, by whom he had two fons and three daughters; of whom the firft was George Treby, efq. of Plymton-houfe, in the town of Plymton, who died unmarried—and the fecond, George Hele Treby, efq. lieutenant-colonel in the guards, who died alfo unmarried and inteftate. Of the daughters, Charity, the eldeft, married Paul Oury, efq. commiffioner of the dock-yard at Plymouth, who had two fons and two daughters. Of his fons, Paul Oury, efq. exchanged his name for Treby, who married Letitia, daughter of Sir Harry Trelawney, bart. by whom he had iffue two fons, in 1790: He refides at Goodamore. George, the other brother, died a minor. Charity, the elder of the two daughters, was married to Montague Edmund Parker of Whiteway: By him fhe had two fons. Montague Parker lives chiefly at Teignmouth. Caroline, the fecond, married Sir William Molefworth, bart. Dorothea Juliana was married to Edward Drewe, efq. barrifter at law, of Exeter; who had by her two children, Edward Drewe, efq. and Dorothea Juliana, married to Arthur Kelly, efq. of Kelly, by whom fhe has two fons and five daughters, 1789. The third and laft daughter was Anne, who married Benjamin Hayes, efq. of Whimbleton in Surry, by whom he has one fon and two daughters.

On a marble ftone in the floor of the chancel:

Here lieth the Body of Mrs. Dorothy Hayman, Daughter of the Rev^d. Mr. Cory Rector of Rattery by Dorothy his Wife, Daughter of the Rev^d. Mr. James Bampfield of the Poultimore Family and formerly Rector of Rattery & Black Torrington in this County. She was the Wife of the Rev^d. Mr. Gawen Hayman many years Rector of this parifh, by whom fhe had 5 Sons & 2 Daughters, one of whom is ftill living, & wife to the Rev^d. Mr. William Mervin Rector of Tiverton and Atherington. She ran thro' the moft different conditions of Life & acted very prudently in all. Few Women underwent greater afflictions; fewer bore them with more refignation to the Will of God who fent them. Seven times was fhe forely fmitten of him in the lofs of a prudent & loving Hufband & fix very dutiful and hopeful Children. She was of a mild and amiable Difpofition, refpected by the rich and beloved by the poor, and in her Temper fhe was remarkably chearful, in her behaviour very inoffenfive, conftant and regular both in her public & private devotions, rejoicing in hope, patient in Tribulation, ferving the Lord with all humility, with whom we truft fhe now refts & by whom confequently fhe is amply rewarded. She departed this Life the 19th day of March 1746 Aged 76.

On another:

Here lyeth the Body of the Rev^d. Mr. Gawen Hayman late Rector of this parifh 45 years who departed this Life the 8th day of Feby. 1735 Aged 74.

In the north wall of the chancel, in Saxon characters:

Hic jacet Dnus. Tomas Briant quondam Rector hujus Ecclefiæ et Portlemothiæ.

This monument is erected to the deferved Memorye of Leonard Darre, Efq^r. & Joan his Wife the Daughter of Sir George Bonde, Kn^t. Alderman of London late Mayor of the faid Cittye in the memorable Yeare 1588. Joan deceafed the 7th of December 1608, whom her hufband followed on the 28th of March 1615 leaving iffue of their Bodyes 2 fons & 3 daughters.

A white marble monument in the eaftern wall of the fouth aifle, with a narrow canopy, a black flab for the infcription:

On the left fide: On the right fide:

2 Boys behind a Man kneeling.   a Woman kneeling—3 Girls behind her.

Underneath an infcription in verfe, part of which is fo obliterated that it cannot be made out.

‡ " *Semar* was feized of *Charlton* at the conqueft, fince Brecell, then Sir William de Brickley, knight, was lord thereof. *Wolfton*, in elder ages *Ulifton* when Colbert held half a hide there, was the inheritance of Richard Crifpin, the 27th of King Henry the 3d, which by the coheirs of Crifpin came to the family of le Baftard; a name that has lived in this fhire fince the conqueft, of which tribe there hath been many worthy men, and the poffeffor of this place liveth in worfhipful eftate." *Rifdon.*

§ " The parifh of Charleton is divided, into, what is called by the parifhioners, the north and fouth fide, feparated from each other by the fpace of about a mile and half. The extreme length of the north part is about two miles and half; the breadth about a mile and half. The fituation is rather high, (for the South Hams). The foil is flate or fhelf, and clay. The fouth fide is in the fhape or form of a triangle, each fide one mile and half, bounded on the north-weft and fouth-eaft by branches of the river which flows from Salcombe to Kingfbridge. This part of the parifh, which is commonly called the Manor, belongs to Lord Boringdon. It is a very low fituation. The foil chiefly flate, and when well manured grows very excellent barley; and is famous for producing great quantities of good cyder. It is an
inclofed

DODBROOK is fituated about 16 miles below Dartmouth, with a harbour for boats. The cuftom of this place, to pay a tythe to the clergyman in white ale, has been, often, mentioned.*

Mrs. Holdfworth of *Widdecomb*, in STOKENHAM, and Mount Galpin, Dartmouth, widow of Arthur Holdfworth, efq. M. P. for Dartmouth, and governor of Dartmouth-caftle, who died in 1787, has 5 fons; the eldeft of whom, Arthur Howe, was born in 1780. Michael Allen of *Coleridge*, efq. married a Mifs Cornifh of that place, and has a numerous iffue.†

SHERFORD (fo called from a clear ftream of water running there, and a paffage thro' it), paid, anciently, after half a hide of land.‡

SLAPTON (as I have already had occafion to remark) is bounded on the fouth by the fea; from which it is feparated by a ridge of fand, having on the infide a very fine bafon of frefh water, of above two miles in length, and abounding with fifh and wild fowl.§ There are the remains of the antient feat of Lord

Guy

---

inclofed parifh; the fields, indeed, are remarkably fmall; the fences are earth banks, planted with thorns. Here are but few trees, a trifling number of elms, fcattered in the hedges, make up the whole. The roads are in general dry, but very narrow. The materials are of the worft kind, a foft flate.—Villages belonging to the parifh of Charleton are five. Goveton and Lidftone, fituated in the north part of the parifh, the diftance between them one mile. In the fouth divifion is Weft and Eaft Charleton, with part of the village of Frogmore. The houfes in thefe villages are chiefly built with mud, and thatched. The principal farm on the manor is the barton of Court, belonging to Lord B. a very compact eftate; but the houfe is very Gothic, and very unwieldy. The other principal farms are Cutland, Burrow, Tor, and Croft, all the north part of the parifh. I underftand Cutland derived its name from an ancient family, the Courtlands. There was a Sir Hugh Courtland who poffeffed this eftate. The remaining part of the parifh is divided into fmall tenements. There is no fort of manufacture carried on by the inhabitants, who confift of farmers and day-labourers. The latter are a robuft hardy fet of men, whofe employment, during the fummer months, is that of procuring fand for manuring the land. The method is—two men in a barge (which will carry about 100 horfe load) go to the entrance of the harbour of Salcombe, and moor their barge in about 18 feet of water, and draw up the fand with a dredge, which is juft the form of an oyfter dredge. The farmers are rackholders and leafeholders, nearly equal in number. The farmers of this parifh oftentimes, during the fummer months, catch large quantities of fifh, called the grey mullet, which proves excellent and cheap food for the lower clafs of people. The number of inhabitants are about 400. Here are fome ftrong inftances of health and longevity, fuch as ninety and ninety-fix, with all the fenfes perfect. Among their cuftoms, they have one very bad one, which is abfenting themfelves, Sunday mornings, from public worfhip, and which (by the bye) is an eternal difgrace to the South Hams in general. They believe firmly in witchcraft and conjuration. Their fports are fkittle playing and wreftling. The church, which is a very neat one, with a beautiful fcreen, is fituated at the fouthern extremity of the manor, on the point of the triangle; built with ftone, and covered with flate. The tower is low, with four bells. Patron of the living, which is a rector, Lord Boringdon; incumbent, William Tickell, L. B. Lift of patrons: the prefent Lord Boringdon; —— Spechard, efq. Incumbents: the prefent William Tickell, Thos. Whingates, Henry Odham, —— Langworthy, —— Garland. The parfonage-houfe is neither an ancient nor modern building, but an uncouth ftructure, fituated about a quarter of a mile from the church." From the rector in 1791.

* " This manor Richard, the fon of Alan, once poffeft—fince the Rohants, knights. By an heir of this houfe, thefe lands, in hereditary right, defcended to the Champernowns, in the reign of Henry the 3d." *Rifdon.*—The Southcotes were lately lords of the manor.— In a place called Court-green, near Court-houfe, are the remains of an old chapel, and the veftiges of a burying-place belonging to it. It is fituated on a triangular plot, where three ways meet. The walls are ftill ftanding, but rooflefs.

† " *Stokenham* ftandeth where the fhoars fhrinking back is made in manner of a bay; and thereby a fpacious pool, which the Britains call *Lin*, the Irifh *Lough*, we the *Ley*, feparated from the fea by a ridge of chefell, fand and gravel, called by fome *Long-fand*. This mere is fed by rills of frefh water, wherein ftore of fifh is taken. This was the lands of Sir Matthew Fitz-Herbert, a valiant foldier in King John's time, who was a younger fon of Herbert Fitz-Herbert, whofe father was chamberlain to King Henry the 1ft. Matthew Fitz-Herbert, his fon, was lord of Stokenham; he was a valiant knight, and of great fervices, and had good knowledge in the wars; he was flain near Montgomery in Wales, by the fall of a ftone from a hill, in the reign of King Henry the 3d. The laft Matthew was called a baron in parliament, in King Edward the 1ft's reign; and he was one of the lords that wrote to the Pope, againft his pretended right to the kingdom of Scotland, the 22d of that king's reign; by whofe daughter this mannor came to the Lord Mounthermer in marriage; of whom Sir Thomas Mounthermer was a man at arms in King Edward the 3d's reign, and ferved in the wars in France, and was flain before Sluice, a fight in the 14th of that king's reign; leaving Margaret his only daughter, married to Sir John Mountacute, brother to the Earl of Salifbury, lord of Stokenham, a valiant man in the wars, and imployed with others by commiffion for defence of this fhire. By the match of the daughter and heir of Mountacute, with Haftings Earl of Huntingdon, it came to that houfe, the ruins of which ancient dwelling remain to be feen. The mannor the earl difmembred, giving part to his fervants, fome for one fervice, fome for another; and for that this hundred enjoys privileges above any in this county, I may not omit them. The lord hath the benefit of all amercements, for not appearing to the affizes and feffions; all felons goods, and *non obftante* the king's pardon, of all forfeitures, wafes, ftrays, wracks, &c. At this place is a fair every Good Friday well frequented." *Rifdon.*

‡ " *Kenedon* was anciently in the poffeffion of Prall. Roger Prall held it, 27th of Henry the 3d. William Prall 24th Edw. the 1ft, and after him, William his fon. In the 18th of Richard the 2d, John Govis held the fame. From Govis, Kenedon came to Halfe, anciently written De Alfe. John Halfe, the judge, was the firft of the name that poffeft this feat: Here the family of Halfe flourifhed for many generations, till Matthew Halfe, efq. in the time of Charles the 2d, made away this and his other inheritance from his uncle, a clergyman of Cornwall, and fettled it on his fifters, their heirs." *Prince.*

§ " *Slapton* fhall not be flighted, where Guido de Bryan had inheritance, which after the death of the Countefs of Wiltfhire, came to the Earl of Northumberland, and was purchafed by Sir Matthew Arundel of Warder-caftle, in Wiltfhire. And Edward Courtenay, Earl of Devon, held a mannor in Slapton, by being chief fteward to the Bifhop of Exeter, at the time of his inthronization in the cathedral church of Exeter, the 7th year of King Henry the 5th.—*Pole* is in this parifh, was once a priory, founded by the Poles. After the furrender, it was fold to Ameredith. And John, the fon of Edward Ameredith, fold it to Sir Richard Hawkins, knight." *Rifdon.*

Guy Brian, called *Pool* or *Pole*. Thefe noble buildings, of a vaft extent, are now crumbling into duft. The houfe of Pool was fold by fome of the defcendants of Lord Brian to the Amerediths, a great family, as appears from their monuments in Slapton church, carved and gilt in a very handfome manner, decorated with various coats of arms, and bearing at one end the date 1610. After thefe, came the Hawkins's (defcendants of Admiral Hawkins, in Queen Elizabeth's days), the laft diftinguifhed family that dwelt here. The houfe of Pool, with a fmall eftate annexed to it, belongs to Henry Fownes Lutterel, efq. exempted from tythe and church rates.* About half a mile from Pool is the parifh church of Slapton, where, on the north-fide, are the ruins of the priory, or college, founded by Lord Guy Brian, about 1350. It was a grand pile of building, as the remains fhow at this day: At the weft end we enter, under a vaft arch, where the gates were hung: the frame-work of which, of pure oak, was exifting in Prince's time. The tower (about 100 feet high) is almoft entire. In feveral windows in the parifh church, are the coats of arms of Brian, painted on the glafs.†

* Slapton-houfe is in the poffeffion of Mrs. Goodridge, widow, aunt to J. H. Southcote, efq.

† The curacy of Slapton (the clear yearly value of which is £.15) was a college in the time of Henry the 8th, valued at £.63 6s. 2d. According to Thes. Eccles. it is in the patronage of Lord Petre (Cath.) and held by fequeftration. The Liber Regis tells us, that the patrons are the churchwardens and principal inhabitants: But this, I conceive, is by the confent and indulgence of Lord Petre.

ARCHDEACONRY

ARCHDEACONRY OF TOTNES.

DEANRY of TOTNES.

IN the deanry of Totton or Totnes, are offered to our obfervation, Totnes, Holne, Buckfaftleigh, Dean-prior, Dartington, Rattery, Brent, Diptford, Harburton, Afhprington, Cornworthy, Holwell, Blackawton, Dittifham, Town-ftall, Dartmouth.*

The fituation of TOTNES, is one of the moft pleafant in the South-Hams. And the hamlets in the vicinity of the town, with a little orchard and garden at every cottage, warmly feated at the bottom of a green hill, or on its fheltered fide, were extremely pleafing, for the content and comfort they feemed to indicate. The town of Totnes ftands on the fide of a high rocky hill, that declines to the river Dart. The defcent of its great ftreet, from the caftle down to the Seven Stars inn, near the river, is in fome places inconveniently fteep; particularly at the old gateway. And a few years ago the pavement was bad; and the fhops by no means attractive.† To the caftle, which ftands on a mound of great elevation, we afcend by fteps, a very fteep acclivity, overgrown with ivy, mofs, and various plants, in a moft romantic manner. From this height, we have a noble view of Totnes and the circumjacent country. Immediately

Vol. III. 2 C under

* " Benefices remaining in charge:

First Fruits. £. s. d.				Yearly Tenths. £. s. d.
29 1 8	Afhprington R. [St. David] Rep. B. Proc. vis. viiid. Syn. iiis. xd. A. D. Proc. vis. viiid. r. V. 180l. -		-	2 18 1
	Patr. —— Holdfworth, efq.			
29 14 4½	Brent alias South Brent V. [St. Patrick] Rep. B. Proc. vis. viiid. Syn. iis. xd. A. D. Proc. vis. viiid. r. V. 280l.			2 19 5¾
	Patr. Dr. Amyatt.			
19 1 0½	Buckfaftleigh V. [Holy Trinity] Rep. B. Proc. ivs. viiid. A. D. Proc. iid. r. V. 110l. -		-	1 18 1¼
	Patrs. The KING and —— Fownes, efq. alternately.			
21 0 0	Dene Prior V. [St. Mary] Rep. B. Proc. vs. Syn. iis. xd. A. D. Proc. vs. r. V. 140l. -		-	2 2 0
	Patr. Edward Yarde, efq.			
36 4 4½	Dartington R. [St. Mary] Rep. B. Proc. vs. Syn. iis. vd. A. D. Proc. vs. r. V. 250l. -		-	2 4 10
	Patr. Arthur Champernowne, efq.			
34 15 0	Dittifham R. [St. George] Rep. B. Proc. vis. viiid. Syn. iis. vd. A. D. Proc. vis. viiid. r. V. 160l. -		-	3 9 6
	Patr. Earl of Buckinghamfhire.			
29 2 1	Dopeford alias Diptford R. Rep. B. Proc. vis. viiid. Syn. iis. vd. A. D. Proc. vis. viiid. r. V. 140l. -		-	2 8 2½
	Patr. Mr Nofworthy.			
49 2 1	{ Harberton V. [St. Andrew] with Halwell Chapel [St. Leonard] Dean and Chapter of Exeter, Penf. xxvis. viiid. Rep. B. Proc. vis. viiid. Syn. iiis. viiid. A. D. Proc. vis. viiid. r. V. 300l. - - }			4 18 2½
	Patr. Dean and Chapter of Exeter.			
8 5 5	Holne V. [Ded. unc.] Rep. B. Proc. ivs. Syn. iis. id. A. D. Proc. ivs. r. V. 90l. - - -		-	0 16 6¼
14 10 0	Rattrey V.—Rep B. Proc. vis. viiid. Syn. iis. xd. A. D. Proc. vs. viiid. r. V. 140l. - - -		-	1 9 0
	Patr. John Bidlake Herring, efq.			

Difcharged.

King's Books.			Certified Value.
15 8 9	Blackauton V. [St. Michael] Rep. B. Proc. vis. viiid. A. D. Proc. vis. viiid. r. V. 80l. - -		- 25 0 0
0 0 0	{ Cornworthy V. [St. Peter] Rep. B. Proc. vis. viiid. Syn. iis. vd. A. D. Proc. vs. This vicarage is en- dowed with a portion of the great tythes of Abbot's Kerfwell. r. V. 90l. - - - - - }		10 0 0
	Patr. Humphrey Prideaux, efq.		
12 8 9	Totnes V. [St. Mary] Rep B. Proc. vis. viiid. Syn. iis. vid. ob. A. D. Proc. vis. viiid. r. V. 90l. -		- 24 6 8
	Patr. The KING.		
12 15 5	{ Townftall [St. Clement] with St. Saviour's in Dartmouth. Rep. B. Proc. vis. viiid. Syn. iis. vd. A. D. Proc. vis. viiid. r. V. 140l. - - - - - - - - - }		29 6 8
	Patr. Mayor and Bailiffs of Dartmouth."		

Thes. Prov.

† " The fuburban town of *Totnes*. This was fometimes walled, whofe foundations and gates yet appear. A minute enquiry at its antiquity, is a tafk that would take up much time, having fuffered alteration under Britains, Romans, Saxons, Danes, and Normans, neverthelefs

under the eye, the white town roofed with flate; beyond the buildings, the river Dart winding amidft the rich hills, and the blue heights far beyond it, have a fine effeft. A few miles down the river towards Dartmouth, a white fpot gleaming through tufts of verdure attracts obfervation—Sharpham, the beautiful feat of Mr. Edm. Baftard: and the towers and foreft trees, villages, and orchards, interfperfed thro' a fcene of meadows and cornland, difcover a well peopled and highly cultivated country. Of the lordfhip of Totnes, I have already fpoken.* The church here is a good ftructure, and the fcreen, which is of ftone, is very elegantly carved, painted, and gilded. The pulpit alfo is of ftone, but plain. The pillars which divide the nave from the aifles are light and handfome; which mode of architecture generally prevails in all the churches in thefe parts, as at Lamerton, Taviftock, &c.†

HOLNE (from Holly, or Holm, that grows here in great abundance) lies on the Dart, which feparates it from Withecombe and Afhburton, on the north-eaft.

Holne-

---

verthelefs flourifheth to this day. Geoffrey of Monmouth dareth avouch, that the Trojan Brute arrived here, and Haviland ftiffly maintaineth in thefe verfes.

> *Inde dato curfu Brutus comitatus Achaiæ,*
> *Gallorum fpoliis cumulatus navibus æquor*
> *Exarat, & Superis auraque faventibus ufus,*
> *Littora fœlices intrat Totonefia portus.*

'Tis faid moreover, when Brute impofed names to regions, rivers, and towns, he called this place *Tout, al èffe*: which interpreted in our vulgar tongue, (as fome will have it) is *all at eafe*; and in tract of time, without any great alteration, hath been changed into *Toutanefs*, now contractedly *Totnefs*. This conjecture would I embrace, could I believe Brute fpeak as good French, or that the French tongue was then fpoken at all; therefore I am the more eafily perfwaded to lean to the other opinion, that would have it called *Dodoneffe*, which fignifieth the rocky town, according to that learned antiquary Leland; for its fituation hath the afcent of an hill both ftony and rocky declining to the river." *Rifdon.*

* " Henry the 2d gave the lordfhip of Totnes unto Sir Reginald de Brues, and King John re-affumed it again upon difpleafure taken againft Brues; and delivered this caftle to the keeping of Henry the fon of the Earl of Cornwall: But afterwards the Brues had this land again; and the laft left it unto Eva his youngeft daughter, wife of the Lord Cantilupe, from whom it came to Eudo de la Zouch, and there remained before John Lord Zouch was attainted for taking part with King Richard the 3d. Then King Henry the 7th, beftowed Totnes on Sir Richard Edgcombe, whom he held in efpecial favour, in whofe pofterity it remained unto Piers Edgcombe, that fold this mannor unto the Lord Edward Seymour; unto the lords whereof this town was in great fubjection, in regard of divers fervile offices, which they ought to perform before they redeemed them. King John gave them power to elect a mayor, and King Henry the 3d, inabled them with many immunities; they have a Saturday's market, well ftored with neceffary provifions, and fairs on May day, St. James and Simon and Jude days: They fend two burgeffes to the parliament, and its greateft honour is, that the town is become the title of an earl, which is born by that noble Sir George Carew, baron of Clopton." *Rifdon.*—The prefent lord is the Duke of Somerfet.—" *Bowdon*, (fays Prince) is a pleafant feat, about a mile to the S. W. of the town, ftanding on an high ground." It is fituated, partly in Totnes, and partly in Afhprington. John de Bowdon lived here in the time of Edward the 2d. William Giles of Totnes, purchafed Bowdon about the beginning of the reign of Henry the 8th, and made it the feat of his family. Sir Edward Giles had the honor of knighthood, fays Sir W. Pole, conferred upon him in his father's life-time. On his return to Bowdon, after this acceffion to the title, his father received him with ludicrous folemnity, placed him at the head of the table, and faluted him with Sir Edward Giles at every word; till at length enquiring: " Pray, Sir Edward, who muft difcharge the fees and charges of your knighthood;" and the fon anfwering, that he hoped his father would be pleafed to do that:—" Nay then, (fays the old gentleman) come down Sir Edward Giles, and fit beneath me again, if I am he that muft pay for thy honor."—In the year 1670, John Giles, efq. died, and left this eftate to Mary, his only daughter and heirefs, married to Sir Richard Gipps of Suffolk, knight. In 1722, a handfome houfe was built here by Mr. Trift, its then poffeffor; and the grandfather of Browfe Trift, efq.

† At the Angel inn dining-room was fome curious old wainfcot, faid to have been brought from Berry-Pomeroy caftle, confifting of pannels about a foot or fomething more in length, carved after the fafhion of the fine Gothic windows which remain in moft cathedral churches.

Here, (among many others), is a monument of Blackall; written to comfort him for the lofs of one of his wives—a lofs which he endeavoured to repair, by taking to himfelf in due fucceffion three others—kneeling ftatues of which are exhibited in refpectable freeftone:

> Ad
> Chriftopherum
> Blackall armigerum
> in obitum uxoris fuæ
> pientiffimæ fororis meæ
> chariffimæ Sufannæ Blackall.

> An doleam, an moriar, nihil eft, ego miror ademptam
> vix reddent fponfam fidera noftra parem
> proh dolor, interiit foror, haud equanda forori
> et conjux illa conjuge nulla prior—
>   O foror O conjux (quid ni clamemus amantes)
> hic Jacet hæc conjux hic Jacet illa foror
>   Robertus Halfwell Fraterrimus.

Under this, (we are informed), Chriftopher Blackall lies buried, with his four wives.

The fine elms in the church-yard would perhaps long fince have felt the keen effects of the axe, but for a difpute to whom they belong, being claimed by the impropriator, the corporation, and the vicar,—a happy circumftance for the rooks, who have remained, and we hope will continue, in poffeffion of their fummits for fome centuries.—In the church-yard are fome handfome tombs, one of black marble to the memory of Ley and Southcote; with the emphatic word engraved on it: *Refurgemus.*

A.C. Esq.r delin.t

T. Bonner Sculp.r

DARTINGTON HOUSE,

The Seat of Arthur Champernowne Esq.r to whom this Plate is Inscribed

By his Obliged Servant R. Polwhele.

Holne-bridge, lightly thrown over the Dart, gives a charming relief to the hollies and the birch woods that occupy the fcene. A fmall houfe of granite, called Cote, or the Cottage, is a romantic hunting-feat of Sir B. Wrey:*

The parifh of BUCKFASTLEIGH is chiefly remarkable for its abbey, which I have already defcribed.† The manor of Brook belongs to the Earl of Macclesfield. The church is inconveniently placed, about half a mile from the village.‡

In DEAN-PRIOR,§ is Dean-court, belonging to Fr. Buller Yarde, efq.

In DARTINGTON, ‖ the objedt moft attractive is *Dartington-Houfe*, which ftands in the centre of eight hundred and fifty acres of rich land, wood, water,

and

* Here *Edulph*, then *Otheline*, inherited half a hide of land. After him, *William Bozun*—then, *Nicholas de la Yeo*. In 1644, the manor was poffeft by Henry, Earl of Bath; at prefent by Sir Bourchier Wrey.

† The hiftorians of this religious houfe were a poor, tho' happy family. The father was an old man, upwards of 90 years of age. He had a florid countenance; and received us with a fmile of welcome. Sitting in the chimney-corner over a few cheerful embers, with a tame lamb for his companion—he was full of traditionary tales; and I wifhed for an opportunity of further converfing with him.

‡ Tradition fays, that the fpot originally defigned for the church was clofe to the fcite of the prefent village—that ftones for building it were conveyed from the quarry, but that the devil carried away by night what the workmen brought thither by day.

§ *Dean-Prior*, fometime the inheritance of Fitz-Stephen, was given by Sir William Fitz-Stephen, in the time of Henry the 3d, to the priory of Plymton, and after the diffolution was purchafed by Giles of Totenays, and is now the inheritance of Sir Edward Giles, where he hath his manfion-houfe. *Sir W. Pole.*—In the wall over the chancel door, was erected to the memory of Sir Edward Giles and his lady, (1642) a very handfome monument. See *Prince*, p. 334.

‖ " *Dartington* takes its name from the river Dart; on the weft banks of which it is fituated, and reaches along them for about three miles, from Totnes to Rattery, north-weft. From thence it hath Harberton fouth, till it joins Totnes again. Its length between four and five miles, and its breadth about two and half. The ground is fertile and well cultivated; and being partly hilly and partly flat, is proper for agriculture and pafture. The low ground a ftiff clay; the hilly ground a rich foil on a dun-ftone, marble, lime-ftone, or flate. Of the two laft, there are feveral very fine quarries. There are two county bridges, one over the river Dart, called Staverton Bridge, (tho' the whole bridge is in the parifh of Dartington), near three miles north from Totnes, on the Afhburton road; a very fine ftrong building of hewn moor-ftone, containing feven arches. The other is a bridge of one arch only, called Skinner's Bridge, about mid-way between Staverton-bridge and Totnes. There is a turnpike road thro' this parifh, over Staverton bridge to Afhburton; and the other roads in the parifh are in general in good repair, and are made either of dun-ftone, the chippings of the lime-ftone, or coarfe gravel from the river Dart. This parifh, in general, is very well wooded, having fine oak, afh, and elm, and fome very fine chefnut trees; of which there was formerly great plenty; the roof of the church and parfonage-houfe being built entirely with that timber. This parifh is remarkable for producing good rich cyder, which of late years is greatly mended, by increafing the propagation of fweet and bitter-fweet apples, inftead of the rough harfh fruit formerly in ufe, and by mixing the beft forts together, and by a different procefs in treating their cyder than was formerly the cuftom. This parifh is furrounded by inclofures of about fix or eight acres on an average, except the barton, where there are fields from twenty to an hundred acres. The kind of inclofures are banks of earth thrown up between four and five feet high, and planted with afh, halfe, withy, alder, white and black thorn, which fupply the farmer and the poor with fuel. On the barton above-mentioned are feveral noble and beautiful woods, well filled with exceedingly fine and large oak, afh, and elm. There is fuppofed to be ten thoufand pounds worth of timber on this barton, four thoufand pounds worth of which is on the decline. The oak in this parifh is fuppofed to be the beft for fhip building of any in the county. There were formerly many fubftantial leafeholders, but the farms are almoft all now dropt into the lord's hand, and occupied by rackholders. There are about fifty families of labourers and manufacturers, of different trades and employments, befides farm-houfes, which are between twenty and thirty. The people in general healthy. The great houfe hath been, fince the beginning of the fixteenth century, the property of Champernowne. There was a good print of *Dartington-houfe* taken in 1742, by the Bucks, tho' they miftake in the infcription under, that it once belonged to the Knights Templars —Hood-houfe, in Domefday, Hode, and poffeffed at the conqueft by Jordanys de la Hode, is a large old ftrong building, flated, the property of Richard Jackfon, efq. *Allerton-houfe*, the property of John Searle, gent. whofe anceftors have poffeffed it fince the latter end of the 15th century. *Venton-houfe*, an ancient large building, flated, now the property of Mr. Wm. Tucker, was, probably, formerly poffeffed by fome great family, as the north aifle of the chancel belonged to that eftate, and was repaired by the occupier, till the prefent poffeffor difcontinued to repair it. The church neat, well-built of ftone, and flated, is fituated almoft at the eaft end of the parifh, and feems to have been placed there folely for the eafe and convenience of the proprietor of the great houfe, to which it almoft joins. The church is feventeen yards and a foot to the fcreen, exclufive of the chancel. From the fcreen to the end of the aifle fixteen feet and half. Breadth of the aifle ten feet and half. Breadth of the nave eighteen feet. Length of the chancel eleven yards and four inches; breadth five yards eight inches. The roof, which is built entirely of chefnut, is fupported by fix fluted pillars of the Tufcan order, ornamented with feftoons. The chancel is ornamented with an handfome carved oak wainfcot altar-piece, on which is written the decalogue, creed, and Lord's prayer. A refpectable marble monument to the memory of Henry Champernowne, efq. and Dorothy his wife, daughter of Sir George Trenchard, and dated 1656, on the fouth fide of the chancel. On the north fide a monument of plaifter work, erected in 1578, reprefenting ten figures, fix men compleatly clad in armour, two women, and two children, feven kneeling and three ftanding; ornamented with feveral coats of arms, but no infcription. Without the communion rails, on the fouth fide, near the chancel door, is a decent white marble monument, to the memory of Rawlin Champernowne, efq. who died in 1774, in whom the male line of that family was extinct. The church is dedicated to St. Mary, but no date when built: The walls ftone, rough cafted, and roof covered with flate. The windows originally Gothic, but lately repaired and modernized. A fingle munion branched to a Y, inclofed with which are the remains of all the painted glafs that could be collected. Screen and pulpit of carved wood, and painted with different colours. Over the pulpit a wainfcot canopy. The communion plate filver, given at different times by the Champernownes. The tower 17 feet fquare, and 56 feet high. Height of the church 22 feet, from the leads to the roof 21 feet. The parfonage-houfe is a good old ftone building, flated, near one hundred feet in front, containing five rooms on a floor, with proper offices behind. The patron Arthur Champernowne, efq. Incumbent, Francis Yarde, who fucceeded Dr. Andrew, who only held it one year. He fucceeded Francis Champernowne, who fucceeded Mr. Ackland, who fucceeded John Champernowne, who fucceeded Nic. Rook in 1732, who fucceeded John Ford in 1677. In the laft 62 years have been 832 baptifms, which makes 13 a year and 26 over; 234 marriages, 3 a year and 48 over; 600 burials, 9 a year and 42 over." From the minifter in 1792.

and lawn. Its poffeffors have been perfons of diftinction, from Falaife to Champernowne.*

RATTERY, or *Ratree,* was called by the Saxons, *Ratrew.*†

" The river Avon, rifing in Dartmoor, fwalloweth, in its folitary courfe, a ftream called Wellabroke, one of the boundaries of the foreft; after which it bendeth towards" SOUTH-BRENT, fays Rifdon. The town of Brent lies fix miles from Totnes, in the road between Exeter and Plymouth.‡ South-Brent is a richly endowed vicarage.§

Of DIPTFORD, ‖ and HARBURTON, ¶ I have nothing worth noticing.

About a mile to the weftward of the place, where " Harbourne fheddeth itfelf into the Dart," ftands ASHPRINGTON.§† In Afhprington is *Sharpham.* It ftands upon an eafy afcent, on the weftern banks of the Dart. It is half infulated by the river; of which it hath a charming profpect up to the town of Totnes.

* " *Dartington-houfe* is a pleafant and noble feat, ftanding on the weft fide of the river Dart. It is a ftately quadrangular building, much in the ftyle of a college. The quadrangle is about an acre of ground. The hall is very fpacious, being nearly 100 feet in length, with proportionable height and breadth. Round the houfe lies one of the beft bartons, both for the number of acres and richnefs of land, in this county." *Prince.*—Dartington-houfe was always the habitation of a noble family. The firft that poffeft it after the conqueft, fays Sir W. Pole, was William de Falaife, who held it in the 20th year of William the Conqueror. But foon after it came (on what occafion I do not find), to Martin de Turonibus, Lord of Camois in Wales, and of Comb-martin, and his heirs; who had both dwelling and barony in this place. He was lineally fucceeded by Robert, Robert, William, Nicholas, and Nicholas, who married Matilda, daughter and heirefs of Lord Henry Tracey of Barnftaple, and had iffue William; who by Eleanor, daughter of Herebert Fitz-Peter, had iffue William Lord Martin, who died without iffue, 19th of Edward the 2d. He was fucceeded by James Lord Audleigh, fon of Nicholas Lord Audleigh, and of Joan, fifter of Lord William Martin. James Lord Audleigh entailed Dartington, among his other lands, on the iffue male of his body. He had many fons; yet, all dying without iffue, Dartington efcheated to the crown, and was given by Richard the 2d to John Lord Holland, Earl of Huntingdon and Duke of Exeter, and half brother to the King. Lord Holland being detected in a confpiracy with his brother, Earl of Kent, and other lords, againft Henry the 4th, was beheaded, and his lands, caftles, and other poffeffions were confifcated to the King. He left iffue Richard, his eldeft fon, who, after his father's death, was feized of a large eftate in this county, which fell not under confifcation—as Bovey-Tracey, Northlieu, Barnftaple, Holdfworthy, Langacre, as Dugdale calls it—perhaps Langtree, Comb-martin, Fremington with the hundred, Southmolton with the hundred, Dartington, Blackburg, Bolhay, and Winkley. But Richard dying unmarried, 4th Henry 5th, John his fecond brother became his heir, and was reftored in blood, and to the earldom of Huntingdon, as heir to John his father, and Richard his brother. John Lord Holland married three wives. His firft wife was Anne, widow of Edmund Mortimer, Earl of March, daughter to Edmund, Earl of Stafford. His next wife was Beatrice, the widow of Thomas Earl of Arundel, illegitimate daughter to John, King of Portugal. On the death of Beatrice, he married Anne, the daughter of John Montague, Earl of Salifbury, who furvived him many years. He had iffue by Anne his firft wife, only Henry, his fon and heir; and by Anne his laft wife, a daughter called Anne, married firft to John Lord Neville, fon and heir to Ralph Neville, fecond Earl of Weftmoreland, by whom fhe had no iffue; and fecondly, to Sir John Neville, knight, uncle to her former hufband. Henry, the only fon and heir to his father, John, Duke of Exeter, inherited his father's titles, with his lands. He married Anne, daughter of Richard, Duke of York, and fifter to Edward the 4th. Anne, at her own fuit, was divorced from him, 12th Edward 4th, and having no iffue furviving, became afterwards the wife of Sir Thomas Saintleger. Sir Thomas and his lady fometimes refided at Dartington-houfe. On the deceafe of the Lord Holland, Duke of Exeter, Dartington fell to the crown, in which it remained till purchafed by a Mr. Ailworth of London, who exchanged it for the abbey fcite of Polflo, near Exeter, with Sir Arthur Champernowne, knight, the fecond fon of Sir Philip Champernowne of Modbury, by a daughter of Sir Edmund Baron Carew of Mohun Ottery. Sir Arthur was the firft of the Champernownes who fettled at Dartington; where his defcendants continue to this day in great efteem." *Prince.*

† " Anciently the inheritance of Alwin the Saxon; in William the Conqueror's time, the lands of William Fallaife. In King Henry the 1ft's reign, Rob. Fitz-Martin, Dartington, and Camoys, who gave mannor to the abby of St. Dogmaels in Wales, which he founded to the honour of St. Mary of Camoys there; which grant of his, King Henry the 1ft confirmed, whereunto he gave the churches of Tregent, Waldre, and the chapel of Cockington, with two farthings of land there, whofe father, Martin de Turon, that worthy warrior, had over-run all the country of Camoys in Wales, reputed a barony; for in it, befides three boroughs, are 20 knights fees, and 26 parifh-churches, all which he left to his pofterity." *Rifdon.*

‡ *Brent,* before and after the conqueft, belonged to the abbey of Buckfaftleigh. After the diffolution it was purchafed by Sir William Petre, and is the inheritance of Will. Lord Petre of Writtle, grandfon of the faid Sir William.

§ " *Monumentum fui aere perennius.* To refcue from oblivion, and perpetuate the memory of an edifice, which was raifed on this fite, this mural monument was erected in October, 1781. At what period of time, this edifice was raifed, or for what ufe can neither be afcertained by tradition or record; tho', with refpect to the latter, as it retained the name of chapel, it is more than probable, that it was originally defigned for religious purpofes. However that be, it was conftructed with fo much art, as (notwithftanding its expofed fituation) enabled it to refift the ravages of all devouring time, thro' the ruthlefs tract of unnumbered ages, and was in great prefervation 'till fome time in February, 1777, when, by the refiftlefs power of the artillery of heaven, an inftant period was put to its exiftence." The above is Mr. Tripe's infcription on a monumental wall, to preferve the memory of what was fuppofed to be an antient chapel, in the parifh of Brent.

‖ " *Dupeford* belong'd to Tingwike, antiently called *Dupeford,* granted with the manor of Tingwike to John fon of Lucas Boteler, by H. 2, & by K. John upon ye revolt of Normandy, refumed & granted to Euftachius de Courtenay. But H. 3, granted it to Sr Theobald de Englifhvill, afterward 30 E. 1. The Lord Jno. de Mules was lord thereof, in whofe lineage it defcended by Botreaux & Hungerford to Henry Hafting, Earl of Huntingdon, who fold it." *Sir W. Pole.*

¶ At Harburton church, the pulpit is one fingle excavated ftone.

§† In an advertifement of 1755, the manor and lordfhip of Afhprington are defcribed as lying in a very good country, pleafantly fituated on the river Dart, containing about 48 tenements (befides cottages) of very good land and orchards, making the beft of cyder; together with a very fine fifhery, in the faid river Dart (where great quantities of falmon, fea trout, and other fifh are caught every feafon). The whole being worth about 1700l. per annum.

Totnes.* Sharpham is the refidence of Edmund Baftard, efq. This gentleman married Mifs Pownal of Sharpham, only child of Philemon Pownal, efq. a captain in the navy; who, I have been informed, about 1763, bought Sharpham of —— Cockey, efq. and rebuilt it.

The picturefque fcenery of a rich and beautiful tract of land, which forms part of the banks of the Dart, in the parifh of CORNWORTHY, feems to be entitled to a particular defcription. But the peculiar grace and beauty of this river, and the country thro' which it flows, even the pencil would vainly delineate. And it remains only to obferve, that the church, which is a neat regular ftructure of the gothic order, fituated on a hill at the head of the village, was, fome years fince, repaired at the joint expence of the landholders of the parifh, and ornamented with great elegance of tafte by the liberal and pious munificence of John Seale, efq. of Mount Boon, the patron of the vicarage, and impropriator of the great tythes.†

Refpecting HALWELL we have little on record.

Nor is there any particular very interefting in the account of BLACKAWTON,‡ or DITTISHAM.§

VOL. III.   2 D   DARTMOUTH

* "Sharpham, in the time of Henry the 4th, was the property of Robert Winard, who had iffue Anne, the wife of Robert French. They had iffue Amy, fecond wife of John Prideaux of Addifton, near Modbury, who had iffue Joan, married to Will. Drewe, and Elizabeth to Will. Someifter of Nether-Exe. Sharpham fell to the portion of Joan, from whom defcended Edw. Drewe, efq. ferjeant at law to Queen Elizabeth." This far *Sir W. Pole.*—"Serjeant Drewe made confiderable purchafes in Combe-Raleigh, Broadhembury, Broadclift, and elfewhere; and fold Sharpham, which had large demefnes belonging to it, to John Giles, efq. of Bowdon." *Prince.*

† Near Afhprington, the Harburn receives a fmall brook, and about a mile lower joins the Dart; on the fouth fide of which, in the way from Totnes and Afhprington to Dittifham, we come to Cornworthy.—"The priory, which was founded in this place by the Edgcumbes, was purchafed at the diffolution by William Harris, efq. and became the habitation of himfelf and family. His fon, Sir Thomas Harris, ferjeant at law, and his grandfon Sir Edw. Harris, of the fame profeffion, enjoyed this inheritance; when it was divided between the daughters and heireffes of Sir Edward. The houfe is almoft in ruins." *Prince.*—"In the chancel of the parifh church of Cornworthy, is erected a large and beautiful monument to the memory of Sir Thomas Harris, and of Sir Edward his fon." See *Prince*, p. 379.

‡ "The moft antient fpelling of the parifh that I have met with, is *Blackawton,* tho' I have heard, it hath been called *Bleak-awton,* probably from the coldnefs of its fituation; as on its north fide it is very high, and expofed to the moor hills; on its eaftern fide it is alfo high; but on the other fides its fituation is rather low. Its length from north to fouth is about 6 miles and half; and from eaft to weft, on its north fide, about 4 miles broad: but towards the fea, on its fouth fide, it is little more than one mile. It abounds with good fprings, and many brooks or rivulets, over which there are four bridges of one arch each, built with ftone, one of which is repaired by the county, the others by the parifh. The waters that run under the three laft-mentioned bridges unite, and fall into a large pond of frefh water, (which is feparated from the fea by the bank of fand, called Slapton Sands), and extends in length to two miles and half; a fmall part of which is within this parifh, and the remainder in Slapton and Stokenham. The parifh is quite enclofed, with high hedges, like moft other parifhes in this part of the county: It is but indifferently wooded, and the trees that flourifh beft are the oak, afh, and fycamore. The roads are in general tolerably good, as there are plenty of fmall hard ftones to repair them, but abound with many hills. However, it is a pleafant healthy parifh, and affords many good and extenfive views. There is no town, but what is commonly called the Church Town, confifting of about forty dwellings, but many villages, viz: Woodford, half a mile diftant weft from the church; Hutchely, one mile and half from ditto, weft; Milcomb, half a mile fouth; Burlefton, two miles and half fouth; Street, four miles fouth, and one mile from the fea; Down, two miles fouth by eaft; Wadftray, one mile and half eaft; Dretton, one mile and half eaft by north. In each of thefe villages, except the laft, (where is only one) are two or three farm-houfes, built chiefly of ftone, and many of them flated, though the greater part are thatched: They are far, in general, from being compact or neat; each hath a kitchen garden and orchard belonging to them, and the farms are from £.30 to £.120 per ann. and are well cultivated. The number of paupers are about 30, and of daylabourers above 100, rackholders 15, leafeholders 12, and freeholders about 24. The number of inhabitants collectively amount very near to 1000, among whom are no manufacturers of any kind. There are four gentlemen's feats, Oldfton, Fuge, Wadftray-houfe, and Cotterbury. The firft of thefe is poffeffed by William Cholwich, efq. who rebuilt the antient manfion-houfe, and confiderably enlarged it about ten years fince. The proprietors of this, as far back as I can trace them from the regifter, I have here extracted:

1610 The 10th of March was baptifed Andrew the Son of William Cholwich.
1673 The 30th of May was buried Andrew Cholwich, efq. of Oldfton.
1720 Septr. 8th. was buried William Cholwich, efq. of Oldfton.
    N. B. His birth is not noticed in the regifter, fo probably was born in another parifh; but it muft be in year 1668, as he is faid on the monument of the family to be 52 years old at his death.
1691 July 12th. was born William Son of William Cholwich, efq. of Oldfton & Mary his wife.
1764 March 8th was buried William Cholwich, efq.
1730 Thomas Son of William Cholwich, efq. of Oldfton & Petronel his wife.
1768 Auguft 24 was buried Thomas Cholwich, efq.
    This man dying without iffue, the family eftate, which is very confiderable, devolved, purfuant to his father's will, to the Rev. Dr. Samuel Cholwich, who married Grace his third daughter.
1775 Auguft 26 was buried the Revd. Samuel Cholwich, D. D. Rector of Ermington, who leaving no iffue, it fell to the prefent gentleman, William Cholwich his brother.

The fecond feat, Fuge, is a neat modern houfe, about two miles from the fea, poffeffed by Charles Hayne, efq. and built by his grandfather, Cornelius Hayne, in the year 1725, who was a very opulent merchant, and built another handfome houfe, about the fame time, in the town of Dartmouth.—Wadftray-houfe is a very neat fmall feat, built about four years fince, by Mr. Andrew Pinfon, a refpectable

merchant

DARTMOUTH includes what was formerly called three towns, Clifton, Dartmouth, and Hardnefs. The mother-church is called Townftall, and is fituated on a hill, three quarters of a mile from the town, N. W. The tower of the church is 69 feet high, and is of good ufe as a fea-mark. Dartmouth-Caftle is very antient; for a chapel has been in it ever fince the time of Edw. the 3d, and belongs to Stoke-Fleming church, two miles to the W.; but the ftone tower and fpire are modern. In Townftall, is *Mount-Boon*;* as, alfo, *Norton*.†

merchant in Dartmouth, who purchafed the eftate, which was a freehold farm, and thought to be the moft barren of any in the parifh; but, by his manuring and improving it, it is now become as fruitful and compleat a farm as any in the parifh. The houfe is erected on a plot of ground fituated very high, at the north-eaft end of the parifh, (where there was no building of any kind before), about half a mile from the farm-houfe, and commands a very extenfive profpect both of fea and land.—Cotterbury, which is inferior to either of the other feats in point of architecture, was purchafed, about feven years fince, by Mr. Peter Ougier, another refpectable merchant in Dartmouth, of Mr. John Pinhey, who now refides in Exeter, and is fheriff for the city, whofe anceftors have inherited the eftate (which is pretty confiderable) for feveral ages. All thefe houfes are built of ftone and flated, and are fituated in the manor of Blackawton, the property of Arthur Holdfworth, efq. who is a minor of 10 years old: His father was a reprefentative for the borough of Dartmouth, and governor of Dartmouth Caftle. The whole manor, together with the impropriation of both great and fmall tithes, and the patronage of the church, was left to this prefent young gentleman's great grandfather, by the will of William Roope, efq. who was buried Dec. 20, 1745. His anceftors, who, I am informed, did purchafe the above from the Earl of Bedford, have left no other memorial on the regifter than the following:

1655 The firft of October was borne Nicolas the Son of Mr. John Roope & Mary.
1721 Septr. 8 was buried Nicholas Roope, efq.

The church is fituated about a mile and half nearer to the north than fouth fide of the parifh, but almoft equally diftant from the eaft and weft extremities; is dedicated to St. Michael; is built with ftone, and roofed with flate; is 94 feet 8 inches in length, including the chancel, 53 feet in breadth, and only 19 feet in height, owing to its flat cieling, which is placed on in the manner of a common room. There is only one monument, which was erected in the year 1759, by the late Wm. Cholwich of Oldfton, containing no other infcription than the names of his deceafed anceftors, beginning with his grandfather Andrew, &c. The tower is a plain fquare building, without the leaft kind of ornament, containing fix bells, and is only fixty-five feet in height. The church yard is nearly half an acre, exclufive of a fmall fpot of ground on the north-fide of the church, which hath always been ufed as a fporting place. Neither the church nor churchyard afford any epitaphs or infcriptions deferving notice. The regifter is as antient as any in the kingdom, fince it begins with the year 1538. The vicars, as far back as I can trace them, are as follow:

1586 Auguft 28 was buried Edward Clifford, Vicar.
1620 The xiith of April was buried Robert Clarke, Vicar.
1653 The 8th of November was buried Mr. Thomas Friend, Vicar.
1688 April 27 was buried Thomas Embery, Vicar.
1688 January 5th was inducted into the Vicarage & Parifh Church of Blackawton, John Adams.
1732 March 10th buried Mr. John Adams, Vicar of Blackawton.
Augt 6, 1733 was inducted into the vicarage &c. of Blackawton, Philip Neyle.
July 30, 1752 was buried the Rev^d. Mr. Philip Neyle, Vicar of Blackawton.
Auguft 18, 1752 I Thomas Adams was inducted, &c. There is no memorial in the regifter of either of the firft four vicars induction prior to my father's.

The vicarage-houfe is fituated exactly one quarter of a mile due fouth from the church, is a modern fmall houfe, erected by myfelf in the year 1753, on the fame fpot where the old houfe ftood, and which was too far dilapidated to be capable of repairing. Tho' it is ftiled a vicarage, neither the great nor fmall tithes belong to it; and the vicar hath only fixteen pounds per ann. This, from the impropriator: with a fmall glebe of eight acres, and ten pounds per ann. given by one William Wotton of Exeter, with about 20 guineas a year iffuing from the fheaf of Sherford, purchafed with Queen Anne's bounty, is his fole income, befides the furplice fees. There is no diffenter of any kind in this parifh." From the minifter, 1791.

§ " 27 Henr. 3. Nicholas de Halton held *Dittifham*. Nicholas had iffue de Halton, whofe daughter Joan brought this manor to Roger Ingpen her hufband, who had iffue Nicholas Ingpen, who by the daughter of Sir John Cobham of Blackburg-Bolhay had iffue John, whofe daughter and heirefs Ricarda was married to Sir Thos. Fitchett of Spaxton, whofe heir-general is by Hill and Cheyney Walgrave of Suffolk. But in the latter end of Edward the 3d, William Huifh was Lord Dittifham, whofe heir general by Trefilian and Hawlegh is Copleftone. Sir Anthony Rowfe was lately Lord of Dittifham, which is now defcended to Will. Rowfe his grandfon, by his fon Ambrofe. —Bofumfhele, in the parifh of Dittifham, was the dwelling of Edmund Bofum, in the time of Richard the 2d; who had iffue John Bofum, by the daughter of Sir John Wadham. John Bofum married Rofamond the daughter and heirefs of —— St. George, and had iffue Elizabeth, wife of Sir Baldwyn Fulford, and fecondly of Sir Will. Huddesfield, attorney-general of Edw. the 4th. From the faid Elizabeth is lineally defcended Sir Francis Fulford, who is now poffeft of Bofumfhele." *Sir W. Pole.*

* *Mount-Boone* is fituated on an eminence, at a little diftance to the north of the town of Dartmouth, commanding a very beautiful fea profpect. It is an ancient ftructure, erected by the family of Boone, who formerly held with it a confiderable property in that neighbourhood, now in the poffeffion of John Seale, efq. a defcendant from the family of Seale, in the county of Northumberland, whofe anceftors diftinguifhed themfelves by their loyal attachment to the crown, as well as by their warlike atchievements in 1426. Richard Sheale was a chief in the famous battle of Cheviot Chace, and the bard of that memorable action. He bears arg. three wolves' heads fable & the fame embrued arg. charg'd with a ducal coronet, which diftinguifhed mark of honor was beftowed upon Robt. Seale of this family in 1559, for his fervices in guard and defence of the queen's perfon. After the death of Queen Elizabeth, the fame Robert fettled in the ifland of Jerfey, his only furviving fon Thomas marrying Ann, fourth daughter of Col. Philip Carteret, chief juftice of the ifland, and governor of Mount Orgiel Caftle, who was from the noble lords of St. Owen and Longville. By this lady he had feveral fons, from the eldeft of whom defcended one only fon, John Seale, late of Mount-Boone, efq. who was fent over to England in his minority, and for whom was purchafed " this godely heritage." He married Mary, daughter of Charles Hayne, efq. of Fuge, in this county, and had one fon, who died at an early age. He then married Elizabeth, daughter of John Fownes of Nethway, efq. by whom he had three fons and two daughters. He afterwards married Anna Maria, fourth daughter of Sir John Rogers of Blachford, bart. Thomas, Henry, and Dorothy all died unmarried. Elizabeth, his only furviving daughter, married Chas. Fanfhawe, efq. and has left one fon. John, the prefent gentleman, married Sarah, daughter of Chas. Hayne of Lupton, efq. by whom he has fix children, three fons and three daughters.

† " In the reign of Henry the 2d, Fitz-ftephens dwelt at Norton, and was fucceeded by three defcents. The Fitz-ftephens being extinct, this land came to the Dawneys: And Nicholas Tewkefbury held the fame of Sir Nicholas Dawney, in the time of Edward the 1ft. Afterwards, Edward, Earl of Devon, poffeft Tunfhall, thro' his wife, the daughter and heir of Dawney. In the reign of Henry the 6th, Anne, Countefs of Devon, then married to John Botreaux, held this manor and the manor of Northpole." *Sir W. Pole.*—Norton-houfe belongs at prefent to Thomas Bond, efq. a man of confiderable fortune.

ARCHDEACONRY OF TOTNES.

DEANRY OF IPPLEPEN.

IN Ipplepen, we have the parifhes of Ipplepen, Littlehemfton, Staverton, Broadhemfton, Torbryan, Woodland, Denbury, Wolborough, Newton-Abbot, Abbotfkerfwell, Kingfkerfwell, Coffinfwell, Mary-church, Tor-mohun, Cockington, Marldon, Paignton, Berry-pomeroy, Stoke-gabriel, Churfton, Brixham, Kingfweare, Stokefleming.*

Though IPPLEPEN give name to the deanry, it is by no means a large parifh.†

LITTLEHEMSTON

* " *Benefices remaining in charge:*

First Fruits. £.	s.	d.		*Yearly Tenths.* £.	s.	d.
11	1	3	Abbots-carfwill V. [St. Mary] Rep. B. Proc. iv*s*. Syn. ii*s*. v*d*. A. D. Proc. ivs. r. V. 100*l*. - - - Patr. The KING.	1	2	1½
25	6	8	Broadhemfton V. Rep. B. Proc. iii*s*. Syn. ii*s*. v*d*. A. D. Proc. v*s*. r. V. 120*l*. - - - - Patr. The KING.	2	10	8
18	19	7	Bury-Pomeroy V. [St. Mary] Rep. B. Proc. vi*s*. viii*d*. Syn. iii*s*. iii*d*. A. D. Proc. vi*s*. viii*d*. r. V. 120*l*. - Patr. Duke of Somerfet.	1	17	11½
12	7	6	Denbury R. [St. Mary] Rep. B. Proc. iii*s*. iv*d*. Syn. ii*s*. v*d*. A. D. Proc. iii*s*. r. V. 100*l*. - - - Patr. Duke of Bedford.	1	4	9
19	15	2½	Littlehemfton alias Arundell R. [St. John Baptift] Rep. B. Proc. v*s*. Syn. ii*d*. A. D. Proc. v*s*. r. V. 120*l*. - Patr. The KING.	1	19	6¼
52	1	0½	Panton alias Paignton V. [St. John Baptift] with Marldon Chapel. Alleyn Belfield Penf. xxvi*s*. viii*d*. Rep. none in Charge. Pec. of the Bp. - - - - - - - - Patr. James Templer, efq.	5	4	1¼
32	14	9½	Staverton V. [St. George] Rep. Dean and Chapter of Exeter Penf. xxvi*s*. viii*d*. No other in charge. Pec. of the Dean and Chapter of Exeter. r. V. 180*l*. - - - - - - - Patr. Dean and Chapter of Exeter.	3	5	5¾
31	6	0¼	Stoke Fleming R. [St. Peter] Rep. B. Proc. vi*s*. viii*d*. Syn. ii*s*. v*d*. A. D. Proc. vi*s*. viii*d*. Stoke Fleming is in the Vifitation Books charged in the deanery of Totnes. r V. 250*l*. - - - - Patr. John Henry Southcote, efq.	3	2	7¼
20	14	7	Torbrian R. [Holy Trinity] Rep. B. Proc. v*s*. Syn. ii*s*. v*d*. A. D. Proc. v*s*. r. V. 160*l*. - - - Patr. —— Trift, efq.	2	1	5½

Difcharged.

King's Books. £.	s.	d.		*Certified Value.* £.	s.	d.
52	15	0	Brixham V. [St. Mary] with King's Wear Chapel [St. Thomas Becket] Rep. B. Proc. vi*s*. viii*d*. Syn. iv*s*. vi*d*. A. D. Proc. vi*s*. viii*d*. r. V. - - - - - - - - - Patr. The KING.	42	2	2
26	2	3½	Ipplepen V. [St John Baptift] with Woodland Chapel. Rep. B. Proc. vi*s*. viii*d*. Syn. ii*s*. v*d*. A. D. Proc. vi*s*. viii*d*. r. V. 100*l*. - - - - - - - - - - Patrs. Dean and Canons of Windfor.	49	10	10¾
31	11	5½	St. Mary Church V. with Carfwell alias King's Carfwell, and Coffinfwell Chapels. Rep. none in charge. Pec. of the Dean and Chapter of Exeter. r. V. 140*l*. - - - - - - Patrs. Dean and Chapter of Exeter.	45	0	0
16	11	10½	Stoke St. Gabriel V. Rep. none in charge. Pec. of the Dean and Chapter of Exeter.—The great tythes of Stoke Gabriel are vefted in the Chancellor of the Church of Exeter. r. V. 100*l*. - - - Patr. Sir Stafford Northcote, bart.	47	0	0

Not in charge.

Wolborough Don. [St. Mary] Rep. none in charge. Patr. Lord Vifcount Courtenay.			
Cockington Cur. Rep. none in charge. Patr. Mr. Mallock.			
Newton Abbot [St. Leonard] Chapel to Wolborough. Rep. none in charge.			
Kingfweare [St. Thomas Becket] Chapel to Ipplepen. Rep. none in charge - - - - -	0	14	0
Woodland Chapel to Ipplepen - - - - - - - - - - -	20	0	0
Marldon Chapel to Paignton - - - - - - - - - - - -	34	0	0
Tormohun Ch. Rep. none in charge.			
Churfton Ferrers Ch. to Brixham - - - - - - - - - - -	38	0	0"

Thes. Eccles.

† " By an infcription in the church, as far back as 1573, the parifh was called *Ippellpen*. It is about two miles and a half from eaft to weft; from north to fouth about two miles. Situation high. Springs many. Parifh chiefly enclofed, with feveral open commons. Not much wood. Roads good, chiefly of marble rock. From a hill, the one fide of which is nearly perpendicular, and forty feet high, is a fine view through the vale of Torbryan, terminated by Denbury church. On either fide of the valley are hanging woods. On the left is a very pretty profpect of the village of Torbryan, entirely furrounded by orchards. The view is much heightened by a peep of the church amongft fome lofty elms, and immediately under a hill. The fpot from which this view is taken is called Orley-rock. From this place feven churches may be feen; the fartheft of which is about four miles diftant. Ipplepen is the church-town. The hamlets are, Coombe-

fifhacre,

LITTLEHEMSTON belongs to the family of the extinct Duke of Bolton.*

STAVERTON is a very extenfive, fertile, inclofed parifh, abounding with hills and vales, well wooded and watered. Its produce is chiefly corn, cattle, and cyder,† of which laft article there is fome years a great plenty, and of excellent quality.‡

The parifh of BROADHEMSTON § confifts of fmall inclofures, in the higheft ftate of cultivation.

At

fifhacre,* Dainton, and Ambrook. The houfes are fome of ftone, others of mud: Some are flated, others thatched. Orchards many. Two or three large farms, the reft fmall: in general well cultivated. The parifh populous. Much weaving by the women. The men, many of them employed in the Newfoundland trade. Inhabitants remarkably healthy, and live to a great age. The laft incumbent, fave one, held the living fixty years, as appears by the regifter. Gentlemen's houfes, three: Ambrook, Bully, and the parfonage-houfe. Ambrooke and Bully built many years: the parfonage rebuilt in 1789. Materials of all three marble rock. Ambrooke belongs to the Rev. William Neyle, and has been inhabited by him and his anceftors I fuppofe for 150 years.† Bully is going to decay: It is inhabited by the farmer who rents the barton: It is the property of Nicholas Brooking, efquire, who is collector of Dartmouth. The parfonage belongs to George Drake, efquire, who holds the great tithe. It has been inhabited by him and his family probably for 150 years: he rebuilt it. The church is on the weft fide of the parifh; it is dedicated to St. John Baptift. When built unknown. Materials ftone; unlike any in the parifh, or nearer than Painton. On Gurrington Sands, in Painton parifh, is rock like it. It is of reddifh rock, which looks like a concretion of coarfe fand. The roof is timber, covered with flate. The church about one-third of the height of the tower. The tower is nearly ninety feet high, fquare, and has five bells. It is about thirty-five yards in length, and fifteen yards in breadth. In the church-yard the remains of a large crofs: The church-yard about the third of an acre. The great tithe held by George Drake, efq.: The vicarage by William Cofens, clerk, as vicar, who is paid a fettled fum, by the perfon holding the great tithe, in lieu of the vicarial tithe. The patrons are the Dean and Chapter of Windfor. The firft incumbent mentioned by the regifter is the Rev. Richard Ham. To him fucceeded in the year 1672, by the Rev. John Shears, who died in 1707. To him fucceeded the Rev. Jof Taunton, who died in 1723; and he was fucceeded by his fon, the Rev. William Taunton, who held the living till 1783. After him the Rev. George Willis held it, till 1789, when he vacated it by accepting another living; and the prefent incumbent, the Rev. William Cofens, was prefented the fame year. The vicarage-houfe is feparated from the church-yard only by a road: It is an old building, but has been much altered by the prefent incumbent, who is making it a modern houfe." From the vicar in 1791.

* This family has great property in Littlehemfton and Bigbury. Dec. 25, 1794, died at Hacwood, Hants, the moft noble Harry Powlett, D. of Bolton, M. of Winchefter. He fucceeded his brother Charles, in 1795. He married Catharine Lowther, fifter to the prefent Earl of Lonfdale. By his duchefs, (now living), he left two daughters, Catharine, Countefs of Darlington, and Lady Amelia. Sir William Powlett, his anceftor, was 30 years lord high treafurer of England: He was created Lord St. John of Bafing, Hants, by Henry the 8th; and Earl of Wiltfhire and Marquis of Winchefter, by Edward the 6th, and died aged 97. The family having been inftrumental in forwarding the revolution, the then Marquis was, by William the 3d, created Duke of Bolton, in Yorkfhire The earldom of Wiltfhire and marquifate of Winchefter have defcended to a coufin, George Powlett, of Amport, Hants.

† " Staverton ftands between the two Hempftons, a place paffing fruitful, infomuch that (report giveth out) there are more hogfheads of cyder made, (communibus-annis) than are men, women, and children living there.—Sparkwell was the lands of Henry de Sparkwell the 27th year of King Henry the 3d, from which name it defcended unto Richard de Barnhoufe; and in the time of King Edward the 1ft, William Barnhoufe was lord thereof. After divers defcents in that name, William the laft had two wives; by his firft, he had iffue Agnes; by his fecond, he had a fon named Thomas, whom he difinherited, and conveyed his land unto his daughter, wedded to John Rowe, ferjeant at law, to whofe pofterity Sparkwell and Hempfton is defcended." Rifdon.

‡ " It is bounded on the fouth by the river Dart, in which is plenty of trout fifh; on the weft by Afhburton; on the north by the parifhes of Woodland and Broadhemfton; and on the eaft by the parifh of Littlehemfton. There is alfo a hamlet belonging to Staverton, confifting of four farms, to come to which another parifh muft be paffed through. A great part (except four capital bartons) of this parifh is farmed under the Dean and Chapter of Exeter, to whom the patronage of the church living alfo belongs. The prefent incumbent is Dr. Thomas Baker, whofe father held it many years before him. The bartons above alluded to are called Kingfton, Pridhamfleigh, Barkington, and Blackler. Kingfton-houfe, which was erected by John Rowe, efq. a papift, in 1743, is a fpacious four-front modern-built houfe: its materials confift of hewn marble ftone, cemented with lime and fand, with an elegant cornice of hewn marble ftone all around it; it is three ftories high, befides the attic ftory; with large arched vaults underneath; and adjoining to it is a large walled alcove garden, &c. with a lawn and avenue in it. It hath been occupied fince the faid Mr. Rowe, by Jofeph Champion, efq. but now the refidence of Mr. Thomas Bradridge, the purchafer and proprietor thereof. Pridhamfleigh is a fpacious antique houfe, formerly the property and refidence of Wm. Drake Gould, efq. but now the property of Lord Afhburton. Barkington was antiently the eftate of —— Worth, efq. fince of John Prefton, efq. This houfe now belongs to Sir Frederick Lemon Rogers, bart.; and Blackler now is, and has long been, in the Woolfton family. The church is fituated near the fouth-eaft end of the parifh; it is dedicated to St. George; about 45 broad and 70 in length, befides the chancel; built of ftone and lime, covered with flate, and plaiftered within. A fquare tower, without fpire or fteeple: It has fix bells. The church-yard occupies nearly two acres of ground, having many fprings around it, and in it. There is this infcription on a ftone of the wall on the outfide of the church: Sub hoc tumulo fepultum corpus Johes. Rowe armigeri filii et heredis Johes. Rowe fervientis ad Legem qui obiit 10 die Augufti Anno Dmi. 1592 et Ætatis fuæ 82 et ampliús. The number of paupers may be eftimated at one hundred. Day-labourers three hundred: A great many go to Newfoundland in the feafon, and on their return home employ themfelves in the woollen manufacture, in the inferior branches of it. Rackholders 30. Leafeholders 50. Freeholders 20. And the parifh collectively may contain two thoufand fouls." From the minifter in 1791.

§ " Hempfton-Magna, olim Hempfton Cauntelowe, alias Hempfton-Borard. Its length three miles and half, breadth one and half. Situation rather low, with the following hills, viz. Torcorn, Beacon, Stout-hill, and Rowdon-hill. Several good fprings of water in this parifh, and in general the houfes well watered. The village called Hempfton Church Town is fupplied with good pumps and wells. This parifh is bounded on the weft fide by a brook, which rifes in two rivulets, about a mile or more from the fpot they meet at; (the one in the parifh of Staverton, the other in that of Woodland). The rivulet arifing in Woodland, has its rife about a mile and half from the above fpot, and ferves as a boundary on the north fide, about the one-fixth of a mile. Near the fpot where thefe two rivulets join, is a farm-houfe, called Oldwalls—and the brook has the name of Hems, alias Hempfton Brook. It is confiderably augmented before

* Combe-fifhacre. We learn from Sir William Pole, that the family of Fifhacre flourifhed in this place, in the time of Henry the 2d. There were feveral knights of this family; as Sir Martin Fifhacre of Combe-fifhacre, in King John's days, who, by Ifabel, daughter and heirefs of William de Wadeton, in the parifh of Stokegabriel, had two fons that were knights, Sir Wm. Fifhacre of Combe-fifhacre, and Sir Peter Fifhacre of Morleigh.

† " Rev. Wm. Neyle, of Ambrook, has, 'tis faid, 1000l. a year. His father was bred an agent in London; but his elder brother, who was a counfellor at law, and had been of Exeter College, Oxford, dying young, he fucceeded to the eftate: When it came to the prefent poffeffor, it was encumbered, and he fold a deal of it, and cleared it."

At Torbryan, were lately feen, (fays Prince), near the church, fome remains of that ancient noble houfe, which was the feat and habitation of the Bryans.*

before it leaves this parifh, with three or four fmall rivulets, and in its courfe is crowned with five bridges, viz. Blackler-bridge, Port-bridge, Bow-bridge, Langford-bridge, and Ford-bridge. The former four are built with the rough marble ftone and lime, have one arch each, and are repaired by the parifhes of Broadhempfton and Staverton jointly. The fifth and laft is built of like materials, has one arch, and is repaired by the county. There is another bridge in the fouth-eaft extremity of this parifh, (and for the moft part within it), over a brook called Littlehempfton brook, (it has its rife in the parifh of Torbryan, near the church, and joins Hem's brook before it enters the Dart juft below Ford-bridge). This bridge is called Fifhacre-bridge, is built with like materials of Ford-bridge, &c. is compofed of four arches, and is repaired by the county. Near this bridge is a farm called Fifhacre, which was fold by the Waldron family to Arthur Holdf-worth of Dartmouth, efq. about 14 years ago. An inclofed parifh; the inclofures well proportioned to the fize of the parifh, and its foil, having none exceeding 10 or 12 acres, in general much lefs. The fences are chiefly made of earth and ftones, well planted with wood. The woods are very few in this parifh, the whole not exceeding 12 acres in the different parts of the parifh. The trees, fuch as the oak, elm, afh, beech, &c. flourifh indifcriminately; the greater number I think of the elm is now ftanding. The roads in general very good, made with the rough black marble, and a ftone which is here called the dun-ftone. The views are very pleafing from different parts of the parifh, particularly on the afore-mentioned hills, where we have an extenfive land profpeét, I think for no lefs than 9 miles towards the fouth, including the park at Berry, with other objeéts fo beautifully interwoven with hills, vales, houfes, and villages, as to form a defi-rable landfcape. The vicar has a beautiful view from his garden, of Totnes, Dartington park and pleafure grounds, &c. The villages are fix in number, viz. Hempfton Church Town, Ford alias Forder a Green, Bearton, Werton, Halfwill, and Bicaton. The farm-houfes are thirty-two, viz. Pool-houfe, Lower Handfnaps, Well, Hern, late Goodridge's, Long's Tenement, Stoop, Radfords, Abrahams, Echa-lauz's, Fifhacre, Ford alias Forder, Brook, Downe, Two Waytown's, Higher and Lower Forder alias Ford a Green, Younghoufe, Half-will, Oldwalls, Finneys, late Alexanders, Oak, Dansford, Lee, Knowl, Lake, Purcombe, and Two Bicaton's. Thefe houfes are all within the manor of Broadhempfton, and built with the black marble ftone, in general flated, and tolerably compaét; each has a garden belonging to it, and the parifh well fupplied with orchards, which are large, and from which vaft quantities of excellent cyder is pro-duced. The ftone which is raifed in this parifh, and which bears a moft excellent polifh for tombs, &c. is likewife ufed, when burnt to lime, for manuring the ground, allowing ten hogfheads to an acre, from which the cuftom is to take three crops of corn or grain, one only whereof to be of wheat. Thofe who farm their own eftates ufually allow twelve hogfheads to the acre. The inhabitants are in number, &c. as follows, viz. 1 furgeon, 15 yeomen, 23 rackholders, 3 butchers, 3 taylors, 3 blackfmiths, 7 carpenters, 5 fhoe-makers, 2 ftone-mafons, 3 mafons and helliers, 4 thatchers, 21 feamen, 3 coopers, 1 innholder, 86 weavers, 18 fpinners, 34 day-labourers, and 18 pau-pers. The number of inhabitants, including men, women, and children, is fix hundred and fixty-nine. Gentlemen's feats, only one in our parifh falls immediately under this defcription, which is Bearton-houfe, fituate in the village of Bearton; and that not on account of its ftruéture, but merely as the ancient refidence of the Rowes, a collateral branch of the houfes of Kingfton and Sparkwell in Staverton. There are two others, very neatly built with the marble ftone; one of which (Pool) together with Beafton-houfe, is built with hewn ftone. Beafton-houfe was built 40 years ago, by Mr. Auftin Rowe; Pool-houfe was built about 17 years ago, by John Tozer; the other, Lower Handfnaps, was built about 3 years ago by Mr. James Garrett; it is rough-cafted in front, &c. contrary to the two former ones.—John Huffey, efq. is the prefent proprietor of Beafton-houfe; he is the fon of Mr. Auftin Rowe above-mentioned, by a fifter of the late Giles Huffey of Marnhull, in Dorfet, efq. (whofe eftate, &c. he now enjoys): It has been in this family for thefe 220 years and upwards. Pool-houfe is in the poffeffion of Mr. John Tozer, whofe anceftors, by the mother's fide, of the name of Williams, enjoyed it for 80 years and upwards—before them Mr. Wm. Mann, who held it a very fhort time: he purchafed it with other lands of Thomas Preftwood of Butterford, efq. Higher Handfnaps is in poffeffion of Mr. James Garrett, furgeon, who purchafed a fpot of land called Higher Handfnaps, and built thereon. Thefe houfes are all within the manor.—The manor is the property of Mr. John Tozer, who came to it, by purchafe, 7 years ago;—before him in poffeffion of Sir John Duntze, bart. Sanders, and Hamilton, bankers of Exeter, who held it jointly 6 years;—before them it was in that of Mr. Jofeph Champion, who held it 8 years;—before him in that of John Rowe of Kingfton, efq. whofe anceftors, John Rowe of Kingfton, efq. and John Rowe, gent. his fon and heir apparent, purchafed it of the Hon. William Weft, knt. Lord Delaware, and Thomas Weft of Jertwood, in Hants, efq. in 1570. "Sir Thomas Weft married Eleanor, the daughter of Nicholas Lord Cantelupe, by whom came the manor of Hempfton Cantelowe into the Weft family." Vid. Rifdon. Now, its a query to me whether Earl Delaware's eldeft fon, who is now ftiled Vifcount Cantelupe, fhould not be Vifcount Cantelowe, as its pro-bable he derives his title from this their ancient inheritance. In an original deed given by the above Lord Delaware and Thomas Weft, efq. to John Rowe, &c. bearing date the 9th September, 1570, this parifh is written Broadhempfton, alias Hempfton Canntelowe, alias Hempfton Borard.—No prefbyterians, nor any other feét befides the eftablifhed church, excepting John Huffey, efq. and his family, who are of the Roman Catholick communion, 6 in number, including three fervants.—The church is fituated nearly about the centre of the parifh : It is built with the marble ftone, and a courfe of brown flate. The roof is flated. The height of the walls on the infide is 20 feet nearly. Height of the tower is 62 feet, is in the form of a fquare, and very plain, it contains 5 good bells. Length of the church on the infide is 74 feet, breadth 45 feet, and is well feated. The fcreen is lofty, ornamented with carving and painting, in the centre are painted the arms of Great-Britain, done A. D. 1715. On the fides are printed the Lord's Prayer and ten commandments, with fcriptural fentences in that of the aifles. The altar-piece is fmall, and very neat, having painted on it the fun; over fome fentences taken from St. John's gofpel. The font very plain, with different arms on it, but nearly defaced. The only painting on glafs is in the eaft window of the manor aifle, which are the arms of the Rowes', viz. Azure, three lambs argent, bearings ftandards gules, between a chevron gules; creft, two wings of a bird joined proper on a wreath of colors." From a correfpondent in 1791.

* " The principal eftates in Torbryan parifh are Tornewton, (which is lord paramount, and is the feat of John Wolfton, efq.) Tor-court, Higher and Lower Yeat, Venn, Wotton, Pool, Broadmead, Brimridge, and Norton.—The parifh of Torbryan formerly belonged to the Lord Bryans, (of whofe feat near the church not a ftone remains). There is an old man in this parifh who remembers to have feen the ruins of a very large building: and he was always told by his grandfather and others, that they were the remains of the feat of the Lord Bryans. From the Bryans, the eftate defcended to the Kitfon's, and from them to the Petere's.—Rifdon fpeaks of a Sir William Petere born here, who was privy counfellor to Henry the 8th, Edward the 6th, Queens Mary and Elizabeth.—I have examined the parochial records, and find a Wm. Petere to be interred in the church in April 1614; and that there was a John Petere born in 1566; and another of the family buried in 1606. Their feat was at Tornewton, of whofe family it was purchafed by the anceftors of John Wolfton, efq.—Torbryan church is fituated nearly at one end of the parifh, among rocks and torrs, and is in length 71 feet, breadth 31 feet. The chancel is divided from the church, as Broadhempfton is, and repaired by different hands. This church, for its fymmetry in ar-chiteéture, I take to be one of the moft handfome edifices we have in this neighbourhood—all the minutiæ of the walls are in proportion to each other; it is not plaiftered over head, but is well feated, and has a handfome gilt pulpit. Near this church, is a very fine fpring of water, which is remarkable for its warmth in winter, and that it never diminifhes in the dryeft fummer. On the top of a hill or common belonging to a few allodial eftates in this parifh, and in the direét road from hence to Ipplepen, is a moft beautiful and romantic view of this church and village, amongft rocks, torrs, and woods."—" John Digby Fowell, M. A. has the living of Tor-brian : His immediate predeceffors were Browfe Trift, James Trift, Nicholas Trift, John Holwell. John Wolfton the prefent patron."

WOODLAND had anciently lords fo named; of which family was Sir Walter Woodland, who was knighted by the Black Prince.

In the church of DENBURY, is a monument containing an elaborate defcription (in Latin) of the abilities and virtues of the grandfather of the prefent Thomas Taylor, efq. Jofeph Taylor, who was a captain in Queen Anne's wars. This Jofeph Taylor married a Reynel, who brought him Eaft and Weft Ogwell. He was fucceeded by his fon Jofeph Taylor, who was M. P. for Afhburton for about two years, and died in 1746, leaving two fons, Thomas Taylor and Jofeph. Jofeph had the livings of Bridford and Weft-Ogwell, and died a batchelor in 1772, aged 39. Thomas Taylor, efq. of Denbury, has one fon, Pierce Jofeph Taylor, efq. who married Mifs Charlotte Cooke, one of the beautiful daughters of Dr. Cooke, late Dean of Ely, and Provoft of King's College, Cambridge. Mr. Pierce J. Taylor has feveral children.

WOLBOROUGH was " the inheritance of Will. de Brewer, a judge and counfellor of ftate in Richard the 1ft's time. He enjoyed large poffeffions " in this fhire by the king's gift, and by his wife Matilda de Vallibus," fays *Rifdon.**

In

---

* In Domefday VLVEBERIE. & called a part of TERRA BALDVINI VICECOMITIS. In an old Regifter beginning Nov[r]. 15th, 1558 (1ft Eliz.) it is Wolborough. In Cleaveland Hift: Courtenay's—Wolleborough. The market-town of Newton-Abbot, is in the parifh of Wolborough, and joined to Newton-Bufhel, in the parifh of Highweek, by a ftone bridge of one arch over the little river *Leman*. The market and burrough-rents belong to Thomas Lane, of Coffleet, efq. The manor of Wolborough to the Right Hon[ble]. Wm. Lord Vifc[t]. Courtenay. Ford-houfe, in the manor of Wolborough, is an old built houfe of ftone, rough-cafted, and flated: It was built by Sir R[d]. Reynel: and Sir Wm. Courtenay marrying his grand-daughter, had the houfe and manor of Ford with other lands. Ford was, a fhort time fince, inhabited by Lord Charles Somerfet, who married Elizabeth, daughter of the late, and fifter to the prefent Lord Vifcount Courtenay. The chapel of St. Leonard is in Newton-Abbot, where fervice is performed in bad weather, when the inhabitants are hindered from going to Wolborough. There are no endowed fchools. One meeting-houfe for prefbyterians, and one for methodifts. The church of Wolborough is an old Saxon ftruĉure of three aifles, covered with flate, in very good repair. The tower is fquare, not very lofty, without fpire, and has 4 bells. There is a table in the chancel, which memorizes the gift of Lady Lucy Reynel, of 4 alms-houfes to 4 poor clergymen's widows. Thefe were but flenderly endowed according to the prefent value of money, and were very low, and confifted of but one room under, and one chamber over: Hence no one applied for them. Wherefore the late Lord Courtenay rebuilt them as two only, and appropriated the whole income to thefe two. There are a few tablets of monuments, but none of any great note, except one on the north fide of the chancel, near the communion table, to Sir R Reynel, his lady, &c.

Aprill 1652. The 20th Day was buried the Right Worfhipfull Ladie Luce Reynell of Ford. (Old Regifter).

The monument erected in memory of S[r] R. Reynel and Lady Lucy and two children, has a marble arch, white, veined with red, blue, and other colours, fupported by black marble pillars, with white marble capitals, and bafes of the Ionic order. On the farcophagus or tomb are his, and his lady's effigies. On the fide is a younger lady's figure; and at the bottom a little child on a cufhion. At the head ftands a female figure of juftice, with her fcales negligently placed near her fide, and no bandage over the eyes (as is ufual). At the foot —Time with his fcythe and hour glafs (but the latter is *broken*, whether by defign, or accident, I know not). The infcription is truly in the ftile of James the 1ft's pedantry, full of acroftic and anagram.

In Memoria Dni Rici Reynell de Forde Milit? extincti Ian:[ry] 24⁰
A⁰ Xpi 1633 Æ[s] fuæ 77⁰ & Dnæ Luciæ Vx.[ris] ej? charifsj.[æ] nec nō Dnæ
Ianæ Filiæ ipo. (nuper Dnō Guliel Waller Militi Conjug) Quæ
Obiens ap[d]. Rathon Mai 18⁰ A⁰ Xpi. 1633⁰ nunc ibi iacet fub Statuâ qm̄ pulcrâ Tumulata Etiam Iohis Reynell eo. Filii qui
Londin moriens Infantulus in Eccletia Scæ Bridæ Sepult. eft
hoc extruĉtu erat Monumentu A⁰ Dni 1634.

Friend You that read our Names that Counfell take
W[ch] wee being dead our living Names doe fpeake
Richard Lucye Reynell
CARE LERN LIVE DYE RICH.

Who Care to LLive who Live & love to leaRne
Who leArne to dyE fhall in their Death's difcerne
Such CaRes rewaRde thVs live You all in whiCh
Yu fhall liuE happy aNd beE and dyE RycH.

<table>
<tr><td>

Had this rare Knight, which now here fleeps in Reft
Twelve pretious Stones like Aaron on his Breaft
All graven to Epitaphs They might in Part
Come neere though not reach home his knowne Defert
But when his holie Life his Heavenlye Learning
His Hebrew Tounge his Head deepe Thinges Deferning
Free Heart free Hand full Age with Honnord Hairs
Great with his Cowntryes Praife and Clergies Prayers
Have but one Stone to fpeake it cant fpeake all
His Worths fo Great alas one Stone's too fmall
Wouldft know him more firft learn live dye the fame
Follow him to Heaven there reade his perfeĉt Name.

</td><td>

For the ReLIgeous LaDy LVCy (onLy VVIfe of y[e] VVIfe
SIr RICh. ReyneL KnIght) Who Left Earth on y[c] ResVreCtIon Day Ap[l] 18. 1652.

L oe Here sat Majesty with Meeknesse Crownd,
V aild vnder Reverence Was Courtship Found.
C ompofd Were All such Graces in Her Mind,
Y ee Knew in Morralist or Christian Shind.
R efuge of Strangers, Prophets Ioynturesse.
E afy Chyrvrgion, Poore Mens Treafvresse.
Y ouths Awe & Ages Honor: To God (When
N ot thus to Man) Imployd in Prayers or Penn
E ate Through This Marble if Time fhall She Hath
L eft Vpon Living Stones Her Epitaph.
ÆTATIS SVÆ 74.

</td></tr>
</table>

In ABBOTSKERSWELL (which is faid to have belonged to Torr-abbey) is Aller. This barton, occupying one quarter of the parifh, was in poffeffion of Mr. Bealy's family for upwards of 150 years. It was fold, a few years ago, to Mr. Baker.

In MARY-CHURCH, is *Shiphay*, the feat of the Kitfons.*

TORMOHUN was anciently called *Tor-Brewer*, from the Brewer family. But fince the marriage of one of the daughters and heireffes of this houfe with Mohun, it hath been ftiled *Tor-Mohun*.† It is now commonly called *Tor-moham*. Sir Lawrence Palk is the prefent lord of the manor. Finely fituated in the bottom of Torbay ftands that beautiful edifice called *Torr-Abbey*, already noticed among religious houfes.‡

At COCKINGTON, fo famous in elder days, the fine manor and park are ftill confpicuous.§

The

1558. Mathew Sandeland, Philip Smith, John Comming, Thomas Fofter, Thomas Johnfon, *William Eafton*, *Thomas Downing*, *William Yeo*, John Buckley, John Reynel, 1685, Martij 5°. (Thefe are taken from the old regifter, but the prefent one has a different lift). I apprehend that thefe, whom I have marked with italics were all during the great rebellion, becaufe all except William Yeo are omitted in the following lift.—1620. Mr. Stocks.—1622. The Rev. Thos. Johnfon.—1648. Wm. Yeo, preacher of Wolborough.—1685. Rev. John Buckley.—March 5°, 1685, Rev. John Reynel.—1700. Wm. Eveleigh, minifter.—1701. Gualterus Elford hujus Parochiæ Rector Annos viginti & Sex.—1727. Ei fucceffit Robertus Sadler.—1731. Ei Manifter Barnard.—1732. Ei Robertus Chute.—1739. Ei Honorab: Carolus Bertie, L.L.D.—1746. Ei Gulielmus Buckland.—1760. Ei Gulielmus Davie.—1778. Ei Thomas Hugo.

* Henry the 3d. This manor belonged to Thomas de Cirencefter, and to Walerond de Cirencefter, fheriff of Devon. Edw. the 3d. After two defcents of the Cirencefters, it came to James, Lord Audley; from which family, by Thomazin the daughter of Sir Richard Hankford, and the wife of Lord Fitzwarren, the manor became the inheritance of the Bourchiers, Earls of Bath.

† For Alice, one of the youngeft daughters of Lord William Brewer, having married Reginald de Mohun, left this eftate, which fell to her part, to her youngeft fon Sir William de Mohun, knight.

‡ With regard to the abbey, I refer my readers to Dugdale's Monafticon, where is the original charter of its foundation, privileges, &c. The church is in ruins; but the greateft part of the abbey has been converted into the prefent manfion. Some of the moft ancient parts of the firft endowment remain in their original ftate, and ftill ferve for offices. The old barn meafuring 123¼ feet in length, and 33½ feet in breadth, and a gate-way are in perfect repair.—*Tor-Abbey* came by alienation into the poffeffion of Sir Thos. Ridgeway, knight, who had a houfe hard by, defcended to him from his anceftors. He re-edified thofe decayed buildings in a better form; and his feat hath a pleafant fea and land profpect. Sir Thos. Ridgeway married the daughter of Southcote. His fon, Sir Thomas, was created Earl of Londonderry in 1614.—" An elder brother to George Cary of Cockington, heir to Sir George Cary, lord deputy of Ireland, in the time of Elizabeth, was Sir Edward Cary, fometime of Stantorr. He was knighted in the Irifh wars. His fon Sir George Cary was of Torr-Abbey; whofe eldeft fon, Edward Cary, efq. now flourifhes there." *Prince.*—This Edward Cary married Mary, fecond daughter and coheirefs to Richard Pelfont, by Anne his wife, relict of Thomas Saville, Earl of Suffex—and had iffue George Cary, who married Ann, daughter of Lord Clifford, and left no iffue. He was fucceeded by the prefent Mr. Cary, whofe name is George, and who is fon to William Cary (4th fon to the above-named Edward), by Dorothy Rowe of Stoke Gabriel. The faid Mr. George Cary has been twice married: firft, to Cecilia Fagnani, of an ancient family in Italy, who has left him four fons and two daughters; fecondly, to Frances Giffard, relict of Thomas Giffard of Chillington, Staffordfhire, and daughter of Thomas Stonor, of Stonor, Oxfordfhire, by whom he has two fons and two daughters.

§ " *Cockington* in the Conqueror's time was written *Cochinton*, when Alric the Saxon was diffeized of three hides of land there, which was beftowed on William Fallaife, one of the Conqueror's followers. Sir Walter Woodland, who was ufher of the chamber to the Black Prince, was lord of this land about the latter end of King Edward the 3d, unto whom the Prince gave the wardfhip of John Blomonfter, fon and next heir of Sir Ralph Blomonfter, knight, that held of him in chief; afterwards the Prince knighted him, and for the more eafe of his charge, granted him the mannors of Morefley, Tywarnaile and Penzance in Cornwall; and promifed an hundred mark land to him, and to the heirs of his body, for the maintenance of his eftate, 26 Apr. 24 King Edward the 3d; fince it is become a feat of the Caries for divers defcents, a family that have flourifhed in great efteem, and have taken deep root, whence many noble branches are budded forth, and by tranfmigration planted themfelves elfewhere." *Rifdon.*—Sir Robert Cary of Cockington was the eldeft fon, among a numerous iffue, of Sir John Cary, one of the barons of the exchequer in the time of Edward the 3d, by Anne, daughter and heirefs of the Lord Guy de Bryan. Sir Robert married Margaret, daughter of Sir Philip Courtenay of Powderham-caftle, by whom he had iffue Philip; who by Thomafin his wife, one of the daughters and heireffes of William Orchard, efq, of Orchard, in the county of Somerfet, had iffue Sir Wm. Cary, who had two wives; firft, Anne, daughter of Sir William Powlet, by whom he had iffue Robert Cary of Cockington, who had three wives, and iffue by them all. Sir Wm. Cary had for his fecond wife Alice, daughter of Sir Baldwin Fulford of Fulford, from whom defcended the noble families of Cary in the eaftern parts of England, of which there were at the fame time two earls, Monmouth and Dover, Vifcount Faulkland, and Baron Hunfdon. Robert Cary, on whom his father fettled Cockington, married three wives. By Jane his firft wife (daughter of Sir Nicholas Baron Carew), John Cary was his eldeft fon, who married Anne, daughter and heirefs of Edmund Devich, or Devyock, efq. of Keckbear, in Okehamton, and fettled there. His pofterity continued in that place feveral defcents; when this part of the family became extinct. Robert Cary of Cockington aforefaid, by Agnes his fecond wife, (the daughter of Lord Chief Baron Hofhe), had iffue Wm. Cary of Ladford, in the parifh of Shebbear, near the Torridge. This branch of the family is gone. By his third wife, Margery, daughter and heirefs of Foukroy of Dartmouth, he had iffue Robert, to whom he gave Clovelly, where the Carys' continued in Prince's time. The fecond fon of Robert Cary of Cockington, by Jane his firft wife, was Thomas Cary, efq. who had fix fons, the eldeft of whom was Sir George Cary, knight, and lord deputy of Ireland in the time of Elizabeth. Sir George firft married Wilmot, daughter and heirefs of John Gifford of Yeo, the divorced wife of John Bury of Colaton, near Chimleigh; by whom he had iffue one fon, Sir George Cary, knight, married, but flain in the wars of Ireland, without iffue before his father's death, and one daughter, married to Sir Richard Edgcumbe of Mount Edgcumbe, without iffue. Secondly, he married Lucy, daughter to Robert Lord Rich, Earl of Warwick; but, having no iffue by her, he adopted George, the third fon of his fecond brother, Robert, according to Sir W. Pole, whom he made his heir. George Cary, efq. of Cockington, the heir of Sir George, married Elizabeth, daughter of Sir Edward Seymour

of

The moft confiderable part of the parifh of MARLDON is juftly faid to confift of the richeft and moft fertile land in the fouth of Devon: and the whole is upwards of 2000 acres.* The manor of Marldon belongs to Sir L. Palk. That ancient and venerable fabric, called Compton-caftle, now in poffeffion of James Templar, efq. was formerly the Gilbert's. It was once a feat of confiderable magnificence. *Mudge's-place*, in this parifh, is a fmall neat houfe, the prefent owner of which is Nicholas Adams Bartlett, efq. whofe family, on the mother's fide, have poffeffed it more than 270 years. The church of Marldon is a light and handfome ftructure, built with hewn ftone.†

PAIGNTON‡ (as Rifdon truly obferves) is " one of the moft fruitful lordfhips in all this county." The village of Paignton is finely fituated: It lies in the bofom of Torbay, about four miles eaft of Totnes.§ *Blagdon-houfe* paffed by purchafe from the Blunts to Montague Edmund Parker, efq.‖ In Paignton is

Torbay-

of Berry-caftle, bart. by whom he had a fair iffue, fons and daughters. His eldeft fon, Sir Henry Cary of Cockington, was ruined in confequence of his loyalty, in the civil war of Charles the 1ft, and was obliged to fell all his eftates. His fecond fon, Dr. Robert Cary, was eminent as a man of literature. " The youngeft fons became foldiers of fortune, and died, I think, beyond fea, without iffue." The houfe and manor of Cockington was purchafed of Mr. Mallach, a rich merchant of Exeter, whofe fon Rawlin Mallach, efq. new built the houfe, enclofed the park, walled round the warren and large gardens, reftored the ponds, and made it as convenient a feat as moft others in the county. At his deceafe, about the year 1690, he left Cockington to Rawlin Mallach, efq. his fon, by Elizabeth his fecond wife, the daughter of Sir John Collins of Hampfhire, knight—" now living here," fays *Prince*. At prefent, Cockington-houfe belongs to Roger Malloc, efq. whofe father, the Rev. Samuel Malloc, in 1779, received it, by will, from his coufin, the faid Rawlin Malloc, or Mallach.

* " Into Torbay a brook fheddeth itfelf, that breaketh forth from *Marldon*, fo called belike of the quality of the foil; for here all about it confifteth of a kind of marl and chalky fubftance. In this parifh is *Compton*, the lands of Angier anciently, whofe daughter and heir Alice was the wife of Ralph de Pole, in the time of King Henry the 2d, which remained in that family until King Henry the 3d: In the 27th year of which king's reign Ralph de Dodefcombe was lord thereof, whofe male line extinct, it was left to daughters; whereof one, as I am informed, was wife unto one of the Worths. A name that enjoyeth lands here at this prefent. This lady Alice Pole gave another Compton unto one of the family of Peter, whofe pofterity took name of the place; and after it had continued fix defcents in that line, William the laft left two daughters, Joan married to Jeoffry Gilbert, and Sufan unto Richard Chiderly; this land fell to Gilbert's part, and hath ever fince been the inheritance of that family, where they have a houfe feated low in a valley between two hills.—*Stontor* may not be filenced, where Stephen Stontor held half a fee in King Henry the 2d's days, where that family inherited, and where they in-habited, before Pierce Stontor married Ifabel the daughter and heir of Sir William Vernon in Wiltfhire." *Rifdon.*

† " One of the Gilberts built the church. It is a very handfome and uniform pile. The arms of Gilbert may be feen in feveral of the windows belonging to this church." *Prince.*

‡ " The parifh of Paignton is about 4 miles long and 3½ wide: it is fituated near the centre of Torbay, by which it is bounded for nearly three miles; the lands near the fea are in general low, gradually rifing into hills, which on every fide furround the parifh on the land fide. The whole is inclofed with hedges, banked up 5 or 6 feet high, on which trees are planted. The lower lands abound much with hedge row elms, which thrive remarkably well; but there are no woods. Roads tolerably good: Materials in general marble. The parifh con-fifts of one village, that of Paignton, and five or fix hamlets, with many farm-houfes interfperfed in different parts. The greater part of the houfes are built of mud walls, and covered with thatch, but not remarkable for neatnefs or commodioufnefs. A great quantity of or-chard ground. Farms in general fmall, from 20l. to 50l. fome few 100l. and one 300l. per year. Cultivation tolerably good. Number of inhabitants in the parifh fuppofed to be about 2000. Number of paupers about 100 names, but including under many of them very large families. No kind of manufacture. Many farmers of each defcription, of rackholder, leafeholder, and freeholder, particularly the laft. Nothing particular as to health, character, cuftoms, &c. One wake or fair on Whitfun-Tuefday, which lafts 2 or 3 days. In the village of Paignton, about half a mile from the fea, are the ruins of what is recorded to have been a palace belonging to the fee of Exeter; nothing but the walls now remain." 1792.

§ " From Brixham we went to Paignton, fix miles, turning down on the right, and driving along the beach before the front of Mr. Shard's houfe, which commands a full view of the bay and fea, with Brixham at one extremity, and Torkay at the other—with the bold abrupt rocks of the fhore; and which muft be a noble fight, when a fleet of men of war, or large fhips, anchor in the bay. Immediately behind his houfe, is a marfh—but the village of Paignton, with its handfome church, and the hills and fields above it, well cultivated and wooded, make a pleafing appearance from the back part of the houfe; and altogether, from the view of land and water, this muft be a delightful fituation as a refidence in the fummer: But in the winter, it muft wear, I fhould think, a dreary afpect. Soon as we had paffed the rock beyond Mr. Shard's, we turned up a road on the left hand, and in a fhort way, then took the firft road to the right, which brought us through a village called Tormount, and in about four miles to Torquay, where we dined at the fign of the anchor. We paffed by Mr. Cary's, Torr-abbey, fituated near the quay; which, with the avenue of chefnut trees in full bloom, looked beautiful." Sketch of a MS. tour in 1792.

‖ " *Blagdon*, the ancient dwelling of the Dennis's, knights. By Agatha, the fifter, and one of the heirs of Sir Robert Le Dennis, it came, with Colaton Clavell, to Sir Nicholas Kirkham her hufband, and defcended, in the name of the Kirkhams, from Edward the 1ft's age, to the days of Rifdon. *Blagdon in the Moor*, an ancient houfe, the long continued feat of the Kirkhams. Sir Nicholas Kirkham of Blagdon, had iffue Sir Nicholas, from whom defcended Robert Kirkham, efq. who married Elizabeth, one of the four daughters and co-heireffes of Robert Scobhul (anciently Scobahul) of Scobhul, in the parifh of South Pool. From Robert defcended Nicholas Kirkham, efq. who by Joan his wife, the daughter and heirefs of John Wray of March, in Newton St. Cyres, had iffue Sir John Kirkham, knight, Nicholas, and Thomas; and Margaret, firft married to John Cheyney of Pinho; fecondly, to William Bampfylde of Poltimore, efq.; thirdly, to Grenville of Stow, in Cornwall. Sir John Kirkham, (famous for his benefactions in the time of Henry the 8th), married firft the daughter of More of Morehays, without iffue; fecondly, the daughter of Sir Thomas Fulford of Fulford, without iffue; thirdly, Lucie, daughter of Sir Thomas Tremayle of Sand, in the parifh of Sidbury, and had iffue Thomas, and Richard of Pinho. Thomas Kirkham of Blagdon, married firft Margaret, daughter and heirefs of Richard Ferrers of Fenniton, efq. and of Jane his wife, daughter and heirefs of

William

Torbay-houfe, (a very large elegant one), belonging to Francis Freke, of Loddifwell, efq. the refidence of William Shard, efq. who has a leafe in it.   Here
alfo is a handfome feat, Primleys, the feat of the Rev. Finney Belfield, M. A.
In Prefton village are two genteel houfes, one belonging to Robert Butland,
gent. and the other to John Diftin, gent.   In the aifle on the fouth fide of this
church was buried Sir John Kirkham, whofe noble benefactions to the town of
Honiton have rendered his name immortal.   I meet with no memorial of this
gentleman here, unlefs, perhaps, on the tranfverfe wall, which feparates the aifle
from the church.   Here are feveral ftatues or figures of men, finely carved in
ftone—which were doubtlefs intended as the reprefentations of fome of the
Kirkham family.*

The parifh of BERRY-POMEROY joins with that of Totnes by a fair bridge of
eight arches, ftanding over the river Dart.   It is a large parifh, richly cultivated, and finely wooded.   The caftle of Berry Pomeroy (fays Prince) is fituated in a deer park, upon a rock, on a rifing ground from the eaft and north,
over a pleafant rivulet, that, running through the park, empties itfelf into the
Hemms at Little Hemfton.   There the Pomeroys had their dwelling from the
Norman Conqueft to the days of Edward the 6th.   The name was varioufly
written, as de Pomerio, de Pomeri, de la Pomerai, and then Pomeroy.   The
firft of the name in England, was Ralph de Pomerai, who came over with the
Conqueror, and greatly affifted him in his conqueft of England.+   Here he built
his caftle; which his pofterity enjoyed to the reign of the 6th Edward; when
Sir Thomas Pomeroy ‡ fold the manour to Edward Seymour, Duke of Somerfet.
Lord Edward Seymour, the Duke's eldeft fon, refided here.   " The fon of Lord
Edward, Sir Edward Seymour, knight and baronet, made the caftle (fays Rifdon)
a very ftately houfe, and here lives Sir Edward Seymour, knight and baronet,
his fon."   It is ftill in the Seymour family; being the property of the Duke of
Somerfet.   The ruins of this caftle are an object of great curiofity to travellers.
The north view feems the moft romantic, from the old fragments of the caftle
breaking thro' the deep umbrage of the fantaftic woods.   The ftone wall is ftill
traceable round the park of about 500 acres.   *Loventor*, (the ancient inheri-

William Malhert of Finniton, and had iffue George, James, and others.   Secondly, Thomas Kirkham married Cicely, the only daughter
of Sir William, and fifter and heirefs of Sir George and Sir Philip Carew of Mohun Ottery; and had iffue Henry, William who had no
iffue, and Thomafin married to Thos. Southcote, efq. of Bovey-Tracey, by whom the Southcotes became lords of Mohun Ottery.   George
Kirkham of Blagdon, married Margaret, the daughter of Sir Thomas Dennis of Holcombe Burnel, and had iffue Elizabeth, a dwarf, who
died without iffue.   James Kirkham, the fecond fon, married, and had iffue Margaret, firft the wife of William Weftofer; fecondly, of
Edmund Argenton.   Richard Kirkham of Pinho and Blagdon, married Agnes, daughter of John Cape of Somerfet, and had iffue Richard,
who died without iffue, Sir William, and others.   Sir William Kirkham of Blagdon and Pinho married the daughter of Tichborn, and
had iffue; firft, Richard; fecondly, Francis, on whom he fettled Pinho; thirdly, Edward, and others.   Richard Kirkham of Blagdon,
efq. married the daughter and heirefs of Oldham, near Tilberry, in Effex, and had iffue Mary, his only daughter and heirefs, married to
Sir George Blunt of Sodington, in Worcefterfhire, bart. by whom he had iffue feveral children, the eldeft of whom was Sir George Kirkham
Blunt of Blagdon and Sodington, bart." *Prince.*

    * The church, fituated in the village of Paignton, about half a mile from the fea, is a very good plain well-built church; the materials
ftone, and the roof flate; about 133 feet long by 46 wide.   The tower is fquare, about 90 feet high, has 6 bells.   There are many charitable donations, but none worth fpecifying.   Vicarage; the right of prefentation is tripartite divided between the Earl of Cork and ——
Poyntz, efq. jointly, Sir Stafford Northcote, bart. and James Templar, efq.   Prefent incumbent, Rev. Samuel Belfield, who fucceeded Mr.
Champernoun, whofe predeceffor was Mr. Milmen.

    † The Conqueror, in gratitude, conferred on him a noble eftate, no lefs than 58 lordfhips, in Devonfhire, or the greateft part of them,
as Sir W. Dugdale tells us in his Baronage of England.   Some of thefe lordfhips are thus named in Domefday: Wiche, Dunwinfdon,
Brawardin, Pudeford, Horwood, Toriland, Holcome, Peremore, Beri, Affton, Otrye, Chivedon, Smaridge.   See *Prince*, pp. 489, 490.

    ‡ The Right Hon. Arthur Pomeroy, Vifcount Harberton, in Ireland, is defcended from the Pomeroys of Berry-Pomeroy: His anceftor,
in the reign of James the 1ft, owned Ingfdon; which, after the death of the Rev. Robert Tapfon, M. A. in 1750, was purchafed by
Charles Hale, efq.

tance of Algar) was lately the refidence of the Rev. Thos. Baker, L. L. D. who had the livings of Staverton near Totnes, and Rinmore near Modbury. In the chancel of Berry Pomeroy church there is a monument of the Pomeroys.*

In STOKE-GABRIEL, is *Sandridge,* a very pleafant feat, ftanding on a gentle afcent, on the eaft fide of the Dart, which furrounds nearly three parts of it.†

CHURSTON-FERRERS is a very fmall parifh. Churfton-Court (the old feat of the Yards) is at prefent poffeft by Francis Buller Yard, efq.‡

In the parifh of BRIXHAM are feveral feats, the refidence of old families ; and now the property of people of confideration.§   At the barton of *Nethaway* was

a

---

* *Berry Pomeroy.* Some arms and other coloured glafs remain in the windows here. The fcreen is of wood, elegantly carved, painted, and gilded in good gothic tafte. The porch before the fouth door feems coeval with the church, which I never obferved at any other church. The roof confifts of fpringing arches in the two key ftones, on which is infculp'd a human face and a fhield of arms, (viz.) a lion rampant—quere, if not the bearing of Pomeroy ? I fhould guefs the church was built temp. Edw. the 3d.—John Edwards, LL.B. is the prefent vicar of Berry Pomeroy, to which he fucceeded in 1781, on the death of Jofeph Fox, M. A. who held it 57 years, being the immediate fucceffor of Mr. Prince, (the author of the Worthies), who poffeffed the vicarage 56 years. Fox was a foolifhly fuperftitious man : he ufed to fow his peas and other pulfe on a Good-Friday, from a perfuafion that they would *rife again,* an earlier crop than if fown on any other day.

† This place had lords called after its own name. Stephen de Sandridge held here three parts of a knight's fee, of the Bifhop of Exeter, fo far back as the time of Henry the 2d ; Martin de Sandridge held the fame, 27th of Henry the 3d ; William de Sandridge 24th of Edw. the 1ft ; Richard de Sandridge 8th of Edward the 2d ; and Henry de Sandridge 19th of Edward the 3d—in all near 200 years. After this, *Sandridge* became the inheritance of Pomeroy, moft likely a younger fon of Berry-caftle. Afterwards, Sir Henry de la Pomeroy of Berry, having no heirs of his body, fettled his lands upon Sir Thomas Pomeroy of Sandridge ; who had married Joan, daughter of Sir James Chidleigh, knight, by his wife Joan Pomeroy, fifter of the faid Sir Henry. Sandridge is at this time (fays Prince) the dwelling of Roger Pomeroy, efq. It belongs at prefent to Lady Afhburton.—*Wadeton,* in Stoke-Gabriel, belonging to Sir F. L. Rogers, bart. was purchafed by his father, Frederic Rogers, efq. younger brother of Sir John Rogers, bart. (whom, in 1773, he fucceeded in title and eftate), I believe in 1756, of Mrs. Shepheard, widow of Francis Shepheard, efq. who died in 1735, aged 31. The Rev. Francis Shepheard, vicar of Dean-Prior, is of this family.

‡ " Beyond Tor-abbey, a beach of feveral miles ftretches itfelf onwards towards the fouth ; in the centre of which the town of Paignton is diftinguifhed. Above the cliffs, as foon as the fouthern arm of the bay commences, among groves of ancient trees, appears *Churfton,* a feat of Sir Francis Buller. About a mile further, in a recefs, is feen the fifhing-town of *Brixham :* And foon after, in Berry-point, this rocky arm terminates. Churfton had long been in poffeffion of the Yards ; and by an heirefs is now the property of Sir Francis Buller, whofe fon has affumed the name of Yard. Judge Buller having purchafed the modern-built feat of *Lupton,* from Mr. Hayne, more towards the centre of the peninfula, (about a mile from Churfton), has there taken up his refidence." MS. Sketch of a tour in 1792.

§ " *Brixham,* or *Britbrickfham,* beareth more to the fouth, which Ulfe held in holy King Edward the Confeffor's time, Raphe, in the Conqueror's time ; afterwards it became the inheritance of the Vaultorts, and from that family it defcended to the Lord Peter Corbet, by Beatrix his mother, and to Henry de la Pomeroy, from Avife his mother, being the fifters and next heirs of Roger de Vaultort, Baron of Harborton, who died in King Edward the 1ft's age.—*Lupton* lieth in this parifh, the ancient dwelling of the name of Peverels, of which tribe I find ten defcents to have inhabited here. John Peverel's iffuelefs deceafe left it to Agnes his fifter, married to John Upton, of which family was Nicholas Upton, the learned civilian, an excellent ornament ; who wrote alfo of heraldry, colours and armories, with the duties of chivalry, whence our modern writers have taken great light : The now inheritor is Arthur Upton, efq. Charles Hayne, efq. poffeft this place. He fold it about the year 1788, to Sir Francis Buller. A moiety of the manor of Brixham went with this to the judge : The other moiety belongs to Henry Fownes Luttrel, efq.—*Greenway,* a pleafant and commodious feat, ftanding on the eaft fide of the Dart, upon a rifing ground, about a mile above Dartmouth : It commands a fine profpect of the Dart, with the boats and barges paffing and repaffing on that delightful river. A large fcope of lands, and the royalty of fifhing and fowling belong to it. *Prince.*—Greenway in William the 1ft's time came to the fhare of Walter de Doway, a noble gentleman ; but for many defcents fince the inheritance of the Gilberts, and now the delightful dwelling of that knightly family. Sir Humphry Gilbert, the famous fea officer in the reign of Elizabeth, was born at this place ; the fecond fon of Otho Gilbert of Greenway, efq. by Catherine his wife, daughter of Sir Philip Champernowne of Modbury, knight ; who dying young, his relict became the fecond wife of Walter Raleigh, efq. of Fardel. Sir Humphry Gilbert married Anne, the daughter of Sir Anthony Agar of Kent, knight, by whom he had nine fons and one daughter. His eldeft fon was Sir John Gilbert of Greenway and Compton, knight. According to Sir W. Pole, he married the daughter of Sir Richard Molineux of Shefton, knight, without leaving any iffue ; as did all his brothers, except the laft, whofe name was Raleigh Gilbert. Raleigh Gilbert, by the daughter and heirefs of Kelly, left iffue Agar Gilbert, efq. who by his wife, the daughter of Edmund Waldrond of Bovey, had iffue Humphry Gilbert, efq. of Compton ; who, by Joan his wife, eldeft daughter of Roger Pomeroy, efq. of Sandridge, had iffue. *Prince.*—*Nethaway,* an ancient and retired feat, lying fomewhat low, and almoft furrounded with hills ; to which belongs a large demefne of feveral hundred acres of land, extending to the river Dart, that alone parts it from the town of Dartmouth. William Cole held Nethaway in the time of Richard the 2d ; to whom fucceeded John Cole ; whofe daughter and heirefs Margaret, was married to Sir John Hody, and thus brought Nethaway to the Hody family, in which it continued about 12 defcents. The houfe becoming ruinous, John Hody, efq. repaired and made it a commodious dwelling for himfelf and family ; but before he had quite finifhed it, he fold every inheritance from his pofterity, about the year 1696, to John Fownes, efq. Henry F. Lutterel, efq. is the prefent proprietor. The firft of the Luttrells mentioned in the annals of the country, we find among the Norman chiefs, who attended William the Conqueror to England, in 1066, and was prefent at the battle of Haftings. Soon after the conqueft, the Luttrells became lords of Hooten-Pagnel, in Yorkfhire ; and in the reign of King John, were barons by tenure ; in that of Henry the 3d, they inherited the barony of Irnham, in Lincolnfhire, together with large poffeffions in the weft, from Maurice de Gaunt, one of the moft potent fubjects of his time : They paid fines in the fame reign for a confiderable property in Ireland ; and Ralph Luttrell was lord chancellor of that kingdom in 1237. In the 23d year of Edward the 1ft, 1295, Robert Luttrell, Baron of Irnham and Hooten-Pagnel, was fummoned by writ, and fat alfo in the king's council. Sir John Luttrell was a diftinguifhed officer in the battles in France, in Edward the 3d's time. Sir Hugh Luttrell was in the wars under Henry the 5th, and a counfellor to the prince. Sir John Luttrell was a knight of the bath, 1399 (at the inftitution of the order) as was Sir Hugh Luttrell in the reign of Henry the 7th. Two branches of this family remain, one at Nethaway, Devon, and Dunftar, Somerfet, a caftle inherited in the reign of Henry the 4th, from the Mohuns, Lords of Dunftar, and Earls of Somerfet, and which came by a fole heirefs, about the year 1750, to Henry Fownes, of Nethaway, efq. The other branch is that of the " Luttrells of Luttrells-town, Ireland, and Warwickfhire." John Fownes Luttrell, efq. fon of Henry, was born in 1752, married a Mifs Drewe of Grange, and has 8 children : He has three brothers, Alexander, Francis, and Thomas.—Mrs. Cutler of Upton, (widow of John Cutler, efq. who died in 1799), has two fons, John and Francis, and five daughters.

a chapel fuffered to fall to ruin, by Mr. Huddy, who ufed the font as a pig's trough. There was alfo a chapel at *Lufton*, the ancient feat of the Uptons.

KINGSWEAR "was a pretty fifhing town," in Leland's days, " of which Sir Geo. Carew was lord." H. Fownes Lutterel, efq. is the prefent lord of the manor.

STOKE-FLEMING belongs to the Southcotes.*

---

* " *Stoke-fleming*, mounting up with high clifts, had that addition of a nobleman of Flanders, lord thereof, that lived here in King John's time; the laft of which tribe gave his lands to the Lord Reginald Mohun, in King Henry the 3d's reign, which Reginald beftowed it on his younger fon William, that had two daughters; the one married to Sir John Carew, Lord of Carew, in Pembrokefhire, the other to Merriot, who died without iffue: Eleanor had iffue Sir Nicholas Carew, who died iffuelefs, but before his death conveyed his land unto his brother John, which his father had by the daughter of Talbot; in memory whereof the houfe of Carew hath ever born the Mohuns arms quarterly. Albeit, they are not defcended from them, yet had they a large inheritance, by reafon of that marriage. This land defcended unto Sir Peter Carew, who conveyed it unto Mr. Thomas Southcote, that had married his niece, the daughter of his only fifter Cicely, which mannor remaineth in that name.—*Stoke*. In the church, are the ftatues of a man and woman fairly figured in brafs, and arched over with this French infcription :——

Amis qui paffes par John Corp & Elienor fils de fon Fitzancy pers dieux pur charite qui de eur Alms avie mercy. Amen,
Obiit in die Sancti Job. Evang. Anno Domini 1361.
Obiit in die Sancti Georgii, Anno Domini 1391." Rifdon.

ARCHDEACONRY

DEANRY of MORETON.

IN this deanry, are Moreton, North-Bovey, Manaton, Luftleigh, Hennock, Bovey-Tracey, Ideford, Teigngrace, Kingfteignton, Highweek, Newton-Bufhel, Afhburton, Bickington, Buckland, Widecombe, Ilfington.*

In the parifh of MORETON † there is much coarfe ground, though turned to great advantage, in the culture of potatoes. Here, on the banks of the Teign, is an abundance of coppice wood. The town of Moretonhamftead, about 13 miles to the fouth-weft of Exeter, is fituated upon an eminence, in the midft of a vale; which, tho' not fo rich as the vales to the eaft of the county, yet bears fimilar marks of cultivation.‡

NORTH-BOVEY § and MANATON‖ exhibit the fame general features of moor-land and coppice.

LUSTLEIGH

* " *Benefices remaining in charge:*

First Fruits. £. s. d.		Yearly Tenths. £. s. d.
38 8 11½	{ Afhburton V. [St. Andrew] with Buckland and Bickington Chapels. Pec. of the Dean and Chapter of } { Exeter. Rep. Dean and Chapter of Exeter. Penf. v*l*. iii*s*. iv*d*. No other in charge. r. V. 250*l*. - } Patrs. Dean and Chapter of Exeter.	3 16 10¾
26 2 1	{ Boveytracey V. [St. Thomas Becket] Rep. to the King Penf. x*l*. B. Proc. vi*s*. viii*d*. Syn. ii*s*. v*d*. A. D. } { Proc. vi*s*. viii*d*. r. V. 150*l*. - - - - - - - - - - - } Patr. The KING.	2 12 2½
17 13 9	Iddesford R. [St. Mary] Rep. B. Proc. iv*s*. Syn. ii*s*. v*d*. A. D. Proc. iv*s*. r. V. 160*l*. - - -	1 15 4½
17 9 7	{ Ilfington V. [St. Michael] College of Ottery Penf. xiii*s*. iv*d*. Rep. B. Proc. vi*s*. viii*d*. Syn. ii*s*. x*d*. A. D. } { Proc. vi*s*. viii*d*. r. V. 150*l*. ▲ - - - - - - - - - } Patrs. Dean and Canons of Windfor.	1 14 11½
28 13 9	{ Kingfteignton V. [St. Michael] with Highweek Chapel [All Saints] and Newton-Bufhel Chap. Rep. B. } { Proc. vi*s*. viii*d*. Syn. ii*s*. v*d*. A. D. Proc. v*s*. viii*d*. r. V 150*l*. - - - - - } Patr. Preb. thereof in the church of Sarum.	2 17 4½
16 7 6	Liftleigh R. [St. John Baptift] Rep. B. Proc. vi*s*. viii*d*. Syn. vii*d*. A. D. Proc. vi*s*. viii*d*. r. V. 80*l*. - - 1 2 9 Patr. Lord Egremont.	1 2 9
13 12 8½	Manaton R. [St. Wenefrid] Rep. B. Proc. v*s*. Syn. ii*s*. v*d*. A. D. Proc. v*s*. r. V. 100*l*. - - Patr. George Carwithen, clerk.	1 7 3¼
49 19 7	Moreton Hampftead R. [St. Andrew] Rep. B. Proc. vi*s*. viii*d*. Syn. ii*s*. x*d*. A. D. Proc. vi*s*. viii*d*. r. V. 350*l*. Patr. Lord Vifcount Courtenay.	4 19 11½
22 10 5	North-Bovey R. [St. John] Rep. B. Proc. v*s*. Syn. ii*s*. v*d*. A. D. Proc. v*s*. r. V. 200*l*. - - Patr. Lord Vifcount Courtenay.	2 5 0½
5 9 4½	Teyngrace R. [St. Mary] Rep. B. Proc. ii*d*. Syn. ii*d*. r. V. 80*l*. - - - - - Patr. John Templer, efq.	0 10 11¼
25 13 9	Withicombe V. [St. Pancras] Rep. B. Proc. vi*s*. viii*d*. Syn. ii*s*. x*d*. A. D. Proc. vi*s*. viii*d*. r. V. 140*l*. - Patrs. Dean and Chapter of Exeter.	2 11 4¾

Difcharged.

King's Books.		Certified Value.
16 0 0	Hennock V. [St. Mary] Rep. B. Proc. v*s*. Syn. ii*s*. ix*d*. A. D. Proc. vi*s*. r. V. 120*l*. - - Patrs. Mayor and Chamber of Exeter.	49 0 0
	Buckland in Mora Chapel to Afhburton. - - - - - - -	26 0 0
	Bickington Chapel to ditto - - - - - - - - - -	22 0 0
	Newton Bufhel Ch. to King's Teignton."	

Thes. Eccles.

† " *Moreton* was the land of the Earl of Ulfter, and afterwards the dwelling of Sir Philip Courtenay, knight, younger fon of Hugh Lord Courtenay, and brother of Hugh Courtenay the firft Earl of Devon of that family. Sir Philip dying without iffue, this land came to the Earl of Devon, and was given by Hugh Earl of Devon to Sir Philip his younger fon, and hath ever fince continued in the family of Courtenay of Powderham." *Sir W. Pole.*—In Moreton, is Hill, belonging to James Fynes, efq. uncle to the Rev. Charles Fynes, LL.D. prebendary of Weftminfter.

‡ It is remarkable, that this town is nearly equi-diftant from fix other towns, Okehamton, Exeter, Crediton, Newton, Afhburton, Chudleigh. And the periphery of a circle about four miles round the town, would run thro' fourteen parifhes.

§ " *North bovy* hath been very antiently the land of Pipard, of w. name I find thefe y*t* follow fucceffively to have enjoy'd this Manr. Willm, S*r* Willm, S*r* Willm Pipard K. his Son 27 H. 3. Edmond, w. had iffue Thomas & John, Thomas had iffue Willm, w*ch* died witht iffue 29 E. 1. unto whom fucceeded John his Uncle, & had iffue John, w*ch* had iffue S*r* Willm Pipard K. w*ch* left iffue Margaret

wife

Lustleigh is all hill, valley, and rock.*

In viewing the parifh of Hennock,† I was conducted by two very pleafant and ingenious friends (animæ neque candidiores, &c. &c.) to the heights of

Vol. III. 2 G Bottor.

wife of Gerald Lord Lifley & Matild wife of Sᵣ Ofbert Hameley K. Sᵣ Warren Lord Lifley fucceeded in this Land, & had iffue Margaret wife of Thomas Lord Buckleigh, whofe Daur Elizabeth Brought this Manr to Richard Beachamp Earl of Warwick whofe Daur Elizabeth brought this Manr. to George Nevill Lord Latimer her hufband, in wᶜʰ name it continued unto Jnɔ Nevill Lord Latimer, unto whofe Daurs it defcended." *Sir W. Pole.*

‖ " The parifh of *Manaton* is in length from eaft to weft about feven miles, in breadth about four. That part of it toward the weft is fituated very high, is a wild uncultivated tract of land, and is bounded on that fide by the foreft of Dartmoor. Toward the north it is bounded by the parifh of North Bovey, and the river Bovey divides it from Luftleigh, on the eaft, which river has a fubterraneous paffage for about fifty yards. It is here well wooded, and highly cultivated. The river Becca bounds it on the fouth, and divides it from Ilfington. This river rifes within the parifh, and runs thro' a moft romantic valley, till it joins the river Bovey, four miles below its fource : In its way it has a beautiful fall of about 40 feet ; it then proceeds thro' the parifh of South Bovey, and empties itfelf into the Teign. The roads are infamoufly bad ; made with a loofe fand, which every hard rain wafhes away. The village confifts of about fix or eight houfes, adjoining the church, fituate near the eaft end of the parifh, fronting the fouth. The farm-houfes but few in number, but in general remarkably neat and good, built with ftone, and thatched. The farms in general from 40 to 80 pounds per annum, and thefe moftly occupied by their owners, which will of courfe denominate them freeholders. Few or no orchards. The manorial rights are divided into thofe of the eaft and weft ; the former belonging to Mr. Lane of Coffleet, the latter to Lord Courtenay. The number of inhabitants are about 200, remarkably healthy, ftrong, and long lived. The parifh is very flightly burdened with poor, not above 10 applying for relief, and thofe very old. The church is of hewn moor-ftone ; its height about 40 feet, length 42 feet from the fcreen to the weft wall, breadth 33 feet. The tower is 103 feet high, fquare built, with a ring of 4 bells. The rectory is worth about £130 per annum. The parfonage-houfe is a very old building, going faft to decay, built with ftone, and thatched." From the minifter in 1791.—The church was built in Will. the Conqueror's time by Bowerman, who lived at Huntorr, and had iffue 12 daughters, the eldeft Winifrid : But, having no male heirs, the eftate was divided between the daughters. *Milles's* MSS.

* " Luftlegh was the inheritance of Sir Will. de Widworthy, and of his fon Hugh de Widworthy, knight, who was fucceeded by Emma, wife of Sir Robert Dinham, knight. William Prous held the fame 8th of Edw. 2d ; and 19th of Edw. 3d, Walter Horton. 4th Edw. 3d, Alice, daughter and heirefs of Sir Will. Prous, widow of Roger Mules, conveyed this manor to John Damerell and Alice his wife, her daughter, and to the heirs of the body of the faid Alice, who had iffue Clarifia, wife of John Biry, and Joan, wife of John Dernford. 4th Henry 5th, William Burlefton conveyed this manor to Sir John Wadham and Joan his wife, and their heirs ; from which time it hath continued in the name and family of Wadham, unto Nicholas Wadham, efq. who left it to the heirs of his three fifters." *Sir W. Pole.*—In Luftleigh church Lord Dinham is fuppofed to have been buried. His and his lady's picture are to be feen, fays Rifdon, very glorious in a glafs window, having their armories between them, and efcutcheons on their furcoats. But Dugdale tells us, that he was buried in the Gray Friars church, near Smithfield, London.—Liftleigh belongs to John Mudge, M. A. who fucceeded, in 1792, Robert Tripp, who, in 1778, fucceeded William Trivett, who, in 1775, fucceeded Thomas Hutton.

† " Hennock, antiently *Hennycke*, and fo now pronounced by the inhabitants—Sax. *Hen-nock*, Old Hill. Its greateft length feven miles ; its breadth where wideft about one, in many parts not a quarter of a mile wide. It extends five miles on the weftern banks of the Teign. It afcends over the ridge of hills that feparates the Bovey from the Teign. Bridges three, all acrofs the Teign : Crookham, built of moorftone, two arches, connecting Trufham with Hennock ; Chudleigh-bridge, built of limeftone, two arches, connecting Chudleigh with Hennock ; Newbridge, of limeftone, two arches, connecting Bifhopfteinton with Hennock. An enclofed parifh, even the downs all enclofed ; well wooded, fome of the woods extenfive, particularly thofe in Netton Cleave. The kind of enclofures various : on the downs, principally the black thorn. Roads bad, tho' amidft the beft of materials. All the roads in. the parifh, as meafured a few years ago, 20 M. Views : the vicarage garden, Bottor Rock, Netton Cleave ; the two former extenfive, the latter picturefque. Villages five : Knighton, confifting of 30 houfes, on the great weftern road ; Warmhill, 7 houfes, on the Bovey and Exeter road ; Greenhill, 3 houfes, ditto ; Church Town, 20 houfes, on the Moreton and Chudleigh road ; Kelly, 5 houfes, on the Moreton and Bovey road. Total of cots and farm-houfes, 76. The houfes mud built, thatched, not neat. Orchards to all the farms ; except thofe on the downs. The farms very fmall, the property divided, in good ftate of cultivation. 56 farms. Thefe farms are occupied by 6 freeholders and 44 rackrenters. Twenty years ago there were 19 refident freeholders. Number of fouls 511. The form of the parifh long and narrow. The church is fituated in the middle, on the high ground of the parifh, oppofite Haldown. The church is neat ; the feats new and uniform. The altar-piece given by one of my predeceffors, Mr. Harris, unornamented, but decent. The carved work, the painting, and the letters were executed by a clergyman, Mr. Madge. The building confifts of three roofs, flate healed, forming 3 aifles : Its length in the clear 59 feet, its breadth 35 feet. The tower fquare, plain built, its height to the parapet 44 feet, in which are four bells. Number of paupers that have cafual pay 12, conftant pay 35, fix of whom have families of children.* (Forty-four years fince the overfeer paid the poor with one pound feven fhillings a month—now the overfeer expends 15l. a month.)—The parifh of Hennock has been regularly inhabited by a peafantry—the property divided into freeholds, as far back as the regifter gives any information, without a manfion-

* 1598. *Extracts from the Poor Books of Hennocke.*
A copy of the Preambule of the firft rate that appears upon the oldeft book :
Hennocke, ⎱ 1598. A Rate for the reliefe of the aged & impotent poor People within the faid Parifh as are not billited or appointed to be relieved by
⎰ the Inhabitants *in their Houfes*, for the Year following, fett down by the Overfeers of the Poor & Church Wardens.
The Sum expended this Year was 5l. 2s. 11d.—and the Number of paupers relieved was 22—and three Children were bound out apprentices.—The Parifh paid with the Apprentice 3s. 4d—No extraordinary Expences. The Money is all paid to the Poor except 8d. for writting yᵉ Account.

A Lift of 21 Years Expenditure.			A Lift of 21 Years, commencing 1668.			A Lift of 21 Years, commencing 1732.			A Lift of 21 Years, commencing 1770.		
A.D.		£. s. d.	A.D.		£. s. d.	A.D.		£. s. d.	A.D.		£. s. d.
1598	(yᵉ Years Expend.) ..	5 2 11	1668	(Expenditure)	34 14 11½	1732	(Expenditure)	58 2 5	1770	(Expenditure)	81 7 11
1599	....	5 10 8	69	....	19 17 4	33	....	42 8 0	71	....	98 19 6
1600	....	4 17 3	70	....	23 16 0	34	....	57 14 6	72	....	97 5 6
01	....	5 4 0	71	....	23 15 11	35	....	64 8 7¼	73	....	120 15 6
02	....	5 10 6	72	....	27 15 4	36	....	50 5 9¼	74	....	149 4 5
03	....	5 3 6	73	....	37 0 5	37	....	50 1 3	75	....	138 14 2
04	....	5 18 11	74	....	38 7 10	38	....	51 7 3	76	....	141 2 5
05	....	7 11 0	75	....	42 1 4	39	....	59 4 3	77	....	134 1 6
06	....	6 8 5	76	....	54 16 10	40	....	56 19 9	78	....	146 2 1
07	....	7 2 4	77	....	49 19 0	41	....	70 19 9¼	79	....	200 3 10¼
08	....	9 12 3	78	....	50 13 7	42	....	60 0 1¼	1780	....	145 7 0
09	....	8 6 9	79	....	32 10 10	43	....	61 3 7	81	....	164 9 7½
1610	....	8 3 10	1680	(25 Paupers)	29 4 8	44	....	58 1 11	1782	....	166 8 2¼
11	*	7 14 1	1681	....	28 8 13	45	....	52 7 10	83	....	193 19 8
12	....	6 19 3	82	....	30 1 8	46	....	45 16 4	84	....	177 15 11
13	(13 Paupers)	9 5 6	83	....	31 4 0	1747	....	36 11 7	85	....	166 0 8
14	(37 Paupers)	19 5 3	84	....	17 3 10	49	....	36 4 3	86	....	165 5 5
15	....	14 6 6	85	....	37 9 9	50	....	32 12 5	87	....	162 3 7
16	....	11 19 4	86	....	31 10 2	51	....	37 9 1	88	....	131 4 0
17	(25 Paupers)	11 11 9	87	....	23 8 0	53	....	43 18 1	89	....	172 9 5¼
1618	(48 Paupers)	23 11 8	1688	....	29 0 9	1754	....	59 7 0½	1790	....	169 8 7

* There were fome Legacies diftributed thefe Years, 30s. each Year.			Number of Paupers.
			1791 ⎱ Cafual Pay ...... 12 ⎰ 47 ⎰ Conftant Pay .... 35 ⎱
Hennock, Feb. 6th, 1791.			

Bottor. Here, the oak growing on the clefts of the rock—and the mountain afh fhooting up thro' the chafms, and overhanging the precipice, had a fine effect.* *Hennock* was by the Saxons written Hannoch, when *Alnode* held one hide there.† Matthew Lee, junior, was, a few years fince, lord of the manor.

BOVEY-TRACEY is called *Tracey*, from having been the inheritance of the Traceys, Barons of Barnftaple.‡ It is a very extenfive and populous parifh. The town is a ftraggling collection of houfes, more than half a mile, I fhould conceive, in length. At fome diftance it had a picturefque appearance. The hamlet of *Knighton* had, in times paft, a chapel belonging to it.§ The manor lately belonged to the Putts. *Indio*, once a priory, became the feat of the Southcotes, knights, after the fuppreffion. They poffeft it in the reign of Charles the 1ft. Here was built a large houfe; in 1772 much altered, and applied to the purpofes of the pottery manufacture.‖ The church is of a good fize: It has a curious fcreen, a roodloft entire, and a pulpit chiefly of freeftone richly gilt and coloured. Here are a variety of armorial bearings.

In

fion-houfe, or refident lord of the manor—indeed the parifh is made up of the fkirts of other manors—the manors of Hennock and Knighton, the property of James Templer, efq.; South-Bovey, Lord Courtenay; and Cannonteign, Hellyer, efq. but few eftates ac-knowlege either lord. The families in poffeffion of eftates at the commencement of the regifter * were the Credifords, Wrefords, Harris, Balls, Pinfents, Loveys; and their families are now in poffeffion of property, or are inhabitants in the parifh. It is remarkable, that the families on the downs, and the interior parts of the parifh, are the families that remain—I cannot account for this, but that the inhabi-tants of the downs, and the unfrequented parts of the parifh, not having fo frequent opportunities of obferving the advantages of fituation, have lefs defire to emigrate. and, however lefs pleafing, grow attached to their own fituation.—Qu. If this obfervation is verified by the inhabitants of the unfrequented and retired parts of the county.—There are the ruins of a chapel at Knighton, now converted to a barn; it is fituate in the middle of the village. There was a field that belonged to this barn, half a mile diftant, that is called Chapel Park; it is now fold off, and feparated fome few years fince. The length and breadth of the chapel, in the clear, 24 feet by 13½ feet. The eftate that it belongs to is called Lower Town Eftate, perhaps fo called from the higher town of Hennock; but the village is now called Knighton, from the manor.—A vicarage: Incumbents, Hill, Hitchins, Harris, Tompfon, Weeks, Loveys, Lane. Patrons, the Chamber of Exeter. The houfe in the church village, about two hundred yards diftant, an old houfe, repaired at various times; cob, ftone, and thatched. Every man fervant pays 1s. maid ditto 6d. as Eafter dues, annually, to the vicar.

* The bearings from *Bottor Rock* to the north—Sir Robert Palk's tower—the line of Haldon—Whiteway—the Obelifk—Chudleigh—the fea off Teignmouth—Shaldon hill—Marychurch hills—Knighton Heath and Bovey Heath—a beautiful valley, that from the two heaths of Knighton and Bovey runs down to Torbay—Highweek and Stover—Mr. Templer's canal winding by Teigngrace church, the fpire of which makes an elegant appearance—Torbay—Ipplepen tower—Ingfdon plantations—Ilfington—the Berryhead—the opening at Dartmouth—line of hills from Dartmouth to Plymouth—Brent Torr—High-torr—Dartmoor along to Drewfteignton—Manaton and North-Bovey churches—Laplode barton—Whitftone church—Mary-pole Head—Stoke hills—and Sir Robert Palk's tower again.

† " Not long after the Conqueft, Roger, furnamed de Hemiock, held the fame; whofe fon William, Lord of Hemiock, had iffue Bea-trix, wife of Sir Gerrard de Clift, knight; from which family, by Ifabel, the daughter of Will. de Clift, it came to Richard Tremanel, and by the heir-general of that name to Dymock. The abbot of Torr had a manor in Hennock, as appears from the following : Will. de Clift, Mil. fil. Willielmi, fil. Geraldi de Clift, falut. Noverint me confirm donationem quam Philippus de Salmovilla, et Beatrix avia mea, et Willielmus Pater meus fecerunt Abbati de Torr de Ecclefia de Hannocke." *Rifdon.*

‡ Notwithftanding the tradition of a duel between *Bovey* and *Tracey* !!!

§ " Of this tything, William de Clift was Lord, in the time of Henry the 3d; whofe heir general was married to Frankcheiney. It was the inheritance of this family to the reign of Henry the 8th; when John Frankcheiney had one only daughter, called Elizabeth, married to Strode. In the reign of Edward the 3d, the Dean and Chapter of Exeter recovered certain rents againft Rob. de Knighton and others, iffuing out of Knighton and Fen." *Rifdon.*

‖ Sir Popham Southcote, Sir John Stawell, Bale, efq. Inglett, efq. (by purchafe), Geo. Forfter Tuffnel, (by purchafe), efq. have been poffeffors of Indio.

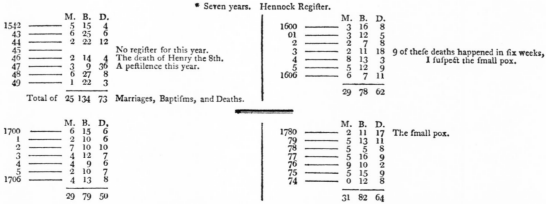

* Seven years. Hennock Regifter.

	M.	B.	D.
1542	5	15	4
43	6	25	6
44	2	22	12
45	No regifter for this year. The death of Henry the 8th. A peftilence this year.		
46	2	14	4
47	3	9	36
48	6	27	8
49	1	22	3
Total of	25	134	73

Marriages, Baptifms, and Deaths.

	M.	B.	D.
1600	3	16	8
01	3	12	5
2	2	7	8
3	2	11	18
4	8	13	3
5	5	12	9
1606	6	7	11
	29	78	62

9 of thefe deaths happened in fix weeks, I fufpect the fmall pox.

	M.	B.	D.
1700	6	15	6
1	2	10	6
2	7	10	10
3	4	12	7
4	4	9	6
5	2	10	7
1706	4	13	8
	29	79	50

	M.	B.	D.
1780	2	11	17
79	5	13	11
78	5	5	8
77	5	16	9
76	9	10	2
75	5	15	9
74	0	12	8
	31	82	64

The fmall pox.

The form of the entry in 1542, in the reign of Henry the 8th, was in Latin, (Natus fuit atque eodem die baptizatus erat.) and fo it continued till the year 1544, then the entry was made in Englifh; but in the firft of Mary, the Latin form was refumed, without the (*eodem die* baptizatus erat), fimply baptizata eft,—fepultus eft,—and fo it remained till 1576, the 18th of Eliz. From this laft date, the entries are all in Englifh.

STOVER LODGE.

The Seat of James Templer Esq.r To whom this Plate is Inscribed
Bye his Obliged Servant R.R. .....

Drawn & Engraved by J. Bonner

In TEIGNGRACE, is *Stover-lodge*, built by James Templer, efq. about the year 1781. It is of granite from Hightorr down. It is a ftrong and regular pile of building. The chimney-pieces, in the upper rooms, exhibit the different marbles of the county.* James Templer, efq. of Stover, in 1776, married Mifs Mary Buller, fecond daughter of James Buller, efq. of Morval, Cornwall, and King's-Nymton, Devon; by whom he has George, William, Charles, John, Frederic, Edward, Francis, and four daughters. His brother John married Mrs. Line, by whom he has no iffue. His brother George (M. P. for Honiton) married Mifs Paul of Somerfetfhire, and has iffue. His brother, Henry Line, a major in the army, is married to Mifs Rogers, daughter of Sir F. L. Rogers, bart. and has iffue. Mifs Templer married Sir J. W. de la Pole, bart. The church and fteeple, remarkable for their beautiful fimplicity, were built a few years fince, at the expence of the Templers and Sir J. W. de la Pole.†

KINGSTEIGNTON,

* " *Ting Graas*, anciently *Tingbruer*, was, in the time of Henry the 2d, the land and dwelling of Anthony de la Bruer, whom fuccef-fively followed William, Sir Jeffery, and Sir William de la Bruer, who had iffue Eva, wife of Thomas Graas and Ifabell, wife of Ralph de Donne, between whom the manor was parted. The one part, after its owner, was called *Tinggraas*—the other retained its old name, *Tingbruer*. Of the name of *Graas* were John, fon of Thomas and Eva, Theobald and John, whofe daughter Catherine was married to John Copleftone. Sir Ralph Donne and Ifabell de la Brewer had iffue Pafchafe and others. Pafchafe had iffue Hugh, who had iffue Amy, wife of Henry Ledred, and Ifabell, wife of John Holcombe." *Sir W. Pole.*

† A monument, white marble:

Sacred to the Memory of | Mrs. Mary Templer | For a Period of 35 Years the affectionate Wife | & of two Years the afflicted Widow | of James Templer, Efq. | the Duties of every Relation which Providence affigned her | fhe ftrictly & chearfully difcharged | a faithful Partner in all the Viciffitudes of Life | She participated his pleafures, fhe divided and mitigated his Pain | Her Difcretion was his Refource in difficulty | her Tendernefs his Confolation in Diftrefs | that animated Senfe of Duty to her Creator & her Fellow-creatures | that Pru-dence tempered with Generofity & Good-humour | which threw a Luftre & Dignity on her own Life | She inculcated by Precept & Ex-ample on her numerous Progeny | The Efficacy of fuch Virtue was not reftrained | to the narrow Sphere of parental and conjugal Duty | Her Piety was diffufed & Exemplary, her charity univerfal | To her domeftics fhe was a gentle Miftrefs a condefcending Friend | They who poffeft her Confidence never failed to partake her Bounty | To the poor her Liberality had no Bounds | When fhe faw Diftrefs, what-ever fhape it affumed | Then fhe faw an Occafion to pity and to relieve | Having thus performed the Part of a good Mother and a pious Xtian | mature in Virtues as in Years | When the tendereft Tie which bound her to this Earth was diffolved | She readily refigned that Being of which the better Part was extinct | & amid the Embraces of her forrowing Children expired | on the 21ft of June 1784, aged 59 years.

Another marble monument:

To the Memory of James Templer, Efq. of this Parifh | whofe Abilities were eminently exerted in improving | the Arts which contri-bute to the Conveniency | or Embellifhment of human Life the fame Simplicity | of Tafte which was the Ornament of his Genius | Shed its Influence on every Part of his Character | averfe to the falfe Refinements of Vanity & Luxury | he devoted himfelf in modeft Retire-ment to the | humble Practice of all moral and Xtian duties | the good Gifts which Providence put into his | Hands, were diftributed by an active & well | directed Benevolence. He gave his Advice with | great opennefs, his Charities with great Secrecy | was warm & conftant in his friendfhips mild | & gentle in his Authority never provoked by | any Thing but Vice Happy in the Efteem of all | good Men, fupremely fo in the exalted Comforts | of every domeftic relation he faw thofe Ties | about to be diffolved with Refignation though | not without Regret & when a robuft | Conftitution aided by Habitual Temperance feemed | to promife a much longer Continuance of Time | on the 4th of March MD.CC.L.XXXII in the fifty-ninth Year | of his Age He obey'd the laft awful Summons with a Conftancy & Compofure which nothing | but religious Hope in the Recollection of a | well fpent Life could infpire. May this faithful | Stone com-memorate his Virtues for the | Information & Inftruction of future Times | for they furely can want no Teftimony to convince them how he lived who witneffed | how he died.

Another marble monument, on the north fide:

In Memory | of Mr. Charles Templer | youngeft Son of J. Templer, Efq. | of Stover | who perifhed in the Ship Halfewell | bound to Bengal | which in the awful Night of January the 5th, 1786 | was wrecked on St. Alban's Head in the Ifle of Purbeck on the Coaft of Dorfet | This Stone, alas, denotes only his Name | for his Body is buried in the Caverns of the great Deep | while his Virtues remain engraved on the Hearts | of his furviving & afflicted Friends who with pious care & fond Regret | will ever cherifh the Recollection | of thofe gentle Manners & brilliant Talents | which haftening to Maturity | feemed to merit a longer Term of Years | At the Inftant when he entered on the firft Duties of Life in the 15th Year of his Age | he was removed to a better State | by a Decree of that Providence | which always determines every thing for the beft | Whofe Way is in the Sea, whofe Paths are in the great Waters | & whofe Footfteps are not known. |

Stern Minifters of Death, ye winds, ye waves!
Who in your wild and pitilefs Career,
Deaf to the Cries of Youth, of Innocence,
With headlong Rage your tender Victims hurl'd
On the rude Rocks—could no lefs Sacrifice
Appeafe the King of Terrors? Oh forbear!
Tis impious to repine—fo Heaven ordain'd,
Whofe Sovereign Word the liftening Storms obey:
Tis Man's! with meek Submiffion to receive
Affliction's bitter Cup—fo Heaven ordain'd;
Father of all, we bow to thy Decree,
Severe yet merciful—thy will be done.

KINGSTEIGNTON, or Kingftenton, (as it was once written), extends to within about a mile of Chudleigh town; whence Kingfteignton church is five miles S. E.   It is four miles and half from Teignmouth.*

HIGHWEEK, a daughter church to K. ftands on a hill, which commands Teignmouth Bar.   The village is a thoroughfare from Teignmouth to Afhburton.   Newton-Bufhel is in the parifh of High-week.†

" On the eaft bank of a ftream that ftrengtheneth the Dart, ftands ASHBERTON," fays Rifdon; now *Afhburton*.‡   The parifh of Afhburton is about five miles and half in length.   The number of inhabitants in Afhburton were upwards of 2500 in the year 1785.   They were numbered by Mr. Tripe.§   The tower and church were built about 500 years ago.   The church was an appendage to the abbey of Buckfaftleigh.‖

Of BICKINGTON ¶ and BUCKLAND IN THE MOOR, little occurs worthy of notice; except that the latter, a fmall parifh, and well wooded with coppice, difplays, in fome places, the moft romantic fcenery.   Here, a favourite fpot of Mr. Baftard, unrivalled in its combination of torrent, rock, and foliage, hath charms that might attract to its recefs the pencil of a Salvator Rofa.

" The Dart (fays Rifdon) paffes through the moor by a long folitary courfe, until it watereth WIDECOMBE."   Withecombe is a very extenfive parifh—including a great part of Dartmoor—from eaft to weft about fourteen, and north to fouth eight miles. *†   Here, in Edward the Confeffor's time, Edric held half a hide of land: And in this tything, Walter Widecombe, in 43d year of Edward 3d, granted lands to William his fon.   The chief manor was long fince in the family

mily

* " *Kingfteignton*, anciently the demefne of the crown, was given by Henry the 1ft to Richard de Burdon, together with the moiety of the hundred of Teignbridge.   After fome defcents in that family, the laft left iffue Cicely, his daughter and heir, married to Sharp; from whom, by defcent, this land came to the Cliffords." *Rifdon.*

Epitaph in the parifh church on Mr. Adlam, minifter of the fame, fuppofed to be written by himfelf, 1669:

Apoftrophe ad Mortem.

Damn'd Tyrant, cant profaner Blood fuffice,
Muft Priefts, that offer be the Sacrifice?
Go tell the Genii that in Hades lie,
Thy Triumphs o'er this facred Calvary;
Till fome juft Nemefis avenge our Caufe,
And teach this Kill-Prieft to revere juft Laws.

† Newton-Bufhel was, by Henry the 2d, given to John, the fon of Lucas his brother, and upon the revolt of Normandy refumed by King John, in whofe time Euftachius de Courtenay held the fame.   Henry the 3d, in the 31ft year of his reign, granted Newton-Bufhel to Theobald de Englifhville, who granted it to Robert Bufhell his kinfman and fofter-child: And this grant was afterwards ratified by the faid king.   Robert Bufhell had iffue Theobald, who had iffue William, who had iffue William, John, and Elifote.   William died without iffue.   John his brother had iffue John, who in the time of Richard the 2d died without iffue.   After whofe death this land fell to Thos. Yard, the fon of Roger and the faid Elifote.   The faid Thos. Yard had iffue Richard, who married Joan, daughter of William, and one of the heireffes of William Ferrers of Churchftone, and had iffue Gilbert; who had iffue Roger; who had iffue Richard; who had iffue Thomas, who by his firft wife, Elizabeth, daughter of John Levefton of Warwickfhire, ferjeant at law, had iffue Edward; and by his fecond wife, Joan, daughter of William Hurft of Exon, had iffue Thomas, to whom he conveyed this land.   He died without iffue; and Gilbert his brother hath iffue Gilbert, (fays Sir W. Pole), now of Bradley and Teignweek.

‡ *Afhburton* is faid to be fo called from the quantity of afh that ufed to grow there.   Whether this be true or not, it is certain that a great quantity of afh formerly flourifhed there.

§ On the 12th of June, 1790, died Mr. Tripe of Afhburton.   I have mentioned him, as a man of learning and ingenuity.   But whilft we fpeak of his highly cultivated mind, we remember with tears of regret his truly focial fpirit.   It may be juftly faid, that, hofpitable to his acquaintance, charitable to all who needed help, his delight was in the happinefs of others.   Afhburton will never witnefs fuch another townfman.   Yet he has left a fon, who inherits all his talents—all his virtues; and who has more ample means of gratifying the benevolence of a good heart.

‖ It is in length 103 feet, and in breadth 43 feet 5 inches on the infide.   A very handfome monument in this church was lately erected to the memory of Lord Afhburton.

¶ " In this parifh Furzland inhabiteth; one of whofe anceftors well increafed his eftate, by marrying Avifia, the daughter of Whitchurch." *Rifdon.*

*† The boundaries of the parifh are not exactly afcertained.   In 1789, a man of the name of Cater, living on the Moor, near Two-bridges, had built feveral houfes there, and inclofed a great part of the moor: But as it was undetermined whether his eftate lay in this parifh or in Lidford, he paid no poor-rates, nor was fubjected to any parifh affeffment.

mily of Shillingford; and thence defcended to Sir William Hudesfield, knight. *Park*, Lady Afhburton's, is the only feat of confequence in Withecombe. The church is a handfome gothic ftructure. The tower about 90 feet in height, is very light and elegant.*

ILSINGTON, firft the land of the Beaumonts, from Edward the 1ft, continued in the name of Dinham till it came to the four fifters of John Lord Dinham. *Ingfdon*, in this parifh, is a fine old houfe of Mrs. Hale. The perfpective thro' the fuite of rooms is ftriking. The lawn is pleafing, with good trees, and fome beautiful objects in profpect. Penwood-hill, covered with thick oaken foliage, from the foot to the top of it, has, from the road, a very rich appearance.†
The church is a building ‡ worth examination.

---

* From the altar-piece to the finging loft, more than 80 feet, confifting of three aifles. It has been damaged feveral times by lightning —of which a particular account is given in the Natural Hiftory.—Mr. Lyde, who was born at Loventor, in Berry Pomeroy, and who is faid to have been " the fixth of ten fons, every one of whom faw no lefs than five fifters"—was many years the vicar of this parifh. He died at a good old age, in 1673, and was buried in the chancel of Widecombe church.

† Mr. Topfham of Ingfdon, got poffeffion of this wood by the fingular generofity of a gueft. A gentleman, quite a ftranger to Mr. T. accidentally led to his houfe, was there very courteoufly entertained; but obferving a fcantinefs of fuel not anfwering to the plenty of other things, on his return home had this wood conveyed by a deed of gift to Mr. Topfham, as a mark of gratitude for his hofpitality. It now belongs to Hale of Ingfdon.

‡ " There are the veftiges of a rood-loft in the church of Ilfington over the fcreen, which divides the chancel from the body of the church, and winding fteps of ftone which lead up to it. And on the right hand of the altar, as you approach to it from the body of the church, there are two feats in the wall, both made of ftone, the one raifed about half a foot above the other, divided from each other by a fmall pillar of ftone, about three feet high, a little bigger than a man's arm; and another pillar like it on the other fide of the higher feat. On the fouth fide of the chancel lie the family of the Pomeroys, who lived at Ingfdon. In the regifter, I find many of this family baptized Hugh, which was a name common to that family, which came over with William the Conqueror, which founded Bury Caftle, Buckfaftleigh Abbey, and Afhburton Church; from which I conjecture that the one family might have fprung from the other. The firft patronage of this church was in the collegiate church of Saint Mary Ottery, and afterwards, I believe, in the monaftery of Plympton St. Mary; now it is in the church of Windfor. The following account of the vicars is from the regifter, as far back as the beginning of Queen Elizabeth's reign, 1555.—William Bickford, April, 1565. George Sweete, May, 1580. Benedict Parker, Auguft, 1595, buried Feb. 1596. Radford Mavericke, Oct. 1603. Chriftopher Warren, M. A. buried 1626. Robert Dove, B. D. inducted Sept. 1634. Humphrey Dyer, M. A. Decem. 1646, buried Auguft. 1653. William Stooke, Decem. 1657. Richard Bryan, April, 1675. Philip Nanfon, M. A. April, 1719. —— Bedford. —— Stephenfon. Jonathan Palk, B. A. 1788." 1792.

See also facsimile manuscript index following this printed index.

INDEX.

See also facsimile manuscript index following this printed index.

See also facsimile manuscript index following this
printed index.

CORRECTIONS, &c.

VOL. I.

VOL. II.

VOL. III.

In fome paffages, the marks of quotation are omitted; in others, inferted erroneoufly.

In arranging the prints, the reader will confult his own judgment.

TREWMAN AND SON, PRINTERS, HIGH-STREET, EXETER.

JAMES DAVIDSON's
Manuscript Index to Polwhele

We are grateful to Devon Library Services for allowing us to reproduce, in facsimile, this hitherto unpublished manuscript index to Polwhele, the original of which is in the West Country Studies library at Exeter.

James Davidson (1793–1864) of Secktor, Axminster was a diligent antiquary and bibliographer who devoted himself to the history of Devonshire. This careful and detailed index will be of immense value to all readers of this work.

Brickdale III 390
Brickhouse III 161.163
Brickley III 476
Bridenpohin III 362
Bridestow I 292 III 440.445
Brodford III 75.76.77 488
Bridgrule III 432.433
Bridgford I 227
Bridges I 223.230 III 155.236.
Bridgwater I 265 306.331.378
Bridwell III 361.
Brien I 204.
Brigham III 270
Brightlegh I 204.224 226.258.265.270 III 142.349.400 406.437.438
Brigwere I 212.
Brimble III 85
Brimmer III 271
Brimridge III 487
Brindley III 83
Brion III 136
Briouus I 203.210 213.224.228.437
Bristol III 51.
Bret III 83. I 270.271 303. III 450.454
Brithays III 358
Britricheston 44.194
Britton I 257.293 III 401.
Britville I 206.
Brewer I 212.219.220 267.268.293 294.
Briventorr I 13.
Brixham I 17.308 327. III 485.492
Brixton I 18.228 III 51.457 300. See after bra.
Briar I 223
Bruce III 476
Bruer III 497
Breere I 267
Brees III 480
Brinanburgh I 224
Bruse III 410
Brushford III 387
Bruton II 37.38 III 290.423.424
Brutton III 36.247+ 255.
Bryan III 91.477.478 487.489.499
Bryaut III 115
Bryett III 191.318
Brynlow III 290
Bryon III 412
Buck III 390.393.418 420.424.435
Buckenholt III 408
Buckenton III 207
Buckerel I 222.284 299.247+ 248.273 III 274.

Buckeston III 221.229
Buckhurst III 438
Buckfast I 292
Buckfastleigh I 70.229 230.227.239.293 297.327. III 47.48 49.416.469.472 479.481.482
Buckingham I 253 III 207
Buckinghamshire E. III 47.447.
Buckington III 274.275 403.
Buckland I 228.286 See 268.292.293.297 Buck- 321. III 382 396 land 398.399.402.403 426.464.465.466 470.489.494.498
—— Abbey III 253.449
—— Brewer I 13.278 III 418.426
—— Baron. III 144
—— Filleigh III 412 416.417
—— Monachorum I 307. 228
—— Trill III 301
Buckley I 265. III 489 495.
Buckyet III 210.
Buddle I 1. III 217
Bude I 186
N. Buzeaux I 5
Bulden I 303
Budgell I 202 III 374
Budleigh I 37. 225 261. 267. III 214 216.217.218.221 230.232
Budockshead III 23 115
Bulbeck III 192
Bulford III 102
Buckworth III 319
Bulkworthy III 311 418.426
Bullards III 358
Buller I 309. 313.326 III 31.89.92.98 100.101.102.103 207.393.447.492 497.
Bull hole I 51
Bulloin III 426
Bullworthy III 380
Bully III 486
Bulteel III 455.456 460.462
Buncombe II 4.20
Bundleigh III 388
Bunter III 295
Burchard I 242
Burdon III 120.121.496
Burell III 457.
Burges I 293. II 20 III 333.395
Burgh I 209.263. III 290.341.400.433
Burghet III 334.

Burgheirs III 90
Burgoin III 65.175
Burgoyne III 350
Burian I 313
Burial III 407.408
Burleigh I 257.261 266.
Burlescombe I 225 294.295.296 III 367.
Burleston III 483 495
Burley III 473
—— Dolts I 231
Burn III 249.359
Burnaford III 314 446.
Burnby III 439
Burnell I 230.306 III 40.61.66.197 389.413.
Burnett III 203.204
Burridge III 241.354 356
Burridgewood Castle I 19.
Burrington I 282 II 26. III 36.54.110 130.387.
Burrough III 266
Burrow III 425.477
Burrowe III 183.196
Burrows III 398.
Burston III 375
Burton I 208.270.271 319 III 279 361 362.378.404.437 438.
Bury I 278. II 25. III See 52.320.399.434 Berry 467.489.
Bushell III 498
Bussell III 160.
Butcher III 381
Butcombe III 462
Bute III 403
Butland III 491
Buxton I 267
Butler I 271 II 26 III 147. 327. 353
Butsford III 35
Butter I 197
Butterford III 458
Butterleigh III 174 247+ 248.256.
Buttlesgate I 299
Button I 283.284 See Bitton III 296. 267
Buzon I 206.267.
Byng I 310
Byrdall III 116.117
Byry III 424 See Berry
Bystock III 224.

Cabile I 311.
Cadbury I 187.263.298 III 30.45
Cadhay III 242.243 245
—— bridge III 240
Cadickbeer III 438
Cadiho III 142.143.434 435
Cæsar I 177.
Cadleigh I 200.266 III 42.172.174 343.460.
Cadwell I 320
Cahaignes I 210
Calcite III 372
Calewood III 380
Caliland III 346
Calf III 382
Caldard III 301.415.433
Calmady I 266.311. III 36.37.121.157.337 362.445.456.
Calstock I 39
Calsdon I 253
Calvert I 150
Calverleigh I 277 III 380.381
Calwodeley III 380.381
Camden I 202.323 III 254.284.454.
Camoys I 207.262.263 344.353.482
Campbell I 206. III 388
Campeaux III 394.395
Campes I 82.230
Campeus I 206
Camville I 207.262 263.268. III 401
Canary I 316
Caren III 53.64.441
Cannington III 402
Canonleigh I 225.294 295.297 III 77.81 172.197.198.260 307.365.366.368 369.373.404
Canonleigh I 24. III 74 496
Cairns III 82.
Cantilupe I 206.214 263.275.285 III 78.480.487
Canyng I 251
Cape III 491
Capel III 238
Capellan I 230
Capihays III 284
Cappis III 207
Carbonell III 209.212
Carden III 394.419
Cardinham I 263.268 III 436
Cardmaker I 301
Carew I 227.235.247 248.249.250.253 254.257.258.259 263.264.265.266 267.269.270.272 291.306.311. II 11.19.20. III

Haugher III 457	Harward II 44. III 263.270.273.329	Hearle III 55	Henton III 280
Hauke III 83.265	Hastard III 272.303	Heat I 9.	Herebath III 285
Hankford I 262.265 270.271.326 II 11. III 425.426 378.398.410.411 489.	Hastings I 251.262 III 194.212.263 319.456.460.477 482.	Heath I 320.326 327 III 50.82 198 230.240.465	Herbert III 458. I 308
Hanne III 41	Haswell III 30	— Barton III 57	Hereford I 218.295 ³¹⁰ II 3.15.56.77 III 224.
Hannington III 344	Hatch I 270. III 82 254 304.305.391 434.	— Bridge III 37	Hereward I 264 III 99.100.186 413.
Hanworthy III 371		Heathfield III 210 213.353.355	
Harberton I 262. III 421 479.482.491 492.	Hatherleigh I 4.19 42.228.281. II 17 39. III 314.433 437.439.442.	Heavitree I 185.222 276. III 21.22.104	Herford III 451.457
Harbord III 88	Hatton III 174.	Hebarden II 31.44 III 191.446.	Herle I 264.265.270 303.326. III 205 389.400
Harbours I 16	Haverfield III 247+ 276.	Hecham I 205.261 III 342	Herliow III 229
Harburn I 24	Haviland III 374.449		Herlyn I 267.
Harcombe III 237.259	Haw I 43.296	Hedges III 444	Hermandsworthy III 436
Harcourt III 136	Hawell I 296	Hedhayne III 312	Hernaman II 45
Hardeskull III 400	Hawkchurch I 22	Hedreland III 224	Hernedewth I 207
Harding I 296. III 282.399.405.410	Hawker III 331	Hegpen I 205	Herpath I 224
Hardness I 238.484	Hawkridge III 405 407	Heighe III 195	Herridge III 287
Hardwick I 256.293	Hawkins I 257.259 266.275.302.353 III 353.421.454 466 468.469.473 474.477.478.	Heighen III 98	Herring III 69.479
Harepath I 183.		Heighes III 29	Herrington III 185
Harford I 183.285. III 451.457.		Heines II 7.	Hertford I 259.292
Haringworth I 264	Hawley I 249. III 193 312.445.484.	Hele I 266.270.297 311. III 15 .142 150 175 192.194 251 323 332.367 371 391.416.419 442 454.455.456 457.463.476.	Hertland I 236.186 292.294.296.297 210.286.272.277 280 III 209.418 421. See Hartland
Harise III 46			
Harleigh II 207	Hawtrey I 13.36 III 203.242	Heleigh I 264	Heron II 24
Harlestone III 466		Helemoor III 363	Hervey III 419
Harlewin I 259.265 III 234.367	Haydon III 200.201 211.225.226.242 243.245.246.247 272.293.294.312 390.473.	Helion I 211.212. III 46.84.312.372	Hethen III 312
Harman I 289.291 II 46.			Hewett I 235
Harness III 380		Helter III 76.	Hewgoe III 77.81
Haroldstone III 450		Hembury Fort I 74 183 188.189 III 267 274.	Hewish I 264. III 247+ 266.451.464
Harpford III 201.224 226 227.230.234	Hayes III 43.45.98 219.230.455.464 468.469.476.	Hemeanton III 207	Hewon I 293.
Harptrew III 58.	Haylebarton III 248	Hemington I 228	Hext I 253. III 196.392
Harridge III 344.346	Hayman III 272.476	Hempston I 264 III 486	Heynes I 290.291.292
Harrington I 264.265 III 58.179.316 343 394.404.476	Hayne I 311. II 44 III 30 54.186.263 445.471.483.484 492.	Hemton III 207	Heyton III 159.163
		Hemyock I 193.263 264 267.291. III 334.496.	Heywood I 311. III 448.450
Harris I 259.266.271 296.311.319. III 43.45.59.71.89 270.364.380.390 419.432.433.434 435 440.445 483 495.496.	Haynton III 412		Hiansleton I 206
	Hayridge I 261	Henbeer III 358	Hickman III 267
	Hays I 266. III 300 301	Hengescot III 432.434	Hicks II 29. III 44
Harrison III 473.	Hayter III 73	Hengestmore III 331	Hide III 116.290
Harrowbridge III 449.		Hengham I 271.	Hidon I 263. III 41 753 332.334. 335.336.
Harston III 207.457	Hayward III 89	Hennig Down III 301	
Hart I 266. III 97 371 461.462.	Haywood I 265.266	Henley III 257.274.285	Hidron III 136.
	Head I 251	Hennaborough I 186 230	Hiford III 266.
Hartford III 224	Heale I 266. II 35. III 89 266 267.270 284 350 360.361.	Hennock I 49.70 230 291. III 494 495.496.	High Bickington I 240 — Bray I 53. III 396 401.
Hartland I 231. III 386.403.414. see Hertland			— Buckington III 403
— Abbey III 435	Heales III 394	Hennyoke III 495	Higherline III 387
Hartleigh III 416	Heamton III 396	Hennycastle I 230	Higher Thorn III 212
Hartnoll III 43.354 382.	Heanton I 263.265 266 III 51.222 461	Henrietta I 306	— Torr III 455
Hartop III 222	— Court III 398	Henscote III 31	Highford I 186
Harvey I 257. II 11.40 III 37.46.190 365.378.	— House III 416	Henshaw II 39	Highamton III 437.439
Harwood III 163.	— Punchardon III 396.397.	Henstyll I 292	Highhouse III 475
			Highlly III 394
			Hightorr I 2.
			Highweek III 124.488 494.498.
			Hillers I 266
			Hilion I 207.263. III 46.308